A CULTURAL HISTORY OF THE SEA

VOLUME 5

A Cultural History of the Sea
General Editor: Margaret Cohen

Volume 1
A Cultural History of the Sea in Antiquity
Edited by Marie-Claire Beaulieu

Volume 2
A Cultural History of the Sea in the Medieval Age
Edited by Elizabeth Lambourn

Volume 3
A Cultural History of the Sea in the Early Modern Age
Edited by Steven Mentz

Volume 4
A Cultural History of the Sea in the Age of Enlightenment
Edited by Jonathan Lamb

Volume 5
A Cultural History of the Sea in the Age of Empire
Edited by Margaret Cohen

Volume 6
A Cultural History of the Sea in the Global Age
Edited by Franziska Torma

A CULTURAL HISTORY OF THE SEA

IN THE AGE OF EMPIRE

VOLUME 5

Edited by Margaret Cohen

BLOOMSBURY ACADEMIC
LONDON • NEW YORK • OXFORD • NEW DELHI • SYDNEY

BLOOMSBURY ACADEMIC
Bloomsbury Publishing Plc
50 Bedford Square, London, WC1B 3DP, UK
1385 Broadway, New York, NY 10018, USA

BLOOMSBURY, BLOOMSBURY ACADEMIC and the Diana logo
are trademarks of Bloomsbury Publishing Plc

First published in Great Britain 2021
This edition published in Great Britain 2024

Copyright © Bloomsbury Publishing, 2021

Margaret Cohen has asserted her right under the Copyright,
Designs and Patents Act, 1988, to be identified as Editor of this work.

Cover image © *The Tugboat*, Gustave Le Gray © The J. Paul Getty Museum, Los Angeles

All rights reserved. No part of this publication may be reproduced or
transmitted in any form or by any means, electronic or mechanical,
including photocopying, recording, or any information storage or retrieval
system, without prior permission in writing from the publishers.

Bloomsbury Publishing Plc does not have any control over, or responsibility for,
any third-party websites referred to or in this book. All internet addresses given
in this book were correct at the time of going to press. The author and publisher
regret any inconvenience caused if addresses have changed or sites have
ceased to exist, but can accept no responsibility for any such changes.

Every effort has been made to trace copyright holders and to obtain their
permissions for the use of copyright material. The publisher apologizes for
any errors or omissions and would be grateful if notified of any corrections
that should be incorporated in future reprints or editions of this book.

A catalogue record for this book is available from the British Library.

A catalog record for this book is available from the Library of Congress.

ISBN: HB: 978-1-4742-9908-4
       Set: 978-1-4742-9910-7
       PB: 978-1-3504-5128-5
       Set: 978-1-3504-5130-8

Series: The Cultural Histories Series

Typeset by Integra Software Services Pvt. Ltd.
Printed and bound in Great Britain

To find out more about our authors and books visit www.bloomsbury.com
and sign up for our newsletters.

CONTENTS

LIST OF ILLUSTRATIONS — vii

GENERAL EDITOR'S PREFACE
Margaret Cohen — xi

Introduction
Margaret Cohen — 1

1 Knowledges
   Natascha Adamowsky — 27

2 Practices
   Richard J. King — 55

3 Networks
   Siobhan Carroll — 81

4 Conflicts
   William Boelhower — 105

5 Islands and Shores
   Ian McCalman — 131

6 Travelers
   Adriana Craciun — 155

7 Representations
   Charne Lavery — 177

8 Imaginary Worlds
   Cannon Schmitt 203

Notes 229
Bibliography 234
Notes on Contributors 253
Index 256

ILLUSTRATIONS

0.1 J.M.W. Turner, *The Fighting Temeraire tugged to her last berth to be broken up,* 1839   11

1.1 "Profils ou Coupes du Bassin de la Mer," from Louis Ferdinand Marsili, *Histoire physique de la mer,* 1725   30

1.2 "Lima Tenera," from Alfred Fredol, *Le Monde de la mer,* 1865   31

1.3 "The Pholas boring through the rock," frontispiece from John Harper, *The Sea-side and Aquarium; or, Anecdote and Gossip on Marine Zoology,* 1858   42

1.4 "Pheromona carpenteri Wyv. Th.," from *Wissenschaftliche Ergebnisse der Deutschen Tiefsee-Expedition auf dem Dampfer Valdivia 1898–1899,* vol. 4, 2, 1904   46

1.5 Édouard Riou, "Giant squid attacking the Nautilus," illustration in Jules Verne, *Twenty Thousand Leagues Under the Sea,* [1870] 1976   48

1.6 "Group of Alcyonidae," from Baron Eugen von Ransonnet-Villez, *Ceylon: Skizzen seiner Bewohner, seines Thier- und Pflanzenlebens und Untersuchungen des Meeresgrundes nahe der Küste,* 1868   51

1.7 "Portrait instantané d'un scaphandrier," from Louis Boutan, *La Photographie sous-marine et les progrès de la photographie,* 1900   52

2.1 Melville's Cape Horn ships: *Acushnet,* USS *United States,* and *Meteor*   56

2.2	Details of 1833 Chart of Cape Horn by Richard Holmes Laurie	58
2.3	Log pages for the 1841 passage of the whaleship *Acushnet*	61
2.4	"And ice mast-high, came floating by, / As green as emerald," drawn by E. Duncan (engraved by H. Harral) for Samuel Taylor Coleridge, "The Rime of the Ancient Mariner," 1857	64
2.5	Detail of "A Squall off Cape Horn," Currier and Ives, *c.* 1860	66
2.6	Chart of the South Pacific, 1849	74
3.1	"An interesting scene, on board an East-Indiaman, showing the effects of a heavy lurch,–after dinner," George Cruikshank, 1818	86
3.2	Map of the *Kent*'s Global Connections	89
3.3	William Daniell, *The Kent Indiaman on Fire, in the Bay of Biscay*, 1825	97
3.4	Letter written by Lt. Gen. Sir Duncan MacGregor, March 1, 1825	102
4.1	*Imperial Map of the British Empire*, 1886	108
4.2	*Death of Capt. Ferrer, the Captain of the Amistad*, 1839	116
4.3	Katsushi Hokusai, *Under the Wave off Kanagawa*, *c.* 1829–33	124
4.4	J.M.W. Turner, *Slave Ship (Slavers Throwing Overboard the Dead and Dying, Typhoon Coming on)*, 1840	126
4.5	*Whale Chart*, 1851	129
5.1	*Vue de la Rivière d'Endeavour fur (sur) la Cote de la Nouvelle Hollande où le vaisseau fut mis à la bande*	133
5.2	Narcisse Pelletier	140
5.3	O.W. Brierly, *HMS Rattlesnake, First Arrival of White Men Amongst the Islands of the Louisade Archipelago*, *c.* 1860	141
5.4	Residence of E.J. Banfield on Dunk Island, 1935	147
5.5	Aboriginal man with an outrigger on the beach at Lockhart River, Queensland, *c.* 1930	148

6.1	"Fastened to an Iceberg," from Elisha Kent Kane, *Arctic Explorations in the Years 1854, '54, '55*, 1856	160
6.2	"Instruments," from William Scoresby, *An Account of the Arctic Regions*, 1820	161
6.3	"First Communication with the Natives of Prince Regent's Bay, Drawn by John Sacheouse," from John Ross, *A Voyage of Discovery*, 1819	168
6.4	Aron of Kangeq, from serialized *Robinson Crusoe*, in *Atuagagdliutit*, 1862	171
6.5	François-Auguste Biard, *Vue de l'Océan Glacial: pêche aux morses par des Groënlandais*, 1841	172
6.6	"Et Ego in Arctis," from Lord Dufferin, *Letters from High Latitudes*, 1873	173
6.7	*Spitsbergen Gazette*, July 1897	175
7.1	Eastern and Associated Telegraph Companies map, 1914	181
7.2	"A whale entangled in the submarine telegraph cable, Persian Gulf," from *The Illustrated London News*, 1873	181
7.3	Photograph of the crew of *Cawdor* including four African Lascar crew members, 1884	183
7.4	"Giving chase to a dhow in the distance," *The Illustrated London News*, 1881	184
7.5	William Lionel Wyllie, *Lascars Manning the Sails*	187
7.6	"Divers Preparing for Work," from *The Illustrated London News*, 1873	194
7.7	A piece of the 1873 submarine telegraph cable, encrusted with marine life	196
7.8	Alphonse de Neuville, "Hunting in underwater forests of Crespo," engraved by Hildibrand, from Jules Verne, *Twenty Thousand Leagues Under the Sea*, 1870	200

8.1 Extract from Erskine Childers's *Vixen* log, 1897 — 205

8.2 E. Boyd Smith, "Reading *Woodstock* aloud," from Richard Henry Dana, Jr., *Two Years Before the Mast: A Personal Narrative*, 1911 — 211

8.3 "Chart of Juist, Memmert, and part of Norderney," from Erskine Childers, *The Riddle of the Sands: A Record of Secret Service Recently Achieved*, 1903 — 214

8.4 "East Friesland and the German or East Frisian Is.," from Erskine Childers, *The Riddle of the Sands: A Record of Secret Service Recently Achieved*, 1903 — 215

8.5 "Diagrams illustrating the Battle of the Saintes," from Captain A.T. Mahan, *The Influence of Sea Power Upon History, 1660–1783*, 1890 — 221

8.6 "Approaches to Harwich, Hanford Water, the Stour, Orwell, and Deben Rivers," from Frank Cowper, *Sailing Tours: The Yachtsman's Guide to the Cruising Waters of the English Coast*, 1892–6 — 227

GENERAL EDITOR'S PREFACE

MARGARET COHEN

Over the past thirty years, oceanic studies has emerged in the humanities as a leading interdisciplinary field. It owes its importance to its capacity to give an account of globalization spanning millenia that is robustly cross-cultural. As this new field has taken shape, it has both incorporated and revised an earlier generation of scholarship, which attended to maritime transport, naval warfare, and global exploration, often within a framework of national history. Contributions of oceanic studies range across scales: from showing how maritime transport and marine resources join separated lands into water-based regions to resurrecting how a meeting on a beach between societies never before in contact could create intractable structures of domination to revealing the impact of a single photograph from outer space of the earth as a blue planet. Today, oceanic studies aims to tell the stories of all who have traveled the seas: professionals, adventurers, passengers, forced migrants—and animals.

Further, this emerging field recognizes that the seas are a rich realm for the imagination, all the more so given the paradoxical tension between their remoteness for many people and yet their life-sustaining importance. It is telling that a poet, the Nobel prize-winning Derek Walcott, has penned the memorable phrase, "The Sea is History."[1] At the same time, the imagination of the seas is not purely fanciful but rather takes shape in relation to located marine environments and how humans practice them, leading humanists to engage the reality of the physical world. When modern oceanography and marine biology took shape in the nineteenth century, these sciences established the oceans as nonhuman natural realms, despite their prehistory in mixed, practical knowledge conjoining environmental curiosity with the pursuit of power and wealth. Since this disciplinary cleavage, the sea has time and time again shown us the need to recognize its existence for and with humans, as well as in itself.

In the twenty-first century, the importance of the sea in world-defining developments, including second-wave globalization, postcolonial conflict and climate change, has become so evident that its social and cultural reality cannot be ignored. In the words of Franziska Torma, volume editor of *The Global Age*, such developments have "forced us to 'think science and humanities' together, because science provides data and humanities 'translate' them into social and academic interpretation; this opens up historical perspective on the oceans from antiquity to the present" (Franziska Torma, personal communication, May 2020). Whether drawing on nautical archaeology resurrecting sunken cities and shipwrecks, or using scientific research about the impact of climate change on coastal communities, oceanic studies is taking the lead among humanities fields in pursuing this urgent, if vexed, disciplinary crossing.

In editing *A Cultural History of the Sea*, I have been fortunate to work with volume editors who have made major contributions to setting the agenda of oceanic studies in its twenty-first-century form. Taken together, their expertise encompasses the oceans of the globe, notably the Mediterranean, the Indian Ocean, the Atlantic, and the Pacific and includes the history of science and the environment as well. We have launched our project from our institutional homes in transatlantic universities, even as we mark our starting point at once to acknowledge and brush against the grain of Western-oriented perspectives. Further, readers will see that the abstraction Western itself fractures when subjected to the pressure of water-based movement and seafaring practices. Thus, maritime travel creates far-flung contact zones across thousands of kilometers, which cannot be reduced to the orientation of the West, even if Western Europe may have been a point of departure. These contact zones are characterized by extreme social complexity, which modify those whom they involve, and the importance of the physical environment in such contact zones creates yet another set of considerations. The demands of sea-oriented life, moreover, unmoor those who work on ships to the point where they may be a culture unto themselves, unnervingly apart for their societies, due to such factors as the rigors of shipboard living and the multicultural *habitus* even on vessels enforcing the routes of empire.

Our interest in conveying the heterogeneous histories that meet on the sea extends to the themes we have chosen for our series' organization. A unique feature of the Bloomsbury *Cultural History* series is to devise eight chapter headings for each volume that can run from antiquity to the present. These headings address culture understood in its expansive, anthropological sense: as designating the diverse realms of practices organizing the structures of a society. In the case of the seas, important aspects include but are not limited to war, technology, and trade at sea, scientific knowledge, as well as myth and imagination. We defined our themes in a fashion that would enable contributors to present a democratic history. Thus, for example, we framed histories of "War and Empire," at sea as "Conflicts," to take account of the many scales of violent struggles at sea, including frames of state-supported navies, non-state actors, and the violence of shipboard life, ranging from mutinies to treatment of passengers and transport of the enslaved. Or thus, we reframed the theme "Science and Technology," as "Knowledges," to provide an opportunity to include knowledge beyond the strict boundary of science. Such knowledge ranges from philosophical speculation in classical antiquity to sea knowledge and practice outside Western paradigms.

In organizing the chapters, we have respected conventional Western historical periodization, which has been shaped by events on land. At the same time, readers will find within the volumes chapters that take up the question of whether such periodization stops at shore, due to the previously mentioned pressures of a sea perspective on concepts whose operations are focused toward the land. Thus, the history of Egyptian seafaring and contacts with other cultures of the Mediterranean basin traverses the land-based periodization of this particular culture, traditionally understood in terms of its ruling dynasties, from Greek prehistory through the classical period and into Roman times, roughly the second millennium BCE to the first century CE. Within the modern era, to take the example of a single technology, the years from 1769 to 1989 form one period in the history of navigation, although this epoch runs across three volumes in the series. In 1769, British engineer John Harrison perfected a chronometer that would keep accurate time over a long traverse. With the ability to compare noon during a ship's traverse and noon at an arbitrarily defined starting point—it became the Greenwich Meridian by convention—navigators could finally establish their longitude while a ship was sailing, a development that would vastly improve safety at sea, even if it took decades to expand beyond naval circles. Celestial navigation would remain the best practice for establishing a ship's location until the invention of the global positioning system (GPS) in the third quarter of the twentieth century, which could be dated to 1989, when the US Department of Defense launched a satellite system that would become GPS, replacing with the touch of a few buttons the arduous calculations needed for celestial navigation.

Another dimension to the specificity of sea-based periodization is the timescale of the oceans as a physical environment. For eons marine history moved at a geological pace, but in the age of the Anthropocene we are learning about the human impact on a realm of the planet long considered an inexhaustible resource and a vast power beyond human reach. Such an impact can occur within a person's lifetime, as is the case, for example, with melting ice caps at the poles, which have drastically diminished in satellite visualizations, dating back to 1979 (Starr 2016). This impact in turn is affecting societies, from Indigenous inhabitants of the Arctic to farmers around the world, who depend on weather patterns disrupted by global warming. Yet further entangling human and geological timescales at sea, melting ice caps open up new shipping routes through the Arctic, which present potential for a greater human footprint there.

The global consequences of polar ice melt exemplify how a sea perspective reorients terrestrial units of geographical analysis, which is the case not only for the oceans as an environment but also for the oceans as an arena of human practice. Chapters across the series reveal how state-drawn borders may be less important for cultures at sea than fluid spaces defined by natural features, and how islands or coasts eccentric from the perspective of land-based history may play an outsized, formative role in a nation's oceanic ambitions. Further, sea transport produces states that are at once joined under the same flag yet are also territorially disconnected, with unique and uniquely difficult administrative features. Yet another challenge, at the lexical level, is that when we try to express oceanic phenomena with language from the land, we reach to unsatisfactory imagery that impedes understanding. A good example today is the great "garbage patch" of pollution in the Pacific Ocean. The figure of a "patch" misleadingly limits its reach and does not capture the microscopic pervasion of plastic in sea water.

The seas are vast expanses, whose study drives home the point that any research is necessarily fragmentary and located. Contributors to these volumes include established and emerging voices, who have written chapters that are original research around our central themes rather than summaries of secondary literature. Volume editors have encouraged their contributors to present their insights in whatever way they thought would best bring out the originality of their topic and suit their disciplinary expertise. Some have used the narrative of a survey. Others have taken a single event as their canvas, whether the event is exemplary or tellingly anomalous. Yet others have spun out their questions at the scale of one marine environment.

Such flexibility is also important because "the sea" of our series' title is not one thing. Rather, the saltwater element is culturally constructed and imagined in widely different ways, depending on who is engaging with it and to what ends. This range is evident as well in the rich imagery accompanying the chapters, which is another feature of the *Cultural History* series. Thus, readers will see how in antiquity, the sea was never represented directly but rather suggested metonymically on frescoes and vases, with depictions of fish, ships, or mythological sea creatures. Grand seascapes, exhibiting the ocean as a theatre of awe, in contrast, compelled audiences in Enlightenment and Romantic eras. One constant across centuries are practical charts, which have used a variety of methods, shaped by different epistemes and environments, to find and mark paths across the waters, all nonetheless sharing an aim of safety. To draw a parallel between navigating vast, and in many cases, untracked waters and emergent areas of scholarship: as readers constellate the diverse subjects and approaches collected in this series, I hope they will gain a better understanding of the abiding, pervasive human interface with the seas as well as recognize new and future directions for oceanic studies.

Introduction

Currents, Riptides, and Eddies: The Global Meets the Local in Technological Modernization at Sea

MARGARET COHEN

In the nineteenth century, the Industrial Revolution took maritime globalization to a new scale. By 1900, people and goods crossed bodies of water with a rapidity and reliability inconceivable when the century began. In the first decades of the nineteenth century, the fastest North Atlantic crossing for the ships that routinely carried mail and goods called packets from Liverpool to New York was twenty-one days, and a slow crossing would take twenty-nine days. By 1900, the average crossing was less than a week, with the ocean liner the *Mauretania* setting a record in 1907 at four and a half days. In 1840, trade across the world's oceans was 20 million tons. By 1887, it was 140 million tons (Stopford 2009: 23). Communications too dramatically transformed. In 1800, a message between Liverpool and New York would have traveled at the speed of a swift sailing ship, and the time for the message to arrive and be answered would hence take many weeks. By the end of the century, due to a submarine transatlantic cable, messages could be sent and responded to in a single day.

As a result of technological modernization, maritime connectivity multiplied and thickened routes, freight transport, and mobility, expanding and diversifying the numbers and types of travelers. The waters of the globe went from a highway to a massive transport system with intensively practiced hubs and nodes. The reference points used to date technological modernization at sea both occur within the general time frame of the Industrial Revolution on land, yet innovations are also specific to seafaring, taking into account the demands of season, weather and tide, and the myriad cultures brought into contact in the marine environment. In the realm of transport, a steam engine was first used to push a locomotive in 1802, which was the same year that a steamboat, the *Charlotte Dundas*, designed by Scottish engineer William Symington, did the work of horses for towing on the Forth and Clyde Canal. From its use on canals, the steam engine took on open waters, and in 1807 American Robert Fulton launched a paddle-wheel steamboat, the *Clermont*, with an engine made in Birmingham, England, to navigate the Hudson River. Cross-ocean travel by steam dates to the 1840s. In 1890, London, New York, and Buenos Aires were the leading port cities of global maritime transport, in a geography of shipping whose hubs included, among others, the European cities of Hamburg and Marseilles, the Asian cities of Calcutta (present-day Kolkata), Rangoon (present-day Yangon), and Hong Kong, and the Australian port of Sydney (Ducruet 2013).

The nineteenth century is termed the age of empire in the volume's title. On sea and on land, modernization promoted imperial expansion and capitalist profiteering, just as imperial profits drove modernization. In *Heart of Darkness* (1899), Joseph Conrad has his most famous narrator-protagonist Marlow flag the role of steam in enabling colonial expropriation and despoliation, starting with Marlow's search for employment that launches him on his ill-fated adventure. Casting about for some sort of work, Marlow realizes: "Dash it all! […] They can't trade without using some kind of craft on that lot of fresh water – steamboats!" ([1899] 2006: 8). Already, traveling down to Africa on a French steamer, Marlow observes, "she called in every blamed port they have out there, for, as far as I could see, the sole purpose of landing soldiers and custom-house officers" (13). To cite historian Mark Larabee, "Steam power […] made it much easier to navigate the Congo and other African rivers than would have been possible under sail. This change came just in time for the opening of the vast waterway of the Congo and its tributaries – 7,200 miles in all – to European trade" (2018: 22). Modernization had a similarly important role in amplifying Western hegemony amidst the long-standing trading and travel patterns shaped by the environment and *longue-durée* sociability in other regions of the globe. Thus, Indian Ocean historian Michael Pearson observes that starting in the early nineteenth century, elemental environmental elements such as "monsoons, currents and land barriers are all overcome by steam ships and steam trains in the service of British power and capital" (2003: 11).

As these cases suggest, Western nations dominated global maritime transport in the volume's age of empire, above all Britain, in a century characterized by the Pax Britannica, when British naval power reigned on the global oceans. Yet in the "Conflicts" chapter, volume author William Boelhower emphasizes that such maritime supremacy was in fact more the ability to police ocean traffic than to control a vast part of our planet that, in our time as well, remains with large areas of unregulated waters. Thus, among his examples, while the British patrolled the Atlantic off West Africa following the 1807 abolition of the slave trade by both Great Britain and the United States, many ships evaded their reach, in an era when abolitionism coexisted with what historians call the age of Second Slavery. The area between the South China Seas and the Bay of Bengal was particularly contentious in the later nineteenth century, which is moreover still the case today. In the span covered in our volume, coveted goods passing through this area were textiles and opium, at once illegal and profitable to traders of many nations, starting with Great Britain and the United States; in the twenty-first century, the most valuable commodity is oil.

The Pax Britannica dates to 1815 with the end of the Napoleonic Wars. Throughout the nineteenth century, the United States competed with Great Britain on the seas but the Pax Britannica would only definitively dissolve at the turn of the twentieth century, when Russia, Japan, and Germany, as well as the United States and France, challenged Britain's hegemony. An important document in drawing geopolitical attention to the oceans was American Alfred Thayer Mahan's *The Influence of Sea Power on History, 1660–1783* (1890) that conceptualized the importance of naval dominance in international hegemony. While Germany was the foremost emerging naval power in Western waters, Japan and China clashed off the Korean Peninsula in the first Sino-Japanese War (1894–5). The Japanese then pursued their bid to control Pacific Rim waters in the Russo–Japanese war (1904–5), which came to an end with a decisive naval victory of the Japanese fleet over the Russians in the Battle of Tsushima. The inventive strategies used by Admiral Heihachiro Togo, such as "crossing the T" in front of the Russian battleship line, were studied around the world, and this battle can date the inauguration of a new era of naval warfare.

With our twenty-first-century awareness of the Anthropocene, the volume's title, "The Age of Empire" takes on a scale beyond national ambitions. The nineteenth century was also the era that saw the project to expand what historian Rosalind Williams has called "human empire" (2013) over and into the seas of the planet. Both the technologies and planetary scale of the Industrial Revolution at sea gave an impetus to marine science, which, as Natascha Adamowsky discusses in the volume chapter "Knowledges," emerged in its modern form across the long nineteenth century. American seaman and scientist Matthew Fontaine Maury's *The Physical Geography of the Sea* (1855) is commonly used as a reference point for the first work of modern oceanography, with its aims to render intelligible the world's oceans as a planetary ecosystem. Such oceanography was at once pursued for science and was of practical use to all who plied the seas, whether from motives of curiosity, power, or profit. Even as it served national and commercial ambitions, the take-off of oceanography also was entangled with the development of other modern earth sciences at this time. Indeed, Charles Darwin's first theory, before evolution, concerned the composition of coral atolls, which he conceived while a young naturalist on the voyage of HMS *Beagle* (1831–6), undertaking a surveying circumnavigation.

As Adamowsky underscores, marine sciences further discovered the diversity of the ocean's third dimension in the mid-nineteenth century. The ability to study and exploit the depths transformed the long-held view still prevalent in the early nineteenth century, where, as historian Helen Rozwadowski has observed, "the open sea was understood by Europeans as a wild place and a great void outside society" (Rozwadowski 2005: 40). Despite such ambitions, the ocean depths have resisted human curiosity due to the unbreathable, weighty aquatic atmosphere of this realm that Jacques Cousteau would call a century later a "world without sun." The black box still unlocated of Malaysia Airline flight 370 that went down in 2014 is a vivid reminder that the planet's oceans confront us not only with the triumph but also "the limits" of human empire, to cite from volume author Cannon Schmitt, in his chapter on the nineteenth-century ocean imaginary.

Moreover, what the nineteenth and much of the twentieth century conceived as human domination through modernization is now revealing itself as impact without mastery, for in our era of climate crisis, we can understand the nineteenth-century extension of human empire at sea as a facet of the Anthropocene. Across millenia, the "histories of navigation" and "environmental history" have been inextricable (Armitage, Bashford, and Sivasundaram 2017: 11), and the Industrial Revolution invented technologies such as steam serving navigation that impacted the environment at a planetary scale. From the perspective of transport innovation, the long nineteenth century ends in the fatal encounter in 1912 of the White Star Line's "practically unsinkable" RMS *Titanic*, with an iceberg that calved from Greenland. If Greenland is melting today at an unprecedented rate, the Industrial Revolution's greenhouse gases have played a catalyzing role, even as these gases have been intrinsic to the thickened web of global maritime interconnectivity across the era covered in this volume.

The cultural histories of the seas as explored by volume authors occurred against the backdrop of technological change. Yet long-period historical transformations did not happen uniformly, nor should such a top-down view obscure the fact that the environments of the planet's oceans are extraordinarily diverse and located, as are the people who came into contact with them and each other. I offer in this introduction an overview of technological modernization to help readers make connections among the multitude of events, practices, and fantasies described by authors in the chapters. The introduction develops three concepts to organize this multiplicity, with recognition that they are unavoidably schematic and reductive: *complexity*, *unevenness*, and *eccentricity*. By *complexity*, I mean the fact that no single technology worked in and of itself or separate from cultural relations involved in its development and implementation. By *unevenness*, I mean that technologies were not uniformly utilized or adapted, as soon as they emerged. And by *eccentricity*, I mean that there were at the same time seafaring practices and societies that ran counter to these global currents or proceeded with different investments. As I hope to suggest by explaining these concepts with reference to details from the chapters, volume authors both unfold and also complicate the master narrative of the nineteenth century spreading Western and human empire, and they use both case studies and more panoramic surveys to enable their elucidations.

COMPLEXITY

The baseline of technological change is steam; to cite Richard King in his chapter on "Practices," "the greatest single influence on our relationship to the ocean was surely the marine engine." At the same time, the marine engine worked in tandem with a number of other new technologies and processes that enabled its success and multiplied its impact exponentially. Thus, for example, the steamship was developed in an era when shipbuilders started to use iron to build ships. Iron ships were cheaper to produce than wooden vessels, and the material of iron also enabled construction of larger and longer ships that could carry more cargo and passengers and that required fewer workers.

One net effect of iron ships when coupled with the maneuverability introduced by steam were reduced costs for time in port. Thus, in the freight sector,

> as metal steamships came to dominate ocean shipping, productivity growth accelerated. Industrial technology also reduced shipping costs by rapidly lowering the price of metal steamships, which in turn lowered freight rates by close to half a percent annually. Together productivity improvement in ship operation and lower ship prices brought freight rates in 1910 to just over 40 percent of their 1855 value at the same time general prices rose slightly.
>
> (Harley 1988: 862)

Passenger transport as well increased exponentially on these larger, more reliable ships, where the speedier voyage also decreased the chance of mortality at sea.

Taking the case of one type of passenger, the immigrant from Europe to the United States, economic historian Raymond Cohn notes a reduction in the cost of passage, "a rise in volume," and an expansion of "the areas in Europe from which immigrants came" with the advent of steam travel (2005: 470). Cohn has further found that the types of people who immigrated diversified. In the era of sail, immigrants were primarily families traveling together. Thus, Siobhan Carroll's "Networks" chapter features such a family in tracing the lines of ocean connectivity with the case of the 1825 wreck of the East Indiaman *Kent* that caught fire bound for Bengal during a heavy storm in the Bay of Biscay. British colonial officer Duncan MacGregor brought with him his wife Elizabeth, who undertook the arduous voyage only a month after she had given birth, with her baby, assisted by her unmarried sister, Agnes Joanna Dick. Among other passengers, Carroll notes as well MacGregor's superior, Colonel Fearon, and his daughter Margaret. With steam transport, more men came "on a temporary basis […] to work for a period of time and then return" (469–70), even while families continued to make up a large share of immigrant transport.

Across the nineteenth century, the ports where ships were built and where they docked were expanding to handle larger shipping capacity, using steam-powered dredging as well as new underwater construction techniques. Helmet divers were important in laying the supports of port structures, as well as in bridge and lighthouse construction. For dive historian Robert Marx (1990), a reference date for the emergence of modern helmet diving is 1839, when British engineer Augustus Siebe patented the closed helmet that fastened on to the suit providing a watertight seal for the head. Helmet diving relied on industrial technologies such as steam and pistons to send compressed air down into the greater depths of water pressure beneath the sea. Another technology improved for underwater engineering in the middle decades of the nineteenth century were diving chambers, such as the caissons used to build New York's Brooklyn Bridge, which opened in 1883. Caisson's disease was the name given to the devastating injuries, and in some cases death that befell workers involved in its construction who spent prolonged time underwater. This disease is today known as decompression sickness, but it would not be until the twentieth century that people understood the dangerous effect of the atmosphere of water on human physiology; the nitrogen bubbles released in the blood stream under the greater pressure beneath the surface necessitate a decompression stop in shallow depth to let the body readjust.

Steam-powered dredging was one important industrial technology in the land excavations needed to create the Suez Canal. Opened for navigation in 1869, the Canal connected the Atlantic with Indian Ocean regions via the Red Sea and the Mediterranean. Steamships could pass through this waterway on their own power, and the intensifying need of capitalism for global transport fostered investment in such an ambitious undertaking. Canal transport at the scale of nations had been known across history and became important to the Industrial Revolution with the advent of the need to convey the goods of industrialization. As David Landes observes about Great Britain, "In two decades (1760–80), navigable water and solid roads linked the major industrial centres of the North to those of the Midlands, the Midlands to London, and London to the Severn basin and the Atlantic" (1988: 47). A canal through the isthmus of Suez dates to 1900 BCE and "monuments testify to the will of every powerful ruler—Egyptian, Persian, Greek, and Arab—to preserve that instrument of prosperity and power," until the eighth century CE when it was closed (Mollard and Gauthier 2018: 10). Construction of such a canal similarly interested modern empires and multinational capitalists. This massive engineering effort, undertaken by French entrepreneur Ferdinand de Lesseps, took ten years to accomplish (1859–69).

A critical technology expanding shipping along with the ability of freight and passengers to travel with more regularity were—and are—undersea cable networks. As Carroll reminds us in her chapter, using figures from 2015, today more than 98 percent of our international data travels through submarine space (UN General Assembly 2015). In the nineteenth century, there was no access to the air, hence, the ocean was, in Carroll's words, "the crucial natural space across which international communications, warfare, and trade were projected." This information would start to be transmissible underwater with the inception of transoceanic cable networks, whose circuit was linked up continuously in 1866 across the Atlantic. In 1870, overland and undersea links were joined up to enable cable transmission from London to Mumbai, creating another medium of passage between Atlantic and Indian Ocean worlds. Such circuits promoted imperialism and revolutionized shipping logistics. The ability of shipping companies to have information about the locations of their ships around the world, for example, expanded the tramp steamer business, where even small subcontractors could carry cargo to a distant port and pick up another job, much like Uber drivers depend on the global positioning system (GPS) and internet today. Given the high cost of telegrams, London at the center of both the overseas cable network and global finance was also the center of this business. In 1869, shipping company H. Clarkson & Co. "spent more on telegrams than on wages" (Stopford 2009: 32).

Industrial technologies revolutionized transport in war as in business. The Civil War battle of the ironclad ships, the United States *Monitor* and the Confederate *Merrimack* (March 9, 1862), is regarded as opening the era of industrial battleship warfare, although both ships, while iconic, had flaws in their functioning and were not particularly effective. While ironclads were used in the Civil War and during the subsequent Russo–Turkish conflict, the later nineteenth century was an era experimenting with how to use these new technologies in combat, as navies had neither "the technical impetus" nor the "tactical lessons of a major naval war" (Kemp 1988: 267). In contrast, after the 1905 Battle of Tsushima, navies around the world noted not only Admiral

Togo's strategy but also the offensive advantages of speed and barraging artillery to overwhelm an armored ship's defense. The Japanese battleship *Mikasa* was a precursor of the battleship that would dominate warfare in the twentieth century, called the dreadnought, after the eponymous vessel launched by the British in 1906. The battle of Tsushima further showed the power of modern communications technology in warfare at sea. Thanks to effective wireless telegraphy invented in the preceding decade, the Japanese knew when the Russian fleet was approaching and also were able to maintain formation in darkness and mist (Sterling 2007: 460).

The submarine was another military technology drawing on nineteenth-century technological innovation, which would remain a work in progress in this era. The submarine had been an inventor's dream for centuries going back to the notebooks of Leonardo da Vinci. Along with the battle of the *Monitor* and *Merrimack*, the Civil War was the occasion for the first successful use of a submarine. The *H. L. Hunley* sank a Union sloop, the USS *Housatonic*, in 1864, although the *Hunley* sank in the attack as well. The nineteenth century beneath the waves closed with a successful submarine launched by John Philip Holland in 1897, and rapidly acquired by the US, British, French, and Russian Navies. The German Navy then invented the U-boats that would be deadly in the First World War.

The most famous submarine of the nineteenth century was a fantasy—invented by an author rather an engineer. This submarine was the proto-nuclear *Nautilus*, imagined by Jules Verne in his novel *Twenty Thousand Leagues Under the Sea* ([1870] 2017). Verne conceived of his powerful technology inspired by sea literature, technological modernization, and the nineteenth-century takeoff of marine biology and oceanography. He further was inspired by glimpses of the undersea kingdom afforded by the new mass spectacle of the public aquarium. While fish had been kept in bowls since antiquity, new innovations such as pumping systems to keep water flowing facilitated self-sustaining, large-scale displays of aquatic life. Victorian biologist Philip Henry Gosse designed and oversaw the installation and curation of the first public aquariums, opened in London in 1853. Aquariums spread to other sea-loving cultures with industrial techniques, as Adamowsky discusses in her chapter on "Knowledges," at first in Europe and North America. In Japan, the first public aquarium was opened in 1882.

The underwater worlds exhibited in aquaria were controlled environments, yet they opened the public's eyes to the vibrant life in depths thought sterile at the century's beginning. Aquariums were so popular that they featured as attractions in international exhibitions celebrating modernization, such as the many World's Fairs later in the century. Verne was a visitor to the three massive aquarium tanks of the 1867 World's Fair in Paris. These tanks were a celebrated crowd-pleaser at an event that between 11 million and 15 million people are estimated to have attended. The International Fisheries Exhibition, held in London in 1883, was another global crowd-gatherer that featured the largest public aquarium to that date. The exhibition was at once a cultural and commercial spectacle to promote the age-old industry of fishing and encourage its modernization.

Fishing techniques that developed across the century evince the complex aspects of technological modernization discussed in this section, ranging from the changing transport practices already described to portside management of catches. Canning was invented in 1809 in France using glass bottles, and tin-coated iron cans were developed in Britain the following year. With the ability to preserve perishable goods, canning expanded the ability of fisheries to preserve and hence expand the quantities useful to catch, and it was rapidly adapted on both sides of the Atlantic, with American and European scholars disputing which nations took the lead (Dias and Guillotreau 2004). The canning industry for tuna, the great pelagic fish today threatened by overfishing, would not be established until the twentieth century. However, the destructive potential of industrial-scale fishing was evident to those involved in the North Atlantic fisheries on both sides of this ocean by the mid-nineteenth century. Eminent British scientist Thomas Huxley played an equivocal role in debates about overfishing launched as early as the 1860s, when he was part of a Royal Commission to decide whether trawling should be regulated. The Commission advised that such matters should be left to the market, and that "any act of legislative interference is simply a superfluous intervention between man and nature" (quoted in Bolster 2012: location 2923). Nonetheless, when Huxley gave his opening address to the audience at the International Fisheries Exhibition of 1883, he did raise the question: "WHETHER FISHERIES ARE EXHAUSTIBLE; AND IF SO, WHETHER ANYTHING CAN BE DONE TO PREVENT THEIR EXHAUSTION?" (Huxley 1883, emphasis in the original).

The International Fisheries Exhibition may also have drawn visitors, as its aquariums suggest, due to public interest in the sea as both a conduit of empire and now, in the nineteenth century, a new destination for leisure. In the early modern era, most people feared the sea—when Robinson Crusoe built a place of relaxation on his island, he tellingly constructed an inland bower. Historian Alain Corbin has shown how in the later eighteenth century, this aversion began to shift, to what he calls "the lure of the sea" (1994) emerging together with an interest in the coast as a site of leisure and hygiene. Initially, only upper classes had the means to visit and vacation; by the mid-nineteenth century in Europe, however, railroads enabled the middle classes to reach coastal towns, and resorts proliferated. There, people enjoyed swimming, sailing small boats, and taking in the beauty of the seashore, collecting specimens for their home aquariums.

Aquariums as well as coastal observation led the general public to take an interest in an undersea realm they had no way to observe directly. Helmet diving remained the province of professionals—more comparable to mining than scuba, which quickly was taken up by amateurs after its invention in the twentieth century. Unknown creatures fished up by engineers laying transatlantic cable lines in the 1850s led scientists to realize that the depths of the seas were in fact richly inhabited. However, scientists only observed creatures from the surface, and rendered them through preserving them or through drawings in the static tradition of scientific illustration. While beautiful imagery of marine life by biologists such as Ernst Haeckel influenced the decorative arts in the later nineteenth century, moreover, scientists had no technology to exhibit the reality of the environment beneath the sea. From the perspective of submersive spectacle, the nineteenth century of marine observation concludes with the invention of underwater photography by French marine biologist Louis Boutan in the early 1890s. Initially of interest primarily as a technical feat, this invention came to mass notice with a 1914 documentary using undersea footage recorded by Scottish-American engineer J.E. Williamson, who invented a submersible that could hold a camera operator able to film underwater. Williamson contributed undersea footage to the first Hollywood adaptation of Verne's *Twenty Thousand Leagues Under the Sea* into film in 1916, directed by Stuart Paton. The photosphere's ability to exhibit to mass audiences on land the submarine environment, rather than curated marine gardens, marks the advent of a new era of undersea spectacle.

UNEVENNESS

Because of steam's impact, the transition from sail to steam is a phrase commonly used as shorthand for the massive transformations of the Industrial Revolution at sea in the nineteenth century. One of the most famous icons of technological modernization is J.M.W. Turner's *The Fighting Temeraire tugged to her last berth to be broken up* (1839) (Figure 0.1). This scene, by arguably the premier Western painter of the sea, shows a "98-gun, 2nd rate ship of the line which fought at [the battle of] Trafalgar," when Nelson defeated Napoleon's navy in 1805 (Kemp 1988: 861). In Turner's image, the sailing ship and the tugboat come alive as creatures, personifying the clashing energies of history. Figureheads were an age-old ornamentation of ships, expressing the mariners' sense that "a ship needed to find her own way across the waters, and could only do so if she had eyes" (302). Investigating the source of Turner's painting, Sam Willis suggests that there is "some sketchy evidence that the *Temeraire* did not have a figurehead at all," but nonetheless, Turner has turned the entire bow of the ghostly white *Temeraire* into a downcast marine monster. (2012: 97). The prow and forecastle of the *Temeraire* moreover rhyme with

FIGURE 0.1 J.M.W. Turner, *The Fighting Temeraire tugged to her last berth to be broken up,* 1839. Oil on canvas. © Wikimedia Commons (public domain).

the smokestack and paddlewheels of the stubby, compact, energetic steamboat towing it. The steamboat's countenance, colored in the rust brown of iron and the orange black of smoke and fire, gives a sense of Vulcanesque personality, although tellingly steam vessels, in contrast to sailing ships, did not have figureheads.

Turner's painting is prescient: steam would indeed take over sail in work and war by the end of the long nineteenth century covered in this volume. However, at the time it was painted in 1838, Turner conceived a technofantasy about a transition that was by no means achieved. While promising, industrial technologies were a work in progress, and sailing crafts persisted both in complement and in competition across the nineteenth century. Indeed, we can find that persistence in the *Fighting Temeraire*. Steam tugboats were used to tow large sailing vessels into harbors, whether they were decommissioned or not. Thus, the activity of towing is the subject of *The Tugboat* on the cover of this volume, an 1857 photograph by Gustave Le Gray. This innovative photographer is known for having created a single image joining negatives of different exposure times to capture the beguiling luminous marine atmosphere and the surface of the sea. With the image of a steamship leading a furled sailing ship, Le Gray's photo conveys the same sense of transfer as Turner's painting, although in fact sail and steam are complementing each other in the scene captured by Le Gray.

Indeed, the transition from sail to steam is not only shorthand but commonly substitutes for the complexity described in the previous section. Such shorthand is convenient and also may express an "emphasis on discovery" that, historian Gerald Graham speculates, has been responsible for such descriptive and reductive phrases as "The Age of Iron and Steam" (1956: 74–5). Yet at the same time, it is deceptive, not only because of the complex processes described in the previous section but also because of the persistence of the sail in the work of the sea. As Graham observes, as long as routes to Asia and India demanded going around the Cape of Good Hope, "the commercial steamer could not hope to compete"; "the great days of sail lie not before but after the middle of the century" (75). This extends as well to routes in the Pacific and to the West Coast of the United States in this era of sea transport whose conclusion might also be marked with the 1914 opening of the Panama Canal. Further, such emphasis on innovation backgrounds the continued use of other forms of maritime travel amidst the cultures encountering each other on the seas of nineteenth-century globalization, including the variety of Indian Ocean vessels encompassed by the term *dhow*, the outrigger canoes in the Pacific, and the kayaks in polar seas that readers will find discussed in the volume's chapters.

In sum, modernization in the nineteenth century is at once purposeful and proceeds at difference paces in different frames of reference, in a fashion that resonates with the cohabitation of old and new technologies in the digital revolution we are witnessing today. It is fitting that an aging James Bond who came of age in the analog world and a young Q intuitively at home in digitally-enabled crime, surveillance, and defense first meet in front of *The Fighting Temeraire* in Sam Mendes's *Skyfall* (2012). Along with noting the complexity of the Industrial Revolution at sea, readers should note its *unevenness*. The events, people, and processes described in chapters are enmeshed in nuanced, environmentally specific, highly diverse practices.

In Marxian social theory, unevenness designates the coexistence of different levels of modernization within a single time frame, as access to technologies of modernization are distributed according to wealth. Access to new technologies in many cases is determined by wealth in the history of the sea. A good example is the use of the marine chronometer in the first decades of the nineteenth century, whose revolutionization of navigation King explains in the "Practices" chapter. This life-saving technology finally permitting the calculation of longitude in the course of an open sea voyage had been invented in 1769. These timepieces required fine craftsmanship and were expensive. At the start of the nineteenth century, they were primarily purchased for the navy. Even in this service so foundational to the British rule, the chronometer only became widely used on navy ships in the early 1820s, and its use was not widespread on ocean-going vessels until the middle of the century. Indeed, most of the many chronometers on HMS *Beagle* critical to its scientific mission of observing location accurately were paid for personally by its captain Robert FitzRoy.

However, unevenness had other reasons that will be familiar to all of us living at a time when so many old and new technologies coexist. Inertia of long-established practices can have an irrational impact on the adoption of life-saving innovations, as was the case with the chronometer. In Carroll's chapter about the wreck of the *Kent*, she highlights the ongoing concern of the British government about shipwrecks, which threated both the empire's wealth and reach. When a Parliamentary Committee on Shipwrecks of 1836 inquired into the use of chronometers, it discovered that many captains believed the technology was hard to use and took them on voyages only so that, in the words of one captain, "the passengers will see I have a chronometer on board, with which they will be satisfied" (Betts 2017: 59).

Further, new technologies could be slow to implement, particularly when entrepreneurs were uncertain whether their investments would pay off. The uneven pace of steam implementation in cross-Atlantic immigrant transport from Britain to the East Coast of North America offers a good example: Cohn notes that during the Great Famine in the early 1850s, 99 percent of Irish immigrants arrived on sailing ships (in "Conflicts," Boelhower includes in his discussion of human trafficking the notorious "coffin ships" where so many refugees from the famine died). Cohn takes the case of Quebec, where immigration remained stable in the late 1850s to 1860s, to show that it was possible to implement the transition in several years. He cites information from Basil Greenhill that "in 1858, 138 sailing ships carried 9,104 steerage passengers from Britain to Quebec and 16 steamers carried 1,912. In 1860, 37 steamers carried 6,932 passengers, 20 sailing ships carried 904" (quoted in Cohn 2005: 478). In one of the world's busiest ports, New York City, in contrast, "the transition that had started as soon as the early or mid-1850s was not finished by 1867; in fact, it did not completely finish until 1874 or so" (Cohn 2005: 476). Thus, "almost 47,000 immigrants still arrived at New York City on sailing ships [in 1867], as many as in 1861 and not many fewer than the 69,000" arriving on sailing ships in 1858 (476). In explaining the slowness of this transition, despite available technologies, Cohn weighs different factors. Among the most likely are the cost of passage and the type of travelers. On this route serving immigrants, poorer travelers could sacrifice speed to price, and choose a sailing vessel if it was less costly, and while steerage had been introduced in the 1860s, sailing ships still retained a portion of the immigrant market. Another important factor is the cost of capital improvement. A steamship took months to build, and steamship companies had to decide that this investment was profitable.

They were hesitant until the mid-1860s, when immigration to the United States started to rise sharply, which prompted companies to order new ships. Until all those new ships were built, sailing ships took up the slack.

Established practices further might encode hard-won knowledge that would come with the perspectives and biases of those responsible for its achievement. Thus, accurate ocean charts had been accumulated over centuries by seafaring nations. In the nineteenth century, the leading producer of charts was the Admiralty of Great Britain, which "understood deeply the interrelation between scientific knowledge and naval, mercantile, national, and imperial power" (Smith 2018: location 716). When American Admiral Perry led an exploratory American voyage to scope out the possibility of using Japan as a toehold in the Pacific, cross-cultural contact also helped Japan access state of the art scientific and technological practices. As Japan escalated its maritime ambitions, Japanese geographers noted that Kyoto should be the location of the prime meridian for their nation, much as Greenwich for England or Paris for France. However, Japanese geographers were keenly aware that the Japanese had "not yet sailed abroad and therefore have not measured the longitudes and latitudes of various places" (Frumer 2018: 127). They thus found it expedient to adapt the British charts whose prime meridian ran through Greenwich, all the more so because "comparison tables brought to Japan [...] all measured time according to Greenwich" (127). Simultaneously, the Japanese were entering into competition with European (as well as other East Asian) nations for oceanic dominance and, indeed, as Frumer observes, "the Greenwich-based global time reinforced the Japanese idea of national time," and thus a national sense of identity (127).

As the ongoing viability of sail for long ocean transport across the century shows, noting the exigencies of specific marine environments is critical to understanding the uneven appearance of ocean practice across this century of transition. Further, as Davis, Gallman, and Gleiter observe, "Far from being driven from the seas by the advent of steam, the sailing vessel reached its apogee—in technological development, numbers, and importance—more than fifty years after oceangoing steamships began to arrive regularly at Continental ports" (1997: 261). They credit this development to "the pressure" of competition that "leads to improvements in the traditional technology that keep the old way competitive for a substantial period of time. Such was the case for sailing vessels" (261). The swiftest sailing ships ever built were clipper ships perfected in the 1840s and 1850s, over three times faster than other ships of the era. The clipper ship expanded the design of a type of schooner "built in Virginia and Maryland, known as the Baltimore clippers [...] which became famous during the War of 1812 as blockade runners and privateers and subsequently notorious as slave ships carrying human cargoes from Africa to the U.S.A"—counter to US law, which had outlawed the slave trade starting January 1, 1808 (Kemp 1988: 172).

Swift, maneuverable ships, such as schooners and subsequently clippers, played an important role in enabling the age of Second Slavery discussed by Boelhower; historians estimate that slavers abducted between three-quarters of a million and over a million people before the trade in fact stopped, possibly as late as 1880. Such vessels could dodge British and American warships, and their ability to maneuver was abetted by switching flags. Thus, while it was illegal to transport slaves onboard American ships, ships plying the slave trade could sail to Africa under the flag of the United States, and then switch to flags of other nations, such as Brazil and Cuba. The Cuban schooner *Amistad* was the setting for one of the most notorious instances bringing to public attention the ongoing trade, when captives from Sierra Leone rebelled in 1839, killing captain and crew. *The United States v. Libellants & Claimants of The Schooner Amistad* in 1841 exonerating the rebels became a rallying point for abolitionists. Historian Marcus Rediker contextualizes both their rebellion and their cruel treatment when they landed in the United States, emphasizing the complex legacy of racism and freedom in the seafaring world (2013). As Rediker has documented throughout his work, ships were at once the vessels of the Middle Passage and tolerated free Blacks as seamen in the age of slavery, enabling an avenue open to talents, even while Black seamen were most often given lower status work. Frederick Douglass, who would eventually escape to freedom donning the disguise of a sailor, captures this contradiction in his autobiography when he describes looking out at the sailing ships on the Chesapeake Bay while still enslaved, likening their white sails at once to the shrouds of ghosts and "freedom's swift-winged angels" (1845: 66).

The streamlined clipper ships that took sail to its apogee after the mid-century were used across the globe in transport of high-value cargo requiring swift delivery, with narrow hulls that sacrificed space to speed. Shipbuilder Donald McKay's extreme clipper *Sovereign of the Seas* claimed the record of 22 knots, "a speed that steamships would not reach until the 1890s" (Worrall 2018). Tea is famed as a high-status commodity traveling by clipper, but in recent years, historians have delved into the importance of clipper ships as conduits of illicit cargo, such as the opium that made fortunes for traders and solidified British dominance in India. One of the first famous British opium clippers was the *Red Rover*, built in 1830 on the Hooghly River in Calcutta, named ironically after a sea novel by James Fenimore Cooper celebrating eighteenth-century piracy by American colonists as the antecedents of the American Revolution. Nations profiting from the opium trade were foremost Britain and the United States, even as the drug also profited traders in long-established Indian Ocean networks. Regional crafts continued to ply the routes of the opium trade, including, in Chinese waters, ocean-going junks, flat-bottomed river boats and hybrid sailing/rowing boats known as "crab boats" that carried opium upriver and to other coastal harbors, from ports of entry such as Macao.

The role of the environment, at once physical and social, in determining vessels used for sea transport, emerges across the wide variety of navigations found in the volume. In the chapter "Practices," King, for example, differentiates among three types of working vessels sailing around Cape Horn in the two decades 1840 to 1860. Through the lens of Melville's passages around a storied environment of danger in the history of navigation, King explains first sailing around the Horn on a whaleship, in Melville's case, the *Acushnet*. When Melville rounded Cape Horn a second time in 1844, he was on a US Navy ship, the USS *United States*, nearly "twice the size of the whaleship *Acushnet*." In 1860, Melville was a passenger on the clipper ship *Meteor*, captained by his younger brother. King observes that even when steam engines made it easier to maneuver around Cape Horn, some of "the last merchant vessels under sail alone still sailed around [...] [it] up until the 1932, even when the Panama and Suez Canals had been well established."

From the Southern tip of the Americas, nineteenth-century seafarers found in this volume span to the Great Barrier Reef and the ice floes of Arctic waters. Iain McCalman includes both Western and Aboriginal vessels in his survey of human interaction with the Great Barrier Reef across the nineteenth century, in his chapter on "Islands and Shores." In 1858, two years before Melville sailed around Cape Horn on the *Meteor*, French cabin boy Narcisse Pelletier was on a workaday French sailing ship when it was wrecked on the Great Barrier Reef. Adopted by Wanthaala Aborigines, with whom he lived for seventeen years, as McCalman details, Pelletier learned to build and navigate in outrigger canoes, which could paddle out sixty-five kilometers to the Outer Reef, and were used to hunt dugong.

In her chapter on "Travelers," Adriana Craciun includes the use of sea kayaks well adapted to ice, when she explores the diverse navigations of Polar waters. Thus, kayaks were the craft of choice for the Inuit Qitdlarssuaq, who crossed from the Canadian Arctic to northwest Greenland in the mid-nineteenth century. Once there, Qitdlarssuaq's expedition spent six years, intermarrying with the more isolated Inughuit, and teaching them arts that they had forgotten over generations, such as how to build kayaks. As Craciun details, Qitdlarssuaq learned of Greenland from a European searching for the lost expedition of Sir John Franklin, a British voyage to find the Northwest passage (1845–8), whose sunken wrecks have recently been found thanks to the collaboration of Inuit knowledge and nautical archaeology. Craciun notes that "European travelers in northern seas considered ice as a bitter foe, while Inuit travelers used sea ice as a highway connecting communities across great distances." Among modes of transport suited to the polar environment, Craciun also describes the arduous practice used by whalers of hitching their ships for a ride on an iceberg.

Whaling was one industry where the use of sail for its renewable power lasted across the century. By 1851, the year when *Moby-Dick* was published, and when the industry was at its height, due to the demand for whale oil, blubber, and bone, the whale populations had been decimated in the Atlantic. As Melville accurately depicts, whalers would go out for years on end, tracking their prey across the planet. Because of the lengthy time away from land, whalers continued to use sailing ships, with auxiliary steam added late in the century. Indeed, the last wooden whale ship in the world was a sailing ship, the *Charles W. Morgan.* Currently restored and on view at Mystic Seaport in the United States, the *Morgan* was built in 1841 and had an eighty-year career, with voyages lasting three years or even longer. The *Morgan*, as the Mystic website specifies, was "built for durability not speed" ("Charles W. Morgan" n.d.).

This value of durability adds another factor to incorporate in the history of modernization at sea framing this volume, which is that in extreme environments such as the oceans, excellence in transport does not reside in speed alone. Joseph Conrad recognized the complex and uneven nature of technological change at sea in his nonfictional *The Mirror of the Sea* (1906), a historical and philosophical memoir with insights derived from his two-decade career sailing on a range of types of vessels around the world, including schooners and clipper ships, barques, steamers, and a steamboat up the river in the Congo. When Conrad writes about sailing ships in "her days of perfection," he notes that what is meant by perfection is "not the perfection of speed" but rather "build, gear, seaworthy qualities, and ease of handling" ([1906] 1924: 47). Conrad notably mentioned the importance of copper-sheathing the hull of wooden ships, a practice that developed in Britain in the 1760s and was in use in the Indian Ocean by the 1780s. Copper sheathing was an effective way to slow down the growth of marine organisms on the submerged part of the hull, which would not only eat away at it but also add drag. As Conrad writes in *The Mirror of the Sea*, "Everything has been done to make the iron ship perfect, but no wit of man had managed to devise an efficient coating composition to keep her bottom clean with the smooth cleanliness of yellow metal sheeting. After a spell of a few weeks at sea, an iron ship begins to lag as if she had grown tired too soon" (47–8). In keeping with Conrad's insight that speed is not the only criterion of effectiveness, renewability is a twenty-first-century term for one important seaworthy factor developed across this section on uneven modernization. Thus, although it was too obvious in the nineteenth century to need highlighting, sailing ships ran on renewable energy. In seeking to reduce greenhouse emissions today, engineers in the shipping industry are again looking for ways to travel using wind power as well as solar energy.

Sail was also used late into the century in scientific voyages of surveying and research, which sought out inaccessible, remote ocean locations. In

"Knowledges," Adamowsky emphasizes the "'discovery' of the underwater biosphere as a source of creation and a subject of marine biology." A milestone in marine science of the depths was the first government-sponsored oceanographic expedition, the British HMS *Challenger* expedition, between 1872 and 1876, which used a corvette, a small navy ship, outfitted with a scientific laboratory as well as with an auxiliary steam engine. The expedition circled the globe taking samples of marine life, as well as sounding and gathering topographical information about hitherto unfathomed depths. An indication of the voyage's thorough study, despite rudimentary tools for undersea charting by today's standards, was its location of the Mariana Trench, which is still recognized as the deepest place on our planet.

Volume author King reveals yet another facet to the unevenness complicating a narrative of technological modernization when he observes that the dangerous, mercurial conditions at Cape Horn could thwart the improvements offered by new technologies. While the whale ship *Acushnet* had a wide hull "built for cargo rather than speed, she was only a few days slower than Melville's passage [around the Horn] two decades later" on the *Meteor*. Nor did clipper ship travel make this crossing any less austere. In his "first fictionalized narrative *Typee* (1845)," Melville described a "horrid headland," but as King points out, in his journal entries about sailing around Cape Horn on the *Meteor*, Melville's language had turned infernal, portraying "horrible snowy mountains" and gorges of a "hell-landscape."

The violence of weather is noted by Boelhower, and indeed is one form of conflict he adds to the more familiar histories of violence that he includes in his chapter. Thus, Boelhower discusses Conrad's novella *Typhoon* (1902), where Captain MacWhirr runs into a typhoon of unprecedented magnitude, because, despite an ominous barometer, he cannot imagine natural forces capable of overwhelming his steam ship, as well as due to pressure by shipowners that he waste neither coal nor time. Survival in this tale results from luck, MacWhirr's unflappable stubbornness, and above all the deft handling of the engine by crew member Solomon Rout. *Typhoon* admonishes readers not to equate better technologies with domination of the ocean environment. It also shows that such forces care nothing about capitalism and are disrespected at human peril.

In the chapter on the ocean imaginary, Cannon Schmitt underscores the theme of both practice and imagination coming up short in confronting the diversity of ocean environments throughout literature of and about seafaring. Using the fictional library of the *Dulcibella* in Erskine Childers's novel *The Riddle of the Sands* (1903) to elaborate the diverse kinds of sea knowledge valued in the nineteenth century, Schmitt emphasizes the mesh between fantasy and practical experience. In addition, the library of the *Dulcibella* includes detailed technical knowledge essential to a real as well as the imaginary navigation of the treacherous intertidal environment of the Wadden Sea off the coast of Germany depicted in the novel. Yet the environment repeatedly betrays the skill of its captain, Davies, who runs aground despite precautions on a daily basis. This ability of the marine environment to exceed imagination together with control, Schmitt suggests, may have been more evident to writers evaluating the state of marine knowledge at the turn of the twentieth century, like Childers, in contrast to those referred to by Rosalind Williams from an earlier generation (Jules Verne, Robert Louis Stevenson, and William Morris), when she develops her concept of the triumph of human empire.

Volume author Charne Lavery too observes how writers in the second half of the nineteenth century draw energy from the contradictions of modernization at sea, even as some nineteenth-century popular fiction celebrates technological shifts and the "virulent expansion of maritime empire." Lavery opens her chapter "Representations" with Conrad's *Lord Jim* first published in *Blackwood's* (1899–1900), which foregrounds the role played by modern communications technology in revealing the crime that is the subject of the first part of the novel. Transmission of information across the Indian Ocean became possible with a linkage of overland and undersea cables in 1870. When the motley crew of the *Patna* amble into an Eastern port in Conrad's novel, their lies have been preceded by "that mysterious cable message from Aden," where the disabled steamer that they abandoned, claiming it sunk, has been towed ([1900] 2002: 27). The submarine cable lines reaching to Mumbai were laid to foster British control of India and contributed in myriad ways to Western imperialism in the Indian Ocean. *Lord Jim* reverses this power flow in the dereliction of duty that is put on trial in the first half of the novel. There, the cable reveals the racism and incompetence of characters belonging to a class of European seamen in such service that Conrad characterizes as endemic to Eastern ports, preferring to the craft of the sea "short passages, good deck-chairs, large native crews, and the distinction of being white" (10). Their laxness, Conrad implies, propagates as they evade the protocols of European merchant shipping amidst a pre- and coexisting Indian Ocean commerce pursued by Arab, Indian, or in Jim's case, Chinese shipowners.

Heart of Darkness, initially serialized in *Blackwood's* in 1899 as well, offers a related, environmentally based complication of technological modernization. After revealing the importance of steam in implementing imperial bureaucracy, Marlow takes his listeners to a treacherous river, where, along with colonial incompetence and greed, the environment, including the jungle and tropical disease, destroys the supply chain essential to colonial mastery. When Marlow reaches his command, he finds it sunk at the bottom of the Congo River, perhaps due to one of the snags whose danger Marlow, like Mark Twain in his *Life on the Mississippi* (1883), points out to us as he works so hard to avoid it. While steam promotes speed in contexts administered efficiently, Marlow is forced to wait for months for the needed materials due to the complete breakdown of bureaucracy at the Central Station, with mounting frustration about such enforced idleness. Another environment whose forces outstripped modernization at the end of the nineteenth century were undeveloped areas of Panama, which initially thwarted the French project to build a canal joining the Atlantic and Pacific, led by the entrepreneur who constructed the Suez Canal, de Lesseps. In this ambitious project, technology still could not sculpt the land nor tame malaria and yellow fever, and the French abandoned their efforts after almost a decade (1881–9), with more than 20,000 deaths. The United States would subsequently succeed where the French had failed, leasing the land from Panama, as part of its challenge to the Pax Britannica, seeking to consolidate American empire on both the Atlantic and Pacific Oceans. The dangerous effort of construction lasted from 1904 to 1914, killing thousands of workers and maiming many more. Casualties from yellow fever were alleviated due to the understanding of the disease as mosquito-borne rather than bacterial, proved by the experiments of Walter Reed in 1901.

I have focused in this section on the unevenness in modernizing work at sea across the nineteenth century. Such unevenness further encompasses the fact that amateurs as well as professionals played a role in emergent new forms of sea practice, notably in the marine sciences. Influential observations about coastal waters were made by attentive amateurs, whose work was then absorbed by professionals. Carroll, for example, starts her chapter on the networks of transoceanic travel with a bottle found by an unnamed Black man, presumably enslaved, in the waves off a beach in Bathsheba, Barbados, in 1826. The bottle turned out to contain a message sent from the *Kent*, bound for British India, in the Bay of Biscay, eighteen months before. Two early citizen scientists, the unnamed bottle's finder, and James Surles, a white man swimming with him, perhaps his master, brought the bottle to the attention of the newspapers. Thanks to journalism, oceanographers took up the bottle's drift and used it to help map the directions of ocean currents.

Along with oceanography, as Adamowsky emphasizes, "modern marine biology owes many of its roots to the natural studies of passionate amateurs and hobbyist researchers." One figure in her chapter both excluded from the scientific establishment of her time and contributing to it was the British naturalist Anna Thynne. In 1846, Thynne took her six children and all their collecting equipment down to the seashore in Devon and gathered marine specimens. Transporting the sea creatures home after the summer, and then finding a way to maintain them, Thynne created a small sustainable marine ecosystem in a controlled setting. Jeanette Villepreux-Power is another amateur working in the Mediterranean, who had in the 1830s created small aquariums to observe the paper nautilus and the octopus. She published her findings to the interest of scientists in *Observations et expériences physiques sur plusieurs animaux marins et terrestres* ("Physical Observations and Experiments on Several Marine and Terrestrial Animals").

In Schmitt's chapter, he describes as well the entanglement of amateur and professional practices in the development of yachting in the nineteenth century. While amateur naturalists contributed to marine science, professional seafarers contributed to the growth of sailing for pleasure, as part of expanding water-based leisure. Schmitt notes that the naval officer and the editor who founded *The Naval Annual*, Thomas Brassey, accomplished the first amateur circumnavigation of the globe from 1876 to 1877. Author Jules Verne exemplifies the enjoyment of yachting by a knowledgeable amateur. Verne was born in the port city of Nantes and had grown up surrounded by technological experimentation, as well as work, at sea. As an adult, he pursued a passion for yachting. His boats included the *Saint Michel II*, a thirteen-meter sailing ship for cruising around the Atlantic off of Brittany and Aquitaine, and then the thirty-one-meter *Saint Michel III*, a hybrid vessel with both steam and sail that he would take as far abroad as Italy, North Africa, and Malta.

In discussing the allure of yachting, Schmitt adds the pleasures of adventure without practical purpose, which is yet another facet to the unevenness of sea practice in this century. Adventure was, as Schmitt writes, at once a pursuit different from workaday existence, and a keen existential affirmation "outside an entirely managed, humanized, charted world." The Romantic poets Byron, who swam across the Dardenelles strait, and Shelley, who drowned in a boating accident at the century's beginning, are antecedents of such heroes of extreme adventure as Canadian Joshua Slocum, who circumnavigated the globe on his own between 1895 and 1898. Slocum's *Sailing Alone Around the World* (1899) became a classic in a new genre of narratives of adventure for its own sake, as well as taking a place on the bookshelf of sea literature. This lure of the sea as a path to escape a predetermined social situation at once is in continuity with an earlier fantasy of running off to sea and opens another facet to the cultural history of marine environments in the nineteenth century, which is the potential they have to foster lives lived off the charts, in a quality I call eccentricity.

ECCENTRICITY

From the perspective of this volume's focus on Western and human empire, eccentricity applies to people, events, and processes within dominant formations whose stories have not been told, as well as to those who resist such formations, and those that escape their compass. Indeed, eccentric participants across the volume can belong to more than one of these categories. This is the case, for example, of the Indian Ocean seamen, known as lascars, discussed by Lavery, who played a critical role in the maritime industry. Despite their importance, these seamen have been relegated to the margins of Western saltwater writings about this region. As Lavery points out, their lives have only been reclaimed with the advent of postcolonial perspectives. Thus, recent novels by Amitav Ghosh and Abdulrazak Gurnah restore the alternative modernities of Indian Ocean transport in the nineteenth century, and the prominence of African, Arab, and Indian workers of the sea. Lavery further brings from the shadows the presence of lascars in the Anglo-American canon of nineteenth-century sea fiction, applying Edward W. Said's notion of contrapuntal reading to sea novels by authors ranging from James Fenimore Cooper to R.M. Ballantyne and Rudyard Kipling, along with the most canonical of sea novelists, Melville, Stevenson, and Conrad. Reading such authors contrapuntally opens up new directions for maritime historians, as well as literary critics. Thus, Lynette Russell has used the writings of Melville to recover the agency of Australian Aborigines who participated and profited from the industries of whaling and sealing (2012).

In Schmitt's chapter, he observes that while philosopher Michel Foucault used the ship to illustrate the concept of a "heterotopia," sea geographies are hospitable to diverse and heterogeneous trajectories beyond shipboard settings. An important form of eccentricity that emerges in Indian Ocean contexts is the varied cast of characters who people a hybrid underworld, such as the "failures, drifters, and beachcombers" identified by Lavery. As Lavery notes, such figures are often outcasts from the imperial enterprise, and she relates them as well to counter-bourgeois bohemia on land: "theirs is a kind of *flanerie,* but played out on an oceanic rather than an urban scale." Lavery gives a political significance to these outcasts when she traces how they have been reinterpreted in postcolonial fiction. In the novel *Desertion* by Gurnah (2005), for example, she stresses the uncoupling of the beachcomber from the white traveler or settler, in favor of attending to Black travelers and beachcombers. She also discusses the reframing in this work of the cliché of the white beachcomber, who turns out not only to be a deserter but a wasteful killer of wild animals in Southern Somalia.

The eccentric types that Lavery identifies in fiction come to life as historical individuals in Iain McCalman's discussion of European castaways on the Barrier Reef across the long nineteenth century. In McCalman's account, the story of European castaways begins in the later eighteenth century, as the first expedition of James Cook shipwrecked there, nearly lost to the history of exploration, from the Western perspective, and initiating a history of depredation from the perspective of the people who call the Reef home. For Cook, the Reef was a "labyrinth of terror," while the Guugu Yimithirr encountering his expedition knew its seasons, treacheries, and bounty. In the nineteenth century, McCalman follows the stories of European castaways who washed up on the Reef due to shipwreck and were nurtured by Indigenous clans. McCalman traces the changing attitudes of Europeans toward the Reef inhabitants through the settler reaction to the people they had protected. Giom, whose European name was Barbara Thompson, was "rescued" by the *Rattlesnake* oceanographic expedition in 1849 and reintegrated into white society. Tolerance for her years amidst the Kaurareg Islanders was fostered as well by the open-mindedness of the scientists who received her story. In contrast to Thompson, the French cabin boy, Narcisse Pelletier renamed Anco by Wanthaala Aborigines known today as Night's Island or Sandbeach people, was stigmatized a quarter of a century later, in 1875, when he returned to European society. Although Pelletier left his Aboriginal life, McCalman recounts, he never adapted European values and died at fifty, remaining proud of his prowess in crafts Europeans considered savage, such as spear-making and dugong hunting.

The last beachcomber in McCalman's account is Ted Banfield, a voluntary castaway on an island of the Reef Banfield idealized as a tropical counterpart to Thoreau's Walden Pond. In this retreat, Banfield exemplifies the fondness for islands, which, as John Gillis has described, are a particularly valued imaginative geography of hygiene and restoration in the West (2004). Even as Banfield and his wife purportedly escaped civilization in a Romantic return to a state of nature, McCalman reconstructs the perspectives of locals on the Western castaway story that will become important in postcolonial novels. Banfield's "Dunk Island" was not an uninhabited desert island, despite Banfield's representations, but rather part of an Aboriginal insular network, and Banfield depended for his survival on Aboriginal labor. Indeed, the first figure to appear when Banfield arrived on what he called Dunk Island, was a man named Tom, who regarded this island, Coonanglebah, as a lifelong hunting ground and dreaming place.

Banfield "escaping" civilization on Dunk Island is far from the exile of Robinson Crusoe and the fearsome view of being castaway in earlier centuries. Indeed, Banfield's beachcomber lifestyle takes to a qualitatively different level the turn to the coast for relaxation and leisure that developed across the nineteenth century. Now the coast becomes a refuge from the oppression of land—a version of the use of the water as an escape from bureaucratized, normative society described by Schmitt undertaken by amateur yachtspeople. In Banfield's beachcomber lifestyle, he adumbrates the beach bum culture that will develop in the twentieth century. At the same time, Banfield shows us how the beachcomber lifestyle, for all its apparent nonchalance, could also be a form of dispossession.

In Craciun's chapter on nineteenth-century travelers, she further cautions against the simple opposition of Western and non-Western knowledge in assessing the entangled histories of those who encounter each other on the sea and its coasts across different cultures. She notes that the convergence of Indigenous and European practice of the seas could result in aesthetic as well as practical innovations, requiring a history that would give societies conventionally opposed as premodern and modern shared roles in fashioning practices of the era. One such example to come out of the nineteenth century in the domain of water practice was the development of surfing. Surfing was a millennial old pursuit in Hawaii, and had first been described for Westerners by a ship's surgeon on Cook's third voyage. Across the nineteenth century, missionaries and plantation owners tried to eradicate surfing, on both moral grounds and due to the demand for laborers to work sugar plantations. Yet surfing persisted and three Hawaiian princes brought it to Santa Cruz, California, in 1885. In 1915, Olympic medalist Hawaiian Duke Kahanamoku surfed for crowds at Freshwater Beach in Sydney, Australia. Social and racial tensions, as well as cross-cultural creativity, would accompany surfing's subsequent spread around the globe in the twentieth century (Hough-Snee and Sotelo Eastman 2017).

Whether in the case of beach bums or surfers, the beach lifestyle is a complex formation joining modernization and age-old practices, a refusal of Western values and colonial appropriation, and also yielding new forms of expression. In another iteration, the eccentricity of sea regions could foster nonnormative lifestyles. An example of such hospitality is the previously mentioned participation of women amidst the amateurs who gained access to the scientific establishment through leisure practice of the coast. Through the lens of the professional marine scientist, the contributions of people such as Anna Thynne were what I have called uneven—a residue of amateur naturalism in a field that would become increasingly institutionalized. However, from the perspective of gender norms, their work was path-breaking and exemplifies the heterotopic possibilities of the sea. Certainly, women were present as passengers on sea voyages, however, those women who did manage to find a career amidst the overwhelmingly masculine professions of the sea were exceptions that proved the rule. This seafaring discrimination persisted in science as well, where women were not allowed onboard oceanographic research vessels during the nineteenth century.

The exclusion of women from oceanography contrasts with the hospitality of marine biology to female scientists, from the amateur contributions of Thynne and Villepreux previously mentioned. Women would continue to contribute to the development of coastal naturalism across the nineteenth century. They wrote pedagogic guides for amateur audiences and for children about creatures of the shore and also about marine plant life. An early example is Mary Matilda Howard's *Ocean Flowers and Their Teachings* (1847), which incorporated specimens of marine flora. Anna Atkins's *Photographs of British Algae: Cyanotype Impressions* (1843) was not only a contribution to marine biology but also featured arguably the first photoprints in the history of photography (Armstrong 2004). In the mid-nineteenth century, Harvard biologist Louis Agassiz, followed by his son Alexander, would include women in summer schools such as the Massachusetts retreat on Penikese Island and the

Chautauqua religious movements in Pacific Grove, California (Kohrs 2015). With such encouragement, women would start to enter into the professions of marine biology by the end of the nineteenth century. The Marine Biology Laboratory (MBL) in Woods Hole, Massachusetts, notably, is one scientific institution where in the first two decades of its establishment, 1888 to 1907, 50 percent of its students and 25 percent of the people conducting research were women (Zottoli and Seyfarth 2015).

The prestigious MBL would further influence other marine biology laboratories and attract brilliant young women. Looking forward to the twentieth century, Rachel Carson first spent time there during the summer of 1929, in between graduating from college and undertaking a Masters in zoology at Johns Hopkins University. During this summer in Woods Hole, Carson became captivated by the marine environment. If Romantic wonder and science are joined throughout this long nineteenth-century process of bringing scientific observation to the seas, in Carson's *The Sea Around Us* (1951) readers can find echoes of the amateur tradition of marine natural history of the nineteenth century. In the opening to *The Sea Around Us*, she rewrites the history of technological modernization central to this volume as "man" finding his way back to what she calls "mother sea," looking out on it with "wonder and curiosity," and then embarking on its waters and plumbing its depths. Nonetheless, she declares, "he has returned to his mother sea only on her own terms. He cannot control or change the ocean as, in his brief tenancy on earth, he has subdued and plundered the continents" ([1951] 2003: 19). Her articulation of the ocean as the limit of male-gendered control is a feminist rewriting of Byron's famous lines from *Childe Harold's Pilgrimage* (1812–18) at the beginning of the nineteenth century:

> Roll on, thou deep and dark blue Ocean – roll!
> Ten thousand fleets sweep over thee in vain;
> Man marks the earth with ruin – his control
> Stops with the shore ...
>
> (1819: 372)

Further, Carson, an English major in college, evokes the charismatic, if difficult, "mother sea" beloved by the Victorian sea poet and swimmer Algernon Swinburne, as, for example, in his poem "The Triumph of Time" (1866).

Carson would complicate her notion of the powerful mother sea a decade later in *The Silent Spring* (1962), showing that while humans may not control forces of nature like the ocean, we certainly can affect them. Thus, *The Silent Spring* would address the destructive use of DDT, which, in an example of the complexity and unevenness stressed throughout this introduction, at the same time helped to eradicate deadly mosquitos carrying malaria and yellow fever. Across the nineteenth century, maritime and marine knowledges and practices enabled more people to contend more effectively and safely with a vastly more diverse range of ocean environments than ever before. While mighty environmental powers such as the sea escape our domination, such escape does not imply that they are impervious to human agency, whether that agency pertains to the craft of navigating the seas; to the scientific understanding of their workings; or, as we are now realizing, to the role of the Industrial Revolution in causing today's climate crisis.

Acknowledgments

I am grateful to Adriana Craciun, Richard King, Charne Lavery, and Cannon Schmitt for their valuable feedback on drafts of the introduction.

CHAPTER ONE

Knowledges

Submarine Discoveries: Wonderful Facts and Monstrous Encounters

NATASCHA ADAMOWSKY
Translated by Courtney Blair Hodrick

In the nineteenth century, scientists, artists, literati, engineers, and nature-lovers alike discovered the sea. It was a place of curiosity and a source of inspiration, a hidden world that seemed to await its conquest by modern man. This sentence sounds surprising at first, as the emerging modern age is commonly known to have looked back on a centuries-long tradition of seafaring, of discoveries and conquests, and of fishing, oyster farming, and coral workmanship. The novelty of the modern attention to the sea, however, did not consist in new knowledge about navigation, wind forces, or currents, or in innovations in the construction of ships, bridges, or lighthouses. Rather, what was at stake was a consequential shift in the anthropological and historical meanings of the sea and its capacity to serve as a stage in the domains of aesthetics as well as thought to play out a new dynamic for control over nature

The nineteenth century discovered in the sea, in the words of Matthias Jakob Schleiden (1804–81), "such an inexhaustible generation-power of Nature, that nowhere else on the Earth does she meet us in equal abundance" (1858: 164).[1] Instead of the liquid surface of a midnight abyss, in which only death awaited, the oceanic depths were now described as a hoard of truth, as a thalassic country of origin, both poetically and scientifically awaiting humanity's return. "Every organism comes into being out of a cell, but every cell is maritime in origin," wrote the French physiologist René Quinton (1888–1925) in 1904 in *L'Eau de mer*, "and animal life unfailingly seeks to return to its origins."[2]

This chapter will discuss this "discovery" of the underwater biosphere as a source of creation and a subject of marine biology as well as the emerging theories of evolution, paleontology, and geology. It will pay particular attention to the endeavors, challenges, and misunderstandings that accompanied the different research processes, the knowledge creation practices and visualization techniques, and the new aesthetics of exhibition and attempts to interpret them rationally.

But first a short step back. On many occasions, historians of science have approached the concepts of discovery and innovation ambivalently. Indeed, a widespread consensus reigns in historical scholarship that the underwater realm barely interested most people before 1800, not even those whose lives took place at sea. This idea exists in conjunction with the historiographic trope of a primal human fear of the sea, which is said to have dominated European history for centuries and which was first treatable in the nineteenth century (Corbin 1994; Delumeau [1978] 1989). Nevertheless, for this all to be true, we would have to omit a large part of European cultural history and several central aspects of the history of oceanography. Indeed, it is neither the case that the science of the sea started from nothing around 1800, nor that the Enlightenment thinkers and Romantics were the first to admire a seashell or to grapple with the biodiversity of marine creatures. So it is worth venturing beyond the well-trod narratives and taking a look at the changing human conception of the sea, with its transformations and the continuities alike. The following chapter is a sketch of how such study could occur.

PREVIOUSLY

From a cultural-historical perspective, it could actually be argued that the collective intellectual history of Europe originated in an ancient philosophy of water. After Thales of Miletus had proclaimed water to be the original element and principle of all things, ancient philosophers devoted great attention to water. Scholars occupied themselves with the water cycle, the association of evaporation and rain, the question of underground connections between bodies of water, the salt content of the ocean, the mechanism of ebb and flow, and the directions of ocean currents (Deacon 1997). Admittedly, there were few new "discoveries" on these topics in the centuries between Pliny's *Historia naturalis* and the Renaissance. Nevertheless, the questions surrounding water and the sea remained a continually discussed presence.

With the Renaissance, the sea developed into a consistent object of study of the emerging new sciences. In the sixteenth century, the age of discovery had explosively expanded the realm of natural history and channeled scientific curiosity. The European chambers of wonders and collections welled over with mussels, snails, corals, stuffed crocodiles, seahorses, tortoise shells, shark teeth, narwhal horns, crabs, and swordfish bills. Within a few decades, extensive compendiums emerged, promising to bring this enormous wealth of material, from a world now fraying on all sides, into a new order. Richly illustrated works appeared, detailing everything the underwater world had to offer, from fishes and mussels to even fossils, composed by the most renowned scholars of the time, such as Adam Lonicer (1528–86), Guillaume Rondelet (1507–66), Pierre Belon (1517–64), and Conrad Gesner (1516–65) (see Belon 1555; Gesner 1558; Lonicer 1551–5; Rondelet 1554).

Then, around 1660, the diverse zoological, geological, and physical interests solidified into the first heyday of oceanography. As Margaret Deacon explains, the idea of a "Science of the Sea" soon consolidated into a broadly implemented research program. While the Royal Society looked into the composition of seawater, its gravity, and the patterns of ebb and flow (Derham 1726; Halley 1715; Wallis 1665), the prominent Anglican cleric Thomas Burnett (1635–1715) pondered how the world could have drowned in its own limited water supply during the biblical Flood (Burnett 1684). Meanwhile, Edmond Halley (1656–1742) sat at the bottom of the Thames in a diving bell he had built himself, investigating the way the colors of the water and of the light changed with increasing depth (Halley 1716). The upper surface of his hand, on which the sun shone, was red but the underside glowed green. At around the same time, the Italian naturalist and pioneer of oceanography Louis Ferdinand, Comte de Marsilli (1658–1730), set off into the sea to research below the surface of the Mediterranean (Figure 1.1). His *Histoire physique de la mer* appeared in 1725, the first book to deal exclusively with oceanography. Eight years later, a beautiful folio called *Ueber die Asterien* was published in Leipzig, the first work dedicated exclusively to starfish.

All these extraordinary endeavors and noteworthy announcements were followed attentively by an interested public, who mirrored them in their own efforts and activities. Over the course of the eighteenth century, the coast became popularly understood as a preordained place where enlightened peers could encounter the riddles of the world (see Corbin 1994; Thomas 1983). Heading off to the seashores became a beloved pastime for a populace in search of truths about the earth's past and the origins of life—or at least an idea of the new dimensions of time that the geologists had begun discussing.[3]

Within the context of the revolution regarding the concept of geological time, and in light of the deciding role played by the ocean in the development of nature, the seashore advanced in the second half of the eighteenth century to a place and subject of attentive scrutiny. Nowhere else was it so easy to perceive the multiplicity of natural rhythms, to feel the length of geological time, and to observe the instability of biological boundaries and the astonishingly

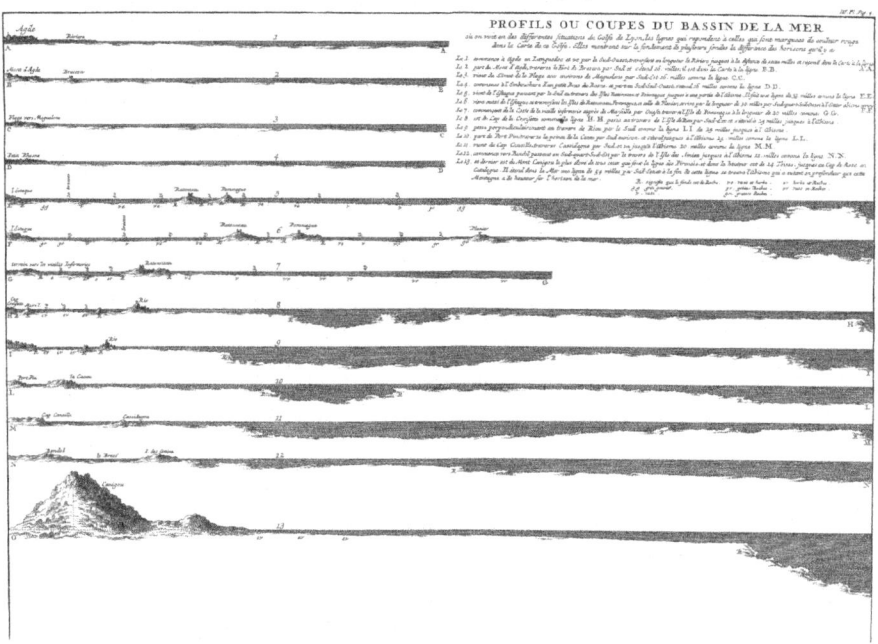

FIGURE 1.1 "Profils ou Coupes du Bassin de la Mer," from Louis Ferdinand Marsili, *Histoire physique de la mer* (Amsterdam, 1725), plate III (public domain).

metamorphosing spheres of life as on the beaches, shores, and cliffs of the maritime world. The new "passion" for the sea of this enlightened age begat a plethora of innovative practices, which combined aesthetic enjoyment with the pleasure of scientific observation and the satisfying feeling of physical exertion. People jumped into floodwaters, collected mussels and fossils, or painted the space where the land and water touched. By the end of the century, a hustle and bustle gradually overtook the shores. Educated as well as amateur researchers rummaged for wonderful curiosities on the bared seafloors and marveled over algae, jellyfish, and zoophytes. They collected mussels and posed questions that had interested no one for centuries. Why are whales beached? What is the explanation for marine luminescence (glowing seas)? Why had God created this fantastic world, only to hide it from human eyes under eternal floods?

EARLY MARINE SCIENCE AT THE SHORE: WALKS ON THE BEACH

In the nineteenth century the collection and study of marine plants and animals counted as a cultured form of amusement. Amateur researchers and educated beach vacationers alike filled their leisure hours with preparation, observation,

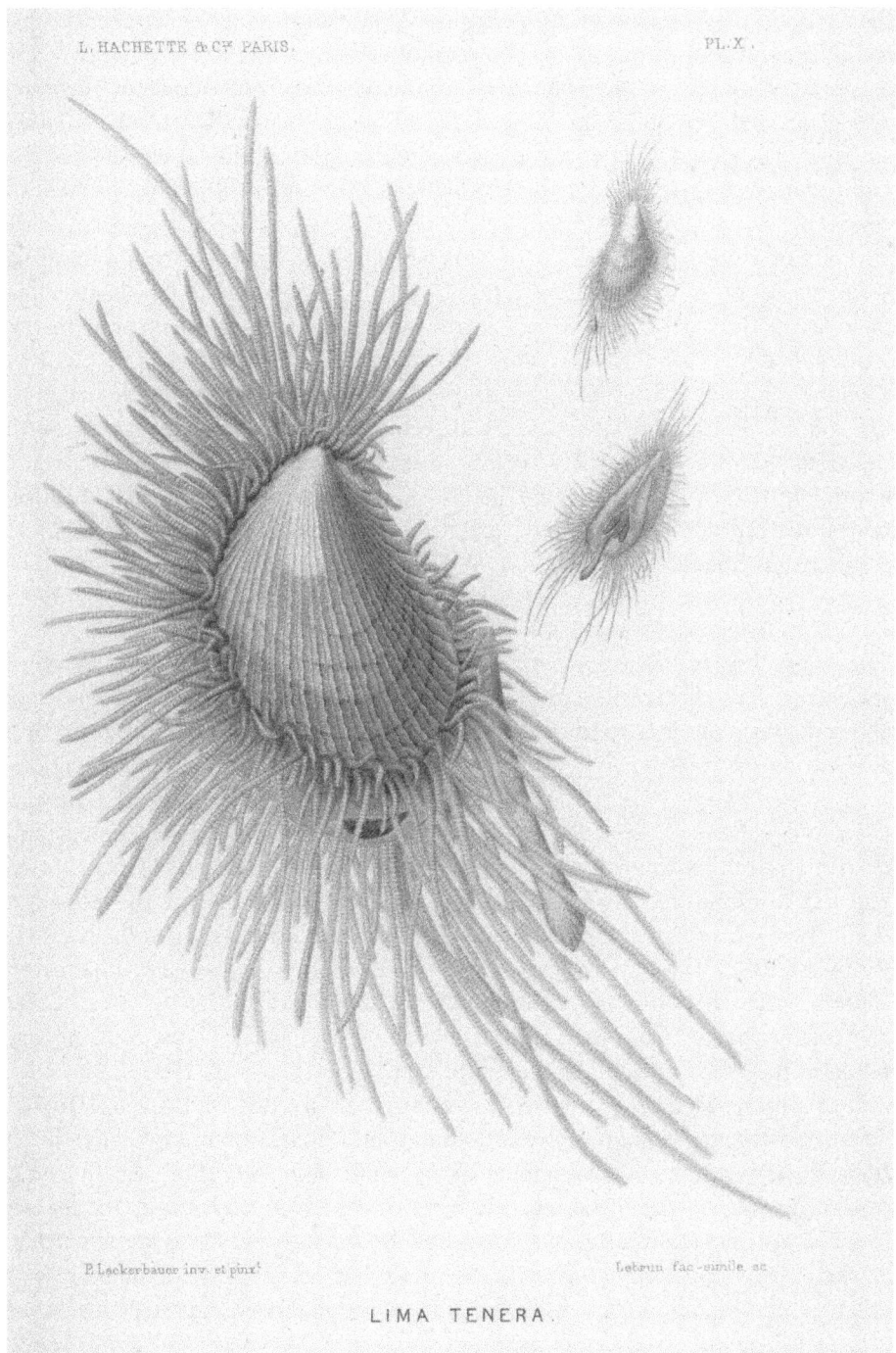

FIGURE 1.2 "Lima Tenera," from Alfred Fredol, *Le Monde de la mer* (Paris, 1865), plate X. © Chronicle/Alamy Stock Photo.

display, and description and brought the ocean into the houses, conversations, thoughts, and dreams of others. This section will describe the walk on the beach as a new epistemic practice, one which tested new forms of seeing and meaning and generated new epistemic objects (Figure 1.2). Using the example of two singular incidents, I will show the decisive meaning that this "discovery" of the frontier between rocks, sea, and sand held for the constitution of a new field of research.

The first incident pertained to fossils and outlined the path from a puzzling stone object to a scientific imaginary. Namely, what emerged was the idea of locating the "depths of time," in the sense of our geological past, in the unknown depths of the seas. The second occurrence advanced this train of thought and popularized the association of the ocean depths with the origin of life and the multiplicity of species. It thereby illustrates a decisive transition in the scientific research practices of the nineteenth century: away from a static natural history, which dissected lifeless material and drew up classification tables, toward a science of living creatures and experimentation upon them (Reiß 2012; Rheinberger 1992).

Fossils

The beginning of the nineteenth century was distinguished by a series of spectacular fossil finds. These are in no way attributable to luck. Rather, they came about thanks to an increased and media-modulated attention from scientists and amateurs alike, who exchanged knowledge among themselves in publications such as the *Organic Remains* (1804–11) or the magnificently illustrated *Mineral Conchology* (after 1829). A flowering market for fossils had developed, and particularly on the English coasts a group of especially talented fossilists (fossil seekers) distinguished themselves. They emerged mostly from the common population who roamed the fields and coasts in search of fossils (Cadbury 2001; Rudwick 2008). Two of the most renowned fossilists of the early nineteenth century were the siblings Joseph and Mary Anning, children of a carpenter and fossil collector from the south of England. Mary was to later enter history books as the "greatest fossilist the world ever knew" (Torrens 1995: 260).

The Anning siblings primarily set to work at the Bay of Lyme in Dorset. There, in thick layers of slate and limestone, also known as "Black Jura" (Liassic), lay the petrified remnants of an enormous primordial sea. In 1811, Joseph discovered there the gigantic head of a fossilized creature, 1.2 meters long, its protracted jaws full of sharp teeth and its bony eyes as large as saucers. A year later, his sister Mary found the torso that presumably belonged to this creature, at which point scientists had at their command a complete, continuous skeleton stretching over 5 meters long.

The peculiar creature was first displayed publicly in Bullock's Museum in Piccadilly in London. This strange "Crocodile" with its enormously large eye sockets and its extremely long jaws, which seemed stretched into a disconcerting smile, was something entirely anatomically inexplicable and created a massive sensation. The long, pointy muzzle was reminiscent of a dolphin; in contrast, the teeth seemed to belong to a crocodile; while the vertebra were slim like in the backbone of a fish. William Buckland (1784–1856), William Conybeare (1787–1857), and Henry De la Beche (1796–1855) examined the creature thoroughly, in a flurry of letters with the French luminary in comparative anatomy, Georges Cuvier (1769–1832). They concluded finally that this must have been a "Sea-Lizard." At the same time, further fossilized remains of this creature were being found in many counties in southwestern England. As De la Beche and Conybeare published their findings in 1821 in the *Transactions of the Geological Society*, they presented the image of a primordial sea, with reptiles over 7 meters long ploughing through the waves. Thus the *Ichthyosaur*, "Fish-Lizard," was named.

Two years later, on the evening of December 10, 1823, Mary Anning discovered the skull of a peculiar "tortoise" with a long snake-like neck at the foot of the Black Ven cliffs. After hours of work, a fantastical creature 2.7 meters in length emerged from its ancient grave. Instead of legs or flippers it had paddles, which were made of countless thin bones. The news of this animal, which Conybeare baptized *Plesiosaur*, "reptile-like," spread with lightning speed, becoming a sensation. Once again, an absolutely unbelievable life-form was at stake, one whose long neck violated the previously known laws of anatomy to the utmost degree. However, further fossil discoveries were soon able to prove the veracity of the Anning fossils. They demonstrated that the Plesiosaur, despite his tiny brain and obscenely long neck, had once enjoyed great prevalence. On February 20, 1824, Conybeare introduced the Geological Society in London to the "miracle that came from over the sea," as well as to the "monstrosity" that had previously been found in the ruins of an earlier world. But what sort of world had it been, in which these two bizarre beasts had roamed, and what was the connection between their disappearance and the waters of the biblical Flood?

Among the peculiar fossils on the beach of Lyme Regis, there were also numerous dark gray figments, shaped like elongated pebbles and boasting a characteristic ripple pattern. They often appeared in the insides of the Ichthyosaurus, and chemical analyses revealed that they were fossilized digested material, which chiefly consisted of the bones of smaller living creatures (see Rupke 1983). One piece at a time, an unsettled public was exposed to the image of a primordial sea full of gigantic sea lizards locked in a relentless fight to the death. The earliest days of Creation appeared to be a horrifying bloodbath. Once Mary Anning discovered the fragile remains of a ghostly creature, half vampire bat, half reptile, with a 1.2-meter wingspan, in December 1828, the fantasies of the public were entirely mesmerized by an antediluvian world of horrors.[4] Not only the depths of the sea, but also the bright heights of the heavens were found to have once been populated by horrifying monsters whose existence resembled a single predatory slaughter. Can one evaluate such unbelievable facts, and how could we understand something that no human being had ever seen with her own two eyes?

To understand the unease and bewilderment of the nineteenth-century public, it is important to recall two things. First, with the fossilized dinosaur skeletons, an absolutely inapprehensible dimension of time became visible, shaking everyone's imagination to its core. In Robert Hooke's (1635–1703) time, humanity was presumed to have a history of about six thousand years. By Immanuel Kant's (1724–1804) lifetime, they were already aware of a past a few million years long. However, the scale of geological time, which now surfaced in the form of gigantic lizards, had such unbelievable dimensions that any attempt to integrate them into the enlightened man's image of Self and Other was inevitably crushed. One reaction to this absurd incommensurability was to project everything outside of the realm of human temporal experience onto something that also escaped the grip of human understanding, but at least was materially present: onto the unknown, still unresearched depths of the sea, out of which the legendary creatures from Lyme Regis must at one point have emerged.

The second point to keep in mind in order to understand this historical moment is the monstrosity of the idea that species could go *entirely* extinct. For centuries, scientists had already been concerned with the problem of the resemblance between fossilized creatures and extant species. Conrad Gessner, in his *Historia animalium* (1558), had already recognized the similarity of the famous *glossopetrae* or "tongue stones," to shark teeth and had depicted both together, fossil and shark tooth. In addition, a space of aesthetic argumentation had emerged with the aforementioned detailed and illustrated natural history compendiums, particularly of fishes, mussels, and fossils. These seem for us today to irrevocably demand a comparative observation along the lines of a visual analogy. But despite the great similarity between many living and fossilized organisms, the thought that the latter could be an extinct species must have been unimaginable to a Western, Christian understanding. Why should plants and animals who could exist and who obviously had existed have disappeared from God's Creation? There was only one logical way out of this dilemma: somewhere in God's wide world, descendants of these species must still exist in hiding. Furthermore, because this concern pertained primarily to sea creatures and exotic marine plants, about whose environment very little was known anyway, this seemed to be the most plausible explanation. In fact, in the middle of the eighteenth century, the first apparently vanished species emerged out of the depths of the West Indian Ocean, among them the "sea lily" (modern: *crinoids*) and *ammonias*, deep sea mussels (Rudwick 2005: 249–53).

This led to one of the most attractive dreams in the Western conception of undersea realms and helped to develop a comprehensive cosmological picture that particularly fascinated the nineteenth century: the sunken world and the fiction of a journey to the beginning of time. Still in the late eighteenth century, someone like Jean-Guillaume Bruguière (1750–98), one of the leading naturalists and a proven expert on fossilized shells, could argue that ammonite, belemnite, and many other fossilized life-forms were not extinct but rather had migrated to the dark night of the deepest ocean. "The vast floor of the sea," as Bruguière put it, "could still be paved with them" (*Histoire naturelle des vers*, vol. 1. [1792], quoted in Rudwick 2005: 257).

Aquaria

Modern marine biology owes many of its roots to the natural studies of passionate amateurs and hobbyist researchers. These were more than just eccentric dilettantes who indulged themselves in a *l'art pour l'art* of collection. Rather, they were sharp observers and careful archivists. With both feet firmly anchored in the Newtonian universe, they were convinced that sooner or later entirely new insights into the principles of life would proceed from the patient comparison of similarities and metamorphoses. In any case, they gladly and extensively reserved for themselves the right to enthusiastic amazement. Charles Kingsley (1819–75) summarized this special *esprit* in *Glaucus; or, the Wonders of the Shore*:

> Why not, then, try to discover a few of the Wonders of the Shore? For wonders are there around you at every step, stranger than ever opium-eater dreamed, [...] wonders [of ...] classification, [...] marvels, which meet us at every step in the anatomy and the reproduction of these creatures.
>
> (1859: 3, 39)

"Wonders of the Shore" were in the nineteenth century essentially more and other than curiosities collected by unoccupied ladies to decorate their boudoirs. They were aesthetic as well as epistemic things.[5] Their miraculous existence manifested in their ability to provoke amazement. Most of all, this lay in marvelous facts such as their specific anatomies and their unconventional reproductive lives. Equally significant was the difficulty of understanding their systematic place in God's well-ordered Creation. But how and in what form were these delicate plants and animals best studied? What options did people have, if they lacked access to scientific personnel or to a furnished laboratory on the sea?

Let's shift back in time by about 150 years. We will set the dial to the year 1846 and go for a walk on the beach of Torquay in Devon, south England. The winter season has just begun and by our side is Anna Constantia Thynne (1806–66), the wife of the prosperous Lord John Thynne (1798–1881), subdeacon of Westminster Abbey (Stott 2003). She is actually on the hunt for fossils, but her six children, laden down with butterfly nets, collection glasses, miniature scalpels, little hammers, forceps, zoological notebooks, and ink and quills, are more interested in the saltwater pools that the low tide has left behind in the stony rocks. But what was so interesting about those pools, which had been resting undisturbed on Devon's coasts for centuries?

If you bent over one of these dark lakes and carefully pulled the seaweed to the side, then maybe a fleshy blood-red sea anemone would wave to you with one of its hundred filigreed tentacles. A crab would probably hurry away into a crack and you would suddenly see the dark luminescence of a stone coral, its edge studded with exquisitely formed brown tentacles whose tips shimmered white. Anna Thynne was equally fascinated by these creatures. At home in Westminster Abbey she already owned a lovely collection of fossilized corals, or *Madrepora*, but she had never thought that these animals could be so soft, smooth, and beautiful in nature. Anna Thynne was a decidedly sophisticated amateur naturalist. Her interest in fossils was bound up in the urgent question of the time, that of the connection between extinct animal bodies and living species. Were they traces of the creatures who had perished in the Great Flood? Was it necessary to accept that the world was older than four thousand years, as the church had calculated?

Some scientists claimed that these fossilized bones were proof of earlier life-forms out of which the present species had developed. Out of which primitive life-form had the stone coral developed? These small creatures, shimmering below in the pool, were clearly recognizable as a descendent of the fossilized madrepores that Thynne had already studied. Moreover, giant life-forms had populated the seas at the time of the fossilized madrepores, the gigantic Ichthyosaurs and Plesiosaurs who had long died out. Why, then, was this stone coral not extinct, and why had it hardly changed? And how did this creature reproduce at all, out of whose dead bodies had giant coral reefs, or entire islands, grown? It was a process that could hardly have been completed in forty thousand years let alone four thousand years, but must rather have lasted millions of years.

Thynne was determined to know more about these animals and collected thirty of them with the help of her children. Next, she placed them on the floor in every available pot and pan, all filled with seawater, and fed them every day with fresh shrimp. As the day of their return trip to London drew nearer, Thynne stood faced with the choice between letting her marine menagerie go in the freedom of the tidal pools of Torquay, or finding a way to bring them back to London with her. She chose the latter and sewed every single stone coral tight to a sea sponge, packed these into glasses full of seawater, and sent them along with the coach to London.

"If Anna could not stay by the sea, she would have to bring the sea to the city," writes Thynne's biographer, Rebecca Stott (2003: 20). Back in London,

Thynne began to resettle her little flock into large glass cases and to care for them with seawater and the smallest pieces of shrimp. Procuring fresh seawater was a problem. Since it was expensive to have new water brought to London every week, a maid was assigned the task of aerating the tank water by hand every day, which meant that the maid spent hours standing by an open window pouring the water from one pitcher into another. It was an unbelievably time-consuming procedure.

In early 1847, Thynne was finally determined to secure a stable home for her sea creatures and ordered a number of maritime plants from Torquay. Within a few weeks she had discovered that seaweed was particularly suited for maintaining the balance of oxygen and nitrogen in her tanks. Two years later, she had an equilibrated sea aquarium whose occupants had now enjoyed a good three years in the best of health.

At this point, questions of copyright emerge. Anna Thynne was without a doubt the first person in history to create within her aquarium a small, special world and to use it as an experimental arrangement. Nevertheless, she never used the word "aquarium" for her seawater tanks and she also didn't publish on the topic. In addition, she was essentially concerned with a single species, stone coral, rather than with the epistemological implications of her arrangement. Still, Rebecca Stott, Anna Thynne's biographer, concludes that Anna Thynne is the yet-unrecognized inventor of the aquarium. Most seriously of all, she further argues that those to whom the invention of the aquarium is usually ascribed are plagiarists (Stott 2003: 135–43).

From Thynne's notebooks, it follows that for two or three months in early 1849 she showed her stone corals in the seawater tank to several people, "professed naturalists and other persons interested in natural history," as Stott puts it (2003: 109). Stott claims that one of the visitors was the London chemist Robert Warington (1807–67), and another the famous naturalist and extremely successful author of popular scientific books Philip Henry Gosse (1810–88). Both are proposed as the inventor of the aquarium in the majority of reference works, and both first give account of their experiments with aquariums in the beginning of the 1850s, a chronology that brings them both into question as plagiarists. On the other hand, this is merely a conjecture, and Stott further reports that naturalists and amateurs from around the world made the pilgrimage to Westminster Abbey to lay eyes on Thynne's stone corals. Her menagerie is said to have been the "talk of zoologists" (115). However, it is impossible to reconstruct who was doing the talking, and when or where it occurred.

In contrast, there is extensive evidence that Gosse was a painstakingly exact historian of his own sources and trains of thought. As early as in his 1854 book *The Aquarium: An Unveiling of the Wonders of the Deep Sea,* he explained over several pages who had first experimented with plants and animals in water, and when. He discussed which successes had been recorded and how the idea had finally occurred to him that it could be possible to establish a balance of oxygen and nitrogen in the water with the right mixture of plants and animals. In the second edition of *The Aquarium*, in 1856, Gosse also mentioned the work of Thynne, who in the same year had bequeathed to him the records of her careful study of the reproductive lives of stone corals. Gosse didn't use the manuscripts for his own research, as Thynne had offered, but provided for their 1859 publication in the prestigious journal *Annals and Magazine of Natural History*, under the title "On the Increase of Madrepores." Last but not least, from Anne Thwaite's extensively researched biography of Henry Gosse, it seems extraordinarily unlikely that Gosse could have laid false claim to such an intoxicating sight as thirty live stone corals in a seawater aquarium in Westminster Abbey for years (Thwaite 2002).

The significance of this whole narrative does not lie in an alleged crime thriller about stolen inventions. More important is the extremely strange fact that the successes of Thynne and other precursors did *not* spread like wildfire. This is even stranger, because in the 1830s and 1840s marine biology was beginning to become a hot topic among naturalists. Although the British Association for the Advancement of Science sponsored several expeditions to dredge for sea creatures and recorded huge forays into marine collecting every year (Rehbock 1979), there is no evidence that they bothered keeping the captured creatures alive for research purposes.

The decisive impulse to reconsider the situation probably came from the field of botanical research. Around 1830, the English botanist and surgeon Nathaniel Bagshaw Ward (1791–1868) discovered that delicate plants such as certain ferns and mosses thrived in airtight glass containers. A stable microclimate would develop in the containers, making the plants independent from external temperatures and protecting them from air pollution. Interestingly, Ward first published his insights in 1837 in a report to the British Association for the Advancement of Science, which tackled the question of economy of air among plants and animals. Then, in 1842, he released *On the Growth of Plants in Closely Glazed Cases*, in which he explicitly discussed the fact "that the animal and vegetable respirations might counterbalance each other" (Ward 1842: 70). Independently thereof, Ward's small greenhouses quickly headed toward production. The fashion of "Wardian Cases" came together with the notorious "fern craze" and ensured that within a short time no British household wanted to forgo its "plumy emerald green pets glistening with health and beadings of warm dew" (Hibberd 1869, quoted in Allen 1969: 62).

However, it ultimately wasn't Ward who established the contact between marine biology and the new science of physiological chemistry, but Robert Warington (1807–67), a member of the London Society of Apothecaries. In 1849 he developed systematic experiments to clarify the cooperation between plant and animal organisms in freshwater. In 1852 he began to experiment as well with seawater vessels, contemporaneously with Gosse. Warington reported on his experiments in the "Annals of Natural History" in November of 1853, where Gosse had already published in 1852. But while Warington limited himself to publishing his results in scientific journals, Gosse caused a furor with his popular-scientific bestseller *A Naturalist's Rambles on the Devonshire Coast* (1853). Both can take credit for having coined the term "aquarium."

While until 1852 aquariums were primarily cylindrical glass cases with a few fish or invertebrates inside, after 1852 they came to be perceived as the living space of a marine biocoenosis and the perfect medium for idealistic submarine landscape designs. Finally, in 1854, Gosse's perhaps most successful work, *The Aquarium: An Unveiling of the Wonders of the Deep Sea*, appeared in print and triggered the so-called "aquarium fever." An 1856 newspaper article with the headline *"The Aquarium Mania"* read:

> In London itself, the mania is raging just now at fever point. [...] In West End squares, in trim suburban villas, in crowded city thoroughfares, in the demure houses of little, unfrequented back streets, and inside the flat, sill-les windows of wretched Spitalfields and Bethnal Green, everywhere you see the aquarium in one form or another.
>
> (quoted in Stott 2003: 132)

In summary, it is clear that we cannot answer the question of the origin of the idea of a self-contained aquarium simply. The practice of examining sea creatures at home in water glasses was widespread among naturalists for decades, and historical research reinforces the impression that fish in glass hardly interested anyone else for a long time. It took a significant charge to the imagination as well as a media-aesthetically diverse design for people to lose their heads and speak about worms and spiny crabs as "Mexican princes" (Anonymous 1855: 505). Without a doubt, other important factors such as the expansion of the rail networks and the abolition of the Glass Tax in England in 1845 also contributed to the "boom" of aquariums. But for aquariums to be perceived as a first-rate epistemic object and a window into the previously uncharted realm of the sea, what they presented needed above all to be connected to the intellectual currents and preferences of the time.

WONDERFUL FACTS: MEDIA, AESTHETICS, EPISTEMOLOGY

From the perspective of media and cultural studies, an aquarium is an imaging medium. It is a technical artifact, a symbolic construction, and a media-aesthetic strategy to render available a space of life usually adjacent to human cognitive capacity. The sea is an extra-human realm, only accessible with considerable technical effort. In their influential book on oceanographic research *The Machine in Neptune's Garden*, Keith Benson, Helen Rozwadowski, and David van Keuren wrote:

> The oceans are a forbidding and alien environment inaccessible to direct human observation. They force scientist-observers to carry their natural environment with them [...]. [O]ceanography's necessary dependence upon technology [...] create[s] a persuasive argument that the machine *is* the garden. That is, what oceanographers have learned about the ocean has been based almost exclusively on what various technologies, or machines, have taught them.
>
> (2004: xiii, xiv)

The history of modernity is thus rich in aqua-nautic as well as oceanographic techniques, in medial arrangements and aesthetic practices, and in maritime instruments and systematics, all designed to transform an ocean space stretching into the depths and around the globe into forms of factual evidence. Against this background, aquariums are a paradigmatic example for the natural-philosophical insight that science can only depict that into which it has already intervened and which it has ordained for its own purposes (see Rheinberger 2001).

In its early years, the aquarium was connected with the metaphor of a journey of discovery into parts unknown. Here, people studied and displayed the treasures and curiosities that they had brought back from the previously uncharted expanses of the sea. But notably, aquariums at the time mostly played host neither to extraordinary nor to unique objects, but to common indigenous plants and animals. For this reason, aquariums were also not an attribute of the powerful elite classes but belong to the first "mass media" of a new medial praxis of collection, observation, and display. Thus aquariums were part of the historical context in which the idea of uniqueness attained a new symbolic meaning and organisms from around the world became a sensation in the house of Mr. and Mrs. Everyman. Uniqueness was henceforth no longer a material quality but a feeling that ensued as a result of interactions and stagings.

With this in mind, it is not surprising that an aquarium was initially not an item that someone could get delivered like a bouquet of flowers. One needed instead to be achieved with patience and dedication. The assembly of the plant and animal community demanded instinct, and the entire preparation and installation of the aquarium was understood as a type of ritual dramaturgy that paved the oceanographer's way from a novice to a discoverer of hidden secrets. A polyphonic sea of texts and a multicolored tapestry of guides and travel magazines enfolded enthusiasts from their first step on the beach, modulating their attention, making recommendations, and regulating individual decision-making processes.[6]

Minute organisms and the metamorphosing organs

Aquariums granted scientists and lay people alike the opportunity to observe "all thinkable proceedings in the life of countless creatures of which it was formerly impossible to dream" (Dohrn, quoted in Simon 1980; 50, 81).[7] The central instrument of this voyeuristic practice of observation was the microscope. Under its lens, the most banal objects transformed into breathtaking creations: "It is not easy to express the pleasure which is excited in the mind of the observer of nature, while contemplating the habit and manners of the Annelida," Thomas Williams wrote in his *Report on the British Annelida*: "Every movement exemplifies the curve of beauty; every tentacle winds ceaselessly and rapidly through a thousand forms of matchless grace" (1852: 271).

Nevertheless, the microscope also offered unsettling discoveries. It revealed on the one hand the sublime textures of brown algae, but on the other hand bizarre monstrosities that subverted the official order of nature and seemed to be sometimes plant, other times animal, sometimes dead and then once again living. The puzzling relationships between the genders were particularly risqué, seemingly leading to the idea of reproduction ad absurdum. A famous case, first thoroughly described by Charles Darwin, was the life cycle and the reproductive patterns of the common rock barnacle (*Balanus balanoides*), a member of the barnacle family.

Common rock barnacles are hermaphrodites, but they cannot fertilize themselves. They live tightly packed so that their penis, which is twice as long as their body, can fertilize the neighboring barnacle. The fertilized eggs then remain in their lime shell until the young hatch and leave their home as free-swimming nauplius larvae (first larval stage). After their transformation into a cypris larva a few weeks later, the creature seeks out a place to spend the rest of its life. To do this, it cements itself upside down to a seashell, a crab shell, a snail shell, or the hull of a ship. After its cementation, the barnacle repeatedly sheds its skin inside its shell until it is fully grown, depositing six slabs of lime that form its conical, covered home. It goes without saying that a process of such complex metamorphoses caused a commotion among the public and presented taxonomists with delicate problems. Thus Darwin described the life cycle of the common rock barnacle in the following terms: the adult animal affixes itself to a rock with its "head," while its "feet" float freely in the water. In the larval stage, on the other hand, its "mouth" was said to be found between its legs; a second "eye" was located above its stomach in the interior of its body (1851). Inevitably, images emerged of these grotesque distortions (Bakhtin 1995; Stott 2000). The visual culture of the second half of the century proliferated bizarre palimpsests of mouths and peculiar orifices, an underwater grotesque with disturbing sexual implications (Figure 1.3).

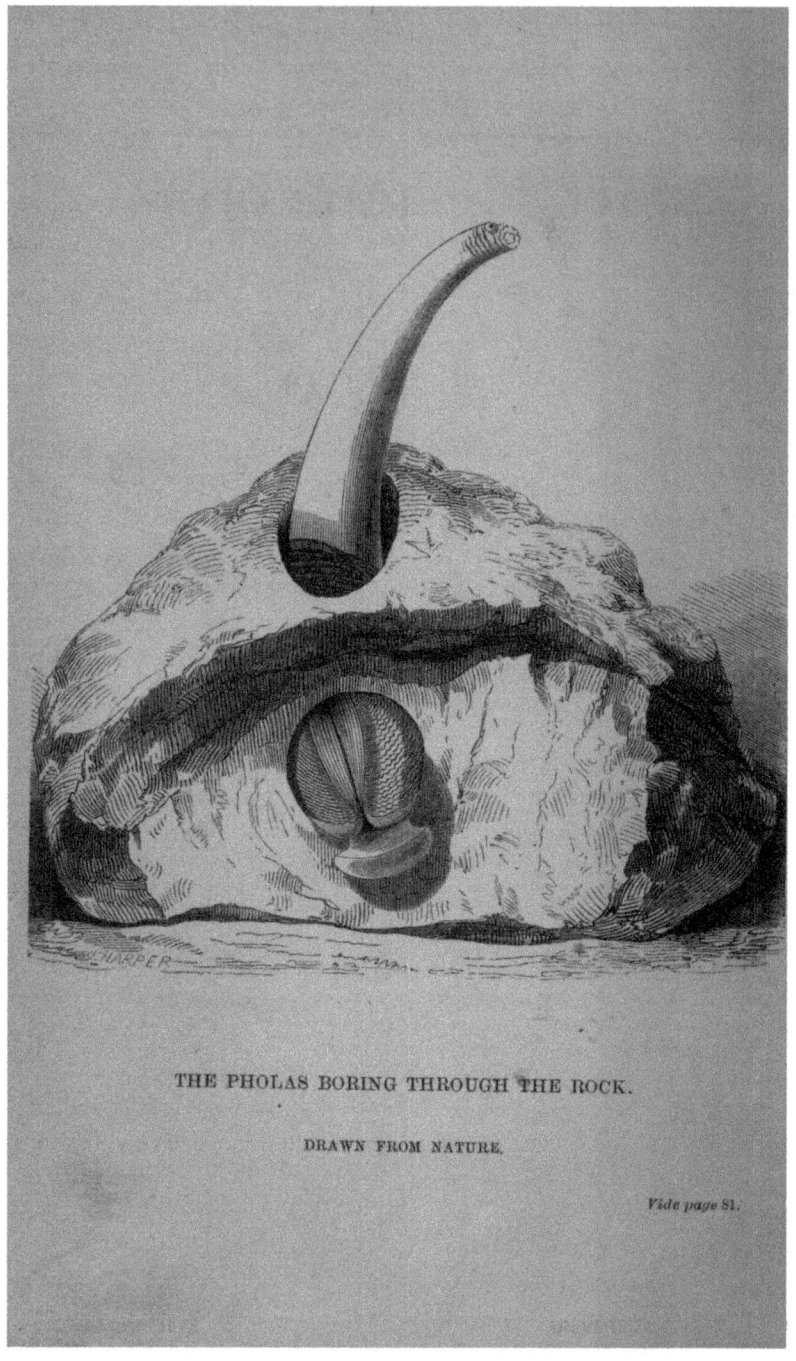

FIGURE 1.3 "The Pholas boring through the rock," frontispiece from John Harper, *The Sea-side and Aquarium; or, Anecdote and Gossip on Marine Zoology* (Edinburgh, 1858) (public domain).

Several of Darwin's contemporaries attempted to play down the obscene goings-on with an anthropomorphizing wink of the eye. On September 14, 1849, Darwin wrote to his friend Charles Lyell, describing a polygamous female barnacle (*Cirripedia*):

> The other day I got a curious example of a unisexual instead of a hermaphrodite cirripede, in which the female had the common cirripedal character, and in the two halves of her shell had two little pockets, in each of which she kept a little husband; I do not know of any other case where a female invariably has two husbands.
>
> (Darwin, quoted in Stott 2000: 315)

Two "little husbands" in two "little pockets." This scene of cozy family life has a much less threatening effect than the idea of a parasitic male existence, which caused Darwin's contemporaries considerable discomfort. On the one hand, marine invertebrates were central for the development of the theory of evolution. On the other hand, their multifaceted form was best suited to take their place behind the ape, the primary icon of descent theory, as a shadow icon of degeneration.

A second method of discursively tackling the grotesque corporeality of sea creatures was transferring them into new registers by associating them with the monstrous/wonderful creatures of past epochs. Cnidaria, entoprocts, and tardigrades (water bears) transformed into adventurous wonder-creatures, as they had been in the Middle Ages, when they had populated the margins of the known world, in the tales of John Mandeville, Gervase of Tilbury, or Marco Polo.[8]

> The Periwinkle (*L. littorea*) [is] marching soberly along beneath his massive mansion, stopping to munch the tender shoot of some Alga, or leisurely circumambulating the pretty tide-pool which he has chosen for his present residence. You may tell that all his movements are marked by gravity and deliberation, for if he does not let the grass grow under his feet, (I beg his pardon, he has but one foot; though, as that is somewhat of the amplest, he is not deficient in *understanding*) he lets it grow over his head. It is with a goodly Ulva or other sea-weed that has taken root on the summit of his shell, so that he habitually sits under the shadow of his own roof-tree.
>
> (Gosse 1854: 30)

The similarities of the "common periwinkle" with the one-legged men in Mandeville's universe, who used their single foot as a parasol, is unmissable. The designation of sea creatures as "foreign peoples" was also widespread. In many cases, the maritime regions were compared to the wild, uncharted territories of Africa. Even a tidepool on the southern coast of England could become an African jungle:

Its upper side is a whole forest of see-weeds, large and small; and that forest, if you examined it closely, as full of inhabitants as those of the Amazon or the Gambia [...]. Countless ages before we appeared on earth the depths of the old chalk-ocean teemed with forms as beautiful and perfect as those, their lineal descendants, which the dredge now brings up from the Atlantic sea-floor.

(Kingsley 1859: 27, 83, 88).

The argumentative device of these and many other passages in popular sea literature consists of the equation of "primitive" and "prehistoric." The "primitive peoples" of the sea thus occupy the place of the "primitive" Indigenous cultures of Africa and Oceania, who were treated as prototypical forebears of the Occident in contemporary anthropological discourse. The study of the "primitives" was said to give some indication as to the past that the Europeans had long left behind. Analogously, the look inside an aquarium was considered the disclosure of a prehistoric landscape, on which the first-borns of Creation walked, as well as of an unknown continent whose primitive cultures were ripe for study and colonization alike. The oceanographic texts of the time stressed time and again the enormous spectrum of strange body parts and mainly revolved around the orifices such as the mouth and the genitals. The monstrous appetite of marine life-forms particularly stands out and corresponds to the colonial narratives of the time, which mobilize cannibalistic and vampire motifs to describe the Other as foreign and exotic (Stott 2000: 312).

In the nineteenth century, the construction and perception of the world inside the aquarium bore both imperialistic features and those that were clearly carnivalesque in the Bakhtinian sense. The underwater obscenities unveiled the arbitrariness of bourgeois ordered relations to an astounded public, and the literary and pictorial culture of marine biology in the nineteenth century was highly fascinated by this play between the natural and the artificial. So it was that the love-life of candy-colored bristle worms and the food consumption of plush green sea urchins could reveal the aesthetic nature of scientific understanding and composition in enticing, capricious, and even provocative ways.

THE DEEP SEA

The "discovery" of the deep sea belongs to the most important discursive events of the second half of the nineteenth century. Even into the 1850s, people were convinced despite evidence to the contrary that the depths of 500 meters of darkness, cold, and pressure forbade any form of life. The image of a lifeless deep was first "officially" and finally refuted in the Fall of 1860 when a defective telegraph cable crusted over with sea creatures was hauled up from

3,600 meters deep off the Algerian coast. A sensation! But it didn't stop there: what the first quickly appearing research expeditions brought up from depths of 1,000 meters to 4,500 meters in the next decades, such as HMS *Lightning*, HMS *Porcupine*, or HMS *Challenger*, shattered the expectations of the time. Instead of the usual microorganisms, only true "giants" were brought to light for the dark reason that they allowed the deep sea to appear as a dreamland of absurd proportions: head-high hydroid polyps, colossal sea crabs, long tail crayfish with 1.5-meter-long feelers, gigantic isopods and spiny crabs, nut-sized malacostraca, pieces of glass sponge bristles extending to a length of three meters, two-meter-long sea-squirt feet, pyrosomes the length of logs, thousands of ostracods, and gigantic forms of mantis shrimp and idiosyncratic decapods as well as countless types of squid (Jäger 1908: 169).

The gigantism of the abyss not only raised multifaceted questions about a life in absolute darkness and under extreme hydrostatic conditions. It also offered abundant fuel for all reflections that saw in the ocean depths a refuge for mythical-prehistoric forms. The overly large creatures simply fit perfectly in the Western ancestral halls of beasts and monstrosities, allowing them to be sorted smoothly into a well-known nomenclature. They outdid everything that had been seen before. But nevertheless, the object status of these organisms, which were mostly shriveled and squashed through the dredging process, was for this reason precarious. On the one hand they were epistemic objects pointing to a completely differently formed, absolutely incomprehensible Creation. On the other hand people associated the depths with phantasmagorical riddle forms, from which a grotesque aesthetic fascination emerged. In the museums of natural history and at the great World Exhibitions excited visitors stooped over mauve sea cucumbers and bright red lacquered crustaceans, and gazed at amazement in fish with their own little lanterns and snake-like beings with horribly toothed pelican heads. Who could wrap their head around it all? Instead of seeking an answer, people above all approached these beings aesthetically and created masterpieces that remain unsurpassed to this day. These creatures were drawn and painted, watercolored and retouched, photographed and modeled, until they swam through the visual culture of the *fin de siècle* in a thousand variations. The dark night had stunningly and eloquently arrived in the fantasies of men (Figure 1.4).

True monsters

Among the most famous fictional works that portray this time period in its complex ambivalence and excitement is without a doubt Jules Verne's (1828–1905) marvelous novel *Twenty Thousand Leagues Under the Sea* (1870) with the congenial illustrations by Alphonse de Neuville (1835–85) and Édouard Riou (1833–1900). In the opening sequence he writes:

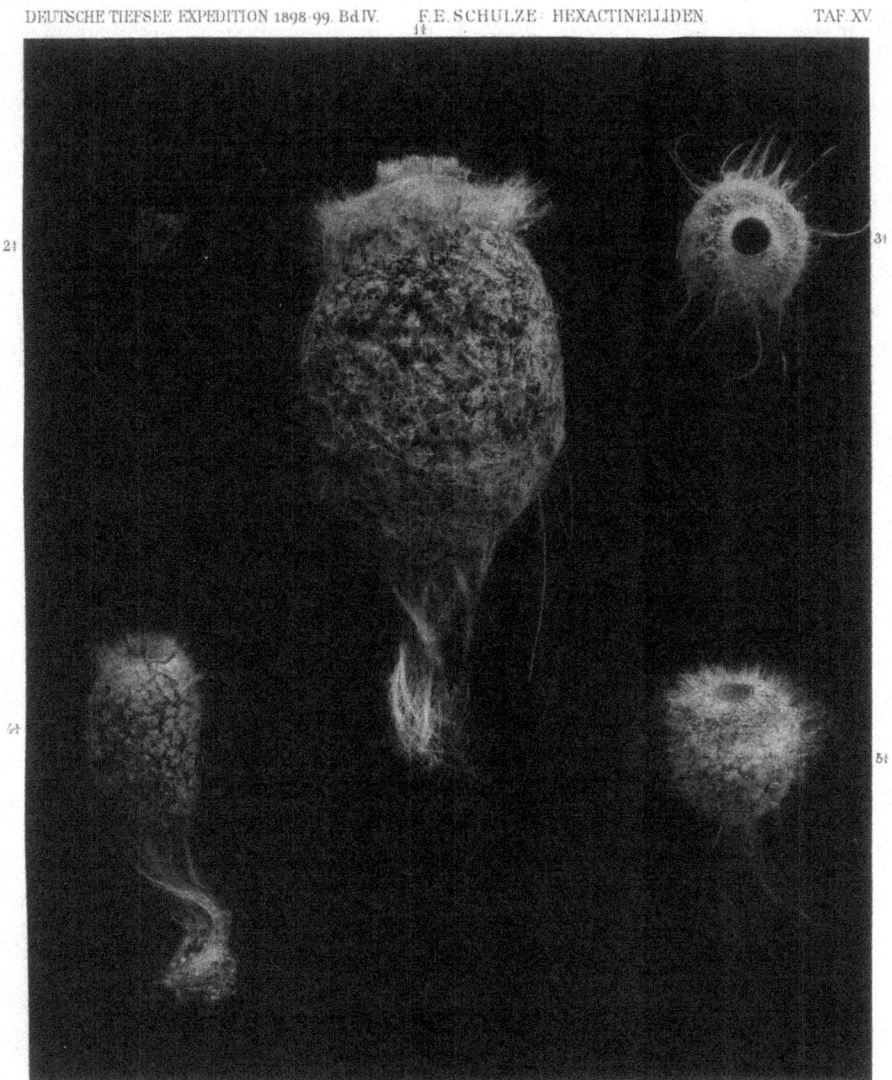

FIGURE 1.4 "Pheromona carpenter wyy. Th.," from *Wissenschaftliche Ergebnisse der Deutschen Tiefsee-Expedition auf dem Dampfer Valdivia 1898–1899*, 24 vols. (Jena, 1902–40), vol. 4, 2, *Hexactinellien*, edited by von Frank Eilhard Schulze (Jena 1904), panel XV (public domain).

The year 1866 was marked by a strange event, an unexplained and inexplicable occurrence that doubtless no one has yet forgotten [...]. For some time already, sea-going ships had been encountering an "enormous thing": a long, spindle-shaped object, which sometimes appeared phosphorescent and was infinitely longer and quicker than a whale.

(Verne [1870] 1998: 5)

Of course, today's readers know that the mysterious object doesn't refer to a sea monster, but to a submarine under the command of Captain Nemo. But in 1870, Verne's protagonists, in their role as audience surrogates, asked themselves whether huge specimens of another era, last examples of titanic species, had been preserved in the unknown depths. This question can, of course, be answered in the negative, as Verne portrayed in his novel with a technological utopia of underwater vehicles and submarine gardens—but only so as to allow the intrusion of the monstrous in the form of the squid to return all the more realistically.

The battle with the giant kraken, which in reality is a squid, not only constitutes an impressive chapter of Verne's novel but also narrates a parable of modern maritime sciences (Figure 1.5). The animal enters the underwater stage as a hybrid of legendary figure and scientific sensation and is characterized as a "horrible monster," as a "freak of nature" (344).

It appears noteworthy from today's point of view that Verne described his monstrosity as both a squid and a kraken, for these are now well known as different animals. Nevertheless, it was not uncommon in Verne's time to use the terms *kraken* and *squid* interchangeably, even in scientific tracts. A pertinent example of this connection is the report of the French consul M. Sabin Berthelot (1794–1880) to the Académie des Sciences, on the occasion of the encounter of the French sailing ship *Alecton* with a giant squid. This consistently interchanges the designations *kraken* and *squid*, although it is clearly a squid that was sighted and described.[9] Verne certainly knew of this report, because he presents the encounter as described in detail by one of his protagonists. Although the novel consistently refers to eight arms, which would suggest a kraken, the illustrations by Neuville and Riou sometimes show an eight-armed creature, sometimes a ten-armed, whose body is always simply "cylindrical" like a squid (Verne [1870] 1998: 344).[10] Beyond that, the legends recalled by Verne's protagonists as a prelude to the battle doubtless point to the myth of the Giant Squid.[11] Here, Verne summons a man of science of impeccable reputation so typical for the nineteenth century with the figure of Pierre Aronnax, the scientist imprisoned by Nemo, who recalls the French biologist Henri Milne-Edwards. Out of his mouth, Verne presents to his readers his research into a giant cephalopod with a long register of mythic as well as scientific records, a long history of eyewitness accounts, and

FIGURE 1.5 Édouard Riou, "Giant squid attacking the Nautilus," illustration in Jules Verne, *Twenty Thousand Leagues Under the Sea* (Zurich [1870] 1976). © Wikimedia Commons (public domain).

a handful of preserved evidence. Nevertheless, the Giant Squid belonged for Verne's contemporaries in the realm of legends. The specific point of this literary "exploration" is that the giant squid even in the year 2019 is among the creatures on this earth most beset with secrets. But to begin with: it really exists. It is called *Architeuthis*, the giant squid.[12]

Giant squids are known to us today as high-performance swimmers (see Aldrich 1992; Ellis 2002; Roper 1998). They have an ammonium chloride solution in their bodies that is lighter than ocean water and ensures their buoyancy—but also the animal's strong smell. Giant squids are therefore disgusting to humans. The sperm whale (*Physeter macrocephalus*), however, is an interested consumer, as one can conclude from the stomach contents of slain creatures. For a long time, whale hunters have wondered about the palm-sized pieces of squid bills, as well as about the giant scars on the sperm whale's skin, which seemed to issue from suction cups that were the size of soup bowls and reinforced with teeth. Even today, people try to account for the size of the squid from the size of the scars that they created in defending themselves; a difficult calculation, because the scars naturally expand with the growth of the whale and its skin over the course of the years. We can be certain of one thing despite all the incalculable factors: giant squids are gigantic. Creatures have been found up to nearly eighteen meters long, but squid researchers consider it possible that even larger examples could live in the depths of the oceans.[13] Even the specific organs of the giant squid are of record-breaking size: the penis is thought to be about a meter long, and the eyes count among the largest in the entire animal kingdom with their diameter of up to twenty-one centimeters. Thus, much of the biology of the giant squid either is unknown or must be reconstructed from present anatomical material and the life-forms of smaller but better known squids. Until a few years ago not a single person had seen a live giant squid. It was first in September of 2004 that a Japanese research team around Tsunemi Kubodera and Kyoichi Mori were able to observe a giant squid 900 meters underwater. Giant squids are still among the largest and at the same time least researched life-forms in our biosphere—but at least we finally believe that they exist. This unequivocally didn't apply to the majority of Verne's contemporaries, who as men of science were stonily convinced of having reason on their side. The French naturalist Arthur Mangin (1824–87) answered quintessentially for his time:

> There is no caprice, as I have already said, in Creation. Nature is subject to certain fixed laws, and to believe that all animals may indifferently exhibit the most arbitrary and irregular dimensions, is an opinion which could only gain credence among persons completely ignorant of natural philosophy. The evidence is indisputable that there exists, besides the degree of development of the different animals and their physiological organization, a

necessary co-relation, in virtue of which it is impossible to place any rational belief in the existence of an *infusoria* six feet long as of a microscopical elephant, in that of a spider as large as a horse, in that of a rhinoceros no bigger than a fly. And it is in virtue of the same law that the existence of a sepia or calamary the size of a whale must appear *à priori* inadmissible.

(1868: 290–1)

Going down

Science in Verne's time was still very far removed from journeying to the depths of the sea with Captain Nemo in his submarine. In one way, this is surprising, as humanity has been diving underwater for over two thousand years for work and combat alike. But over the course of the centuries, the idea of plunging into the water to study the undersea world hardly seem to have occurred to anyone. In the period discussed here only a scarce handful of scientifically motivated dive attempts were documented, beginning with the dive sessions of the French naturalist Henri Milne-Edwards (1800–1880) off the Sicilian coast in 1844 (see Forest 1996; Norton 1999). With the help of an open dive mask with glass windows, a specially lined leather jacket, lead soles on his feet, and a lifeline and an oxygen tube, Milne-Edwards walked around for thirty minutes, four meters under the Milazzo harbor and tried, as it were, to chase the depth of the sea into its most hidden lair (Quatrefages 1857: 15). The innovative potential of his biological fieldwork was thoroughly clear to him: "My opinion as to the inadequacy of research made on animals preserved in alcohol was further confirmed. The observation of living animals allows you to recognise the cause of errors [...] and to correct them" (Milne-Edwards, quoted in Norton 1999: 40).

Some thirty-five years later, Anton Dohrn (1840–1909), the founder of the Zoological Research Station in Naples, similarly recognized that the clear, warm waters of the Mediterranean offered the best conditions for underwater exploratory walks (Jung 1999; Müller 1976). After undertaking his first dive attempts in August of 1878 with his friend Werner von Siemens (1816–92) in the harbor of Kiel, he began his own dive experiments in the summer of 1879 in the Gulf of Naples. With a canoe-bubble device from the Italian Marine Ministry he attained depths of up to thirteen meters even on his first dive attempts and discovered a plethora of new algae and sponge species as well as three new types of flatworm. He excitedly recorded that with the new dive technology, we could increase "our power over the secrets of the sea by 60 or 70%" (Dohrn, quoted in Müller 1976: 142).[14] In fact, a mere two years later the Zoological Research Station was able to present findings on the connection between algae vegetation and incidence of light to members of the still novel scientific field of ecology (see Müller 1976: 143–6). However, the Research Station remained an exceptional case, first, because its work was without a doubt incredibly dangerous and serious accidents repeatedly occurred, but second, because the aquarium still reigned as the experimental success story of the contemporary research landscape. No one doubted until the beginning of the twentieth century that animals in an aquarium behaved identically as they would in open nature. It was first the generation of aquarium-loving researchers such as Oscar Heinroth (1871–1945), the leader of the second Berlin Aquarium and inventor of the field of ethological behaviorism, as well as behavioral researchers such as Konrad Lorenz (1903–89), Niko Tinbergen (1907–88), and finally Irenäus Eibl-Eibesfeld (1928–2018) who attained insight into the constructed character of the aquarium, its synthetic situation on the borders between nature and culture, and the influence of observer and observation conditions on the object of observation.

FIGURE 1.6 "Group of Alcyonidae," engraving from an image by Baron Eugen von Ransonnet-Villez. Baron Eugen von Ransonnet-Villez, *Ceylon: Skizzen seiner Bewohner, seines Thier- und Pflanzenlebens und Untersuchungen des Meeresgrundes nahe der Küste* (Braunschweig, 1868), plate XXV (public domain).

FIGURE 1.7 "Portrait instantané d'un scaphandrier," from Louis Boutan, *La Photographie sous-marine et les progrès de la photographie* (Paris, 1900), plate X. © Wikimedia Commons (public domain).

Nevertheless, in the late nineteenth century there were also a few great incidents of scientific dive sessions, as demonstrated for example by the underwater works of the Austrian amateur researcher Eugen Freiherr von Ransonnet-Villez (1838–1926), a lover of the natural sciences and of painting alike (Hantschk and Kruspel 2001). In the 1860s, Ransonnet-Villez had constructed himself a diving suit in which, seated underwater, he studied the submarine world of the Red Sea and the Indian Ocean, even capturing it in sketch. His observations, complete with a series of extremely aesthetically and intellectually fascinating color illustrations, appeared in 1868 (Figure 1.6). Still, astonishingly, they failed to elicit any great echo in the Europe of the time. Both of his travel accounts were indeed well received, despite their limited circulation, but it would be a few decades yet before others were "crazy" enough to trek under the surface of the water with pen and paper or other recording medium.

A further place among the pioneers of diving marine scientists is without a doubt reserved for the French zoologist Louis Marie Auguste Boutan (1859–1934). In the spring of 1893 he achieved the first pictures photographed underwater in the Bay of Banyuls-sur-Mer, the seat of the French research station Laboratoire de biologie marine de Banyuls-sur-Mer. A few months later, on July 31, his report *Sur la photographie sous-marine* was presented to the Académie des Sciences, prompting a worldwide success in countless magazines and journals.[15] The image of the marine researcher in his diving suit, capturing the wonders of the undersea world on the plates of his camera by the streaming light of his magnesium lantern, entered into the repertoire of images of the scientific-technical culture of success in the *fin de siècle* (Figure 1.7). But what subsequently ensued, even for Boutan, despite the enormous popularity of his underwater photographs, was hardly a crowd of imitators.

In the conclusion to his compendium of underwater photography *La Photographie sous-marine*, published in 1900, Boutan challenged amateurs above all to try their hand at underwater photography and to conduct their own studies during their vacations on the seashore. But even if the number is difficult to reconstruct today, it is doubtful that more than a half dozen followed his lead. It was not until the 1920s that diving photographers came back into the discussion, but then in the company of the first underwater film directors and camera people.

Boutan himself turned back to his zoological studies in the following years. It is not documented whether or not he dove again, but his students are said to have called him the Sea Wolf, because he never missed a chance to head out to sea with them and retrieve new life-forms from the depths. He himself saw his work in the tradition of an explorer from the moon, for whom the atmosphere on earth would have been as impermeable as the water was for marine biologists:

What must he do if he wishes to know something of what exists below the layers of clouds which hide our globe from his view? He would do as our naturalists have done – construct dredges and nets, and, having weighted them, would let them down like the anchor of a ballon [sic], and try and pull them along the surface of the earth. Do you think that with such primitive instruments he would obtain very precise ideas of the terrestrial globe?

(Boutan 1898: 48)

A century later, nothing essential about this situation has changed.

CHAPTER TWO

Practices

Herman Melville Sailed Cape Horn and Lived to Yarn About It: What the Iconic Ocean Passage Teaches about the Practices of Nineteenth-Century Mariners

RICHARD J. KING

By good fortune and favorable weather, I once saw Cape Horn myself. It was from the bow of a seventy-two-meter steel ship named the *Professor Multanovskiy*. This former Russian ship, built for travel around ice, had been repurposed for the ecotourist trade. We were on the way back to Argentina from the Antarctic Peninsula. I was aboard studying seabirds, but I had also brought my copy of Herman Melville's *White-Jacket*. On a late December afternoon of the austral summer, the captain steered the ship toward the infamous crag.

Dead ahead was Cape Horn!

Yet I was the only person up on deck.

Winds blasted from the west at over forty knots. Dozens of angled albatrosses sliced through the air. Crepuscular rays glistened streaks of spindrift and shone down from on high astride wave-lashed rocks.

But, I repeat: I was the only one of the fifty or so passengers who bundled up and held on to the steel stanchions and braced against the wind to revere Cape Horn. Our otherwise erudite and dutiful guides had not given any introduction to help the passengers recognize the sheer significance of this sight.

So I'm attempting here to declare the intense significance of the rounding of Cape Horn, especially to understand the practicalities of travel at sea during the nineteenth century. This rounding of the southernmost tip of South America was the route of choice for most Pacific-bound ships, especially before railroad service across the isthmus of Panama in the 1850s. French contractors began the canal in 1881, but it was not completed by the Americans until 1914. Cape Horn represented a crucial halfway point as a gateway to the Pacific or as the landmark on the return home. For those sailors who actually made the trip, such as Herman Melville, they considered Cape Horn a military, legal, experiential, and even a moral landmark, a Rock of Gibraltar of the Southern Hemisphere. By reputation and often reality, Cape Horn represented the worst and most unpredictable waters for these mariners. The passage around Cape Horn became the sailor's badge of honor, the most respected of rites of passage earned from hard toil amidst the ocean's harshest extremes.

Melville serves as an ideal interpreter of nineteenth-century maritime practice here because he understood the iconic significance of Cape Horn to the mariners of his time. As a writer and a sailor who had lived the experience, he was able to incorporate accurate navigation and seamanship into his fiction and narratives, while he infused the significance of storytelling, the crafting of a mythology of the Horn, and a cognizance of how sailors prepared, navigated, and then interpreted their own stories when they returned. Melville sailed around Cape Horn three times on three different types of ships for three different kinds of maritime endeavors: once as a whaleman in 1841 aboard the *Acushnet*, once as a sailor with the US Navy in 1844 aboard the *United States*, and then a final time as a passenger aboard the clipper ship *Meteor* in 1860 (see Figure 2.1).

Despite the ravenous reputation of Cape Horn, by Melville's mid-nineteenth century, vessels of all types were navigating around these rocks faster and more safely than ever before. The charting of the region was steadily improving, captains were getting experience, and vessel navigation had been advancing. That said, Melville's vessels transiting back and forth around the Horn were still

FIGURE 2.1 Melville's Cape Horn ships, *left to right*: whaleship *Acushnet*, thirty-two-meter-long on deck (watercolor by Henry Johnson, boat-steerer, *c*. 1845; Peabody Essex Museum); frigate USS *United States*, sixty-three-meter-long on deck (battle painting, Thomas Birch, *c*. 1813; Library of Congress); medium clipper ship *Meteor*, fifty-nine-meter-long on deck (Chinese trade artists, *c*. 1852; Australian National Maritime Museum). © Peabody Essex Museum, Library of Congress (public domain), and Australian National Maritime Museum.

operating technologies far closer to those of the eighteenth century than those that we enjoyed aboard the *Professor Multanovskiy* at the start of the twenty-first century. Melville saw men die trying to work the ship, and he knew or read of ships sinking and drowning men, women, and children in the icy waters of what was known then as also "Cape Stiff."

To examine more closely the practices of nineteenth-century mariners, I will examine each of Melville's passages around Cape Horn and then place his trips in the context of the seamanship and navigation of his time. I will conclude with how this fit into Anglophone popular culture and sea writing: how mariners processed, wrote, spun, and re-spun yarns about this most iconic saltwater passage. Melville grabbed the eighteenth-century Romantic tiller from Samuel Taylor Coleridge and handed over the watch to the twentieth-century psychological realist Joseph Conrad.

MELVILLE'S FIRST PASSAGE AROUND CAPE HORN, ON A WHALESHIP (1841)

Beside me I still have the chart that I took on that voyage to Antarctica. It's a British Admiralty chart of the Southern Ocean, updated to the year 2000, which maps depths and coasts from as far north as Valdivia, Chile, to as far south as the Filcher-Ronne Ice Shelf. By Melville's mid-nineteenth century, the Cape Horn region had been fairly well mapped and surveyed, thanks in part to a pair of voyages by Robert FitzRoy aboard HMS *Beagle* in the late 1820s and early 1830s (see Figure 2.2).

While I recorded where and what seabirds we saw on our voyage out of Ushuaia and reread my copy of *White-Jacket*, I also brought out my sextant and navigation tools. I marked our progress each day on my chart. I had a little yellow waterproof handheld GPS too, which was far faster and more accurate than any coastal piloting or celestial navigation I could manage. The GPS is a device, of course, that would have rendered speechless a careful, mathematical navigator such as Captain FitzRoy.

Cabo de Hornos is a gray basalt island that towers about 425 meters high. The island juts vertically out of the sea at longitude 67° 25' west of Greenwich, England, near the same meridian as Bar Harbor, Maine. Cape Horn is at the end of a string of clumps of other rock islands and channels, extending, as the albatross flies, about sixty nautical miles north up to the Beagle Channel. Fly another 145 kilometers or so northwest and you're up to the Straits of Magellan, which separates the mainland proper of the South American continent from the volcanic islands and channels that include Cape Horn, known collectively as Tierra del Fuego.

Aboard the *Professor Multanovskiy,* we had approached the perilous peak of Cape Horn from the south, from the South Shetland Islands. We had steamed

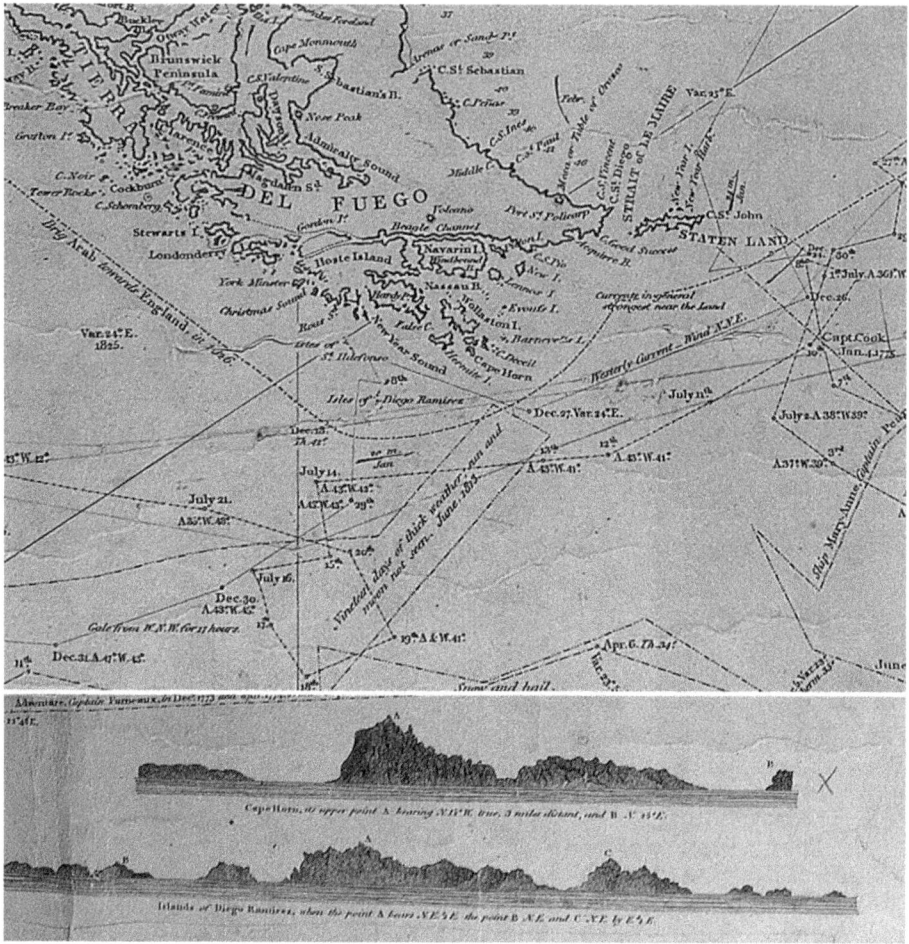

FIGURE 2.2 Details of 1833 chart of Cape Horn by Richard Holmes Laurie, chart seller to the Admiralty (Mystic Seaport Museum). Note the tracks and experiences of previous voyages, such as at the bottom center, "Nineteen days of thick weather: sun and moon not seen June 1813." © Mystic Seaport Museum.

across the Drake Passage, which is about 450 nautical miles wide. At latitude 56° south of the equator, Cape Horn is farther south than Tasmania. It's farther south than New Zealand. Cape Horn is more than 2,100 kilometers farther south than Africa's Cape of Good Hope.

In the nineteenth century, no trade made deep ocean navigation more accessible and commonplace than that of the whale fishery. In January of 1841, at the apex of this global hunt from sailing ships, Melville departed New Bedford, Massachusetts, aboard the whaleship *Acushnet*. He was twenty-one years old. The men of the *Acushnet*, led by Captain Valentine Pease, were bound to the Pacific to try to make a living by killing sperm and right whales. The 1830s through the 1850s were the height of the whaling industry in terms of number of ships involved and the number of whales killed. Whaleships were making regular passages around Cape Horn from Europe and New England, with voyages funded by American, English, French, German, and Dutch merchants. It's reasonable to estimate during these decades well over one hundred whaleships a year, on average, passed around Cape Horn (Clark 1887: 10, 70–1; Davis, Gallman, and Gleiter 1997: 6).

Melville later gave a sense of his first approach to the Cape Horn region aboard the *Acushnet* in his novel *White-Jacket, or The World in a Man-of-War* (1850). Here he describes being on a ship that avoided the transit through the Straits of Le Maire. This approach could be a bit riskier for a ship, a narrower channel, but it provided the most leeward protection and allowed the vessel to get as far west as possible before being fully exposed to the wind and waves in the Drake Passage. Melville describes his first vision of the region in terms that are Romantic and sublime. The narrator, identified only with the nickname White-Jacket, remembers:

> The land near Cape Horn, however, is well worth seeing, especially Staten Land. Upon one occasion, the ship in which I then happened to be sailing drew near this place from the northward, with a fair, free wind, blowing steadily, through a bright translucent day, whose air was almost musical with the clear, glittering cold. On our starboard beam like a pile of glaciers in Switzerland, lay this Staten Land, gleaming in snow-white barrenness and solitude. Unnumbered white albatross were skimming the sea near by, and clouds of smaller white wings fell through the air like snow-flakes. High, towering in their own turbaned snows, the far-inland pinnacles loomed up, like the border of some other world. Flashing walls and crystal battlements, like the diamond watch-towers along heaven's furthest frontier.
>
> ([1850] 1988: 116)

As far as we know, the first European to actually navigate in open water to the south of all the southern rocks of Tierra del Fuego and find their way into the Pacific was not Sir Francis Drake. He stuck his nose down there but never went around that way, transiting instead via the Straits of Magellan. It was a Dutch captain named Willem Cornelisz Schouten and his merchant-commander Jacob Le Maire who first did so in 1616. In *White-Jacket,* Melville's narrator tells his own brief history of the Horn, although his chronology and details are fuzzy. White-Jacket says of this first known transit: "It is a significant fact, that Schouten's vessel, the *Horne,* which gave its name to the Cape, was almost lost in weathering it" (98).[1] In 1741 the English discovery ship *Centurion,* White-Jacket declares, endured during their doubling of the Horn "perhaps the greatest hardships on record" (99). Men on this latter voyage had indeed become frost-bitten, developed gangrene, and others were killed by boarding seas, the rolling of the ship, and the action of the tiller. A couple of other vessels in the fleet of the *Centurion*, who lost spars and parts of their masts, surrendered and went back to the port of Rio de Janeiro. The *Centurion* carried on, slogging to windward through storms and hail for nearly sixty days. A hundred men died due to illness, injury, and scurvy. Groping around for their location, Commodore George Anson and his navigator, Captain Nutt, eventually turned north to enter the South Pacific, yet found themselves still in the region of Cape Horn, over three hundred nautical miles farther east than they thought, further prolonging the agony of the passage. The tragedy became one of the rallying cries for the necessity for better methods to calculate longitude. The invention and refinement of a reliable, accurate, ocean-going timepiece, known as the chronometer, had already begun—but in 1740 it was still almost a century away from reliable and widespread usage at sea (Randier 1969: 76–8; Sobel and Andrewes 1998: 20–5).

In the wake of the English discovery ships of Anson and Captain James Cook, and despite further hellish accounts of the Horn by navy men William Bligh and David Porter, whalemen soon followed around Cape Horn. The whalemen often then did their own exploring, charting, naming of islands, and negotiating the first contacts with Indigenous peoples. In 1788 the Enderby family, an English whaling clan that Ishmael mentions in *Moby-Dick* (1851), launched the first whaling expedition into the Pacific, which arrived by way of Cape Horn. By 1791 fifty British whaleships were sailing in the Pacific, many by way of the Horn (Rigby, Van der Merwe, and Williams 2005: 18). Whalemen were so eager to explore the Pacific, from what Ishmael calls in *Moby-Dick* "the all-grasping western world," because they had so diminished the stocks of right whales, bowheads, and sperm whales from the entirety of the Atlantic Ocean and the Atlantic-Arctic. The whalemen were willing to risk three-to-five-year voyages for the more "lively grounds" of the Pacific. Quickly rewarded for these pioneering Pacific voyages, whalemen learned how to provision their ships for long voyages and how to navigate in the most distant regions. By Melville's 1840s, whaleships hunted throughout the entirety of the Pacific. Although most whaleships entered this most expansive of oceans via Cape Horn, a small portion did sail the far greater distance by way of the Cape of Good Hope and the Indian Ocean.

Mariners kept daily logbooks to learn from past voyages and experiences. They recorded the locations of whales, islands, anchorages, food networks, fresh water, and most importantly kept note of their cruise track and weather trends. Columbus kept a daily logbook, as did the deck officers of the *Professor Multanovskiy*. The logbook from Melville's *Acushnet* has not survived, but there is an abstract of the log that remains (see Figure 2.3).

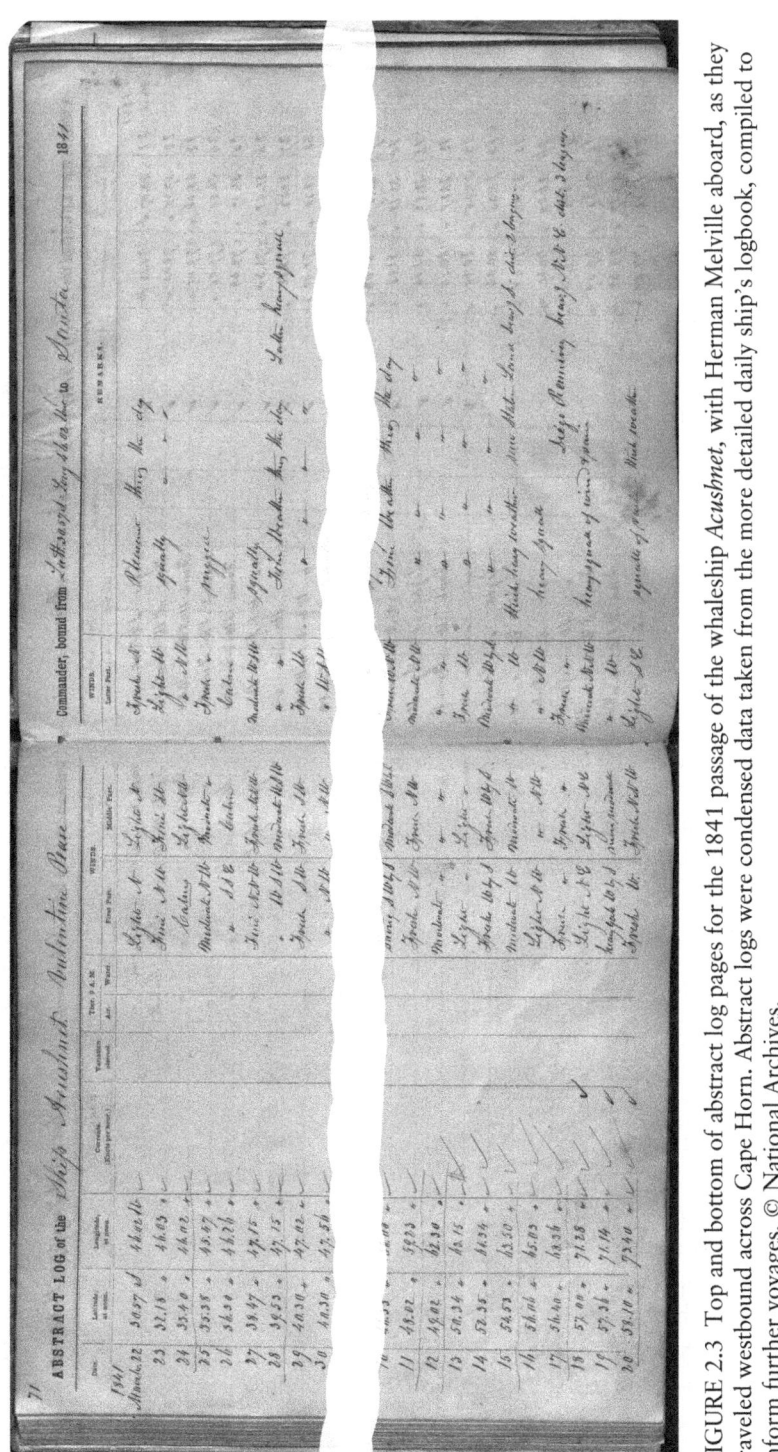

FIGURE 2.3 Top and bottom of abstract log pages for the 1841 passage of the whaleship *Acushnet*, with Herman Melville aboard, as they traveled westbound across Cape Horn. Abstract logs were condensed data taken from the more detailed daily ship's logbook, compiled to inform further voyages. © National Archives.

From the abstract of the log you can tell that the *Acushnet*'s passage around Cape Horn was a speedy, fortunate one, even though they were westbound in winter and encountered "heavy squalls of wind and rain." Captain Pease sailed outside the Straits of Le Maire then steered southwesterly. On April 17, 1841, perhaps using an illustrated profile on his chart (see Figure 2.2), Pease was able to get a line of position, a bearing over his compass, between his ship and a set of dangerous rocks about fifty-five nautical miles south of Cape Horn called the Diego Ramirez Islands. The abstract log records a "Bear[in]g NNE, dist[ance] 3 leagues," meaning that the *Acushnet* was about nine nautical miles away, safely away from these rocks. Pease continued sailing southwest, surely because of wind direction and safety, until they turned to head north a few days later, now well clear and safe in the South Pacific. The *Acushnet* rounded Cape Horn in less than two weeks on Melville's voyage. Despite a wide hull built for cargo rather than speed, she was only a few days slower than Melville's passage two decades later aboard the clipper ship *Meteor* (Heflin 2004: 60–2).

THE SAILOR'S OCEANOGRAPHY AND ECOLOGY OF CAPE HORN

Cape Horn was, and still is, so rigorous for sailing vessels because prevailing winds in the far southern latitudes blow from west to east. To attempt to sail around from the Atlantic, usually means sailing against the wind and current. No land mass checks these winds or currents. Both forces, almost relentlessly, push ships, albatrosses, penguins, fish, and krill back eastbound. The waves have an endless fetch, swelling and barreling all around the world. Adding to these contrary winds and currents are fronts of cold air and storms. Even in the austral summer in January, temperatures average about 8.9°C. Hurricane-force winds or cyclonic systems rarely blow around Cape Horn, actually, although among the islands and channels local "williwaws" can burst down winds of over 160 kilometers per hour, and out at sea in the Drake Passage, for two out of every ten days on average, it is *at least* blowing a gale—meaning the wind is at least between sixty-two and seventy-four kilometers per hour (Murphy 2004: 48). An additional oceanographic feature to consider is that Melville's trips around Cape Horn were at the beginning of the industrial age. We were just starting a period of rapidly increasing deforestation and the burning of fossil fuels. So it was almost certainly even colder when Melville sailed there in the mid-1800s (Burton 2018: 9–10; Schneider et al. 2006: 1).

Mixed with the cold, winds, currents, and occasional floating icebergs is the less visible Antarctic Convergence Zone. As shown on my modern Admiralty chart of the region, this band around the globe where cold Antarctic waters sink underneath warmer waters from the Indian, South Pacific, and South Atlantic Oceans, oscillates between latitude 55° and 60° south. The Antarctic

Convergence Zone splits the Drake Passage, which often creates further unsettling of weather in the region, building fogs and confused waves and swells. My chart labels a distinct eastbound current of one knot (8.5 kmh) along this convergence, which nineteenth-century charts had also identified.

Although an additional complication to navigators, the Antarctic Convergence Zone creates oceanographic conditions that are especially productive throughout the marine food web, supporting vast blooms of krill and other zooplankton that in turn support flocks of seabirds, schools of pelagic fish, and dozens of species of baleen and toothed whales, as well as fur seals, elephant seals, and sea lions. This attracted whalemen and sealers to the region. The published account of Schouten and Le Maire's arrival to the straits and Cape Horn describes a prolific region in January of 1616: "We saw immense numbers of penguins here, also whales by thousands, so that we were compelled to be constantly on our guard, loofing up and with a drag-sail set, in order to avoid the whales and not run into them" (de Villiers 1906: 187). American and European sealers, beginning in the late 1790s, came down in small wood sailing vessels, some less than fifteen meters long, to hunt pinnipeds on the islands off Tierra del Fuego, Patagonia, and down to the Antarctic Peninsula, and then in turn to deliver pelts and oil to China or return to markets back home.

Stories came home too, published and oral, which associated Cape Horn with animals unknown in the Northern Hemisphere, steeping further the mystery and otherness into the perception of the region. The Southern Ocean marine life became identified with this area, especially, most famously, the albatrosses.

For his "The Rime of the Ancient Mariner" (1798), English poet Samuel Taylor Coleridge had his sailor kill an albatross in flight near the region of Cape Horn. The mariner does so, presumably, to improve the weather (see Figure 2.4). Coleridge got at least part of the idea from William Wordsworth, who had recently read a narrative by George Shelvocke titled *A Voyage Round the World by the Way of the Great South Sea* (1726), which tells of how south of Cape Horn a sailor's hands froze and then the man fell off the yard to his death (Lowes 1927: 222–8). Shelvocke also wrote of a "disconsolate black *Albitross*" that followed their ship off Cape Horn for several days. An officer "imagin'd, from his colour, that it might be some ill omen" (1726: 72–4). The officer shoots the bird hoping for a fair breeze. Which never comes.

Melville picked right up from Coleridge in his first fictionalized narrative *Typee* (1845), in which he piled on to the spiritual, supernatural significance of Cape Horn. Melville wrote of their captain who sat back aft and killed seabirds for sport with a shotgun. The sailors were "struck aghast at his impiety" and believed their long passage around Cape Horn was due to his needless shooting of albatrosses, petrels, and other seabirds: "one and all attributed our forty days' beating about that horrid headland to his sacrilegious slaughter of these inoffensive birds" ([1845] 1968: 223).

FIGURE 2.4 "And ice mast-high, came floating by, / As green as emerald," drawn by E. Duncan (engraved by H. Harral) for an 1857 edition of Samuel Taylor Coleridge's "The Rime of the Ancient Mariner" (New York: Appleton & Co.). © Vintage Library/Alamy Stock Photo.

MELVILLE'S SECOND PASSAGE AROUND CAPE HORN, ON A NAVAL FRIGATE (1844)

In 1841 after rounding the Horn, Melville's actual *Acushnet* traveled up along the South American coast and then cruised searching for whales off Peru, the Galápagos, and then for over four and a half months dawdled after whales along the equator before finally anchoring off the Marquesas. Here Melville and a friend jumped ship, lived with the Indigenous peoples for a month, and then joined an Australian whaleship named the *Lucy Ann*. Aboard this vessel, the captain was ill, had too few officers, and the whaling had been poor, so the crew refused duty when they got to Tahiti. Melville went along with the mutiny, escaped from his in-house arrest, hung around the island of Moorea for about a month, and then got a berth on the Nantucket whaleship *Charles and Henry*, aboard which he sailed up to Hawaii. Here he was discharged and took a few odd jobs and explored Oahu until, perhaps, he feared the return to Honolulu of the *Acushnet* with Captain Pease, who would demand his return aboard his original outbound whaleship. Or maybe Melville was simply homesick, out of money, and ready to return to New England, ready for the homeward-bound passage around Cape Horn (Heflin 2004: 193).

In late August of 1843, in Honolulu, Melville signed aboard the USS *United States*. This warship was sixty-three meters long on deck, not including the other nearly thirty meters more of spars that extended beyond the bow and stuck off the stern. The *United States* was nearly twice the size of the whaleship *Acushnet*, and was also wide and bulky in order to store, instead of barrels of oil, ten times as many sailors and an armament of cannon. Melville and the five hundred or so other men aboard the *United States* left Hawaii and traveled around the eastern Pacific for several months before reaching Cape Horn eastbound, homeward bound, a year later. Our best record of this passage is an abbreviated log written by "G.W.W.," who was most likely an ordinary seaman or a private in the marines. G.W.W. wrote of their eastbound passage:

> July 13th [1844] we are making rapid head way for Cape Horn, having a stiff breeze & a heavy sea, the old Ship half burying herself at every plunge. On the morning of the 15th it fell calm and continued so untill the afternoon, when the wind came out from the S$^{d.}$ & E$^{d.}$, which continued with moderate breezes untill the 25th, when the weather became very squally. On the same, Sail ho! was proclaimed from the Mast head, which proved to be the American Ship Natchez under Courses, topsails, topgallant sails, Royals, Skysails [...] we being at the time under topgallant sails and singled reefed topsails. On the 28 blowing a gale, we lay *too*, under Main & Mizen staysails & Fore Storm Staysail, for 6 hours, not being able to carry sail. The wind abated and then shifted in our favour, and we were on our way once more towards Rio under all sail.
>
> (Anderson 1966: 14–15, 65, emphasis in original)

The *United States* sailed in the easier, eastward direction, before the prevailing wind, but this situation can be dangerous too. Downwind steering can be exceptionally difficult, with small margins for error: the ship can turn quickly and broach, or with the waves astern, the ship can pitch, and the rig beyond the ship's bow can be plunged dangerously under the weight and motion of the water, as was the case of the *United States*. For Melville and his navy shipmates, the weather changed dramatically off Cape Horn—from a stiff breeze to a calm and then to a squall so heavy that they needed to "lay too," also known as *heave to*, which meant maneuvering the sails and rudder in a manner that the ship was mostly stopped, drifting in the water with the hull in a favorable, stable position to the seas and wind. In the gale off Cape Horn, the crew of the *United States* struck all their square sails (the downwind rectangular sails that could be aligned squarely, perpendicular to the keel) and set only a few low staysails (triangular sails that ran up wire *stays* supporting the masts, rigged parallel to the centerline) (see Figure 2.5).

G.W.W. reported that before the gale, the *United States* saw a merchant ship named the *Natchez* that recklessly carried all of its canvas, seemingly every sail it owned. The captain was trying, perhaps foolishly, to gain as much westing as quickly as possible. The *United States*, sailing in the opposite direction, exposed less canvas to the wind and set only sails that were closer

FIGURE 2.5 Detail of "A Squall off Cape Horn," Currier and Ives, *c.* 1860. Note all the men climbing up the shrouds and already out on the yards of the square sails, all of which are being struck except the lowest square sail on the foremast (the "fore course"). Beyond the bow, the jib—a type of staysail—has also been brought down, but they are not bothering to attempt to furl it at this time. The noise of all these sails slapping, the blocks clattering, along with the wind and seas, would be terrific. © Library of Congress (public domain).

to the deck for greater stability and safety. The *Natchez*, it turns out, made it around just fine. It was captained by Robert Waterman, known as a famous "driver." Waterman later set a record on this very voyage aboard the *Natchez* for his return passage from China to New York via the Cape of Good Hope (Albion 1939: 201–2; Clark 1912: 74).

In *White-Jacket*, Melville adhered roughly to his actual experience passing eastbound around Cape Horn aboard the *United States*—if only taking some occasional poetic license to spin a better yarn. For example, White-Jacket tells of passing "a fleet of icebergs bound north," a scene that G.W.W. does not mention and that Melville might have only read about or heard in stories from shipmates. Melville's fictional frigate, which he names the *Neversink*, experiences a maddening calm for two days at the latitude of Cape Horn. White-Jacket says: "Cold! It was cold as *Blue Flujin*, where sailors say fire freezes" ([1850] 1988: 101). In light air, but still in rough seas, the ship rolled so dramatically that they needed to send sailors aloft to bring down some of the highest yards so they were not lost overboard. To stave off the terrific cold, all hands were allowed to run around the ship and "skylark"—dancing, playing music, rough-housing, even fighting—to get their blood flowing. One of the ironic hardships of Cape Horn was for those that lived in the cabin, such as the wife of the captain, who had difficulty in managing any kind of work or exercise that could warm them or provide fresh air. Walking the deck would be unsafe. Harriet Swain, for example, the wife of a whaleman, wrote in her journal off Cape Horn in 1853: "Have been sick 12 days, vomiting up everything I took down. During the time it has been a continual succession of gales of wind with rain hail and cold. We have made no headway in the time but have instead drifted back which is very discouraging to all" (Druett 1992: 34).

In *White-Jacket*, using language that's evocative of "The Rime of the Ancient Mariner," the narrator describes a becalmed ship, the *Sultan*, as a sail on the horizon, which retells Melville's actual experience watching the *Natchez*.[2] In *White-Jacket,* Melville's *Sultan* had all its light air sails set too. "Never before," White-Jacket says, "was Cape Horn so audaciously insulted" ([1850] 1988: 105). As the *Sultan* glides past, the navy lieutenant shouted over that they should reduce sail. The *Sultan* does not heed the advice. Melville then creates a series of squalls that pummel the vulnerable merchant ship, "with a suddenness by no means unusual in these latitudes" (105). The squalls rip a couple of their lightest sails right off their stays and yards.

White-Jacket explains that his warship carries on around Cape Horn cautiously, until they are blasted with wind around midnight. All hands are called on deck:

> Here the scene was awful. The vessel seemed to be sailing on her side. The main-deck guns had several days previous been run in and housed, and the

port-holes closed, but the lee carronades on the quarter-deck and forecastle were plunging through the sea, which undulated over them in milk-white billows of foam. With every lurch to leeward the yard-arm-ends seemed to dip in the sea, while forward the spray dashed over the bows in cataracts, and drenched the men who were on the fore-yard. By this time the deck was alive with the whole strength of the ship's company, five hundred men, officers and all, mostly clinging to the weather bulwarks. The occasional phosphorescence of the yeasting sea cast a glare upon their uplifted faces, as a night fire in a populous city lights up the panic-stricken crowd.

(105–6)

Yet the crew survive, and White-Jacket continues on to explain that Cape Horn was an unavoidable evil to get to the Pacific or to return home. Nearly every ship faces these sorts of tempests, he says. It's a good thing that they have half the voyage home to recover—and, it's implied, to forget.

MELVILLE'S THIRD TRIP AROUND CAPE HORN, ON A CLIPPER SHIP (1860)

On Melville's third and last trip around Cape Horn, he was now a man of the cabin. The *Meteor* was captained by Herman's younger brother Thomas, who steered the clipper ship from Boston, bound for San Francisco, to serve the tail end of the Gold Rush and trade markets in China. The *Meteor* was known as a medium-sized clipper ship, built for speed with a lot of canvas and a narrow hull. Shipbuilders crafted the *Meteor* during the brief pinnacle of wooden shipbuilding in America, which hurried to best record passages around Cape Horn to California and take advantage of the high profits in San Francisco. Captain Tom had more than held his own. On his previous voyage as captain of the *Meteor*, he'd set a record run for a passage up to the equator in the Pacific, and he'd made it from New York to San Francisco in a competitive 114 days. By contrast, a clipper ship named the *Golden Eagle*, which left New York two months after the *Meteor*, slogged for an absolutely oppressive ninety days just trying to get around Cape Horn alone (Cutler 1930: 515).

Tom's second trip around the Horn with the *Meteor,* this time with his older brother back aft as a passenger, was easier than the first: he needed only two weeks to sail from latitude 50° south in the Atlantic, around, and back up to 50° south in the Pacific. (The *Flying Cloud*, navigated by Eleanor Creesy, the captain's wife, had a few years earlier blazed around from 50° to 50° in less than eight days.) From aboard the *Meteor,* Herman wrote a letter to his son, Malcolm, then aged eleven, in which he described the geography and their arrival to the region in late July of 1860. This description is an intriguing replay of that recollection in *White-Jacket*, what he saw when approaching for the first time aboard the *Acushnet* two decades earlier:

> As we kept getting to the Southward it began to grow less warm, and then coolish, and cold and colder, till at last it was winter. I wore two flannel shirts, and big mittens & overcoat, and a great Russia cap, a very thick leather cap, so called by sailors. At last we came in sight of land all covered with snow—uninhabited land, where no one ever lived, and no one ever will live—it is so barren, cold and desolate. This was Staten Land—an island. Near it, is the big island of Terra del Fuego. We passed through between these islands, and had a good view of both. There are some "wild people" living on Terra del Fuego; but it being the depth of winter there, I suppose they kept in their caves. At any rate we saw none of them. The next day we were off Cape Horn, the Southernmost point of all America. Now it was very bad weather, and was dark at about three o'clock in the afternoon. The wind blew terribly. We had hailstorms, and snow and sleet, and often the spray froze as it touched the deck. The ship rolled, and sometimes took in so much water on the deck as to wash people off their legs. Several sailors were washed along the deck this way, and came near getting washed overboard.
> (1993: 347–8)

This description, even to his young son, is far more dreary and gothic than the similar territory he recorded in *White-Jacket*. This older Melville was even darker in his journal, in which he wrote of the "horrible snowy mountains" and also the black mountains and gorges that composed a "hell-landscape" (1989: 133).

The next day, as his brother tried to sail the *Meteor* past the dreaded rocks, Melville wrote in this journal: "In a squall, the mist lifted & showed, within 12 or fifteen miles the horrid sight of Cape Horn—(the Cape proper)—a black, bare steep cliff, the face of it facing the South Pole" (1989: 134). Melville saw the region now in dramatic, underworld terms: Cape Horn stood at the end of "other awful islands & rocks—an infernal group" (134).[3]

CAPE HORN AND NINETEENTH-CENTURY SEAMANSHIP

In *White-Jacket*, to close his brief maritime history of Cape Horn and just before his own passage aboard the frigate, the narrator explains, as if to lower the bar: "At the present day the horrors of the Cape have somewhat abated. This is owing to a growing familiarity with it; but, more than all, to the improved condition of ships in all respects, and the means now generally in use of preserving the health of the crews in times of severe and prolonged exposure" ([1850] 1988: 99).

This agrees, and perhaps was even influenced by the pithy entry on Cape Horn in the popular *The Penny Cyclopædia of The Society for the Diffusion of Useful Knowledge* (1836), which Melville owned and used regularly for his books. The reference entry claims, after nodding to the *Centurion*'s struggles and the loss of the entirety of Pizarro's Spanish fleet while trying to round the Horn: "But the improvements in navigation have stripped this cape of its terrors, and the passage may be effected with comparative ease and certainty" (*The Penny Cyclopædia* 1836: 260; see also Hattendorf 1970).

Beyond improvements in the prevention of scurvy, it was not exactly developments in people's foul weather gear that alleviated aspects of the journey—the whole schtick of *White-Jacket* is he has a threadbare, home-patched jacket without any waterproofing—but it was as the encyclopedia states: vessels were simply able to get around faster and more safely. The charting of the region was steadily improving, captains were getting experience in the Drake Passage by repetition, and general ship navigation at sea had been developing.

It's worth emphasizing that for sailing ships it was all about wind. Nineteenth-century readers of Melville and other sea narratives and novels understood, usually from experience, that wind direction and strength were essential to travel at sea—an aspect of weather rendered largely insignificant to the majority of us today. Until quite recently, for the entire history of human passages across oceans and along coasts, the wind has been the beginning, the end, and everything in between. Today, the wind has some impact on modern shipping and air travel, but rarely anything influential to the general consumer or traveler. Unless you regularly commute on a ferry to an offshore island, anything below a hurricane is usually at most an annoyance or a lunge for the barf bag—but nothing compared to the way the wind impacted the lives of mariners and travelers in the nineteenth century. The wind inspires one of Ahab's most profound soliloquys in *Moby-Dick*, paralleling his hatred of the white whale, in which he declaims, "Would now the wind but had a body; but all things that most exasperate and outrage mortal man, all these things are bodiless, but only bodiless as objects, not as agents" (Melville [1850] 1988: 564).

Mariners on nineteenth-century sailing vessels needed to go aloft and out on the yards, the big spars to which the square sails were lashed. The highest of the yards were over ten stories above the surface, and in heavy wind or seas they rocked violently from side to side or in whirls of erratic ellipses and jolts. Melville wrote of characters falling from aloft into the ocean in three successive books: *Redburn* (1849), *White-Jacket*, and *Moby-Dick*. Only White-Jacket himself survives the plunge in the water. Though he read of it often in narratives and fiction, Melville, as far as scholars know, never saw a man die from a fall from aloft during his years working before the mast as a sailor—but while aboard the *Meteor*, Melville saw a man perish from a fall. Right off Cape Horn, a sailor named Ray, from Nantucket, fell onto the deck and died gruesomely, if quickly. "It was in vain to wash the blood from the head," Melville wrote in his journal. "The body bled incessantly & up to the moment of burying; which was about one o'clock, and from the poop, in the interval between blinding squalls of sharp sleet" (1989: 134).

Whalemen were constantly aloft in shifts during the day looking for spouts, and on all square-rigged sailing ships men needed to go aloft often to set, strike, or reef the sails. The necessity to do this could be immediate in response to squalls and storms that shrieked in too quickly for the watch officers to accurately forecast. Often the officers simply waited too long, more concerned with speed, like Melville's *Sultan,* than the safety of the men. The reefing of sails, which meant to reduce the area of the canvas by tying in a new edge, involved teams of men leaning over the yard with one man, often the most skilled, hanging perilously at the very end of the yard, wrenching out a steel ring that was seized into the canvas to make the new edge, the new corner, taut.

With all this in mind, before the development of commercial aircraft, the greatest single influence on our relationship to the ocean was surely the development of the marine engine. A vessel under engine power alone did not need to send sailors aloft. This reduced the size of a crew but introduced a new class of mariner: the firemen and the engineer, characters who would be later championed and explored by Jules Verne, Joseph Conrad, and Eugene O'Neill. By Melville's mid-century passenger vessels crossed ocean by steam and merchant vessels and whaleships often got steam-boat assistance to get in and out of port—but it was not until the late 1800s that the technology was available for ocean-crossing cargo ships, whaleships, or even all warships to have their own steam-powered engines, because it was rarely cost-effective or safe due to the logistics, costs, and impracticalities of storing or replenishing the amount of coal necessary for distant voyages. The internal combustion marine diesel engine, the type of machine that powered the *Professor Multanovskiy,* wouldn't come into commercial use until the early twentieth century. Melville in his writing barely touched the topic of steam power. In 1856, his third transatlantic trip to the United Kingdom, Melville traveled on a steamer across the Atlantic, from New York to Scotland, and during his nineteen-year career as a customs inspector along the wharves of New York City in the 1860s to 1880s, he had a front-row seat to the technological transformation of commercial shipping worldwide.[4]

Steamships with auxiliary sail, beginning with the *California,* began making the transit to the Pacific through the Straits of Magellan as early as 1848. Because of their paddlewheels, and then later their propellers, steamships were able to transit by way of these narrows and deal more safely with the williwaws and leeward rocky edge hazards of the Straits, but even steamships were not without their severities and wrecks.⁵ In general, however, steamships improved sailor safety, saved investors' money on labor, and gave more flexibility in the direction of travel, which in turn saved enormous amounts of time, money, and property. But this was not Melville's experience in the 1840s to 1860s. In fact, some of the last merchant vessels under sail alone still traveled around Cape Horn up until the 1920s, even when the Panama and Suez Canals had been well established. These were enormous ships, later made of iron and steel, filled with large bulk cargos that allowed flexible schedules, such as guano, nitrates, copper ore, and, most commonly, grain. These ships did not have engines, either, so the Drake Passage was still faster and safer than the Straits of Magellan. Adventures on these "Cape Horners" were made famous in narratives, photography, and film in the early twentieth century by author-adventurers such as Irving Johnson, Alan Villiers, and Eric Newby who echoed and furthered the nostalgia of the hard knocks trials and the brutal reputation of the Cape Horn passage.

Square-rigged sailing ships of any age, even the faster clipper ships such as Melville's *Meteor*, can at best travel some sixty degrees on either side of the direction of the wind, even in the most favorable conditions. For example, the logkeeper of a whaleship named the *Commodore Morris* wrote—on his own special day—of how his ship steered about ninety degrees off the wind on the way down toward Cape Horn:

> October 19 1845 Sunday my Birth day these 24 hours fine with weather with the wind to the W[est] ship by the wind to the S[outh]ward all sail set saw several pieces of kilp Falkland Islands bare SW Dist-180 miles thermometer stands on 46 Barometer on 29" 8/10 Latt 49°" South Long 55 West So ends.
> (Logkeeper 1845–9)

The logkeeper kept track of clues in the water, such as coastal species of kelp, to confirm his distance from shore. He took visual bearings across his compass as well as recorded air temperature and air pressure. In this situation, for this whaleship this southerly course in relation to westerly winds was fine, because he wanted to sail south at this point. But once they turned the corner, if the wind continued from the west across the Drake Passage, which it usually does, then the captain would have had to zigzag the ship roughly north-northwest toward the rocks of Cape Horn and then roughly south-southwest toward the cold and rocks of Antarctica, back and forth, to urge his ship to a longitude where it was safe to sail back north and into the South Pacific.

Tacking a big ship with three masts and more than a dozen potential sails is an operation requiring a lot of people hauling and easing lines in order, especially with sails suspended from heavy horizontal yards that must be shifted from one angle to another with some precision. White-Jacket explains that other than to man the guns, this was the reason why so many men were needed aboard a naval frigate. Tacking, also known as beating to windward, requires speed and steerage; heavy seas, light winds, or contrary currents can prohibit a large ship's ability to change direction. In this way, smaller boats, such as sloops and schooners, can be better at tacking and maneuvering closer to the wind and in tighter quarters.[6] Melville wrote in his journal when just off Cape Horn aboard the *Meteor*: "Tried to weather Cape Horn, as sloops weather Castle Garden Point N.Y—but were headed off. Tacked ship to the southward" (1989: 134). In other words, brother Tom tried to steer the ship as close to the wind as possible, with the wind on their port bow, but the *Meteor* was heading toward the rocks of Cape Horn. Before it became too dangerous, he tacked the ship to sail south in the other direction.

After using the trade winds to arrive to the Cape Horn region, vessels then needed to choose their approach carefully and consider when and where to tack, especially if going westbound. As they approached, in anticipation of heavy weather and their desire for maneuverability, ships' crews often took down their topmasts, the upper yards, and stored their light air sails below. "Familiarity with danger makes a brave man braver, but less daring," White-Jacket says. "Thus with seamen: he who goes the oftenest round Cape Horn goes the most circumspectly" ([1850] 1988: 97).

By the 1840s, when Melville started sailing around Cape Horn, more systematic examinations about the best strategies for sailing ships had been published. Matthew Fontaine Maury, a navigator and later oceanographer for the US Navy who became famous for his compilations of mariner's data on weather and whales and who Ishmael cites directly in *Moby-Dick*, wrote the first scientific paper in 1834 about the best practices for going around Cape Horn. Maury had recently navigated the region on a ship of the US Navy. In preparation, he collected logbooks and interviewed experienced captains. In his paper in *The American Journal of Science and Arts*, titled simply "On the Navigation of Cape Horn," Maury wrote dramatically of the trials: "There the tempest, the sea, and the iceberg assume their most terrible character, each presenting dangers almost new in their kind and peculiar to the region" (1834: 54). Of the two basic routes, the "inshore" and "southern" routes, Maury recommended adjusting as winds allowed: if westerly winds kept a ship from hugging close to Cape Horn, a ship should *not* try to wait and weather the area. The captain should not tack back and forth while getting blown back east, but instead should "stand boldly to the south," until below latitude 60° south, despite risks of icebergs. Maury had learned that westerly winds tended to abate significantly farther south and even to shift to a following breeze (61). He believed that March was the most favorable month for a westbound passage from the Atlantic (although a century earlier this had been the month the *Centurion* began its nightmare). November, Maury believed, was the most favorable if crossing eastbound from the Pacific. Regardless of Maury's advice, it seems merchant and whaleship captains seemed unconvinced, or at least unwilling to wait for a given season. For example, Melville passed Cape Horn once in April and twice in July. Centuries of data up through today show that the weather is significantly calmer in December, January, and February—the austral summer (United States Naval Meteorology and Oceanography Command 1995: 3). Aboard the *Professor Multanovskiy*, for example, we traveled at the end of December.

As Melville and *The Penny Cyclopædia* observed, more and more ships continued to travel back and forth around Cape Horn in the mid-nineteenth century, especially whaleships and merchant ships under sail, who in nearly every account describe seeing at least another vessel or two during their passage—without any hint that seeing another sail was anything but expected. From my town of Mystic, Connecticut, a captain named Joseph Warren Holmes (1824–1912) holds claim to a record number of eighty-four passages around the Horn. He sailed on merchant ships, a dozen years aboard whaleships, and was captain of some of the most famous clipper ships of the day (Peterson 1989: 26). Mystic Seaport Museum holds one of his personal charts on which he recorded just some of his track-lines. This chart is, quite frankly, one of the most stunning artifacts of maritime history that I've ever seen (see Figure 2.6).

Captain Holmes, however, was more the exception rather than the rule, of course, but there is surely something to the fact that you have never heard of him.[7] Statistics of shipwrecks around Cape Horn in the nineteenth century are currently hard to come by—a matter for future research—but Holmes's experience at least confirms that the passage could be navigated safely and often if you knew what you were doing.

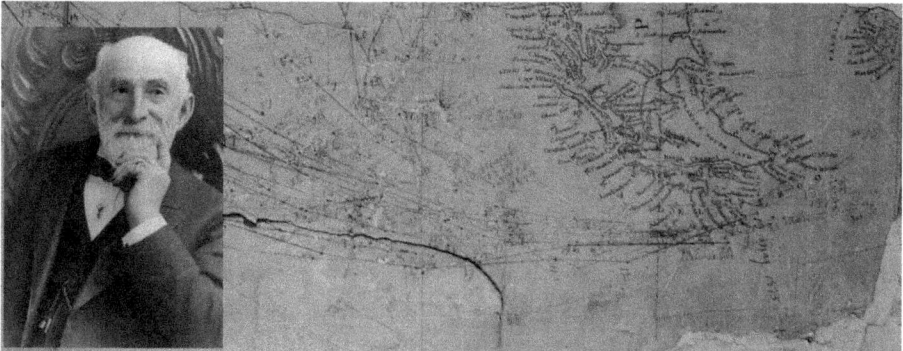

FIGURE 2.6 Chart of the South Pacific, 1849, showing dozens of Cape Horn passages navigated by Captain Joseph Warren Holmes while in his command of the clipper ships *Haze*, *Seminole*, and *Charmer*; Captain Holmes, 1908. © Mystic Seaport Museum.

CAPE HORN AND NINETEENTH-CENTURY NAVIGATION

To sail beyond the sight of coastlines before GPS, mariners such as Captains Holmes, Pease, and Thomas Melville used the sun and stars. Celestial navigation is figuring out where you are on the earth by measuring the height of the sun, stars, and planets. But at no point in history was celestial navigation used for coastal piloting. With celestial navigation, if you regularly got within a few miles of your actual position on the globe you were doing pretty well.

Mariners from several cultures all around the world have for centuries been crossing oceans by measuring the relative heights of the sun, stars, and planets by sight or with a variety of protractor-like instruments. By the nineteenth century, American and European mariners used the octant, quadrant, and sextant, which are all variations of the same tool and were all available to commercial seamen in the 1840s. These tools enabled the measurement of an angle more and more precisely. The sun is handy because it is the most visible object. When you measure the height of the sun at its highest point of the day, it is relatively simple to calculate your latitude, as Ahab does in *Moby-Dick*, especially if you have a copy of the tables that tell you declination. Declination is the earth's tilt in relation to the sun in your location that day. Declination was provided in Melville's time in the ship's reference books and nautical almanacs, easily available to all commercial captains. It's important to understand, though, that you can only get latitude based on the sun's height at local noon, a once a day occurrence.

Getting the ship's *longitude* in the 1800s required more finesse, planning, and mathematics. Mariners usually estimated their longitude using the methods of deduced or "dead" reckoning, provided: (1) the ship owned a sand glass or by mid-century a chronometer; (2) the officers kept reasonably careful track of the direction that the ship was steered, using the compass; and (3) the officers kept track of the speed that the ship was sailing on average over the water, which could be determined by an experienced eye or more precisely using a piece of wood attached to a marked line to measure how quickly the block was dragged away from the ship. Dead reckoning methods are loaded with potential error because of currents, variable helmsmanship, and the sideways sliding of sailing ships, known as leeway. Out in the middle of the Pacific in *Moby-Dick*, Ahab reveals his growing madness when he smashes his quadrant and plans to navigate on dead reckoning alone.

By the nineteenth century, mariners could find their longitude with other methods too. Using their chronometer, they could measure the sun at a few evenly spaced points of the day, called a running fix, but this also had its baggage of variables. Some officers could calculate longitude with their chronometer around the height of local apparent noon or they used the moon as measured in relation to a known star, known as the lunar-distance method. This was more complicated and seems to have been a skill rarely bothered with by working merchant or whaling captains. Stars, planets, and the moon in some ways are more useful than the sun because there are multiple bodies in the sky at once. If you know the time and you get three or more angles at close to the same moment, you can triangulate your location and actually get latitude *and* longitude on the spot, regardless of the ship's course or speed. The catch with this, though, is there are only two short periods during a day to do this, for a time at dusk and at dawn, known as *nautical twilight*. This is when you can see the stars and planets in the sky and while you also have a clean, clear horizon.

My overall point is that, essentially, Melville's brother Tom or even Joseph Warren Holmes or Eleanor Creely could not navigate with any precision when they could not see the sun, moon, stars, and planets in a specific window of time. This was emphasized in that note in the 1832 Laurie chart above (Figure 2.2). If navigators could not get at least one visual bearing off a known landmark, as Captain Pease was able to do to the Diego Ramirez islands from the *Acushnet*, then they were dependent on having a sense of where the ship had been and how the ship had been tracking, all of which were exceptionally difficult to do in the weather and sea conditions in the Drake Passage. Getting a clear view of Cape Horn or another set of rocks was crucial then, hence those coastal profile illustrations on charts of the time. You had to make sure, though, that you were taking a bearing on the correct rocks, or the alternative could be deadly. False Cape Horn is just to the northwest of the actual southernmost island. Several ships bound downwind from the west thought this was Cape Horn—that they were now safe—only to smash up against the true Cape Horn (Murphy 2004: 224–7). No government managed to construct a lighthouse or aid to navigation anywhere around Cape Horn and Tierra del Fuego until a lighthouse structure on Staten Island in the 1880s.

Melville's captains seemed to have known their business and surely had some luck too. They certainly did not sail with nearly the tools and architectural advantages of the *Professor Multanovskiy*. Iron hulls, for example, which are more tolerant of big waves and brushes against rocks, allowed for larger cargoes and greater speed. These construction materials, more cheaply found in the United Kingdom, began to come into regular usage on merchant ships as early as the 1860s. Both sonar—which reveals depth without having to send a sailor forward to huck over the side a piece of lead attached the end of a marked rope—and radar—which reveals the edges of land or other surface objects at night or in restricted visibility—did not come into commercial usage until after the Second World War. GPS technologies did not find their way on to regular commercial ships until the 1990s.

CONCLUSION: MELVILLE'S LITERARY RELATIONSHIP WITH CAPE HORN

Herman Melville never wrote a full story centered around Cape Horn. By the time he wrote *Moby-Dick* in 1851, Ahab's *Pequod* avoids the region altogether. He had already written of a stormy doubling of the Horn in *White-Jacket*, and too many other sea writers had already covered that territory. Even in *White-Jacket*, he acknowledges that Cape Horn material is already well trodden: "But if want the best idea of Cape Horn, get my friend Dana's unmatchable 'Two Years Before the Mast.' But you can read, and so you must have read it. His chapters describing Cape Horn must have been written with an icicle" ([1850] 1988: 99).

Melville and Dana had met in the 1840s and corresponded by letter, with Melville signing off one as "a sea-brother" (Melville 1993: 141). Dana had led the way for Melville as a sailor-author. *Two Years Before the Mast* (1840) is most noted today for it being the first popular narrative of the life of a working sailor rather than a story of admirals, naturalists, or explorer-captains. Melville read *Two Years* before he went aboard the *Acushnet*.

In *Two Years,* Dana described the trip around Cape Horn in both directions, including outbound on a small wood ship named the *Pilgrim*. Dana wrote of enormous seas, maddening calms, wet clothes, and how the sailors managed the ship in such conditions. About the work aloft, Dana wrote:

> The hail and sleet were harder than I had yet felt them; seeming almost to *pin us down* to the rigging. We were longer taking in sail than ever before; for the sails were stiff and wet, the ropes and rigging covered with snow and sleet, and we ourselves cold and nearly blinded with the violence of the storm. By the time we had got down upon deck again, the little brig was plunging madly into a tremendous head sea, which at every drive rushed in through the bow-ports and over the bows, and buried all the forward part of the vessel.
>
> (1840: 38, emphasis in original)

Dana described, too, the sheer necessity for numb endurance. The conditions remained for days. For three entries in a row, for example, he wrote: "The same."

On the way back around in 1836, this time on a larger ship headed downwind, Dana's ship was covered with snow. They sailed near an iceberg that "must have been from two to three miles in circumference, and several hundred feet in height," and then past fields of icebergs of various sizes (1840: 381).[8] The wind unexpectedly switched to coming from the east—for weeks. Dana's captain considered backtracking to transit through the Straits of Magellan, but visibility was too poor to enter the Straits. They eventually made it around after a far more rigorous and brutal passage than it had been going in the supposedly more difficult direction.

Only two decades after Dana penned his descriptions of the region, by the time Melville started to write his own sea stories, Cape Horn had become an objective correlative for harsh conditions as well as a geographic, legal, and moral gateway, in large part due to *Two Years*. In *Typee*, Melville doesn't even describe the passage around, only referring to it in hindsight regarding his captain's taboo of shooting seabirds in the region. The narrator decries when feeling abused by the whaleship's captain: "To who could we apply for redress? We had left both law and equity on the other side of the Cape" ([1845] 1968: 21). In *Omoo* (1847), his narrator describes a nefarious type of beach-combing sailor who "never dream[s] of ever doubling Cape Horn again on a homeward-bound passage. Hence, their reputation is a bad one" ([1847] 1968: 81).

In Melville's novels and narratives, and in some of his later poems, such as "The Fortitude of the North" (1866), "The Admiral of the White" (1885), and "To the Master of the *Meteor*" (1888), Melville drops the reference of Cape Horn as a stand-in for the highest of saltwater struggles, both realistic and metaphoric. In March 1862, two years after his return from his passage aboard the *Meteor*, Melville purchased in New York City two volumes of essays by his older countryman, the philosopher Ralph Waldo Emerson. In one essay, titled "Prudence," Emerson wrote of how outdoor laborers develop complete courage in all weathers: "The terrors of the storm are chiefly confined to the parlour and the cabin. The drover, the sailor, buffets it all day, and his health renews itself at as vigorous a pulse under the sleet, as under the sun of June" (1847: 216). To this, Melville scrawled smugly at the bottom of the page: "To one who has weathered Cape Horne as a common sailor what stuff all this is" (Braswell 1937: 329).

Emerson himself would have known the reference to Cape Horn, as nearly all nineteenth-century readers knew of the region and its trials. Several writers used it simply to evoke suffering and challenge, in the same way we in the twenty-first century throw around the climbing of Mount Everest. For example, in *Villette* (1853), Charlotte Brontë's narrator declares of unimaginable activities: "I had no more presaged such feats than I had looked forward to an ascent in a balloon, or a voyage to Cape Horn" ([1853] 2001: 174). Charles Dickens's only real sea story, *The Wreck of the Golden Mary* (cowritten, 1856) was a ship-meets-iceberg disaster off Cape Horn. "Who has not heard of it? Cape Horn, Cape Horn—a *horn* indeed, that has tossed many a good ship," White-Jacket declares. "You may approach it from this direction or that [...] Cape Horn is Cape Horn," he continues, "Cape Horn it is that takes the conceit out of fresh-water sailors, and steeps in a still salter brine the saltest. Woe betide the tyro; the foolhardy, Heaven preserve!" ([1850] 1988: 96–7)

Cape Horn is so pervasive as a synonym for natural extremes at sea, that it's simply enough to drive the plot of *White-Jacket* forward—merely sailing toward the Horn is enough for a suspenseful narrative. Melville and his shipmates while he was sailing used this for humorous effect too. In *White-Jacket*, the onboard drama troupe post a playbill for the "Cape Horn Theatre." In *Moby-Dick*, Ishmael tosses in the name of "Cape Horn" for both the bewitched and the comical. It is off "the howling Patagonian Cape" where Ahab's madness first develops on his way home from the voyage in which the white whale took his leg. Starbuck explains, without irony—but for the reader's humor—that he's tried to catch whales in a small boat "in a gale off Cape Horn." At "The Spouter-Inn" in New Bedford the entryway painting is a ship foundering off Cape Horn. The tallest glass at the hotel's bar is a "Cape Horn measure."

In sum, Melville's usage and understanding of sailing around Cape Horn was not just wordplay and metaphors from the parlor. Melville understood navigation at sea and wrote of everything accurately to accomplish his larger poetic and narrative goals. What Melville does especially in *White-Jacket*, which is beyond just recycling and embellishing well-fastened cultural impressions of Cape Horn and its trials for mariners, is focus on the psychological impact, the stress of the conditions on the men themselves, which finds its expression in their seamanship and actions in those conditions. At the height of the squall off the Horn in *White-Jacket*, the captain rushes up on deck to issue a command, which the subordinate lieutenant, in charge of the watch, loudly contradicts. The sailors follow the lead of this lieutenant, Mad Jack, who they respect because he knows his work. Melville not only paints the scene dramatically in the action of the squall but then he goes back in to analyze it in the chapter titled "Some Thoughts growing out of Mad Jack's Countermanding his Superior's Order." Cape Horn was the ultimate test for the sailor, working as a metaphor for human behavior back ashore. Here in *White-Jacket*, this scene plays at the level of a commentary on democracy, experience, and labor.

In works such as *White-Jacket,* Melville spun his own yarn from experience as well as on the shoulders of narratives such as those by Dana. Melville portrayed Cape Horn with a realism and understanding of the seaman, taking the region and the human experience there at sea beyond the Romantic fantasy of the place, as was depicted by the likes of Coleridge. By the end of the nineteenth century, the tiller in Anglophone literature of the sea about Cape Horn and extreme weather is passed on to Joseph Conrad, especially in his works such as *Narcissus* (1897) and *Typhoon* (1902), in which Conrad carefully and artfully examines the mariner's decision-making. Conrad's psychological fiction, in which heroes and villains are less clear, focus around seamanship and implications in times of crisis. If you don't have a fundamental understanding of ships and navigation, you miss a significant portion of Conrad's layering (See, e.g., Foulke 2002). In

A Personal Record (1912), Conrad wrote of Cape Horn in comparison to the creative effort of writing a novel:

> A material parallel can only be found in the everlasting somber stress of the westward winter passage round Cape Horn. For that, too, is the wrestling of men with the might of their Creator, in a great isolation from the world, without the amenities and consolations of life, a lonely struggle under a sense of overmatched littleness, for no reward that could be adequate, but for the mere winning of a longitude.
>
> (160–1)

Herman Melville's marginalia to these words of Conrad might have been a bit different than his snarky note to the "Prudence" of Emerson.

CHAPTER THREE

Networks

The Awful Prospect of Eternity: Ocean Networks and the Wreck of the Kent

SIOBHAN CARROLL

"network," *n. and adj. 1. Work (esp. manufactured work) [...] in the fashion of a net.*
(Oxford English Dictionary [OED] Online 2018)

For centuries, "network" was a word associated with fishermen at work on rivers, lakes, and seas. Yet, in our age of social media, it is easy to forget networks' historical link to the watery circulation systems of our planet. We speak of "navigating" cyberspace, but do not often think of how dependent our internet use is on the submarine cables that transmit more than 98 percent of international data (UN General Assembly 2015). If in the twenty-first century, our ability to network remains strongly linked to the ocean, it was even more so in the nineteenth century, when the ocean was the crucial natural space across which international communications, warfare, and trade were projected.

Water networks were particularly important for Britain, the island nation that had emerged from the Napoleonic Wars as the world's dominant maritime power. Britain depended on the ability of its ships to successfully navigate the ocean for its security and prosperity, but even when ships had no human enemies to face, the natural forces that shaped oceanic circulation—tides and currents, wind and rain—could still wreak havoc with its transoceanic networks. Terence Grocott calculates that there were roughly two thousand shipwrecks a year worldwide during the period from 1793 and 1816 (2002: vii), contributing, as

Carl Thompson notes, to an estimated "5,000 Britons dying at sea each year" (2007: 7). Anxiety over shipwrecks contributed to Britain's intense interest in understanding the ocean, prompting what Michael Reidy has described as a major nineteenth-century scientific initiative, in which the British Admiralty collaborated with "the maritime community and the scientific elite [...] to bring order to the world's seas, estuaries and rivers" (2008: 7).

Among their other sources of data, nineteenth-century oceanographers turned to records of shipwrecks to better understand the circulations of the ocean. In this chapter, I do something similar, narrating the 1825 wreck of the *Kent* as a means of unfolding the intersection of human and nonhuman ocean networks in the nineteenth century. The story of the *Kent* shows us how many of the macroscale oceanic networks of the nineteenth century—networks of geography and weather, trade and empire, communications and print culture, war and sociability—impacted individual experience. In reassembling a version of the *Kent*'s story out of primary documents, we can see how the social networks that stretched across Britain's maritime empire were regulated, maintained, and strained at sea; we can also glimpse how those social networks ended up informing scientific understandings of the ocean.

But let us begin with the bottle.

> *"network," n. and adj. 2 a. A piece of work having the form or construction of a net.*
>
> (OED 2018)

On September 30, 1826, a Black man walking along the beach of Bathsheba, Barbados, noticed something in the waves.[1] The man, whose name went unrecorded, was most likely a slave, perhaps a member of the last generation of Africans to be brought across the ocean in chains. If he were lucky enough to live until the end of the year, he would gain the right to own property and give evidence in court; if he lived until 1833, he would witness the abolition of slavery throughout the British Empire. For now, however, he was a slave walking on the shore of an ocean that had, for African slaves, come to represent a space of trauma.

The object proved to be a glass bottle. Deciding it was important, the man walked over to a white man bathing in the waves—one James Surles, who was, perhaps, his master—and handed the bottle to him. Inside was a scrawled note that read:

> The ship, "The Kent," Indiaman, is on fire – Elizabeth, Joanna, & myself commit our spirits into the hands of our blessed Redeemer. His grace enables us to be quite composed in the awful prospect of eternity
> D.W.N. MacGregor
> 1st March 1825
> Bay of Biscay.
>
> (MacGregor 1825a)

Surles and the Black man at his side probably recognized the name of the ship in the message. Already, in 1826, the loss of the *Kent* was on its way to becoming one of the nineteenth century's most famous shipwreck stories. If so, they also recognized that their find had scientific as well as social significance: the *Kent* had sunk near France, and yet had apparently been carried by ocean currents all the way to Barbados.

The *Barbados Globe* titled its initial report on the bottle's recovery "The Currents of the Ocean," indicating the type of interest it knew the bottle would generate. International newspapers soon picked up the story, which emphasized that the bottle had, in "nineteen months, crossed the Atlantic in a S.W. direction" ("We Have Copied the Following from the Barbados Globe" 1827: 2). Recovered at the outset of a new era of oceanographic investigation, the *Kent* bottle provided not only an illustration of the hidden network of ocean currents but also—via its connection to a famous shipwreck—a reminder of why such mapping could be important. Well into the early twentieth century, the story of the *Kent* bottle's drift would be cited as "one of the most remarkable messages from the sea on record" ("Messages from the Sea" 1890: 796) and as a dramatic illustration of how bottles could help map the "direction of sea surface currents" (Allingham 1904: 169).

Yet, even in its initial report, the *Barbados Globe* was keenly aware that the discovery of the *Kent* also had social import. "We sincerely sympathize with the friends of the unfortunate sufferers," the article concluded. Knowing that the social networks of European settlers on the island stretched overseas, the editor also noted that he had "reserved the original M.S." ("We Have Copied the Following from the Barbados Globe" 1827: 2) in case Duncan MacGregor's friends or family wished to recover it.

"network," n. and adj. 5 b. An interconnected group of people.

(OED 2018)

Duncan MacGregor, the man who wrote the bottle's message, had a complicated relationship to the British Empire. Descended from Scottish Jacobites who had fought against the English government in 1745, MacGregor had served in the British Army since the age of twelve (Atholl 1908: 513). He had attained the rank of Junior Major while helping maintain order in Ireland, and in January 1825, he was being sent to Bengal to help consolidate British power in the wake of yet more colonial unrest. Roughly three months earlier, native Indian soldiers had rebelled against their British officers in the so-called Barrakpore mutiny, in part because of the army's rumored plan to transport them by sea: many of the soldiers were high-caste Hindus, who professed adherence to the *kalapani* taboo prohibiting travel across the ocean.[2] For Duncan, himself descended from a group often characterized as colonial rebels, crossing the ocean at the behest of the British Empire had already become a way of life. However, it was one that in 1825, he, too, would have preferred not to undertake.

In late January 1825, Duncan MacGregor was preoccupied with the health of his 34-year-old wife Elizabeth.[3] Elizabeth had given birth to John—the couple's first child—on January 25. Her recovery had not gone well. From the family's correspondence, it appears she was suffering from postpartum depression as well as the physical trauma of attending a nineteenth-century childbirth. Yet, although Elizabeth was still in the period of her confinement, as an officer's wife, she too was expected to undertake the voyage to India. While her husband handled military affairs, Elizabeth was expected to run the household and socialize (that is, network), on behalf of her husband. Ocean voyages were hard on Britons' health at the best of times, and Bengal had a reputation for being "the deadliest province of British India" in terms of disease (Arnold 2006: 44). Gazing out at East Indiaman ships from the window of his lodgings at Gravesend, Duncan could not help but worry about how his ill wife and newborn son would fare on the voyage.

At Gravesend at least, Duncan had help in the form of Agnes Joanna Dick, Elizabeth's unmarried sister. Joanna, as she preferred to be called, had taken over many of Elizabeth's domestic duties during her confinement.[4] But as the time for the MacGregors' departure to India grew nearer, Joanna became increasingly anxious about her sister's health. She reported in a letter to her aunt that "Elizabeth's pulse felt and got lower and lower, for now the thoughts of parting so retarded her recovery, that she seemed to gain little or no strength" (Dick 1825: 29). On the Thursday before the *Kent*'s departure, Joanna had an idea that would change the course of her life. The "thought occurred to me," she wrote, "that if it were possible, I might prepare and go with them." It was a dramatic step for her to take: the MacGregors might not ever return to Britain. But Joanna was from a religious Presbyterian family and it was her duty to care for others. Perhaps the thought of a voyage to India also appealed to a 32-year-old unmarried woman in wintery England. Certainly, she observed, a tad ruefully, her unmarried status meant that there was nobody in Britain "requiring my stay" (29).

As soon as she mentioned the idea to Elizabeth, Joanna's fate was sealed. "No sooner had I hinted at the proposal then her countenance lighted up and the effect was such as left me not a moment to hesitate" (29). Despite the onset of a snowstorm, Joanna took a carriage to London, where she proceeded to buy in the matter of hours all the items expected of a baronet's daughter embarking on an indefinite stay in India. Many of the items Joanna found herself throwing into the carriage—"clothing, shoes, muslins, silks, ribbons, nets, satins, and perfumery etc." (30)—had themselves arrived by ship from Europe, India, or China, via the same stretches of ocean that she was about to travel. Joanna had just finished packing up her clothing when a tap at her door announced that the time had come to depart. Elizabeth was carried down the stairs in a cot, "with [her] baby in her arms [...] and placed in a small boat" (31). Joanna and the other able-bodied members of the family followed and were soon standing on-board the *Kent*.

> "network," n. and adj. 4. a. Any netlike or complex system or collection of interrelated things ...
>
> (OED 2018)

The *Kent* was a ship of 1,332 tons, an "East Indiaman" built in London in 1820 for service with the East India Company. At a time when many East Indiamen were built in India out of teak—a superior wood for tropical waters—the *Kent* was built in London out of oak, the result of shipbuilders' lobbying to move construction from Bombay back to London. Everything about the *Kent*, from its name to the place of its manufacture, to the presence of unmarried, well-born women such as Joanna on its deck, hints at the onset of a new phase of the British Empire, in which opportunities for native Indians to profit from or socially climb within imperial networks would be reduced. At the time, for British readers, the Englishness of the *Kent*'s name and place of manufacture would likely also add a symbolic resonance to the story of its destruction.

Regardless of where it was built, a ship like the *Kent* was a complex machine, intended for moving goods, people, and information across the world. From bow to keel, it measured forty meters long—roughly the length of two bowling lanes put end to end—and thirteen meters wide. Within this space would be crammed 641 people and cargo: 148 crew members, and the ship's passengers, including 344 infantry soldiers belonging to the 31st Regiment of Foot. In keeping with nineteenth-century Britain's increasing attention to the role of domesticity, many of the soldiers' families were accompanying them to India, a group numbering at least 43 women and 66 children (MacGregor 1825c: 4). It was the job of Henry Cobb, the captain of the *Kent*, to oversee the preparations for her voyage, including the stowing of cargo—a notoriously complicated affair that, if poorly done, could have dangerous consequences.

The complexity of the logistics needed to get an East Indiaman underway were brought home to Joanna as soon as she set foot onboard. A departing Indiaman is, she wrote to her aunt, a sight that "altogether astonishes one who never before witnessed anything of the kind" (Dick 1825: 33). The decks were a hubbub of noise and confusion, full of people rushing to perform tasks, and crowded with "soldiers with their wives and children – the stock of poultry pigs geese and turkeys, the confused collection of packages [...] the provisions of all kinds for so great a number as 640 people for four months (having no intention of touching any port before reaching India)" (33). Until that point, Joanna had, like many Britons, thought of the ocean as a space of adventure and potential danger. As a religious woman, she was also used to thinking of the ocean as a sublime site on which God worked his will. She knew that to the East India Company, the ocean was a gateway to wealth and power—a vision evidenced in the ornate carving and gilt edges that covered the *Kent*. But Joanna had not before had reason to attend to the social world of the ocean. Standing on-board the *Kent*, the scale of her new shipboard society dawned on her: an East Indiaman, she wrote, is "like a small town on the waters" (32).

With the decks so busy, Joanna was mostly confined to the family cabins, where she sent and received letters regarding her departure from "friends I never expected to see again" (33). Her decision to travel to India had been a spontaneous one; now that the reality of such a trip was beginning to sink in, she frequently found herself overwhelmed by emotion. She distracted herself by exploring the family's cabins, which were located at the stern of the ship. Two of the small rooms looked out on the sea. The third, larger cabin opened onto the cuddy (the dining room of an East Indiaman). There were venetian blinds on the windows on each side of the cuddy door, and Joanna quickly realized that she could peep through them for an unlicensed look at the soldiers at their dinner. Later, when the weather became rougher, these windows would serve

FIGURE 3.1 "An interesting scene, on board an East-Indiaman, showing the effects of a heavy lurch,–after dinner," engraving by George Cruikshank, 1818. Cruikshank's cartoon alludes to the physical (and social) perils of an East Indiaman cuddy. © Library of Congress (public domain).

as one of her main sources of entertainment. The sisters would try not to laugh as the movement of the waves sent "red coats [...] sliding from one end [of the dining table] to the other [...] getting a sudden overturn, when they and their chairs disappeared all at once under the table" (35).

The scene Joanna describes is not unlike that depicted by George Cruikshank's cartoon, "An interesting scene, on board an East-Indiaman, showing the effects of a heavy lurch,—after dinner" (1818) (Figure 3.1). Based on a drawing by Cruikshank's friend, the novelist and naval officer Captain Frederick Marryat, the cartoon illustrates some of the tensions associated with travel onboard an East Indiaman, where close quarters and prolonged time at sea might lead to the formation of social networks prohibited on land. In the image, a well-dressed woman, unseated by the waves, steadies herself by grabbing one man's thigh, and another man's nose (a body part that frequently stands in for a different male appendage in eighteenth- and nineteenth-century culture). The man whose thigh is grabbed spurts wine into the mouth of a man who crouches to receive it. For Marryat, a man whose cynical attitude toward sexual escapades would earn him censure in 1829, the scene alludes to an East Indiaman's potential as a hotbed of unlicensed sexuality.

When it finally came to Joanna's turn to dine, she discovered a far more decorous scene than that depicted by Marryat and Cruikshank. Henry Cobb, the captain of the *Kent*, sat at the middle of the table, from where he could best oversee the group's conversation, and a "small slip of paper" beside each plate "showed where you were to sit during the voyage" (Dick 1825: 35). Joanna was delighted to discover that she had been seated next to David Pringle, her first cousin, who was traveling to India to join the Civil Service. David was around nineteen years old, a religiously minded youth, and Joanna knew him and his brother Alexander well. The presence of so many family members onboard would, of course, limit the potential for the unlicensed connections Marryat alluded to. It also indicates how tightly intertwined the social networks of oceanic empire could be.

Yet, even if Joanna's experience of the *Kent* would prove less wild than that alluded to by Marryat, the ship still functioned as what Michel Foucault calls a *heterotopia* (1986: 24): a space that produces a differently ordered version of mainstream society. For Joanna, this manifested in her introduction to carpentry. As she explained to her aunt, "every article of furniture" onboard the ship needed to be tightly fastened "with firm cleats below and chords above, so that in rough weather the chairs tables beds etc. might keep their places and not be knocked about over us" (Dick 1825: 37). Even well-born passengers were expected to take up a hammer, which Joanna, unused to home repairs, found fascinating. It "is a great advantage to be able to put in the nail" she marveled, "and well for us was it that the Colonel and Major MacGregor were most expert at the business" (37). Even if the captain's table was well regulated, Joanna was already being introduced to experiences that women of her class would not have on land.

The ship remained at the Downs for almost a week. There, Captain Cobb discovered two stowaways: one a young boy who was trying to follow his father and sister to India, and one of the soldier's wives, who had hidden herself onboard after being told she could not accompany her husband. (The army restricted the number of family members who could accompany the lower-class members of the regiment as paid fares.) Caught, both stowaways were sent back to shore, with the woman "in great distress [...] weeping to think she'd only caused her husband to be punished for his infringement of the rules" (37). Joanna was particularly moved by the woman's situation. Perhaps she felt a pang of guilt over the class dynamics that allowed her, an unmarried member of the gentry, to effortlessly take an unplanned space on the transport as a private passenger, while a soldier's wife was left behind. Whatever the case, Joanna seems to have participated in some behind-the-scenes social maneuvering. After David Pringle, Joanna's dinner companion, wrote a letter to the colonel pleading the stowaway's case; Fearon "granted a pardon to the husband" but would not sanction the woman's return. Captain Cobb then interceded, "generously [promising] to maintain her at his own expense." The woman was "brought back with joy, to her husband," Joanna reported with satisfaction (37).

Finally, the *Kent* was underway. However complex human networks might be, they depend on natural systems, and so the voyages of East Indiaman ships were designed around seasonal wind circulation: ships bound to Bengal generally left Gravesend in December or early January, aiming to round the Cape in order to catch the southwest monsoon winds between April and September. When they arrived in India, the ships would unload their passengers and eastern-bound cargo, and, having loaded up with goods and passengers in Singapore and China, begin the voyage back to Britain in the period between November and January (Sutton 1981: 29). The *Kent* was leaving for Bengal later than tradition dictated, but it was a fast ship. If all went well, they would arrive in India in four months' time (Figure 3.2).

"network," n. and adj. 6 b. A diagrammatic representation of interconnected events, processes, etc.

(OED 2018)

The Bay of Biscay is a section of ocean bounded by the west coast of France and the north coast of Spain, which is known for its violent storms. Winds from North America blow uninterrupted across the Atlantic Ocean into Biscay, generating long waves that average around six meters high. Strong winds can make these waves still higher, leading to the conditions that, in 2016, triggered the abandonment of the *Modern Express*, a 33,000-ton cargo ship, in the face of

FIGURE 3.2 Map of the *Kent*'s Global Connections. Based on locations given in the *Kent*'s 1823 ship's log, this GIS-generated map shows the *Kent*'s intended route as well as the site of the 1825 shipwreck. The yellow arrow traces the probable drift of the *Kent* bottle. © Megan O'Donnell, 2018.

a Bay of Biscay gale (Bates and Spencer 2016). In late February 1825, the 1,332-ton *Kent* was unwittingly sailing into the path of a similar storm.

As Jan Golinski has observed, by the late eighteenth century, the weather had become a topic of considerable public interest in Britain. Atmospheric changes were widely thought to affect humans' psychological and physical health, and attending closely to the weather could be considered a "public duty" (Golinski 2007: 209). Although it would take until the 1850s, and the instantaneous transmission offered by the electrical telegraph, to realize the predictive possibilities of networked weather reports, educated Britons such as Joanna were well aware of the importance of weather observation, particularly at sea.

At first, Joanna was not alarmed by the changing conditions. Her party had been told that the Bay of Biscay "might be crossed in two days with a favorable wind" (Dick 1825: 40). But soon she noticed that "the roll of the vessel [had] increased considerably" (40), making it harder for her to walk. When the ship's company assembled on deck for a funeral, Joanna began to record the weather in detail, noting that the "sky was of green misty appearance" and that the wind "felt mild and warm […] being from the Southwest" (40). Turning her attention to the funeral, Joanna watched as the first of two small coffins were lowered into the rising waves. They were for two "infants [who] had died since we came on board" (40)—an unfortunately common occurrence on ocean voyages. As the first coffin disappeared, the child's mother—one of the solder's wives—started crying out in grief. Elizabeth, herself a new mother, was "much affected" (60) by the scene. Joanna tried to comfort her sister, but she sensed that the ship's atmosphere had—literally and metaphorically—altered.

For the next few days, the gale pounded the *Kent*. The ladies' maids found it difficult to help Elizabeth and Joanna get dressed, and the women soon discovered that it was safer for them to stay seated on the cabin floor. Nevertheless, when Duncan invited Joanna to view the sea, she accompanied him outside, creeping past a porthole through which the sea looked "like a high wall over which the ship rose and fell" (42). There were only a few sailors visible on the deck, and they were tied to their stations, to help them keep their footing. Joanna was less versed in meteorology than her male companion, but she had received a Regency gentlewoman's training in social interaction. "I usually studied the countenances of the sailors as my barometer," she noted gloomily, and "certainly could gather no good omen from them that day" (43).

Even in the middle of a dangerous storm, social rituals needed to be observed. When she entered the cuddy for dinner that night, Joanna found that the room had been altered to help the passengers maintain their balance. There were wooden stanchions for diners to cling onto as the ship moved; glassware was placed on "swinging tables" hung from the ceiling, and the firmly cleated dinner table was crisscrossed with ropes "covered with green cloth for the dishes to stand in" (42). Thus, Joanna wrote, "with some danger from the knives and forks flying about, we contrived to make a tolerable meal" (42).

The dinnertime conversation made it clear that many passengers shared Joanna's concerns over the weather and that, to situate themselves in this strange new environment, they were turning to maritime literature to help familiarize themselves with the possible dangers the ship might encounter. "The conversation turned much upon shipwrecks," Joanna observed, "and Mr. Hay remarked that it was here Falconer met with the awful disaster" (42). William Falconer's poem, *The Shipwreck* (1762), was well known to Joanna. Written by a sailor about an East Indiaman shipwreck he had survived, the poem had originally been composed to educate its British readers in the language and practices of shipboard labor. Written in part to strengthen ties between ocean and land, the poem's initial role as a translator of maritime experience made it a touchstone for Joanna and other *Kent* passengers, some of whom would later use quotes from Falconer's poem in their attempt to describe the events that followed.

On the *Kent*'s final morning, Joanna rose early to trim the oil lamp, "which we were always afraid to let go out as candles were strictly forbidden to be carried about the ship" (45). The lamp in question was most likely a patent lantern—a hand-held pewter lamp—and like many of the objects Joanna was familiar with, it was made possible by the networks of oceanic trade and shipping. It was fashioned from metal mined in Cornwall, fueled by whale oil gathered by Nantucket whalers, and the wick she trimmed was composed of cotton picked by American slaves. After she trimmed the wick, Joanna carefully replaced the lid, which would offer protection against fire if the lamp were dropped.

Joanna then went to check on the MacGregors. Her mind full of shipwreck stories, Elizabeth had been "alarmed with the creaking and shattering noises which she heard all night, and which kept her awake," leaving her "rather depressed and thinking that something was coming over us" (43). Joanna persuaded her exhausted sister to "not attempt rising or having a child dressed until the storm abated" (45). But an hour or so afterward, Joanna watched as a large wave caught the gig-boat hanging beneath their window and "broke some part of it, which seemed to show that the storm had rather increased" (45).

Around noon, third officer William Muir made a fateful mistake. Hearing the thud of loose cargo in the afterhold, he gathered a party of two sailors and descended below. Like Joanna, the men carried a patent lantern for light, its wick newly trimmed. Muir traced the sound to the area reserved for the soldiers' alcohol, where, surrounded by casks of rum and the highly hopped "India Pale Ale" brewed to survive East Indiaman voyages, he spotted a barrel of spirits rolling loose. Catching hold of the barrel, Muir ordered the sailors to fetch billets of wood to help secure it. But as the sailors exited the hold, the ship lurched, and Muir dropped his lantern. Perhaps Muir had not sealed the lid properly after trimming the wick; perhaps the metal was warped from long usage. Whatever the reason, the lamp cracked open, spilling burning whale oil onto the high-proof rum that had already leaked onto the floor. The "whole place was instantly ablaze" (MacGregor 1825c: 7).

"Fire," wrote Captain John Davie, around 1804, "is the most dreadful catastrophe" (1804: 73) that can take place onboard a ship. Fires tend to grow exponentially, and they are particularly dangerous in enclosed spaces, where the CO and CO_2 in smoke can prove deadlier than the flames. So it was with the *Kent*: as William Muir and the sailors tried to douse the flames, thick, suffocating smoke began to spread below decks. Within a matter of minutes, "several of the sick soldiers, one woman, and several children" would die of smoke inhalation (MacGregor 1825c: 8).

In the different accounts we have of the loss of the *Kent*, we can get a sense of how information circulated onboard in a time of crisis. Official information communications followed the chain of command, so that Duncan had just exited the family cabin when a military officer approached him, looking "as pale as death." "Sir," he said, "the ship is on fire in the after-hold" (MacGregor 1825b: 2). Quickly, Duncan made his way to Colonel Fearon's cabin, where, not wanting to "alarm his family" (2), he summoned his superior outside and appraised him of the situation in a whisper. Yet, even as officers such as Duncan did their best to keep the news of the fire contained, news was also spreading through unofficial channels. As Duncan exited the family cabin, Irvine, the MacGregors' manservant, had slipped into the room behind him, and told Joanna and Elizabeth that the ship was on fire. Joanna found this piece of "intelligence [...] so sudden and unlooked for, I could hardly take it in" (Dick 1825: 45). When soon after, Mrs. Fearon brought her children into Elizabeth's cabin, Joanna and Elizabeth shared the news with her. Word of the *Kent*'s predicament was spreading.

Even though he had heard that at sea "the cry of Fire [...] Is almost synonymous with death," David Pringle, who had run onto the deck after seeing the smoke from his cabin, did not at first realize "the danger of our situation" (Pringle 1825: 86).[5] Joining in the fire fight, he was impressed by the level of coordination displayed by the sailors, and he thought the "number of troops on board" made it easier than he had expected to "procure water" (86) and pass it to the afterhold. It was only when Captain Cobb ordered the ship's lower portholes opened that David realized the *Kent* was in desperate trouble. The captain was, in effect, scuttling the lower half of the ship to fight the flames, beginning a sinking process that might easily escape human control. Seeing Duncan preparing to go below to help carry out the order, David asked his cousin-in-law what he thought of their chances. Duncan answered that he "thought we should be prepared to sleep that night in eternity" (MacGregor 1825c: 11). David took the news calmly, and, clasping Duncan's hand in his, declared "my heart is filled with the peace of God [...] yet though I know it is foolish, I dread exceedingly the last struggle" (11). His words would later become one of the most circulated quotations from the narrative of the *Kent*'s sinking.

Joanna had initially responded to the news of the fire by throwing herself more vigorously into her domestic duties, offering help to the refugees from below, who "were clamorous and loud in their cries of despair" (Dick 1825: 47), and trying to find safe places to stow the increasing number of children. As she placed yet more toddlers into Elizabeth's bed,

> [a] sweet little boy (the bandmaster's son) came to me and asked with such innocent simplicity, "Am I to die too? tell me—must I die?" I held up his hands and repeated a short prayer after me, commending his little soul into the hands of his Redeemer, and then he seemed quite pleased and happy.
> (47)

As a Presbyterian, Joanna had, in theory, spent years preparing to die. When David entered the cabin, rushing to tell them the news of the fire, Joanna was struck by her cousin's resolution in the face of death. This, and the incident with the child, prompted Joanna to question her actual readiness for the afterlife. She found herself relentlessly reviewing the conduct of her life, feeling "deeply conscious of my great deficiency in *every point of virtue*" (48, emphasis in original). But there was no time, now, to correct anything. Joanna decided to focus on the work at hand, and trust in God's mercy for what would surely follow.

On the lower deck, it was dark, hot, and suffocating. Duncan encountered one of the mates stumbling through the smoke, who gasped that he had just "fell over three dead bodies" (MacGregor 1825b: 3). Duncan, keenly aware of the danger posed to his family, pressed onward. With the help of two fellow officers, he was able to get the portholes open. Duncan then watched in awe and horror as "the sea rushed in with extraordinary force, carrying away, in its resistless progress to the hold, large chests, bulk-heads &c." (MacGregor 1825c: 8). Duncan and his fellow officers knew that, in opening the portholes, they were risking sinking the ship. Indeed, a few minutes later, they were ordered to close the portholes again, for the "water-logged" *Kent* was proving increasingly hard to control, and the ship appeared to be "settling" prior to going down (9). Captain Cobb ordered the hatches closed, hoping "by the exclusion of the external air to prolong our existence, the speedy termination of which appeared certain" (MacGregor 1825b: 4).

Climbing back to the upper deck, Duncan found it crowded with "six or seven hundred human beings many of whom, from previous sea-sickness, were forced on the first alarm, to flee from below in a state of absolute nakedness" (MacGregor 1825c: 10). Few sights could have been more shocking to a well-bred gentleman. Nineteenth-century European culture was insistently attentive to dress codes, and one of the best-known novels of the late eighteen century, Jacques-Henri Bernardin de Saint-Pierre's *Paul et Virginie* (1788), had featured a climax in which its virtuous heroine dies in a shipwreck after refusing to take off her clothes for the swim to safety. The inhabitants of the *Kent* were evidently less scrupulous. This, and the sight of Roman Catholics performing in front of a mostly Protestant public "the various external acts required by their peculiar persuasion" (MacGregor 1825c: 10), appeared to Duncan as signs of the unraveling of his shipboard society. Practices and body parts people normally kept hidden were being exposed without fear of consequence.

In Elizabeth's cabin, the women had developed an organized response to the fire. Margaret Fearon, the Colonel's daughter from a previous marriage, stood outside the cabin door and "with wonderful self possession watched the progress of the smoke" (Dick 1825: 47), providing encouraging updates to those inside. Joanna looked after the welfare of the room, breaking "all the windows" as the cabin filled with smoke, and giving "out oranges or anything I could find to quench the thirst of the children" (47). When he entered the cabin, Duncan was surprised by the number of people crowded inside, and impressed by Joanna's coordination of the women and servants, which he thought displayed "the greatness of Joanna's mind" (MacGregor 1825b: 5). Joanna, however, felt that in fact it was "insensibility" (Dick 1825: 48) that allowed her to rise to the occasion. The "suddenness" of the news of the fire "prevented my [fully comprehending] all that had happened" (48). It was no wonder, she later wrote, that the fire had made a deeper impression on the refugees filling Elizabeth's cabin, who "were fully acquainted with their danger, and had long pauses to realize it" (48).

Duncan gave his family the bad news in the bluntest possible terms. Saving the ship now seemed impossible. They were about to die by drowning, or by fire, in the Atlantic Ocean, leaving their relatives to guess at their fate.

The family had a hurried conversation about their final plans. Duncan and Elizabeth were "determined to sink in each other's arms" (MacGregor 1825b: 5). Joanna, however, had heard of a plan to "put the women out into which boats remained, and give us whatever chance there was of safety in such a tempestuous sea" (Dick 1825: 49). Dangerous as such a course was, it was one she was apparently prepared to risk. Having decided on their respective destinies, Duncan, anxious to spare his father and siblings "terrible years of anxiety" (MacGregor 1825b: 4), quickly scrawled a short letter to his father. He obtained an empty bottle, and "corking it hard up" (4), he threw his message into the waves. The bottle bobbed away from the burning ship, beginning its long, slow trek to Barbados.

As Duncan watched the waves swallow his final message, a sailor perched near the top of the foremast took off his hat and waved it wildly. "A sail on the weather bow!" (MacGregor 1825b: 6). The ship exploded with cheers. For the first time since he'd received the news of the fire, Duncan felt a spark of hope. It was a small spark: the other ship was far from them, and the fire had been "making progress for some hours" (6), creeping ever closer to the gunpowder in the *Kent*'s magazine. Moreover, "the sea was tremendously high – and as no small vessel and few large ones could be expected [...] to take on board nearly 700 human beings" (MacGregor 1825c: 6). However, Captain Cobb gave the order to hoist the *Kent*'s flag of distress. The waterlogged *Kent* headed toward the strange sail.

"network," n. and adj. 4. a. Any netlike or complex system or collection of interrelated things, as topographical features, lines of transportation, or telecommunications.

(OED 2018)

The *Kent* had gone to sea because of Britain's desire to preserve its empire in the face of colonial unrest; the ship on the horizon had gone to sea because of the collapse of a different imperial power. In 1821, after years of struggle, Mexico had declared its independence from a Spain weakened by the Napoleonic Wars. Eager to rebuild its devastated mining operations, Mexico had almost immediately invited European companies to invest in local silver mining operations, not under the mantle of empire but as part of what Roland Robertson has called "incipient globalization" (1992: 59). The resulting flood of (mostly British) investment created a financial bubble that would help precipitate the financial crisis of 1825. But in early 1825, all seemed well, and the Anglo-Mexican Company, eager to capitalize on its investments, was shipping a group of experienced Cornish miners to Veracruz, onboard a small ship called the *Cambria*.

On March 1, at roughly 2:30 p.m., the *Cambria* sighted a strange ship on the horizon. The *Cambria*'s captain, William Cook, knew immediately that the ship was in distress. Even in the tumult of a gale, black smoke could be seen billowing away from the vessel, indicating the presence of a fire. The ship appeared to be a massive East Indiaman, which meant that it would have a sizable amount of gunpowder onboard. Cook deliberated, then ordered a cautious approach. He did not want to bring his ship in range of the inevitable explosion.

On the *Kent*, the hope afforded by the strange ship's sighting was creating fresh problems. Duncan saw a few of the sailors preparing to "cut away our boats with a view to provide for their own safety only" (MacGregor 1825b: 7). Drawing his sword, he declared that he would "cut down the first man who should touch the boats without orders, or dare to enter them until the means of escape had been presented to the poor women" (7). He stationed two of his fellow officers at some of the other boats, to prevent them being lowered before women and children were aboard. Despite Duncan's precaution, as the sailors began to lower the gig-boat—possibly the same gig-boat that Joanna had earlier seen damaged by the waves—it was impossible to "prevent a rush into the first boat [...] which was in consequence instantly swamped, and the work of death begun" (7). From her station outside the MacGregors' cabins, Margaret watched as the men drowned. This news she did not report back to the women inside the cabin.

The behavior of the *Kent*'s sailors was not particularly unusual. Nineteenth-century shipwreck records show that, during maritime crises, women and children died at much higher rates than men, often because those who had maritime training, like the *Kent*'s sailors, were more than willing to abandon passengers to their fates. The idea that a "women and children first" rule prevailed at sea largely stems from the much-mythologized 1852 sinking of the *Birkenhead* (Burg 1997). Like the *Kent*, the *Birkenhead* was a troop transport ship with a sizable number of armed men aboard who—even if they did not have wives and children present themselves—had communal ties with the families in question. In situations where communal ties were weaker, as was the case on many nineteenth-century emigrant ships, male passengers would join sailors in the rush to safety, leaving women and children behind (Burg 1997). For women and children on the nineteenth-century ocean, survival could thus depend on the strength and size of their shipboard social network.

Captain Cobb ordered a second boat to be lowered, in which would be placed "the ladies, and as many of the soldiers' wives as it could safely contain" (MacGregor 1825c: 18). When Duncan entered the cabin to direct the ladies' evacuation, Elizabeth begged her husband to let her remain with him. After he reasoned "with her calmly for a moment she consented to proceed" (MacGregor 1825b: 7). To Joanna, the farewell "felt as the chill touch of death—as none of us could believe that the *Kent* would [long survive] [...] and we knew his firm determination to do his duty" (Dick 1825: 50). Duncan then "told us to follow him and taking his sword he led us through the cuddy to the side window" (50).

As the women prepared to climb onto the small platform known as the mizzen-chains, some of the party balked. Margaret Fearon, who had just watched a group of men drown after trying to escape in the gig-boat, declared that she "would *not* leave her father" (Dick 1825: 51, emphasis in original). After a moment, her sister, Mary Anne, said that she would stay with her. David Pringle was also present. When Duncan suggested that he, as a passenger might also try to escape in the boat, David, noting that the boat was already battered and "the crowd was so great (in spite of its condition) [...] resolved to remain" (Pringle 1825: 88). From the platform Joanna "begged them to go, not a moment was to be lost, as time was everything in sending back the boats for others" (Dick 1825: 50). Finally, "hearing Elizabeth faintly call for me I hastily stepped in [the boat]" (51). Duncan watched in "agony" as the boat descended "into an ocean so tempestuous that no sailor on board thought it would live for a moment" (MacGregor 1825b: 8).

There were seventeen people in the boat, mostly women and children, with four or five sailors and an officer who was in charge of the company. The lowering process was dangerous: both ends of the boat needed to reach the ocean's surface at the same time for the craft to find stability in the waves, so the women and children were instructed to "lie down below the benches" (Dick 1825: 51) to reduce the boat's center of gravity. Lying at the bottom of the boat, Joanna heard some of the *Kent*'s sailors "[call] out that we were swamping" (51). But the boat successfully pushed off.

Now began the race to the strange ship. As the bottom of the boat filled with water, the ladies were obliged to sit up, the cold water lapping up to their waists. As they approached the strange ship it turned "a little aside," and the *Kent*'s refugees "feared they were not going to let us in" (Dick 1825: 52). But the *Cambria* was merely staying out of range of the *Kent*'s explosives. As they drew alongside the *Cambria*, Joanna saw "the brave Cornish miners stationed outside on the chains ready to draw us up" (52). The first to be saved was the baby, John "Rob Roy" MacGregor, whom Joanna saw dangling by his frock

FIGURE 3.3 *The Kent Indiaman on Fire, in the Bay of Biscay*, colored lithograph by William Daniell, after his painting, 1825. The *Kent* disaster quickly became a popular subject for nineteenth-century artists. Based on Daniell's painting of the same title, this image emphasizes the sublime nature of the *Kent*'s peril. © National Maritime Museum, Greenwich, London.

in the hands of a miner. Joanna's own rescue proved more difficult. Drenched as she was by waves, "my wet clothes had greatly added to my weight (at any time not inconsiderable!)" (53). This included the skirt of gowns Joanna's well-intentioned maid had tied around her waist, and her purse, heavy with sovereigns. "All this together made me *no feather*" (53). Luckily for her, one of the miners, James Warren, was also a champion wrestler from Cornwall. As the boat swung away from the ship "he had but one hand by which he dragged me up till I got safely over" (53).

Immediately upon arriving onboard the *Kent*, Joanna and the other survivors began negotiating for "the valuable lives of those we had left behind" (53). Joanna was relieved to hear that the *Cambria*'s captain and crew had resolved to "take us all in, and would throw over the guns or any part of the cargo, if there was the least occasion for lightening the ship" (53). Joanna joined her voice to others in urging that "no time might be lost in sending back the boat" (52) to save those still onboard the *Kent*.

Despite the *Cambria*'s willingness to help, the social network that coalesced around the *Kent* was growing more frayed by the minute. Of the *Kent*'s four remaining boats, two of them were swamped and sunk, killing "almost all the soldiers and sailors" onboard (MacGregor 1825b: 8), but the other two also safely reached the *Cambria*. Once there, however, the *Kent*'s sailors "sought shelter in the rigging" (9). They were dragged back down by the Cornish miners, who threatened to "throw them into the water" (9) if they did not return to the *Kent*'s assistance. On the *Kent*, when Duncan and his fellow officers saw that the returning boats were reluctant to approach the storm-tossed ship, they "looked around for powder to fire into them" (9)—a detail later left out of the narratives of the *Kent* disaster, which tended to locate conflict solely in among the lower-class sailors onboard.

Eventually, an orderly evacuation procedure emerged. Accepting that it was too dangerous for the small boats to come alongside the rolling ship, the officers adopted a "plan [...] for lowering the women and children by ropes from the stern, by tying them two and two together" (MacGregor 1825c: 20). In the process, "many of the poor creatures were unavoidably plunged repeatedly under water" (20). The women survived, but many of the babies and young children strapped to their backs drowned. Men with large families tried to swim to the boats with their children on their backs, in some cases to ensure that their wives would survive the descent. In many cases they and their children died in the attempt.

By 8:00 p.m., almost all of the men onboard the *Kent* had left the ship. They had settled on two strategies for reaching the boats: diving overboard and swimming or climbing out on the spanker boom and sliding down a rope into a boat waiting below. David Pringle, a competent swimmer, was contemplating the first route. Reentering the *Kent*'s cuddy, he found it a "melancholy picture of desolation" (Pringle 1825: 89). The sailors had dismantled the hen coops and fences to build rafts, leaving the animals to wander freely through the East Indiaman's luxurious cabins. "Some of the geese and other poultry, escaped from their confinement, were cackling in the Cuddy; while a solitary pig [...] was wandering in undisturbed possession of the Brussels carpet that covered one of the cabins" (MacGregor 1825c: 32). David was also struck by the sight of the "little children" who remained on Elizabeth's couch in the after cabin: "some of them had been left by their mothers, who could not take them" (Pringle 1825: 89). He thought they afterwards "perished" (89).

David examined the prospect outside the MacGregor's cabin window. It looked risky: the window was "thirty or forty feet above the water" (Pringle 1825: 89), and many of the men who had tried to swim to the boats had drowned. Deciding the risk was worth it, David climbed out the window and "dropped down" (89) into the cold water. For two minutes he struggled toward one of the boats and finally managed to clamber inside. "I am grieved to say," David later wrote, "that from fear of the boat being swamped, I felt almost totally regardless of those who were perishing around me, so selfish did the love of life render me" (quoted in Tancred 1899: 368). As with his mention of the children he had seen in the cabin, David Pringle was one of the few survivors of the *Kent* disaster to acknowledge, and to express guilt over, his decision to leave others behind.

To Duncan MacGregor and his fellow officers, the spanker boom appeared a safer escape route than the dive into the ocean. The spanker boom was a spar of wood attached to the rearmost mast of the ship. When the *Kent* was being rolled by high waves, as it was now, its spanker boom stood about nine or twelve meters above the surface of the ocean. For those trying to make their escape along the boom, there was not only "the nervousness of creeping along the boom itself, or the extreme difficulty afterwards of seizing on, and sliding down by the rope, which we had to dread" (MacGregor 1825c: 37), but also the movement of the rescue boat, "which the one moment was [...] close under the boom, might be carried the next, by the force of the waves, 15 or 20 yards away" (37). As a result, many of the men missed their first attempt to get in the boat and instead found themselves hanging in midair, where even at "fifteen feet" above the sea's surface, "the next heave of the ship would carry you [...] ten or twenty feet under the water" (MacGregor 1825b: 12). Duncan, who had "pledged myself to the soldier's wives [...] that I would not quit the ship as long as a single woman remained on board" (11), stood with Captain Cobb, who planned to go down with his ship. They watched as Colonel Fearon attempted the climb, and "was so frequently dashed against the side of the boat below, and by the heaving of the ship plunged so deeply into the water, that all thought he was gone" (12). Duncan took careful note of his superior's experience, for when his own time on the spanker boom came.

Around 9:00 p.m., Duncan saw the last woman safely off the ship. This was his chance to escape. But when he approached the spanker boom, he found a collection of men standing on it, paralyzed by their fear of heights, "unable to go either backwards or forwards" (MacGregor 1825c: 13). Despite his "awkwardness" at climbing—he'd been shot through the right shoulder during the Napoleonic Wars, which made putting his full weight on that arm difficult— Duncan "had already encountered too much [...] to be deterred for a moment" (13). When the men would not respond to orders or encouragement, Duncan, catching hold of a piece of standing rigging, climbed "over the heads of the infatuated men" (13). Throwing his leg over the boom, Duncan "slowly crept forward, feeling every step the utmost difficulty to hold on" (13). When he reached the rope, instead of descending "at the moment when the boat was inclining towards us," Duncan instead started his climb as the waves were sweeping the boat away. Duncan timed his descent perfectly, and landed in the boat "without being either severely bruised or immersed in water" (14). The boat he landed in was leaking, "nearly broken up—one large hole at the bottom was stuffed with soldiers' jackets etc. twisted into it" (14), but it reached the *Cambria* safely.

On board the *Cambria*, Joanna and Elizabeth were frantic for news of Duncan. Seeing Colonel Fearon among the rescued, Joanna begged him "to speak to us," but Fearon pretended not to hear her. She later overheard him saying, "'I fear poor MacGregor is gone'" (Dick 1825: 57). Frustrated at her inability to "say anything to satisfy the mind of my poor Elizabeth," Joanna "sat in mute impatience in vain trying to catch some whisper which could give us hope" (57). Finally, "a voice we could not mistake sounded in the small passage which led down to the cabin" (57). Duncan had survived. Delighted and relieved, the reunited family huddled together in the small cabin that had been assigned to them.

From the window in their new cabin, the MacGregor family could still see the *Kent* burning in the water. Joanna was too shortsighted to make out details, but she was told "by others that they could distinguish the poor creatures clinging to the posts furthest from the fire" (Dick 1825: 64). A haggard-looking Captain Cobb, who had given up his plan of going down with his ship, "went on deck, but could not bear the sight, and came down again" (64). Joanna could hear him in the darkness of the hold, counting down the explosions of the *Kent*'s cannon as the fire consumed them. Soon the ship turned into "one mass of fire of a dark and bright flame, which was reflected on the clouds [...] she exploded and sank very low" (64). Soon, "all was darkness" (64). It was around 2:00 a.m. on Wednesday morning.

When daylight came, Joanna was relieved to discover that "there was not one of those I know lost" (Dick 1825: 65). Not everyone was so fortunate. David Pringle, searching for dry clothing, encountered the stowaway he had helped earlier, and learned from her that her husband had drowned while trying to swim to a boat. They were, he wrote, a very "attached couple" who "had no family alive, and [...] seemed only to live for each other" (Pringle 1825: 91). Now, "I never saw a person more distracted with grief" (91). Despite such tragedies, according to Duncan's calculations, of the 641 people onboard, only eighty-two had been lost: fifty-six men (all but two of whom were soldiers), one woman, and twenty-five children (MacGregor 1825c: 63). By the standards of early nineteenth-century shipwrecks, it was a shockingly low body count. Even some of the men that the MacGregors had seen climbing the burning rigging had survived, picked from the water by the *Caroline*, a ship traveling from Egypt to Liverpool. The busy networks of nineteenth-century shipping had, in the end, saved almost all those onboard the *Kent*.

> "network," n. and adj. 2. network [...] Of, relating to, broadcast by, or characteristic of a broadcasting network.
>
> (OED 2018)

Word of the *Kent*'s fate spread quickly. In the immediate aftermath of his ship's sinking, Captain Cobb has begun "dictating a dispatch to the India House"

(Dick 1825: 71), which he sent out as soon as the *Cambria* made contact with England. When Joanna and Elizabeth finally reached shore at Falmouth, they found that word of mouth had already prepared the way for survivors' arrival. The streets were lined with townspeople eager to help carry the survivors, many of whom "were quite unable to stand at first" (73), to the hotel where they'd been directed to stay.

The *Kent*'s sinking soon became one of the biggest news stories of 1825, generating numerous articles and pamphlets. Of the various shipwreck narratives published in the wake of the disaster, Duncan MacGregor's *A Narrative of the Loss of the Kent East Indiaman, by Fire in the Bay of Biscay* (1825) proved the most popular. True to his religious background, Duncan presented the survivors' unexpected rescue by the *Cambria* as an example of "the goodness and providence of God" (MacGregor 1825c: 60)—a message that connected strongly with nineteenth-century readers. MacGregor's narrative went through three British editions in 1825 alone, was soon pirated in Ireland and the United States, and was thereafter translated into French, German, and Italian, ensuring the story's international circulation.[6] In 1826 it was abridged by the Religious Tract Society, in which form it would be reprinted well into the 1880s. In 1895, the periodical *The Leisure Hour* deemed MacGregor's "story of the loss of the *Kent* [...] so familiar" ("John MacGregor ('Rob Roy')" 1895: 43) to readers that it felt no need to recount its particulars. One of the most famous shipwreck stories of the nineteenth century, the narrative of the *Kent* had by then become a tool of religious education, a well-known adventure story, and, as an early example of a successful evacuation of women at sea, part of Britain's national mythology of oceanic chivalry.

Duncan's correspondence reveals a slightly more tortured relationship to the *Kent* than that suggested by his narrative. On the anniversary of the *Kent*'s destruction, Duncan wrote to Joanna, describing how he was still haunted by "the dreadful cries of drowning men," which he found easier to bring to mind than his sense of "Christian peace" (MacGregor 1826: 111) he had felt in accepting his death.

Joanna, for her part, spent the anniversary of the shipwreck in silent reflection. In the weeks after the *Kent*'s destruction she had felt herself paralyzed, "unable to write" (Tracy 2014: 188). A year later, her energy had returned, and Duncan's correspondence reveals that she was determined to see that the "money collected for Warren" would be used to set her Cornish rescuer "up in a shop" (MacGregor 1826: 115). Joanna would never go to India, but she did eventually marry Alexander Pringle, David's older brother, and have a son. When she died in 1878, at the age of eighty-five, she was remembered in American newspapers as a "Scotch heroine" for her behavior onboard the *Kent* ("A Scotch Heroine" 1878: 3).

FIGURE 3.4 Letter written by Lt. Gen. Sir Duncan MacGregor, March 1, 1825. Duncan's battered letter was preserved by his family. It now resides in the National Maritime Museum at Greenwich. © National Maritime Museum, Greenwich, London.

Although he did not realize it at the time, Duncan MacGregor had yet more international headlines in his future. Shortly after returning to active duty, he was transferred to Barbados. (This time Elizabeth, who had recently given birth to another child, did not accompany him overseas.) Soon after his arrival on the island, he was contacted by Michael Ryan, the editor of the *Barbados Globe*, who presented the astonished Duncan with the message he had bottled onboard the *Kent*. Duncan kept the letter, eventually carrying it back to Scotland, where it would eventually hang on the wall of his son's office, a symbol of the unexpected connections of the world of oceanic travel (Figure 3.4).

The news of Duncan MacGregor's recovery of the *Kent* bottle made international headlines, inspiring yet more newspaper articles, and, a decade after the *Kent*'s sinking, a scientific tribute.

On August 19, 1836, the new "*Kent*, troop-ship" threw a message bottle overboard while sailing in the Bay of Biscay, as part of the Admiralty's efforts to map ocean currents (Purdy and Findlay 1861: 272). The experimenters' choice of ship and location served as a subtle reminder of the importance of such scientific attempts at understanding the effects of wind and water at sea. For us, it serves as an indicator of the ongoing relevance of the *Kent* as its story iterated through the print networks of the transatlantic world, and of the nineteenth century's preoccupation with the ocean as a crucial medium for international networks.

Over the course of the eighteenth and nineteenth centuries, organizations such as the British Admiralty came to "know" the macroscale networks of the ocean by gathering in and analyzing message bottles, ship's logs, and letters. In the stories of individual ships and people they learned to glimpse the movements of much larger forces: winds and currents, trade and warfare, and the migrations, forced and otherwise, of human and nonhuman populations. In this chapter I have attempted to restage this process, reconstructing the story of the *Kent* so that, in examining it, we can glimpse the circulations of oceanic trade, the developing science of oceanography, the history of empire and slavery, the reach of transnational print culture, and the often occluded histories of women and children at sea. Just as the *Kent* lingered in the transatlantic imagination as a story that signified the powers of global connection, so too can we view the story of this wreck as a window onto the scale, power, and actions of the oceanic networks of the nineteenth century.

CHAPTER FOUR

Conflicts

Reframing Oceanic Violence: The Pax Britannica and Wild Weather during the Nineteenth Century

WILLIAM BOELHOWER

Before addressing the role of violence in the cultural history of the sea during the nineteenth century, I would like to introduce two premises aimed at explaining the chapter's priorities. Firstly, violence (or conflict) is construed within the broad ecological framework of land and sea and by following the routes of ships across the world's waters. While the land provides ships with a haven of ports and harbors defined largely by departures, arrivals, geographical position, and volume of trade, the trajectories of ships help to reveal the interactions and variegated purposes of ship captains, companies, navies, peoples, nations, and empires. It is certainly true that these two primary elements of land and sea tend to complement each other, but they equally have been seen as antithetic. Since ancient times many continental peoples have considered the oceans out of bounds, a sort of interdicted wilderness, while the land has stood like a seawall against an inconstant and hostile ocean. It is important to keep this perduring tensive relation in mind when discussing oceanic violence. As an Italian proverb explains, "*Chi è in mare navica, chi è in terra radica*" (those at sea go sailing, those on land put down roots). If the land perennially represented security and peace, the sea stood for peril and immemorial fright. Together, their storied rivalry has deeply affected the way we understand the multiple faces of tumult staged upon the world's seas during the nineteenth century.

The second premise is more specifically aimed at expanding our conception of the century's familiar scenarios of oceanic adversity insofar as it requires us to treat the latter not only as a salient set of themes but also as an embracing milieu of signs. Since ancient times the sea, the heavens, and bad weather were the source of various kinds of portents. Interpreting their elusive vibrations was the special office of astronomers, priests, and soothsayers. In the nineteenth century, science-driven positivists began to confine these same meteorological features into distinct systems, reducible to charts and tables. But even the most open-minded of shipmasters continued to experience an indomitable reality—a roiling onslaught of elements that, when taken as a whole, we may helpfully call a semiosphere. In spite of the fact that wild weather was progressively being reduced to identifiable formations and causes, those who experienced turbulence on the high seas stubbornly belied the most authoritative scientific axioms. In acknowledgment of these distinctly nineteenth-century labors, I will consider such meteorological effects in relation to a number of contributing factors belonging to the physiosphere (marine conditions, including winds, currents, waves, storm systems, fog, ice); the biosphere (the interactions of various life systems); the zoosphere (interspecies activity such as whaling and sealing); and the anthroposphere (the actions of imperial navies, the circulation of revolutionary ideas, British impressment at sea, slave smuggling, steamships). These four interpenetrating spheres, when taken together as a commotion of different kinds of signs, generate an oceanic ecology in which violence is inherent. In the wake of my two qualifying premises, the history of ships in the nineteenth century becomes a history of wild weather.

Before wrestling with the seas' many portents, I would like to insist further on the importance of framing land and sea together, even if the former often may remain off stage and in the wings. For centuries, the land has represented a number of positive values such as homelands, sites of memory, the rewards of agriculture, the benefits of civilization, and the triumphs of urban dwelling. At sea, none of these factors hold. According to popular belief, the mythic waters of the deep have always posed an underlying threat to everything for which the land has stood. Obviously, the seas have also represented freedom of movement, the opportunity of cooperative trade, and a bridge to intercivilizational encounters. In the early decades of the nineteenth century, however, this other half of the story proved to be refractory. The planet's oceans and seas—some still unexplored by Western nations—also offered a highly competitive source of extractable goods, primarily in the Pacific. In the first half of the century, during the heydays of the whaling industry and the helter-skelter rush for new resources in the Austral Ocean, among the Pacific islands and along the western coast of the Americas, British, French, Spanish, and American merchants fought and competed with each other for seal and otter skins, sandalwood, opium, and guano as well as tea, textiles, and chinaware from Canton (present-day Guangzhou) (Kirker 1970; Cushman 2013). Piracy, privateering, and European and American annexation schemes accompanied the race to control the new markets, which contributed to make the Pacific an additional arena of global contention. As James Stavridis notes, "The heart of nineteenth-century piracy was in the waters between the South China Sea and the Bay of Bengal" (2017: 107).

THE PAX BRITANNICA

Due largely to a string of stunning victories by Rear Admiral Sir Horatio Nelson—the Battle of Abukir Bay in Egypt in 1798, the destruction of the Danish fleet in 1801, and Trafalgar in 1805—the Royal Navy effectively ruled the waves and oversaw a commercially advantageous form of peace and trade on the world's oceans. Having built up its navy during the Seven Years War, England then thoroughly transformed itself into a marine state. When the political theorist Carl Schmitt used the metaphor of state-as-frigate to epitomize the first global spatial revolution of the early modern period, he was referring specifically to the fundamental transformation of the political-historical essence of England. As Schmitt observes, "It consisted in the fact that the earth was now seen only from the perspective of the sea; the island [England], however, changed from a broken-off piece of the continent into a part of the sea, into a ship" (2015: 79, 46). Schmitt is alluding to the process whereby Britain came to dominate the world by dominating the oceans: "England became lady of the sea and erected upon its dominion over all the seas a British world empire" (80). During the War of 1812 between Great Britain and America, for example, there were more than six hundred of His Majesty's ships in active service and some 140,000 sailors and marines manning them (Toll 2006: 382). Besides its possessions in the Caribbean and the Mediterranean, during the nineteenth century Great Britain also established territorial rule over India, strengthened its hold on Australia, and "covered the globe with a network of naval bases" (Osterhammel 2014: 59; Bayly 2004: 119).

As Great Britain continued to expand, it became the world's largest empire both in area and population (Osterhammel 2014: 450); and by mid-century had treaty ports in China (Hong Kong and Shanghai) and bases in Southeast Asia (with a hub at Singapore) (Figure 4.1). According to Ian Toll, "British warships were kept constantly at sea, on convoy duty, on blockade duty, in commerce-raiding cruises, in shuttling troops and dignitaries from place to place" (2006: 4). This blue-water activism may have allowed the British to control the world's oceans (the Atlantic, the Pacific, the Indian) and seas (the Caribbean, the Mediterranean, the North and the Baltic, the China), but this blanket image of global surveillance and command was illusory. For example, when it came to the slave trade and piracy, control did not translate into omnipotence. According to

FIGURE 4.1 *Imperial Map of the British Empire*, 1886. Creator J.C. Colomb, in *Graphic: An Illustrated Weekly Newspaper*. © Wikimedia Commons (public domain).

Osterhammel, "What it involved was less global maritime supremacy than, as Schumpeter put it, a 'global maritime police'" (2014: 451). England's distracted attempt to punish its rebellious North American colonies in 1776 and again as an independent republic in 1812, proved a colossal miscalculation and a remarkable failure of its pan-interventionism.

***

While the mother country waged war in Europe, Americans used their neutral status to build ships and export American goods across the Atlantic. Already in the first decades of the republic, Gordon Wood tells us, "American ships spanned the world. They had reached China in 1783 and were now sailing all over the Pacific—to Hawaii, Indonesia, Indochina, the Philippines, and India" (2009: 202). To be sure, the fledgling country's merchantmen sailed in waters that were as turbulent as those buffeting its ship-of-state. Early in the century, when the Royal Navy was busy blockading French ports, it had an insatiable need for sailors—requiring about 135,000 hands a year. Further, since between 15,000 and 20,000 British subjects regularly found work on American merchant ships, it had little qualms in stopping and impressing from

American vessels not only on the high seas but also along the fledgling country's coasts. Denver Brunsman notes that between 1793 and 1812 the Royal Navy impressed around 10,000 American seafaring citizens (2013: 249, 241–50). To be sure, it was often extremely difficult for officers to distinguish between Americans and Britains. As a result, many of the republic's sailors were forced to "slave" on British ships. Given the Royal Navy's global ambitions around the world's oceans, impressment became a necessary evil. This practice so irritated the American public that it became one of the chief causes of the War of 1812. Already in the Declaration of Independence, the signers cited impressment as one of the causes for separation from the mother country: "He [George III] has constrained our fellow Citizens taken Captive on the high Seas to bear Arms against their Country, to become the executioners of their friends and Brethren, or to fall themselves by their Hands" (Armitage 2007: 169). Some thirty-six years after the Declaration, it was still a standoff between citizens of a free republic and a tyrannical monarchy.

In his War Message to Congress on June 1, 1812, President Madison complained, "British cruisers have been in the continued practice of violating the American flag on the great highway of nations, and of seizing and carrying off persons sailing under it" (1999: 685–6). As the war proceeded, impressment became "the sole American condition to an armistice, but the British government continued to insist that [it] was a right it would never yield" (Toll 2006: 388; Wood 2009: 659–709). While the British blockade of the country's ports took a heavy toll on the American economy, the US Navy scored a number of stunning victories at sea in a string of single-ship duels that boosted national morale and created several legendary heroes and slogans. Thus, in his duel with the HMS *Shannon*, the mortally wounded Captain James Lawrence, commanding the hopelessly devastated *Chesapeake*, shouted out to his men, "Don't give up the ship. Fight her till she sinks" (Toll 2006: 414, 405–17). These memorable words recalled those of John Paul Jones who, when asked by the captain of HMS *Serapis* if he was ready to surrender, shouted from the deck of the *Bonhomme Richard*, "I have not yet begun to fight!" (Sherburne 1851: 121). It should be said that with the Treaty of Ghent (December 24, 1814) the British maintained all of their previous maritime rights, including the right of impressment.

***

In the first, precipitous decades of the nineteenth century, when the Atlantic's public sphere was thick with ideas of rights and revolution, ship and ocean provided one of the favored emblems for pondering not only life's embattled journey but the sudden upsurge of new nations. Sharing a central role in the founding of the new republic and in the crafting of the Declaration of Independence, the former presidents John Adams and Thomas Jefferson agreed late in life to revive their onceclose friendship in an exchange of 158 letters over a period of fourteen years. Joseph Ellis has called this exchange "the greatest correspondence between prominent statesmen in all of American history" (1998: 286). In an early letter to Jefferson (January 1, 1812), Adams wrote, "It was only as if one sailor had met a brother sailor, after twenty-five years' absence and had accosted him, how fare you, Jack?" (J. Ellis 1998: 286). They had much to remember and much to account for, since their political philosophies remained inexorably different. Once, in a letter to Abigail Adams (February 22, 1787) Jefferson confessed his radicalism in a verbal portrait worthy of Turner's painting *Waves Breaking against the Wind*: "I like a little rebellion now and then. It is like a storm in the Atmosphere" (Cappon [1959] 1987: 173). Of course he was writing from his beloved Paris.

When William Jay brought home what is now called Jay's Treaty (1795), an angry republican crowd gathered outside President Washington's home in Philadelphia to protest. The agreement smacked of a sell-out to Great Britain, but the President knew that the international scene was more complicated: "this government, in relation to France and England, may be compared to a ship between the rocks of Sylla and Charybdis" (Ellis 2002: 137). When Jefferson reflected on the burdens of the presidency to a French visitor at Monticello, he mused, "this exalted station is surrounded with dangerous rocks, and the most eminent abilities will not be sufficient to steer clear of them all" (182). The uses of wild weather and a gale-threatened ship-of-state are too frequent to review in their entirety, but a few more examples will help to depict the international stage on which the young republic was struggling to play a respectable part. Recalling the time when they were "fellow laborers in the same cause," Jefferson wrote to Adams on January 21, 1812, "Laboring at the same oar, with some wave ever ahead threatening to overwhelm us [...], we rode through the storm with heart and hand, and made a happy port" (Cappon [1959] 1987: 291).

In a backward glance of his own, Adams wrote back on February 3, 1812,

> Your life and mine for almost half a Century have been nearly all of a Piece, [...] mine in The Gulph Stream, chaced by three British Frigates, in a Hurricane from the North East and a hideous Tempest of Thunder and Lightning, which cracked our Mainmast, struck three and twenty Men on Deck, wounded four and killed one. I do not remember that my Feelings, during those three days were very different from what they have been for fifty Years.
>
> (Cappon [1959] 1987: 294)

Adams was recalling his frightful voyage to France in the *Boston* frigate in February 1778. Needless to say, the troubled relationship between England and America was not much different in 1812. In his letter of December 16, 1816, Adams affirmed, "Britain will never be our Friend, till we are her Master" (Cappon [1959] 1987: 502). Always an advocate of a strong navy, the former president had written to Benjamin Rush almost a decade earlier (August 31, 1808), "The trident of Neptune is the scepter of the world" (quoted in Toll 2006: 143).

The ship metaphor was equally evoked to philosophize about life as an allegorical journey. In Joseph Conrad's rich trove of sea stories, the critic H.L. Mencken wrote, we have "the symbol at once of man's eternal striving and of his eternal impotence" (Mencken [1917] 1930: 50). Maya Jasanoff cites and synthesizes the youthful visions of the eponymous protagonist in Conrad's novel *Lord Jim* as follows: "Jim had been inspired by 'a course of light holiday literature' to dream of going to sea. He imagined himself leading a 'stirring life in the world of adventure,' fighting pirates, rescuing castaways, suppressing mutinies, 'always an example of devotion to duty, and as unflinching as a hero in a book.'" Of course Jim, "a European trying to make it in Asia," tragically fails (Jasanoff 2017: 135). In Melville's version of the ship metaphor in *White-Jacket*, the narrator says of his experience on the *Neversink*, "As a man-of-war that sails through the sea, so this earth that sails through the air. We mortals are all on board a fast-sailing, never-sinking world-frigate." Then he adds, the "port we sail from is forever astern [...] [O]ur world-frigate is bound to no final harbor whatever [...] our voyage will prove an endless circumnavigation of space" ([1850] 1979: 408). For White-Jacket, the world of the *Neversink* has become the world at large, and both seemed governed by the Articles of War.

After having made several tough turns on a whaler, a man-of-war, and other ships around the world's oceans, Melville's thought-world had become imbued with the inchoate creed of survival of the fittest. An avid reader of Byron, he had stamped these lines from *Childe Harold's Pilgrimage* firmly in his memory (Byron 1819: 372):

> Roll on, thou deep and dark blue Ocean – roll!
> Ten thousand fleets sweep over thee in vain;
> Man marks the earth with ruin – his control
> Stops with the shore; – upon the watery plain
> The wrecks are all thy deed, nor doth remain
> A shadow of man's ravage, save his own, [...]
>
> When for a moment, like a drop of rain,
> He sinks into thy depths with a bubbling groan,
> Without a grave, unknell'd, uncoffin'd and unknown.
>
> (Canto IV, CLXXIX)

A year after completing *White-Jacket*, Melville decided to perch Ishmael, the shadowy narrator of *Moby-Dick*, in "The Mast-head" and have him ruminate as follows: "Childe Harold not unfrequently perches himself upon the mast-head of some luckless disappointed whale-ship and in moody phrase ejaculates: –

'Roll on, thou deep and dark blue ocean, roll!/Ten thousand blubber-hunters sweep over thee in vain'" ([1851] 1981: 162).

* * *

Conflict onboard deep-water ships—whether man-of-war or whaler, merchantman or slaver, sail or steam—proved to be endemic. As Linebaugh and Rediker argued in *The Many-Headed Hydra*, "The ship [...] (as the engine of commerce and the machine of empire) [...] provided a setting in which large numbers of workers cooperated on complex and synchronized tasks, under slavish, hierarchical discipline in which human will was subordinated to mechanical equipment, all for a money wage [...]. All the contradictions of social antagonism were concentrated in its timbers" (2000: 149–50, 152). Given the blustering nature of the oceans and the need for rapid response in carrying out orders, the hierarchy of command on ocean-going ships had to be rigid and discipline harsh. Speaking for all captains, Ahab reminded his first lieutenant Starbuck in *Moby-Dick*, "There is one God that is Lord over the earth, and one Captain that is lord over the Pequod – On Deck!" (Melville [1851] 1981: 484). Richard Henry Dana began his description of the various roles on the *Pilgrim*, a merchantman bound for the California coast, as follows: "The captain, in the first place, is lord paramount. He stands no watch, comes and goes when he pleases, is accountable to no one, and must be obeyed in everything" (1936: 12). Common sailors such as Dana, who were at the bottom of the pecking order, simply had to keep mum and follow orders.

Commenting on ship discipline, Dana at one point abandons his usually judicious tone in order to declare, "In no state prison are the convicts more regularly set to work, and more closely watched" (15). A challenging glance, the slightest sign of disrespect, or a lack of bounce in his step and a sailor could be stripped and flogged without redress before the rest of the crew. In *White-Jacket*, written to expose the injustices of flogging in the American Navy, the narrator reports, "The chivalric Virginian, John Randolph of Roanoke, declared, in his place in Congress, that on board of the American man-of-war that carried him out Embassador to Russia he had witnessed more flogging than had taken place on his own plantation of five hundred African slaves in ten years" (Melville [1850] 1979: 142). Of course there were ways for the crew to let off steam: the officers fought duels, the sailors got drunk when on liberty, and the shipmasters kept to their cabins amidst a choice selection of wines.

There were two extreme solutions to tyranny aboard a ship, namely desertion and mutiny, and both were quite common. In his book *The American Whaleman*, Elmo Paul Hohman studied thirty-six voyages made by thirteen vessels during the years 1839 to 1879, and counted 326 desertions (1928: 62–4). In his book about the *Globe* whale-ship mutiny, Gregory Gibson mentions that Honolulu

Harbor, much frequented by whalers in the 1820s, was so thick with American and European deserters and beachcombers that they formed one of the larger Pacific-island sailortowns (Gibson 2002: 114, 265n.9). Alluding to the ideological climate around the Atlantic at the beginning of the long nineteenth century, Linebaugh and Rediker note, "The sailors of the British navy grew mutinous after 1776 [...]; an estimated forty-two thousand of them deserted naval ships between 1776 and 1783" (2000: 241). On the other hand, Brian Lavery records, "Mutiny was a longstanding tradition in the Royal Navy, but it nearly always took place when the ship was at anchor – the 1789 mutiny on the *Bounty*, when Captain Bligh was deposed, was a notable exception" (2015: 188; Rodger 1988: 237–44). There were two famous incidents of mutiny in the Royal Navy, one in 1797 by the Channel Fleet anchored at Spithead off Portsmouth and another in the same year by various ships anchored at Nore in the Thames estuary. The former won concessions, the second was a complete failure and ended in a hanging (Lavery 2015: 188–94). For the first half of the century, Alexander Starbuck counted sixteen mutinies out of 7,000 whale-ship departures from the United States, almost all of them taking place after 1825 (quoted in Gibson 2002: 114; Starbuck 1878: 133–6). Starbuck also lists a mutiny by eleven Black sailors on June 18, 1818, off the coast of New England (1878: 223).

Sailors working on slavers endured the worst conditions of all. According to Alexander Falconbridge in his frequently cited *Account of the Slave Trade on the Coast of Africa*, "the slave trade may justly be denominated the grave of seamen" (Dow 1927: 164, 145–69). While not a few succumbed to the tropical conditions of the African coast, those who remained healthy enough to man the ships and learn the thankless job of policing the captive Africans often became less than human themselves. As for the ship captains, "it was but a step to treat with equal indifference the rights of the white slaves kidnapped in the slums of Liverpool and Bristol" (171). It is not hard to imagine that for a white sailor to be flogged publicly on a slaver was tantamount to being treated like one of the slaves in the hold, so it often happened. A further issue concerned the living conditions on slavers, which were irredeemably horrible for slaves but also unbearable for the crew. Besides the hovering climate of fear and violence, slavers were known for their pervasive stench, which marked them from a considerable distance.

Worst of all, slave-trade sailors not only had to tend to the sails and guide the ship across an often merciless Atlantic ocean, but also they had to care for the slaves. This care included such degrading tasks as flushing out the ship's hold; emptying the sanitary buckets containing feces, urine, vomit, and blood; feeding the slaves twice a day; guarding them closely when on deck, washing them, and whipping them if they did not dance or sing or refused to eat. They also had to attend to the dead. As George Howe, M.D., recounts in his 1890 article "The Last Slave-Ship," "Notwithstanding their apparent good health, each morning three or four dead would be found, brought upon deck [...] and tossed overboard as unceremoniously as an empty bottle" (Dow 1927: 372). All these tasks contributed to making the Middle Passage infamous, and the slave-trade sailor was right at the heart of it. In the words of Emma Christopher, "Aggression, violence, cruelty, and sometimes sadism were institutionalized in the trade's ethos" (2006: 166).

* * *

Ships were also directly involved in spreading dangerous ideas around the Atlantic and the world at large. In his recent world-historical approach to the American Revolution, in which he traces the infectiousness of ideas about republican government and human rights, Jonathan Israel speaks of "a single Atlantic Revolution" (2017: 4). Indeed, given "the new density of messages" and "unparalleled diffusion of common ideas," C.A. Bayly has claimed that the nineteenth century as a whole might rightly be called "the age of global communication" (2004: 20, 19). A telling example of the pervasiveness of revolutionary ideas comes from the New England ship captain Richard J. Cleveland who, after meeting with a group of disgruntled Creoles in Valparaíso in 1802, encouraged them to follow his country's example. As he proudly recounts, "For the better promotion of the embryo cause, we gave them a copy of our Federal Constitution, and a translation into Spanish, of our Declaration of Independence" (Cleveland 1842: 184). Bayly confirms an earlier observation of Eric Hobsbawm's about the French Revolution being "a universal event" (Hobsbawm 1977: 117) when he states that both the American and the French Revolutions were "of world-class importance, and not simply local revolts" (Bayly 2004: 86). Human rights discourse had an especially powerful impact on the slaves in the Caribbean islands. According to Nick Nesbitt, "The news of the French Revolution came to Saint-Domingue in part via the huge influx of French sailors constantly arriving there, bringing news from Europe as interpreted from those sailors' predominantly exploited, proletarian standpoint." Quoting Julius Scott, he adds, "In 1789 alone, '710 vessels brought 18,000 mariners to the booming French colony'" (2008: 71-2).

As late as 1853, when Frederick Douglass published his account of the successful mutiny onboard the *Creole* brig in 1841, he had Madison Washington, the actual hero of the revolt, say to the white mate, "Mr. Mate, you cannot write the bloody laws of slavery on those restless billows. The ocean, if not the land, is free" (Douglass 2015: 50). Significantly, in *The Heroic Slave* Douglass focused on Madison Washington's transformation from mere mutineer to revolutionary leader. His hero cites the Spirit of '76 to make his point. A brilliant orator and abolitionist, Douglass also participated in other mid-century reform movements on both sides of the Atlantic. In effect, the cause of antislavery became linked with temperance and women's movements, prison reform, republicanism, evangelical revivalism, and the international call for workers' rights. All of these progressive activities had their transatlantic networks and their members were constantly traveling back and forth across the seas. In the 1850s, traces of the French Revolution and the Declaration of the Rights of Man could be found in the ideologies nurturing many conflicts around the world—in China, India, England, and Ireland. As Bayly notes, "The emerging left took particular note of slave emancipation and the coeval Asian rebellions. Karl Marx himself was perhaps the first contemporary to consider the European and Asian rebellions using the same set of concepts" (2004: 166).

***

Although Great Britain abolished the international slave trade in 1807 and the United States followed shortly after, the Royal Navy had a frustrating time enforcing it (see Howard 1963; Rees 2011). As Bayly has noted, "It [abolition] merely drove slave trading into other nations' ships, particularly those of the Spanish and the Portuguese" (2004: 133). Furthermore, the success of transatlantic abolitionism had the effect of veiling the massive smuggling of slaves across a relatively hidden Atlantic. According to Michael Zeuske, Anglo-American historiography tends to refer to the period after the abolition of the slave trade and slavery in the British colonies as the "Age of Abolition," when in fact it was equally the period of "a booming slave-contraband trade and 'Second Slavery'" (2018: 104, 103–35). While the figures on smuggling are disputed, the estimates range from 786,500 to 1.2 million (104). Run by Cuban *negreros* and men operating from the Americas, these ships easily slipped through British and American control by switching flags and record books, and by selling and renaming their ships in a scam that made ownership practically undecipherable. When the Cuban brig *Amistad* set sail with its cargo of slaves, it carried the flags of half a dozen different nations, "used to mislead pursuers when smuggling human beings" (Zeuske 2015: 59). In short, the period of Second Slavery and the horrors of the Middle Passage continued into the 1880s, beyond "the Age of Abolition."

The historian Sowande' M. Mustakeem insists on defining "the sea as a viable and transformative space of history" rather than a mere seaway. Assigning agency to it, she argues, "The ocean was not just *where* the story of slavery transpired [...] but [...] it also became a central conduit for *how* bondage unfolded and consequentially devastated lives" (2016: 5). The ship functioned preeminently as a social space for the production of slaves, while the Middle Passage is aptly described as a "zone of death" (Mustakeem 2016: 5; Christopher 2006:

FIGURE 4.2 *Death of Capt. Ferrer, the Captain of the Amistad*, 1839. © Corbis Historical/Library of Congress/Getty Images.

165–7). Forced into a dark hold, packed tightly, shackled, naked or nearly so, with poor or no ventilation, and neighbored with the sick and dying, African captives began to suffer the sea change that turned them into chattel for the Cuban, Brazilian, and American markets. At the end of the eighteenth century mortality rates during the Middle Passage "fell to some 10–15 percent [...] and finally hit a low of about 5–10 percent during the nineteenth century slave trade." That said, "the ships of the Middle Passage probably claimed the lives of at least 1.5 million Africans" (Taylor 2006: 36–7). The alternatives to the ordeal of the Atlantic voyage were not attractive: suicide, escape, or insurrection. When brought up on deck, it was not uncommon for Africans to try to jump overboard, hoping thereby to return to their beloved homeland. In his book *If We Must Die*, Eric Robert Taylor lists 493 slave insurrections onboard slave ships, which "no doubt pale in comparison to the number that actually took place" (172) (Figure 4.2).

During the nineteenth century countless groups of contract laborers from India and China (Macao, Canton [present-day Guangdong], Amoy [present-day Xiamen]) endured slave-like conditions on ships heading to Cuba, Peru, Australia, the United States, and elsewhere. Bad weather, the long journey, overcrowding, a dearth of water, and harsh treatment at sea led to suicides, mutiny, and mortality rates "comparable to those of slave ships and early Australia-bound British convict ships." Not surprisingly, these transport ships were often called "devil ships or floating hells" (Hu-DeHart 2007: 178, 172). Indian indentured laborers were shipped to the coffee, tea, and sugar plantations of Ceylon (present-day Sri Lanka), Mauritius, and the Caribbean, as well as to

Fiji and Natal (Bayly 2004: 33). Alarmed by the overcrowding of London's Newgate prison, government authorities decided to establish a penal colony at Botany Bay, Australia, 21,000 kilometers away (Pybus 2007: 97–104). The first of the eleven transports arrived in mid-January 1788, and three more (the Second Fleet) in June 1790. Those who witnessed the debilitated state of the convicts when they arrived referred to the conditions of the slave trade to describe them. The ships were overcrowded, the felons stored in small spaces and chained together. The smell in the hold was intolerable. Not only were the ships of the Second Fleet contracted by a slave-trading company but the man who captained one of them was a slave-trader. During the passage to Port Jackson, his ship the *Neptune* recorded a shockingly high mortality rate (Christopher 2007: 109–28). As for the treatment of women, Emma Christopher writes, "When two hundred and thirty-seven British and Irish women convicts were shipped to Australia in 1789, *The Times* of London announced that each sailor of the ship on which they were to travel was 'allowed to select a mate' from among them to be his sexual partner for the duration of the voyage" (2006: 188n89). Predictably, the ship was known as "the floating brothel" (Christopher 2007: 119).

In the year of 1847, when the potato crop failed in Ireland, 296,231 starving Irish arrived in Liverpool on packet boats from Cork and Dublin. Starving at home, they were herded into improvised emigrant ships, with insufficient food and water, scanty clothing, and no medical care. In the words of John Kelly, "The Irish peasantry, having spent the winter of 1847 dying in public works ditches [...] would spend the summer dying across three thousand miles of ocean" (2012: 267). According to statistics, "In 1847, the death rate on vessels on the Liverpool-to-Canada route was over 15 percent; on the Cork-to-Canada route, over 18 percent" (267). At Grosse Island, a quarantine station for the emigrant ships on the upper St. Lawrence in Canada, the Irish left a toll of 5,294 dead. But the ice-infested waters of the North Atlantic also reaped its harvest. As Edward Laxton notes, "On the emigrant voyages to America around 50 emigrant ships foundered during the six Famine years" (1997: 90). It is not clear if it was the poor condition of the ships or the sickly state of the emigrants that led people to refer to these vessels as coffin ships. In his *1847 Famine Ship Diary*, Robert Whyte confessed, "My heart sickens when I think upon the fatal scenes of the awfully tragic drama enacted upon the wide stage of the Atlantic Ocean" (1994: 96). Having a wide range of abominations to choose from during the century of Pax Britannica, the London *Times* drew an obvious comparison: "The worse horrors of that slave trade which it is the boast or the ambition of this empire to suppress at any cost, have been reenacted in the flight of Irish subjects from their native shores" (quoted in Whyte 1994: 98).

FIGHTING WILD WEATHER

In comparison to the writing of national histories, a cultural history of the sea must find the ways and means to recount a liquid world dominated largely by an energetic turbulence of nature's signs. I am referring here to the conflicting systems of meteorological signs that overlay and clash with one another, to the exasperation of sailors and sea captains. In *Two Years Before the Mast* (1840), Richard Henry Dana tells of when his ship the *Alert* was off the Bahamas and heading home to Boston from Cape Horn: "It was blowing no more than a stiff breeze; yet the wind being northeast, which is directly against the course of the current, made an ugly, chopping sea, which heaved and pitched the vessel about so that we were obliged to send down the royal yards, and to take in our light sails" (1936: 375). Riding the strong currents of the Gulf Stream while heading into a relatively light wind caused the ship to buck and rear beyond expectations. A bit farther on, the ship's captain discovers another clash of signs. When they test the temperature of the water, they find it to be a balmy seventy degrees, "which was considerably above that of the air, – as is always the case in the centre of the Stream," Dana notes (375). Showing off his new marine prescience, Dana boasts that the climatic conditions they met up with when crossing the line, which brought them "the usual variety of calms, squalls, head winds, and fair winds," came as no surprise. Why? "It was hurricane month [...] and we were just in the track of the tremendous hurricane of 1830, which swept the North Atlantic, destroying everything before it" (363). Elsewhere, in the Marshall Islands youths learned observational methods of navigation from amazingly accurate "stick charts" that indicated wave patterns and swells and islands (Mack 2011: 116–17).

A neophyte sailor out of Harvard College, Dana spent a good part of his two years before the mast learning to read the signs of various weather systems, from the famed Magellan Clouds portending the imminence of Cape Horn to the sudden onslaught of a south-easter bowling toward the bay of Santa Barbara on the California coast. Frequently, he and his shipmates are told "to keep a bright lookout" for their lives depended on it. When the *Alert*'s captain sees "Old Wilson" (of the ship *Ayacucho*) unfurling his topsails, it was "All hands ahoy!" for Wilson "had been many years on the coast, and knew the signs of the weather" (Dana 1936: 64, 65). Always acutely aware of the ship's bearing and dress, sailors in the age of sail learned the lore that enabled them to interpret and adapt to constantly shifting winds, interoceanic currents, seasonal storms, fog, ice, and countless coastal hazards. Before the arrival of steamers, sailing ships had to calibrate their every move to the unpredictable whip of the oceans. There was never a moment of rest. It is this posture of unrelenting challenge and coping that alerts us to the broad ecology of adversity characterizing the sea's cultural history in the age of both sail and steam.

The sea literature of the century delighted its readers with stories and stanzas about shipwrecks, storms, becalmings, gales, cloud banks, fields of drift ice, and the extraordinary experiences of countless castaways (Neill 2000; Raban 1993). The Romantics in particular favored the sea as their ideal conduit for staging what W.H. Auden has memorably called "the enchafèd flood" (1951). But not until the 1820s do we begin to have exemplars of what the popular journals called the sea novel, a new genre invented by James Fenimore Cooper that successfully captured the peculiar excitements of those who, under the guidance of a John Paul Jones, ran the narrow "Devil's Grip" in a gale (Cooper [1824] 1986: 53–7). Cooper's biographer Wayne Franklin claims that "from 1824 on, anyone who made literary use of the sea did so in Cooper's wake. His fifteen sea tales were an undeniable proof of his fecundity" (Franklin 2007: xxv). At the end of the century, Joseph Conrad wrote, "In his [Cooper's] sea tales the sea inter-penetrates with life; it is in a subtle way the problem of existence, and, for all its greatness, it is always in touch with the men, who, bound on errands of war or gain, traverse immense solitudes" (1921: 76).

By the 1850s, there were enough logbooks and personal narratives about hardships at sea in circulation to encourage writers such as Edgar Allen Poe, Herman Melville, and Victor Hugo to consolidate the genre with new epic-sized twists of plot and psychology, whether "the wooden world" was a merchantman, a man-of-war, or a whaler (Cohen 2010: 133–78; Philbrick 1961: 42–83). Literature and poetry were not alone in reflecting the fantastic dramas occurring daily on the open oceans; there were also the often incredible accounts of those who explored the archipelagoes of the Pacific Ocean and the polar regions. Early in the century and under the Pax Britannica, scientists from several European nations contributed to knowledge of the world's last uncharted waters. In 1846, Henry Piddington wrote an influential handbook on hurricanes and storms for seagoing ships titled *The Sailor's Horn-Book for the Law of Storms: Being a Practical Exposition of the Theory of the Law of Storms* .... Evidently, the author had the entire British Empire in mind, for he covers all the world's oceans and the peculiarities of their storm systems.

Although Piddington claimed to have discovered the law of storms, including the motion of the winds and the various routes that cyclones follow, the most fascinating part of his research may now be his vainglorious attempt to map a typology of cyclones in every part of the world, along with his practical advice for detecting their premonitory signs (thus the chapter "Indication from birds"). We can easily imagine a worried ship captain consulting his Piddington as his sails begin to tatter and the high seas hurl over the bowsprit. Although by then it would have been too late to benefit from the chapter titled "Sailing parallel to, or before the Cyclone track," the captain still may have consulted the one titled "Profiting by a Cyclone." The United States also had its pioneer in studying the mysterious weather systems of the world's seas. In 1855, M.F. Maury, lieutenant in the US Navy, published his innovative *The Physical Geography of the Sea*, which claimed to offer "a philosophical account of the winds and currents of the sea; of the circulation of the atmosphere and ocean; of the temperature and depth of the sea; of the wonders that are hidden in its depths; and of the phenomena that display themselves at its surface" (xv). The immediate importance of this research lay in providing "a universal system of meteorological observations at sea" (dedicatory page), so urgently demanded by the world's blue-water fleets.

Maury defined the method of this new science as follows:

> By putting down on a chart the tracks of many vessels on the same voyage, but at different times, in different years, and during all seasons, and by projecting along each track the winds and currents daily encountered, it was plain that navigators hereafter [...] would have for their guide the results of the combined experience of all whose tracks were thus pointed out.
>
> (v)

Maury called for a collaborative effort of navigators belonging to "the seafaring community of the whole civilized world" (xiii, v, viii). This ambitious effort to render the seas predictable was based entirely on the observational skills of single navigators. If Maury could somehow win the collaboration of the international community, then the venture was sure to result in a resounding victory for marine science: "Every ship that navigates the high seas with these charts and blank abstract logs on board may henceforth be regarded as a floating observatory, a temple of science" (xiii). According to an enthusiastic Maury, now science would provide "a sublime spectacle" capable of surpassing that of the ocean itself (xiii). The evident pay-off was to turn the world's oceans into an atlas of consultable route maps like those already available for travel on land. Observations on storms, currents, and previously capricious atmospheric conditions supposedly allowed Maury to extract laws from nature and turn the watery world into a compilation of reliable charts at the service of global trade. As Maury declared, "We are about to open in the volume of Nature a new chapter, under the head of Marine Meteorology" (271).

Unlike anybody on land, sailors at sea were charged not only professionally but also existentially with the inflexible mandate of watchfulness. In an unending tug of war with a complicated system of sails, they had to keep the ship on course and responding to the fitful winds. They had to both see and foresee what lay around and ahead of them. For the sea was a fickle "friend." While sailors dared not sleep when on watch, they slept very little when below deck. As N.A.M. Rodger explains, ships' crews were methodically divided into watches of four hours and two dog watches of two hours each: "At sea all those in watches had only four hours' sleep at most, and were liable to be awoken at any moment if an emergency required the watch below to turn out and bear a hand" (1988: 39–40). This extraordinary and cagey *pas de deux* between ship and sea compels us to redefine conflict as a systematic and endemic feature of the cultural ecology of the sea in the nineteenth century. Pitted against the ocean's terrific undulating potency, the navigator's vital alertness dramatizes an archetypal battle between human beings and watery nature that far overshadows the themes of naval warfare and famous sea battles.

The nineteenth-century sea was still quite inscrutable, an innervating world of surging signs enveloping ship and crew and creating a circumstantial country of its own. Even when reduced to a scientific order of wrangling meteorological systems, this world of traces and symptoms still remained beyond the reach of the new marine science. Immersed in this oceanic world, a truly skilled sailor was one who had become expert at interpreting its inferential ambiguities—a cloud puff, a slight shift in the wind, a change in the roll of the ship, a sudden calm, sea birds flying overhead. All these required a special craft, a set of hard-earned skills that shaped the sailor's entire being: the way he walked and dressed, the language he used, his special knowledge of rigging and of bending and unbending sails, his ability to bear up under harsh discipline and even harsher living conditions aboard ship (Cohen 2010: 15–58). As a well-known proverb warns, "He that would go to sea for pleasure, would go to hell for a pastime" (Rodger 1988: 60). In his book *The Sea (La Mer)* (1861), Michelet expressed his admiration for Maury's book and cited it frequently. For Maury treated the sea "as a life force and almost as a person" (2012: 60). But when it came to Maury's superb confidence in his ability to regulate the sea's terrifying turbulence, Michelet balked.

* * *

At mid-century, a popular point of debate among marine scientists regarded the origin of "sea spasms," that "sudden turbulence that seems to come from below, and which in the Asian seas are akin to full-scale storms" (Michelet 2012: 63). Not convinced by Maury's explanations or by those who attributed such spasms to volcanic upheaval on the ocean floor, Michelet believed that deep below its surface the ocean was always calm. "Storms are merely transient acts of violence committed by winds, electric forces, or certain intensely critical moments of evaporation," the historian opined (64). As to actually extracting a law from accounts of storms at sea, Michelet was even more skeptical. In a chapter of *The Sea* dedicated to "Storms," he weighed in as follows: "Even the most reliable descriptions provide only vague and general traits but little of what gives each storm its originality or identity as an unforeseen consequence of a thousand obscure circumstances that are impossible to sort out" (65). For Michelet, storms were always singular. This stance also led him to exalt the credibility of sailors over the pronouncements of arm-chair scientists. After all, Michelet was a historian, a craftsman devoted to context and storytelling. If a sailor said he once saw a thirty-meter-high wave, he should not be ridiculed, the author huffed.

This anecdotal matter of "the height of waves" (Michelet 2012: 65) brings us to the very core of what I mean by an ecology of marine violence, for in this single emblematic figure of the wave we have both a minimal and a maximal sign of the oceanic order—both wave and ocean. In this expansive and momentary figure writers from Byron, Cooper, Poe, Melville, and Whitman to Tennyson, Hopkins, Crane, Kipling, and Conrad have invested so vividly to spin their sea tales. In his novel *The Toilers of the Sea* (1866), Victor Hugo gave the contrast between Maury and Michelet a larger purpose: "The sea's forces are mechanisms of infinite power; the ship's mechanisms are forces of limited power. Between these two organisms, one inexhaustible, the other intelligent, takes place the combat that is called navigation" ([1866] 2002: 190).

With the intent to chart this global ecology, an international conference in Brussels was held during which shipmasters from all over the world were encouraged to send their observations to a data collection center housed at the Washington Observatory in recognition of Maury's pathbreaking work on the sea. When making their observations, the shipmasters were told to record them in an "Abstract Log" according to a set of rules spelled out by Maury. Those who cooperated in this international endeavor would receive "a copy of my Sailing Directions, and such sheets of Charts as relate to the cruising-ground of the co-operator" (Maury 1855: 272). The Abstract Log had to record the ship's position, give regular readings of the air and water, of the direction and force of the winds (three times a day), compass variations, and the various currents encountered (272–3). In the free book Maury provided tables about air, water, and weather systems in various parts of the world. The days when the ocean was considered an unpredictable wilderness seemed to be numbered.

But the French historian demurred when it came to accepting Maury's science over personal experience. In *The Sea* Michelet recounts a little incident that happened to him when "quietly sitting on a lovely promontory of about eighty feet. I was enjoying watching the Ocean over a stretch of a quarter of a league, attacking my rock." Every time the incoming waves barreled against the promontory, Michelet felt thunder under his feet. But the point of this story is about waves and his disclaimer about Maury's scientific pretensions. Michelet noted that waves usually break at a height of twenty to twenty-five feet. "However, waves that are impeded and do not move in unison rise up to quite different heights." So it was, for "a large black wave leapt up and crashed down heavily enveloping and soaking me." Then the closer: "I would have very much liked to have had those honorable academicians and engineers who measure the Ocean's battles with such precision by my side" (2012: 66–7).

Although it may not have reached the height of eighty feet, Michelet's wave must have come close. In Melville's novel *White-Jacket*, published a year before Maury's *Explanations and Sailing Directions to Accompany the Wind and Current Charts*, the narrator describes the experience of rounding Cape Horn—or, "this battle with the elements" ([1850] 1979: 107). So intense was the crew's struggle to survive, he says, that "You become identified with the tempest; your insignificance is lost in the riot of the stormy universe around" (109–10).

When Richard Henry Dana recounted his experience of doubling the tip of South America, he spoke of leading "a Cape Horn life," in which the crew of the *Alert* did nothing but "eat, sleep, and stand our watch" (1936: 341). To render even more dreadful this universally feared passage, Dana read Cowper's poem "The Castaway," as popular among shipmates as Falconer's *The Shipwreck* (1762: 204). Sleeping in wet clothes and exhausted by their desperate work in the rigging, Dana says, "we were mere animals [...] little better than the ropes in a ship" (1936: 342). Often in their narratives, sailors chose to compare their own condition with that of the ship or the ocean around them. When the *Neversink* in *White-Jacket* was hit with "a paroxysm of rolling" that sent everything and everybody on deck colliding against each other, "It was impossible to stay one's self." While the deck heaved as if there were "a volcano in the frigate's hold," the water poured over the ship, raising "a hurricane of yells" among the crew (316–7). In circumstances such as these, things got confused and whirled about in a brew of signs. Best known for his history of the French Revolution, Michelet noted, "The waves reminded me of frightful mobs; a horrible rabble [...]. They were like abysmal and unnamed apparitions, creatures with no eyes or ears but only foaming mouths" (2012: 86). Hostage to his imagination, the great historian chose to wield the powers of metaphor against Maury's Abstract Log. In the end he came up with what for him was a crucial nineteenth-century environmental truth, "In the overall furor each wave expressed its own furor" (86). Blue-water sailors undoubtedly agreed.

* * *

In 1830 the Japanese artist Hokusai began printing his masterpiece *Thirty-six Views of Mount Fuji*, which made generous use of the color known as Prussian blue, recently imported from Europe (see Bouquillard 2007). Among these views was the stunning print known as *The Wave* but originally titled *Under the Wave off Kanagawa* (*Kanagawa oki nami ura*) (Figure 4.3). With its foaming white crest and steep blue arch, terrifying yet beautiful, and ready to come crashing down upon a gondola-like fishing boat slicing through the troubled sea with Mount Fuji in the distance, this seductive image of a single majestic wave captures the unassailable power of nature at a time when scientists were intent upon extracting a set of laws from the sea's taunting unruliness. In a peerless

FIGURE 4.3 Katsushi Hokusai, *Under the Wave off Kanagawa*, c. 1829–33. Woodblock. © Wikimedia Commons (public domain).

graphic figure, Hokusai evoked the ocean's wild essence in a seascape antedating Michelet's own rogue wave by some thirty years. Hokusai's work would not be recognized in the West until late in the century. As Britain consolidated its rule over the seas, the United States and Europe's strong nations began to send teams of scientists to explore the Pacific archipelagoes, the polar zones, and the western coast of the Americas as part of a scramble for territorial footholds around the globe (Bayly 2004: 128–47, 227–43).

In 1853, Commodore Perry led a small squadron of steamboats into Tokyo Bay, bearing gifts and imperial ambitions. By that time American whalers had turned to the waters of the North Pacific, off the coast of Hokkaido. In addition, the country's growing trade with China made Japan a perfect base to protect American interests in the region. As James Stavridis notes, "By March 1854, he [Perry] had managed to execute the Treaty of Kanagawa, the first such cross-Pacific instrument that provided […] refueling rights at two Japanese ports" (2017: 26). Who knows what might have emerged if Hokusai had produced his masterpiece *Under the Wave off Kanagawa* under the effects of Perry's treaty. Instead of his sleek fishing boats, he might have wedged one of Perry's spewing steamships under the oncoming cascade of his rogue wave. By 1890 the American naval theorist A.T. Mahan had summed up the effects of the West's competitive advance in an axiom: "Undoubtedly under this second head of warlike preparation must come the maintenance of suitable naval stations, in those distant parts of the world to which the armed shipping must follow the peaceful vessels of commerce" ([1889] 2016: 82).

In Conrad's novel *Typhoon*, the steamer *Nan-Shan*, heading up to the treaty port of Fu-Chau (present-day Fuzhou) with two hundred Chinese coolies in the hold and commanded by a Captain named MacWhirr, ran headlong into one of Piddington's cyclones. MacWhirr believed whole-heartedly in the technological superiority of steam over wild weather, even when "the whole black universe seemed to reel together with the ship" (1953: 318). As Jasanoff observes, "Conrad [...] came to share with his peers the sense that sail and steam represented more than different technologies. They marked different ways of life" (2017: 108). In effect, the *Nan-Shan* relied on engineers and stokers to keep the ship moving forward. There was inevitably a stark division between the men below and "you deck people" (Conrad 1953: 331). Reigning over the ship's chart room, Captain MacWhirr communicated with the engine room below through two speaking tubes while studying the gauges before him. But in a typhoon it was the engineer who counted the most.

While sailing ships scrupulously cooperated with the marine conditions surrounding them, steam ships responded strictly to a schedule drawn up in a distant metropolitan hub. In the age of steam the sailor skilled at furling and unfurling sails was practically obsolete. Ships now had two main points of reference, one the company office and the other a network of coaling stations. At the end of the century, Mahan's book *The Influence of Sea Power upon History, 1660–1783* became the bible for all those nations with interests to defend around the globe (Osterhammel 2014: 471). According to Mahan, "Colonies attached to the mother-country afford [...] the surest means of supporting abroad the sea power of a country" (1890: 83).

* * *

The above imperialist focus on the world's oceans also led some of these nations' premier painters—J.M.W. Turner, Théodore Géricault, Caspar David Friedrich, and Winslow Homer—to choose the sea and shipwreck for their culturally zealous subject matter. As the titles of many of Turner's paintings suggest, storms at sea and shipwrecks were central preoccupations throughout his prolific career. Already in *The Shipwreck* (1805) we have evidence of his early fascination with what became a central subject of Romantic art. This was followed by further masterpieces such as *Disaster at Sea* (c. 1833), *Stormy Sea with Blazing Wreck* (c. 1835–40), and his famous *The Slave Ship* (1840). Positioning himself as artist on the threshold between land and sea, he tried to capture the elemental destructive power of the wind and the waves in atmospheric dramas of light that converted the century's industrious and imperial horizon into a *tourbillon* of wild weather. This sea-accented aesthetic is brilliantly on display in *Waves Breaking against the Wind* (*c.* 1840), where Turner arrests in a single dynamic image the stunning effects of a liquid wind. The Romantic painters evoked shipwreck and the unassailable potency of the ocean to fend off Promethean man's triumphal vision of progress and civilization. In their search for a marine-inspired aesthetic they often cited actual incidents to enforce their thematic effects.

In his dystopian painting *The Sea of Ice* (1824)—also called *The Wreck of Hope*—Caspar David Friedrich alluded to the failed polar expedition led by Sir William Edward Parry, who was blocked in the Arctic ice for months and forced to abandon his search for the Northwest Passage. Barely visible amongst the jagged plates of ice thrust up into a riotous pyramid against an ominous skyline, a small fragment of a wrecked ship provides a moral about the century's unchecked ambitions. In another emblematic painting of the period, Turner's lurid *Slave Ship (Slavers Throwing Overboard the Dead and Dying – Typhoon coming on)*, viewers were reminded of the horrendous case of the slave ship *Zong*, whose captain threw more than 122 slaves into a

FIGURE 4.4 J.M.W. Turner, *Slave Ship (Slavers Throwing Overboard the Dead and Dying, Typhoon Coming on)*, 1840. Oil on canvas. © Wikimedia Commons (public domain).

becalmed sea, hoping thereby to collect the insurance money (Walvin 2011: 2–9, 97–8) (Figure 4.4). *The Times*' art critic complained that Turner had gone too far, both thematically and aesthetically: "Such a mass of heterogeneous atoms were never brought together to complete a whole before" (quoted in Walvin 2011: 7). When Turner first exhibited the painting, he included along with it these lines from his poem "Fallacies of Hope": "Aloft all hands, strike the top-masts and belay; / Yon angry setting sun and fierce-edged clouds / Declare the Typhoon's coming. / Before it sweeps your decks, throw overboard / The dead and dying – ne'er heed their chains / Hope, Hope, fallacious Hope! / Where is thy market now?" ("The Slave Ship" 2020). The combined riot of typhoon and (slave)-market has overpowered the speaker, leading him to "cash in" by throwing the African captives overboard, into the shark-infested waters. A second voice then declares the shipmaster's intentions to be futile; in such seas, the law of the market has no purchase.

At the other end of the century, the American artist Winslow Homer moved to Prouts Neck, a jutting promontory on the coast of Maine. Living alone and on the very edge of the land, he became a devoted sea-watcher and invited the North Atlantic's wildness to storm his art. In *The Life Line* (1884), for example, we see two figures dangling from a rope barely out of reach of the leaping waves. Apparently, they are escaping from a wreck and trying desperately to reach a point of safety; but we see neither wreck nor haven, only the dangling bodies in a trough of licking waves (Flexner 1962: 333–55; Novak 1969: 168–90). This obsessive effort to paint the sea on its own terms led Homer's contemporaries to hail him as the great American painter of the period. In *Gulf Stream* (1890), he broached subject matter that Théodore Géricault had already made famous in *Raft of the Medusa* (*Le Radeau de la Méduse*) (1819) at the beginning of the century. The French artist's handling of an actual shipwreck and the fate of its castaways signaled the failure of French naval power while helping to launch the new sea aesthetic of Romanticism. Homer's canvas depicts a man lying resignedly in a dismasted boat set adrift in the rolling Gulf waters and surrounded by sharks. In the distance we see a water spout whipping toward him and sucking up the sea as it advances.

But it is the painting *Northeaster* (1895) that best epitomizes Homer's profound interest in the battle between a wild ocean and a tattered coast of rocks—in short that liminal zone where land and sea were destined to fight it out forever. In *Northeaster* Homer painted the clouds of spray and foam thrown up from the incoming roarers that were blasting the coast where he stood. In the distance and out to sea there is only a dark army of incoming waves below a matching horizon. In a few years, Britain would concede ascendency in Central America to the United States. The Panama Canal would be completed in August 1914 under the shield of the Monroe Doctrine and according to the geopolitical vision of Theodore Roosevelt and his adviser A.T. Mahan (Beale 1967: 101–8).

* * *

In the early chapter "The Chart" in *Moby-Dick*, Ishmael reveals an important secret about a certain compulsive habit of Ahab's. Evidently, the *Pequod*'s prodigious captain places a wild confidence in what must have seemed a foolproof strategy to catch Moby-Dick. The strategy consists in nightly updating a chart tracing the seasonal distribution of whales across "the unhooped oceans of this planet" (Melville [1851] 1981: 200). Here is Ishmael:

> Had you followed Captain Ahab down into his cabin after the squall [...], you would have seen him go to a locker in the transom, and bringing out a large wrinkled roll of yellowish sea charts, spread them before him on his screwed-down table. Then seating himself before it, you would have seen him intently study the various lines and [...] trace additional courses over spaces that before were blank. At intervals, he would refer to piles of old log-books [...] wherein were set down the seasons and places in which, on various former voyages of various ships, sperm whales had been captured or seen.
>
> (199–200)

In the eyes of Ishmael, Ahab's nightly practice of sitting over his charts is "an absurdly hopeless task" (200). Ishmael then explains the fussy rationale behind Ahab's method. If one could study all the logs of all the whalers across all the oceans over a year's cycle, a resolute whaling captain should be able to identify the feeding grounds of sperm whales at a given time and place. "On this hint, attempts have been made to construct elaborate migratory charts of the sperm whale," Ishmael says, citing in a note the efforts of a certain Lieutenant Maury, of the National Observatory in Washington (201) (Figure 4.5). In effect, Maury's *Whale Chart* was published in 1851, the year Melville published his novel. Ishmael's little secret is that the charismatic Ahab is a covert devotee of the naval officer who believed he could outsmart the currents and storms of the world's oceans. No less than Michelet, Ishmael considers such efforts a "delirious but still methodical scheme," and comical too: "after poring over his charts till long after midnight [...], Ahab would mutter to himself, [...] have I not tallied the whale [...] ?" (202, 204). In the end it was Moby-Dick who tallied Ahab.

Only a diehard captain of science would put such faith in the calculus of Maury's whale chart. But Ahab and Maury were by no means alone in clinging to surfaces. The cultural history of the sea in the nineteenth century was heavily marked by this conflict between those who confided in charts and those who recognized deeper planetary soundings. For people like Melville and Conrad, "going on a steamship wasn't truly going to sea" (Jasanoff 2017: 108). When Benito Cereno asserted to Amasa Delano that everything aboard

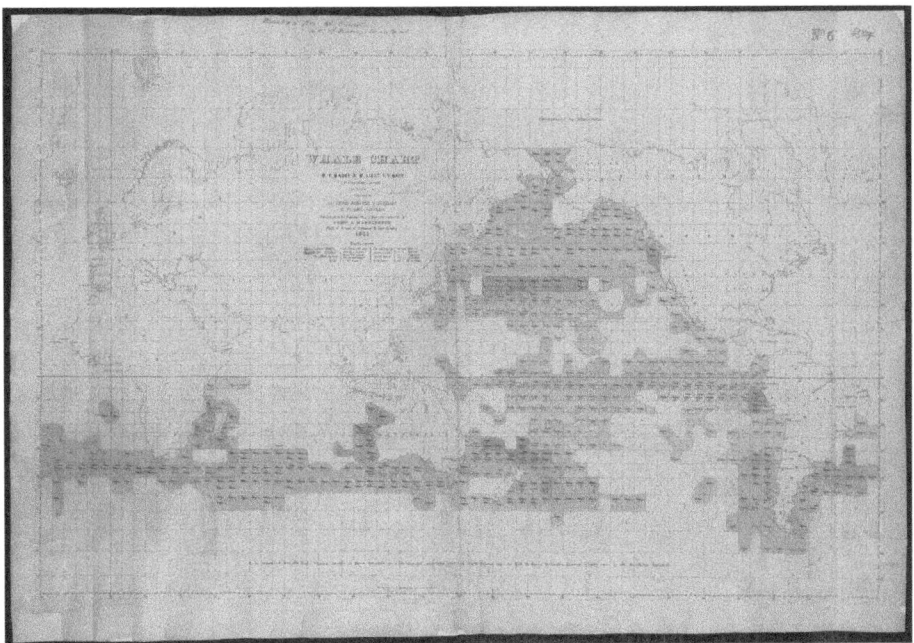

FIGURE 4.5 *Whale Chart*. Colored lithograph, after a drawing by Matthew Fontaine Maury, 1851. © Norman B. Leventhal Map & Education Center at the Boston Public Library.

the *Tryal* was under control, he had hoped that the American would see below the surface of things (Taylor 2016: 139–43). At the end of Conrad's novel *Typhoon*, Captain MacWhirr, the man who believed a ship should run a straight line from port to port, no matter what the weather, confessed, "There are things you find nothing about in books" (1953: 347). The typhoon was one of them. Hokusai's rogue wave and Turner's light-freckled sea storms were meant to push our perception beyond the sphere of positive knowledge to an increasingly bedimmed cosmic dimension of nature.

Both wave and sea point to a rich world of signs that was being obscured by the advance of technology and industry but which offered access to a symbiotic zone where nature and culture interdefined each other. Such was not the case when, at the end of the period, the unsinkable *Titanic* went down after hitting an iceberg. In his essay on history and the social sciences, Braudel writes: "I have sometimes compared [historical] models to ships. What interests me, once the boat is built, is to put it in the water, to see if it will float, and then to make it ascend and descend the waters of time, at my will. The significant moment is when it can keep afloat no longer, and sinks" ([1969] 1980: 45). Stretching from the departure of the prison ships for Botany Bay to the sinking of the Titanic in August 1914, with many middle passages in between, perhaps the century's deep image is indeed Braudel's. Now that the sea itself has become a vast archive for the humanities, it seems to go without saying.

CHAPTER FIVE

Islands and Shores

Living in Reef Country: European Castaways and Indigenous Maritime Societies of the Great Barrier Reef, 1770–1923

IAN McCALMAN

One casualty of the European "discovery" and relentless colonization of Australia from the late eighteenth century through the nineteenth century is the meagre or distorted historical evidence of the ways of life of the numerous clans of Indigenous maritime peoples who then inhabited the coasts and islands of Australia's immense northeastern Great Barrier Reef and Torres Strait Island region. Yet this was by any standards a massive sea country. As well as being the planet's largest organism, and the only natural object that can be seen by astronauts from outer space, the giant coral ribbons off the northeast coastline enclose an area of lagoon, island, and beach larger than England and Ireland put together. The Great Barrier Reef stretches for 2,600 kilometers and encompasses 557,000 square kilometers of sea, sand, and coral, comprising three thousand individual reefs and nine hundred separate islands. Archaeologists and anthropologists have found evidence that few if any parts of this region remained unaffected by the civilizations and cultures of Australian Aborigines and Torres Strait Islanders over thousands of years, yet written records are scanty and unreliable.

Why are there so few European historical records of the mosaic of clans that occupied these coasts and islands, used and nurtured their estates' resources, and navigated the Reef's vast lagoon over the long nineteenth century? There are records of course, but they come mainly from a stream of frontier colonial adventurers, passing sea captains, resource seeking goldminers, pearlers, whalers, *bêche de mer* fishers, and agricultural land grabbers, almost all of whom viewed these clans as obstacles to be removed or labor to be exploited. From around the 1850s this Reef region became a fast-advancing colonial frontier engaged in forcibly dispersing, dispossessing, exploiting, and missionizing Indigenous societies. With few exceptions, European accounts rarely reflect any deep interest in or knowledge of these Indigenous maritime societies, and fewer still are free from racial condescension and biases of their time.

Are the accounts of European castaways any different? Sometimes not. Eliza Fraser's widely reproduced and still celebrated story of her six weeks as a castaway living with small bands of Kabi Kabi speaking Aborigines on Fraser Island at the southern end of the Reef in 1836 was a tissue of fabrication concocted with her predatory second husband and a London hack writer for monetary gain (see McCalman 2013: 55–77). But not all castaways were as ungrateful and grasping toward the Indigenous maritime peoples on whom they invariably depended for their survival. Some, as we shall see, even became deeply appreciative of, or integrated into, the worlds of their Indigenous saviors.

In this chapter I propose to tell the stories of four European castaways, who were diverse in age, background, gender, and circumstance, and to show what they learnt about the life and work of the maritime clans they encountered over the long nineteenth century from 1770 to 1923. I will argue that these castaway accounts, when read with contextual sensitivity, enable us to gain rare and valuable insights into the rich cultures of the Indigenous maritime societies living in Australia's Reef country.

CAPTAIN COOK'S *ENDEAVOUR* CASTAWAYS

Captain James Cook has been called many things but never a castaway, though this is exactly what he and the crew of HMS *Endeavour* became after they crashed their three-masted bark onto a submerged section of the Great Barrier Reef at approximately 11:00 p.m. on June 10, 1770. Though the crew eventually managed to heave the impaled ship off the coral's fangs, the *Endeavour* was leaking at an alarming rate, and was only saved from sinking by the clever expedient of fothering—pulling an external bandage of canvas over the main breach in the hull, which enabled an influx of wool and sheep's dung to act as a temporary caulk.

According to Cook's first editor, John Hawkesworth (who produced the popular Admiralty edition of Cook's papers, which prevailed for the next eighty years), the Captain anticipated the floating of the ship not as a moment of deliverance but "as an event that would probably precipitate our destruction." Should any of the crew escape drowning, he feared that they would be

FIGURE 5.1 *Vue de la Rivière d'Endeavour fur (sur) la Cote de la Nouvelle Hollande où le vaisseau fut mis à la bande.* © Australian National Maritime Museum.

marooned on a "shore without any lasting or effectual defense against the natives, in a country, where even nets and firearms would scarcely furnish them with food; and where, if they should find the means of subsistence, they must be condemned to languish out the remainder of life in a desolate wilderness" (Hawkesworth 1969: 548–9).

After being buffeted and delayed for several days by squally weather, the stricken ship eventually limped the twenty kilometers to the nearest shore at what is now called Endeavour River, the site of today's Cooktown (Figure 5.1). On July 18, the crew dragged the hull up the edge of the riverbank for the carpenters to assess the damage. They discovered that the ship had escaped sinking only through the lucky chance of a lump of coral breaking off and jamming in the largest wound, providing both a partial plug and a nucleus for the temporary caulk. The carpenters thought the damage extensive but fixable, though Cook continued to worry about the ship's ultimate seaworthiness for the extensive voyaging ahead, especially after her central planking and seams sprang a series of new leaks caused by the strains of careening her on land.

Still more concerning was evidence that scurvy had struck. Several of the crew were displaying early symptoms of loose teeth, and both the astronomer Charles Green and Polynesian navigator Tupaia had developed the putrid gums and livid leg spots of the disease's advanced stages. Knowing from experience that the whole crew were in urgent remedial need of fresh meat, vegetables, and fruit, Cook immediately dispatched several search parties on food hunts. He also asked the energetic young naturalist Joseph Banks to use his knowledge to identify suitably local sources of fresh nutrition. Banks soon reported a worrying absence in the soil, which appeared, "by nature doomed to everlasting Barrenness." The total finds were a thin array of cabbage palms, "very bad" beans, fibrous plantains, stone-filled native *wongai* plums that tasted like "indifferent Damsons," and a type of wild kale resembling the West Indian plant called "cocos." Cook, notorious for wolfing down inedible foodstuffs as an example to his sailors, found the cocos roots too acrid to stomach; and he failed to persuade them that the cooked leaves were "little inferior to spinach" (Banks 1963: 113; Bowen and Bowen 2002: 42; Hawkesworth 1969: 562–3).

The animal local life, which was so bizarre as to seem the product of an alternative creation, offered little better. The meat from a giant mouse-like "kangaroo" proved "capital eating," but after this initial encounter the hopping creatures easily outstripped Banks's greyhounds in the long grass. The only later specimens shot consisted of a rank-tasting old male and a tiny joey that offered little meat (Banks 1963: 85). Ducks, cockatoos, bustards, and parrots were equally shy and elusive. Pigeons were sometimes slow enough to be shot, but never in sufficient numbers to feed the hands. Efforts to supply fish using the ship's seine net also proved unreliable, though shrewd Tupaia managed to improve his health by continual fishing.

This paucity of resources became even more alarming when Cook and Banks climbed a hill on July 18, in hope of spotting a passage through the maze of reefs encountered on the way into Endeavour River. "We had an extensive view of the Sea Coast to leeward," Cook recorded, "[but this] afforded us a Meloncholy prospect of the dificultys we are [to] incounter, for in whatever direction we turn'd our eys Shoals inum[erable] were to be seen." Given that a southeast trade wind "blew directly in our teeth," Banks concluded that they could not turn back; a northward passage "among unknown dangers" was the only option. Reports after successive surveys in the pinnace deepened Cook's concern. The Master could find no clear passage in any direction: even if they waited marooned for several months until the trade winds altered direction there was no guarantee of being able return on the track they'd come (Banks 1963: 87; Cook 1955: 360–1; Hawkesworth 1969: 565).

At this point their best hopes of procuring fresh food lay in trading with the local "Indians," who'd been sighted several times, but were markedly skittish and evasive. On July 8 and 9, crewmen and officers eventually made contact with small numbers of naked male warriors carrying wicked-looking lances. Both Cook and Banks formed the impression that these tribesmen were lively, intelligent, and athletic, yet hopes of repeating their successful South Seas pattern of trading beads, mirrors, cloth, and trinkets for fresh food and vegetables were quickly dashed. The Guugu Yimithirr warriors received these enticements with indifference and threw them away as they departed. Only once, when offered a small fish, did the warriors show animation and pleasure, a worrying sign that they put the same value on fresh food as the castaways (McCalman 2013: 23).

The eventual solution to this crisis came literally out of the blue. During one of the Master's many failed attempts to discover a navigable passage, he chanced across and captured numbers of large green turtles basking on the local reefs. Banks described the relief and elation that swept over the crew, for "the promise of such plenty of good provisions made our situation appear much less dreadfull; were we obligd to Wait here for another season of the year when the winds might alter we could do it without fear of wanting Provisions: this thought alone put everybody in vast spirits" (Banks 1963: 90, 94).

Cook was additionally relieved because a stock of live turtles could sustain the next stages of the voyage should they find a way out of their present entrapment. By July 15, Banks was reveling in the turtles' massive bulk—between two and three hundred pounds each—as well as in in their deliciously flavored fat. "We may now be said to swim in Plenty," he crowed (Banks 1963: 90, 94). Neither he nor Cook wondered why there should be such a plenitude of uncaptured turtles so close to the local Aborigines in an area where food seemed scarce. Modern Guugu Yimithirr knowledge custodians point out that the *Endeavour*'s presence in their "country" coincided with an annual period when the clans prohibited the taking of turtle so that their numbers could replenish.[1]

This would also help to explain the Guugu Yimithirr displeasure when their scouts observed the *Endeavour*'s decks crawling with enough green turtle to feed their clan for a considerable time. On July 19, ten warriors armed with spears boarded the ship determined to exert their rights. When Cook refused their leader's request for a gift (or levy?) of one of the thirteen turtles on the deck, angry warriors tried to carry off one or two of the massive creatures to a waiting canoe, but were roughly prevented by the sailors. Cook tried to appease the visitors with an offer of bread, but "they rejected [it] with scorn as I believe they would have done anything else excepting turtle" (Cook 1955: 363).

Hugely outnumbered, the infuriated clansmen leapt ashore and deftly set fire to the long dry grass adjoining the *Endeavour*—an act that threatened the ship's precious fishing net that was drying nearby. Cook retaliated by firing a musket loaded with birdshot at one of the warriors, whom he wounded, but the man ran off briskly leaving behind only a few drops of blood. Nevertheless, this marked a tragically symbolic moment in the relations between the European castaways and the Guugu Yimithirr warriors (McCalman 2013: 24). Instead of negotiating for the turtles as they'd done for half-wild pigs in the South Seas, Cook and his men had taken them without asking. In a sense, the first British–Aboriginal resource war had broken out, and a grim future pattern of bloodshed had begun (Cook 1955: 361–2; Hawkesworth 1969: 582).

Yet luck was again on Cook's side: though the turtles had triggered an environmental skirmish, they also occasioned a formal reconciliation between the castaways and the wronged Aborigines. To be fair, Cook, Banks, and three or four sailors did set off after the fleeing warriors, presumably in the hope of making peace. After picking up some lances that they'd discarded, Cook's party followed the retreating warriors for a kilometer or so, until they stopped beside a tree some distance off.

> We [...] sat down upon some rocks, from which we could observe their motions, and they also sat down at about a hundred yards distance. After a short time, the old man [...] advanced towards us, carrying in his hand a lance without a point: he stopped several times at different distances, and spoke; we answered by beckoning and making such signs of amity as we could devise; upon which the messenger of peace, as we supposed him to be, turned and spoke aloud to his companions, who then set up their lances against a tree, and advanced towards us in a friendly manner: when they came up, we returned the darts or lances that we had taken from them, and we perceived with great satisfaction that this rendered the reconciliation complete.
>
> (Hawkesworth 1969: 582–3)

This reconciliation, which surely cries out for modern commemoration, was underpinned by a further stroke of luck of which Cook and his crew remained blithely unaware. Guugu Yimithirr oral tradition holds that the *Endeavour* had beached at an inlet that served as a hallowed meeting ground for the surrounding clans of the district. Here, under a sign of peace, they traded goods, negotiated disputes, dispensed trans-clan justice, and enacted joint rituals of initiation, marriage, death, and mourning. Failure of the British visitors to share their turtle bounty in such a place was all the more reprehensible, yet it did not override the clan's ultimate sense of obligation to restore peace in this sacred place (McCalman 2013: 25).[2]

Relieved at this outcome, Cook remained puzzled by the sudden deterioration of relations over the issue of turtles. Assuming that the "Indians" might regard turtle flesh as "a dainty"—as did eighteenth-century urban Englishmen—it never occurred to him that these animals were a vital staple of the Guugu Yimithirr, who also considered them produce of their own "country," and therefore could not be taken by strangers without permission—whether white or Black. Neither did Cook realize that these "Indians" practiced food sharing and expected it of others. Banks, at least, seemed to sense something of the kind when he observed that, "they seemd to set no value upon anything we had except our turtle, which of all things we were the least able to spare them" (Banks 1963: 98–9).

Because Cook later wrote admiringly of the Endeavour River Aborigines, historians sometimes claim that he must have viewed them through the prism of a Rousseauvian "noble savage" Romantic, however out of character this might seem for such a practical, plain-speaking Yorkshireman (McCalman 2013: 25). Yet Cook, the seaman voyager, was more than capable of recognizing the abilities of the Guugu Yimithirr to understand and manage an environment where the far greater part of soil "can admit no cultivation," where fresh water was scarce, and where the seas were filled with hazardous coral reefs. After all, in a mere five weeks this harsh environment had tested the European sailors to their limits. As Cook commented in one of his most quoted passages:

> In reality they are far more happy than we Europeans; being wholly unacquainted not only with the superfluous but the necessary Conveniencies so much sought after in Europe, they are happy in not knowing the use of them. They live in a Tranquillity which is not disturb'd by the Inequality of Condition: the Earth and sea of their own accord furnishes them with all things necessary for life, they covet not Magnificent Houses, Houshold-stuff &c, they live in a warm and fine Climate and enjoy a very wholesome Air, so that they have very little need of Clothing and this they seem to be fully sencible of, for many to whome we gave Cloth &c to, left it carelessly upon the Sea beach and in the woods as a thing they had no manner of use for. In short they seem'd to set no value on any thing we gave them, nor would they part with any thing of their own for any one article we could offer them; this in my opinion argues that they think themselves provided with all the necessarys of Life and that they have no superfluities.
>
> (Cook 1955: 399; see also Thomas 2003: 128)

Not surprisingly, Cook praised the Aborigines' ability with spear and boomerang to kill birds, fish, and animals so shy that the Europeans had "found it difficult to get within reach of them with a fowling piece" (Hawkesworth 1969: 637, 642). His description of the technology and use of the woomera, or throwing spear, verged on professional awe.

> Their offensive weapons are Darts, some are only pointed at one end and others are barb'd, some with wood others with the Stings of Rays and some with Sharks teeth &c, these last are stuck fast on with gum. They throw the Dart with only one hand, in the doing of which they make use of a peice of wood about 3 feet long made thin like the blade of a Cutlass, with a little hook at one end to take hold of the end of the Dart, and at the other is fix'd a thin peice of bone about 3 or 4 Inches long; the use of this is, I beleive to keep the dart steady and to make it quit the hand in a proper direction; by the help of these throwing sticks, as we call them, they will hit a Mark at a distance of 40 or 50 yards, with almost, if not as much certainty as we can do with a Musquet, and much more so than with a ball.
>
> (Cook 1955: 396–7)

He was impressed, too, by the Guugu Yimithirr "facility" in the use and spread of fire, and their skills in building outrigger canoes four meters long, using only shell, coral, stone, and the abrasive leaves of the wild fig tree. He even conceded that the hunters' smaller and cruder bark canoes perfectly matched their needs and habitats. "These canoes do not carry above 2 people [...] but, bad as they are do very well for the purpose they apply them, better than if they were larger, for as they draw but little water they go in them upon the Mud banks and pick up shell fish &c without going out of the Canoe" (Cook 1955: 396–7).

This last observation was especially pertinent when Cook and Banks learnt from the Master on July 19, that he'd again found no passage northward or southward that could accommodate a ship of the *Endeavour*'s size and draft. Banks captured the Captain's dilemma with an evocative term to describe their coral reef entrapment, which Cook himself would soon adopt. "We were ready to sail with the first fair wind but where to go?—to windward was impossible, to leeward was a *Labyrinth of Shoals*, so that how soon we might have the ship to repair again or lose her quite no one could tell" (Banks 1963: 2:87–8, emphasis added).

On August 6, after first warping the ship out from the riverbank and then trying hesitantly to follow behind the pinnace on a northeast course, Cook quickly decided to undertake an aerial survey. He dropped the sails, anchored the ship against the buffeting wind, and climbed the masthead. Still he could see no passage: this most decisive of captains did not know where to sail his ship: "as yet I had not resolved whether I should beat back to the Southward round all the shoals or seek a passage out to the Eastward or to the northrd, all of which appear'd to be equally difficult and dangerous" (Cook 1955: 365). Like Theseus he was trying to thread through the Labyrinth, but in his case there was no prospect of an Ariadne to lead them to safety from the horns of the Minotaur (Cook 1955: 365; Hawkesworth 1969: 593).

Subsequent reconnoiters from a headland promontory revealed a further shock—what Banks called a "ledge of rocks" or "a Grand Reef" that blocked them from entering the open sea (1963: 101–3). For the first time they'd sighted the fearsome spectacle of what we today call "the outer Barrier." On August 11, in the desperate hope that "the shoals would end," Cook and Banks rowed to the steepest of three adjacent islands to make yet another survey (102). They named it Lizard Island after its giant Monitors—land guardians, perhaps, of the Labyrinth. "When I looked around," Cook recorded, after he'd climbed to the top of the island's highest hill, "I discovered a reef of rocks, lying two or three leagues without the islands, and extending in a line N.W. and S.E. further than I could see, upon which the sea broke with a dreadful surf" (Hawkesworth 1969: 596). Faint signs of breaks in this vast rampart, however, prompted an accession of hope.

Within hours he and his officers decided to attempt to navigate one of these small channels into the open sea rather than risk being "locked in by the great reef" (Cook 1955: 374–5). That eventuality would mean returning back to their castaway site, losing the prevailing winds to the East Indies and probably dying of scurvy or starvation (Hawkesworth 1969: 598). On August 13, they followed the pinnace into a narrow opening, sounding the depths every few yards. Once through the channel, they were exhilarated to find themselves in a "large sea rolling from the SE," with no ground at 275 meters.

Cook reflected on the unprecedented ordeal they'd come through:

> Our change of situation was now visible in every countenance, for it was most sensibly felt in every breast: we had been little less than three months entangled among shoals and rocks, that every moment threatened us with destruction [...]. But now [...] we found ourselves in an open sea, with deep water; and enjoyed a flow of spirits which was equally owing to our late dangers and our present security.
>
> (Hawkesworth 1969: 601)

We may guess that he and the sailors celebrated that night with a meal of green turtle.

* * *

"WHITE SAVAGES": GIOM OF MURALAG AND ANCO OF THE SANDBEACH

On May 14, 1875, George Heath, Queensland's marine surveyor, was about to embark from the small port of Somerset off the tip of Cape York as part of his regular commitments to mark the Barrier Reef shipping channel against the perpetual stream of shipwrecks since Cook's encounter with Endeavour Reef. In 1849, as a young naval cadet on the British survey ship HMS *Rattlesnake*, Heath had participated in the "rescue" off a nearby Cape York beach of a young Scottish castaway, Barbara Thompson, who'd been living for five years with the Kaurareg people of Prince of Wales Island (Muralag) at the southern end of the Torres Strait. On boarding the Royal Mail Steamer *Brisbane* twenty-six years later, he experienced déjà vu when a fellow passengers turned out to be another recently rescued castaway, a 31-year-old Frenchman, Narcisse Pelletier, who'd just been found by *trepang* traders after living for seventeen years with a clan of the Aboriginal people on a small littoral estate further down the Cape York coast.

Both castaways had been shipwrecked children on the point of death when rescued by Indigenous maritime clans. Barbara Thompson, the Scots-born daughter of a migrant Sydney tinsmith, was only thirteen when saved from drowning by Torres Strait turtle hunters, after her ex-convict husband's ship hit a reef in November 1844. Narcisse Pelletier, the cabin boy-son of a Vendean coastal village shoemaker, was fourteen when his merchant ship crewmates had

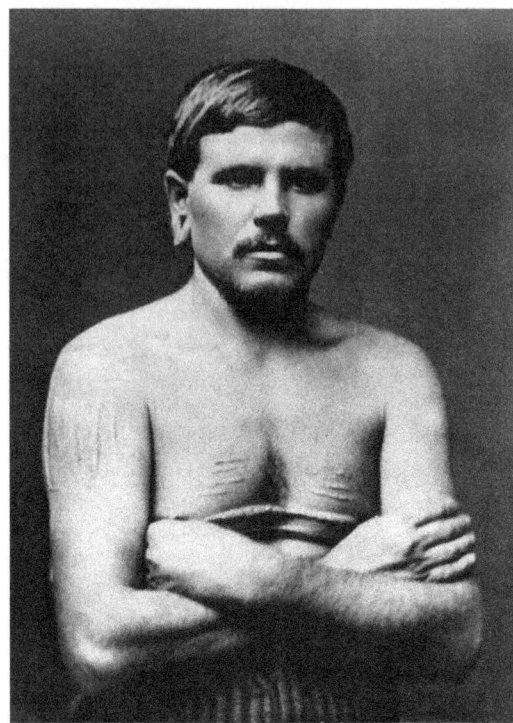

FIGURE 5.2 Narcisse Pelletier. © Royal Historical Society of Queensland.

abandoned him, wounded and dying of thirst, on a Cape York beach in 1858 (Figure 5.2).

Both were inducted into the clan language, customs, values, and kinship structures appropriate to their age and gender. Two of Thompson's male rescuers appointed themselves her surrogate "brothers"; another, Boroto, would become her informal husband; and Peaqui, a senior of the clan, adopted her formally as "Giom," the *marki* or returned "white ghost" of his drowned daughter (Moore 1979: 8). Pelletier, having been saved from certain death by thirst or starvation, was similarly adopted as "Anco," the son of a childless Aboriginal warrior, Maademan, and his wife (Anderson 2009: 153–4). They were Uutaalnganu-speakers of a small fifty-strong clan of Wanthaala Aborigines, known today as Night's Island or Sandbeach people. Despite being separated by a geographic, ethnic, and cultural distance, Kaurareg Islanders and Wanthaala Aborigines had much in common. Both were maritime fishing communities who harvested the coastal and marine environments of the northern Barrier Reef and both were soon to experience the first disruptive ripples of European contact and colonialism.

FIGURE 5.3 O.W. Brierly, *HMS* Rattlesnake, *First Arrival of White Men Amongst the Islands of the Louisade Archipelago*, c. 1860. © National Library of Australia.

When eventually "rescued" from their Indigenous clans by European voyagers, both castaways were subjected to various interrogations about the cultures, values, and behaviors of their supposedly "savage" foster societies. Each, however, had at least one major European interviewer. For Giom, this was Oswald Brierly, an artist onboard the British survey ship HMS *Rattlesnake* (Figure 5.3). For Anco, it was a Nantes medical man and savant named Constant Merland, who published an account of his interview in 1876 called *Dix-sept Ans chez les sauvages: Narcisse Pelletier*. Brierly proved to be a rare model of open mindedness; Merland, though something of a racial ideologue, was not entirely unsympathetic. When interpreted with contextual care, the records of these two interviews offer unique portals into Australian Indigenous maritime cultures on the brink of corrosive frontier change, as well as insights into evolving Western colonial attitudes to Aboriginal and Torres Strait first peoples.

Barbara Thompson was certainly grateful for her rescue and five years of care from the Kaurareg. She conveyed to Brierly a genuine affection for her rescuers, her adoptive family, and for an older woman with whom she lived as a "sister," and who tended to her when she fell ill with fever. Even so, having been with the clan for only five years, she still hoped to return to her family in Sydney and she tried to retain her memory of English language by singing folk songs to herself at night. When discovered half-naked on Evans Beach at the tip of Cape York in 1849 and asked by the *Rattlesnake* sailors whether she would like to stay with the Kaurareg, she declined firmly with the words: "I am a Christian" (Moore 1979: 77).

Her interviews, conducted onboard the ship at Cape York and during the subsequent voyage to Sydney, were frank and fair, showing no inclination either to protect or criticize her clan. She was evasive only when Brierly asked about sexual relationships, avoiding the *Rattlesnake* naturalist MacGillivray's persuasive claim that she'd been Boroto's wife, an admission that a widowed girl of eighteen about to return to European society would have been foolish to make (see Moore 1979: 8–9, 191). However, she answered Brierly unhesitatingly on sensitive subjects such as cannibalism, female infanticide, women's rituals, and even the male domains of boyhood initiation and sorcery.

Much of the credit for the range and quality of information she disclosed must also go to her interviewer Oswald Brierly. His non-judgmental manner, nondirective questions, and meticulous concern for accuracy would have distinguished a modern ethnographer. His method was to ask Barbara a question, take down her answer verbatim in pencil, even including Scottish inflections, read it back to her for clarification on at least two separate occasions, and then write out the final version in ink. As she grew more confident he also prompted her to narrate at her own pace, avoiding any leading questions or interruptions. Above all, he treated her and her subjects with invariable respect and dignity (Moore 1979: 197).

Where he acquired his attitude of tolerant curiosity is hard to say: it was exceptional within the colonial milieu he had earlier inhabited. An Englishman from an upper-middle-class background, part of his fascination sprang from values acquired through his practice of portraiture and maritime art. His journal includes injunctions to would-be sketchers, for instance his shipboard friend Thomas Huxley,

> to record what actually passes under your observation—any characteristic traits or circumstances which transpire under your eyes should be written down while the impression is fresh and as quickly after their occurrence as opportunity may allow—in doing this you will be constantly surprised to find the savage so utterly different from what your preconceived ideas would make him.
>
> (Moore 1979: 64)

By contrast with Thompson, Pelletier was a less frank informant only because of his intense loyalty to the Wanthaala and his awareness of his interviewer's prejudices. After seventeen years, Merland concluded, Narcisse's "naturalization was complete. He was no longer a Frenchman, he was an Australian" (Merland translated by Anderson 2009: 275). Early questioners had observed that he treated his French childhood as irrecoverably distant; and his incoherent struggles to remember French make poignant reading as he groped for words that seemed to have disappeared over a distant horizon. This torment reminded the French Consul in Sydney of Hoffman's tale of the man who lost his shadow (Anderson 2009: 62). Unlike Thompson, Pelletier insisted that he'd been "kidnapped," rather than rescued, by European sailors who'd held him at gunpoint (43). Observers soon after his capture also commented on his discomfort at wearing clothes, his sullen demeanor, and his several attempts to escape back to the Sandbeach.

Even on returning to France, Pelletier retained an intense pride in his clan identity and values. Merland noted that he continued to adhere to Wanthaala norms of beauty, virtue, and valor as well to a strong belief in clan sorcery and flaunted the initiation scarifications on his chest and his ornamental elongated earlobe. He was equally proud of his former achievements as a spear-maker, clan fighter, canoe-crafter, dugong hunter, and fisherman who'd often sailed his outrigger-canoe sixty-five kilometers to the outer reef. As an initiated male warrior there were major realms of secret knowledge and sacral mythology too that he'd sworn never to disclose. One of his earliest Australian questioners, Lieutenant Ottley, a fluent French-speaker noted his deliberate "reticence" about such subjects. "I am inclined to think," Ottley later reflected, "he had definitely made up his mind to give us no more information about the tribe and the language" (Anderson 2009: 307–8). This probably also explains the hostile assessment of a physical anthropologist at Beaujon hospital shortly after he reached France; "he was very mistrustful, sly and probably a liar " (69).

Overall there is no escaping a marked difference in the tone and purport of questioning experienced by Pelletier in the 1870s compared with that of Thompson thirty years earlier. Part of the explanation stems from the advent in Europe during the 1860s of new modes of anthropometric and empirical racial theorizing of the Société d'Anthropologie of Paris, founded and widely circulated by the anatomist Paul Broca at the beginning of the decade. Société members propagated a new racial science of physical anthropology that used comparative craniological and anatomical measurement to assess the "respective position [of races] in the human series" (Anderson 2008: 243). As against monogenists who believed in a single human origin, they espoused a polygenic theory of multiple human racial origins and categorized Australian Aborigines as the most inferior racial type on the ladder of human species. True, Merland himself adopted a mainly ethnographic rather than anthropometric methodology. He was also prepared to concede some aspects of Wanthaala cultural complexity and humanity: he described Maademan as a good and devoted adoptive father; and Sashi, Anco's adoptive cousin, as "a true and faithful friend" (Merland translated by Anderson 2009: 178). Wanthaala women too, he admitted, appeared to show enduring maternal feelings. He was impressed that the clan shared property and revered the dead and that Pelletier's linguistic evidence "proved that the vocabulary of these tribes is truly rich," having words to express scientific concepts such as species and genus (186–91, 217–18).

Other Merland textual interventions, however, shared the ruling assumptions of the Société anthropologists. The Wanthaala, he wrote, were still "in a complete state of nature living a completely animal existence." They were moved only by coarse instinctual and emotional appetites and "their thought never soars towards higher realms, it never embraces intellectual questions." They also lacked any belief in immortality or a higher spiritual order and all higher expressions of sentiment and feeling (167, 193, 199, 231–5). All in all, he concluded, they were frozen in a state of static savagery without any concept of progress or will to improve (273). Pelletier had thus been forced to live for seventeen years as a white savage with his soul in a state of "suspended slumber."

A comparison of the post-rescue lives of Thompson and Pelletier underscores the pervasiveness of this racial hardening during the 1860s. Barbara Thompson appears to have suffered no obvious stigma from living with the Kaurareg and to have assimilated easily back into Sydney society during the 1840s. A year after her return, she married a sea captain and thereafter lived quietly in Sydney into her eighties, eventually dying in 1912.

By contrast, Narcisse Pelletier's life in Saint-Gilles-sur-Vie continued to be haunted by his Sandbeach past. Though his parents welcomed him home initially, they soon became estranged by his supposed savagery, which they tried to purge by having him exorcised by a Catholic priest. Given work as a lighthouse keeper, he was said to have grown morose and solitary, staring wistfully out to sea and flying into rages when locals taunted him with the nickname *le sauvage*. Around 1883 he married a young seamstress, Louise Mabileau, but the couple had no children. He died on September 28, 1894, at the age of fifty of unknown causes. Locals speculated that he'd succumbed either to the long-term effects of Aboriginal sorcery or to primitive nostalgia for his clan and country. Both were assumptions that Anco of the Sandbeach had never ceased to be a white savage.

* * *

TED BANFIELD: A VOLUNTARY CASTAWAY ON A REEF ISLAND PARADISE

In 1908, Western readers were introduced to a new perspective of living on the Reef in a book called *The Confessions of a Beachcomber*. Written by a former Townsville journalist, E.J. Banfield, it told how he and his wife had escaped from civilization to live as voluntary castaways on Dunk Island off the Great Barrier Reef. Named by Captain James Cook after an Admiralty dignitary of his day, Dunk belonged to a small cluster of islands and islets known today as the Family Group.

Edmund James (Ted) Banfield, aged forty-four, and his music-teacher wife Bertha, aged thirty-six, first visited this deserted tropical island of nine square kilometers in mid-September 1896 when looking for a holiday cabin site (Banfield 1907–8: 52–4). No sooner had they landed at the crescent bay at the northern end of the island than a canoe appeared, paddled by a powerful-looking Aboriginal man called Tom. Though born on the island, his family clans of Bandjin and Djiru people were now scattered about the mainland. Yet Tom had somehow learned of the Banfield's intended visit and, in the hope of possible employment, paddled over. To this tall burly man with ribbons of scarification across his chest, the island was Coonanglebah, his lifelong estate, hunting ground, and dreaming place. He knew its legends and habitats intimately, yet could no longer claim an inch of it.

Dunk seemed perfect. It was situated only three kilometers off the opposite coast and possessed two fresh streams, picturesque mountainous, a colorful fringing coral reef, an accessible bay, and a white sandy beach. A few hundred yards inland from the beach grew a forest of vine-entangled forest trees and native figs. Varieties of Acacia, Screw Palms, Pandanus, and flowering Hibiscus shrubs edged the strand, and green webs of native cabbage scrabbled down the beach. Ted stood on a plateau above the strand and ritually fired a rifle bullet into a bloodwood tree to mark the spot where he hoped to build the house. Clouds of colored butterflies hovered over the beach, inspiring him to call the bay "Brammo," after a poetic Aboriginal word for butterfly. Overhead, the trees shivered with colonies of white nutmeg pigeons and metallic starlings (Banfield [1908] 2006: 21–2).

Almost exactly a year later, on September 28, 1897, the couple returned: this time to test the possibility of living permanently on a lease of 128 acres of land they'd acquired from the Queensland government. But in the interim Ted's health had disintegrated. Normally slender, his weight had plunged to a scarecrow 53 kilograms and his Townsville doctor had diagnosed his nervous collapse as the lethal wasting disease phthisis (Noonan 1986: 103–4). When their boat landed at Brammo Bay, Ted was carried from the boat to a blanket on the beach and lay longing for the comforts of Townsville, while Tom, now freshly hired, helped lug the provisions, tools, and materials up a plateau to their hut site.

Ted would later claim that he wakened next morning transformed by the beauty of the sun and beach, but forging a new life actually took much longer than this (Banfield [1908] 2006: 23). He and Bertha initially slept in tents and survived on Tom's daily supplies of fresh fish, pigeon, and scrub fowl under the nearby Bloodwood tree. Though still "in a frail physical state," Ted helped Tom and another hired worker to clear an area of scrub, bolt together a cedar kit home, and begin work on a kitchen and verandah extension. They felled a Bloodwood tree, inched the logs to the site, sawed them into rough planks, laid foundations of local stone and tar, and dug in posts and ridgepoles, which were the scrounged masts of two shipwrecks on the beach. The roof was made from corrugated iron, and the floor surfaced with beaten clay (Banfield 1912: 16–27)

(Figure 5.4). The result, he would later claim, was a tropical counterpart to Henry David Thoreau's famous log cabin built fifty years earlier on the shores of Walden Pond (Thoreau [1854] 1995).

This simple shack, Ted boasted, reflected "the genius of the isle," being "a little shambling structure of rough slabs" that was "hidden in a wilderness of leaves" with geckos, spiders, grubs, and swooping bats sharing the interior (Banfield 1912: 23).

Ted also later claimed that he'd instantly developed a tropical counterpart of Thoreau's Romantic lifestyle, for on a Great Barrier Reef island "the career of a Beachcomber" offered "the closest possible return to nature." All year round Dunk supplied "the tonic of the sea and the majesty of the sun," making it one of the most benign and equable climates on the globe. The debilitating mental and physical sicknesses that had haunted him as a journalist in Townsville were now unknown. Even clothes were hardly needed—he wore only shorts and a large hat to shade his beaky nose. Bronzed and barefooted, he began to acquire the lean muscular physique of a sailor. His weight climbed to 65 kilograms, and he could labor in the sun all morning and swim in the crystal waters of Brammo Bay all afternoon. His entire sensorium had been revitalized. Scents of flowers, shrubs, and birds beguiled his nose; his ears had become attuned to "the hum of the bees and beetles, the fluty plaint of a painted pigeon far in the gloom, the furtive scamper of the scrub fowl among the leaves made tender by decay, the splash of a startled fish in the shadows" (Banfield 1912: 51).

As a beachcomber, he'd cast off civilization's discontents and despised the townsman's pursuits as "devoid of purpose, insipid and dismally unsatisfactory." He and Bertha had shucked off "the poisonous years of the past" to gain a genuine "independence" (Banfield [1908] 2006: 27–8). Unfettered by mortgages, they could live comfortably on fifty pounds a year and, having ditched all schedules, could "dally luxuriously with time" and "loll in the shade of scented trees or thread the sunless mazes of the jungle, or bask on the sand."

> The Beachcomber [...] is an individual whose wants are few—who is content, who has no treasure to guard, whose rights there is none to dispute; who is his own magistrate, postman, architect, carpenter, painter, boat-builder, boatman, tinker, goatherd, gardener, woodcutter, water-carrier, and general labourer.
>
> (Banfield 1912: 47)

Such a person, he asserted, exploited nobody. His daily bounty was thrown up on the sand each day by the chance actions of tides and currents: today, a cedar log; tomorrow a weathered ship's figurehead; the day after, a pearl lying inside the flesh of a Goldlip or Blacklip oyster. Living on an "Isle of Dreams," the Beachcomber's life was rich beyond imagination (Banfield 1912: 29–30). In short, he gained humankind's most precious state: "freedom—freedom beyond

FIGURE 5.4 Residence of E.J. Banfield on Dunk Island, 1935. © The John Oxley Library, State Library of Queensland (public domain).

the dreams of most men in its comprehensiveness and exactitude" (Banfield [1908] 2006: 299).

Yet these idyllic claims were in fact highly retrospective, as was Ted's entire claim to have fled to Dunk Island because of his hatred of commercial civilization. Early letters to family and friends told a different story. He boasted of having made a shrewd investment in low-cost land, ideally suited to the growing and sale of tropical fruits and fresh produce (Ted to Harry Banfield, November 1, 1897). Cheap black labor, fertile soil, a high rainfall, and steady sun would drive this business and a weekly steamer visit from the mainland would transport his produce to ready markets on the nearby mainland (Noonan 1986: 102–3).

In reality, Ted's plan had been easier to imagine than to execute because the couple's early life on Dunk proved far tougher than Ted would later admit. His daily diary entries from January 7, 1898, show that the onset of the rainy season brought them both disabling doses of malaria and dengue fever. Bertha was also afflicted with bouts of internal pain that required an operation and months of recuperation in Townsville's hospital. Money needs struck too when they decided to convert their landholding to freehold. Reluctantly, Ted found himself having to publish freelance pieces for the Townsville newspaper that had driven him to a nervous breakdown (Banfield 1898–1901: 1898:16, 25, 33–6, 39, 41–2, 46–8, 52, 70; 1899:5, 22, 26–7, 71).

More than anything, Ted's diaries reveal the Banfield's utter dependence on the labor, skills, and knowledge of a succession of male and female Aboriginal workers. None of these were granted the dignity of surnames, and we can know them only as Tom, Nellie, Jinny, Mickie, Toby, Sambo, and others. Ted was a hopeless fisherman, dependent on Tom or Mickie to provide daily catches of fresh food by harpooning rockfish, shark, dugong, and coral trout; and he was also an equally bad sailor, who managed, in September 1899, to capsize their skiff and nearly drown Bertha. After this, she refused to sail with him again and he wisely delegated future sailing tasks to Tom, Toby, or Sambo, who visited the mainland ports of Cardwell, Bicton, or Geraldton to pick up weekly supplies or transport produce (Banfield 1898–1901: 77; Noonan 1986: 119–20) (Figure 5.5).

All these Aboriginal workers were poorly paid, and even the daily duties of the "gins," as Ted called the women, were physically grueling. Nellie, Jinny, and Jenny had to weed, hoe, collect shellfish, chop firewood, cook, and clean. The men hacked down trees, cleared and fired scrub, planted vegetables and

FIGURE 5.5 Aboriginal man with an outrigger on the beach at Lockhart River, Queensland, *c.* 1930. © The John Oxley Library, State Library of Queensland (public domain).

tropical fruits, and then harvested, packed, and transported the products for sale on the mainland. They also erected fences against snakes and eagles, built hen and duck houses, bottled and sold the honey generated by Ted's dozen hives of Italian bees, and collected fowl eggs, oysters, crabs, and crayfish to add to the island's exports. As Ted's health improved, he tasked them with a series of ambitious building projects: a boatshed behind Brammo Bay beach, a suspension bridge over the gully, timber rails for a boat trolley, a storage tank and pump, and lines of coconut trees leading up to the Banfield's hut (Banfield 1898–1901). Finally, in January 1900, he decided to replace their hut with a professionally built bungalow. Six months later, he and Bertha gained approval to extend their landholding to 4,050 square meters, so money was needed once again. Swallowing his pride Ted agreed in February 1901 to temporarily take over editorial duties on the *Townsville Evening Star* for six to nine months (Noonan 1986: 120–1).

On returning to Dunk in November 1901, the couple were confronted with a crisis that changed their lives. Ted found that his bees had been wiped out by island birds, depriving the couple of bottled honey, their most lucrative product. After reviewing his philosophy of life, he decided that a honey business couldn't justify the slaughter of two beautiful species of bee eaters. He decided on a new "grand objective": to abandon all forms of commerce and turn Dunk Island into a bird sanctuary.

Other forces had also been pushing them in this direction. Bertha had enjoyed her respite from mosquitoes and loneliness back in Townsville, but Ted had pined for his carefree beachcomber life. Working as a journalist again had also brought one unexpected benefit because he discovered a fresh delight in writing Dunk Island nature pieces. Abandoning commerce now also gave him time for rereading his boyhood love of the Romantic naturalism of Gilbert White's *The Natural History and Antiquities of Selborne* and Thoreau's *Walden*, as well as other more technical works of marine and ornithological science (Banfield [1908] 2006: ch. 8; 1907–8: 59–60).[3]

Most importantly, Ted now also had time to explore the island under the guidance of his Aboriginal workers, though he still held stock colonial beliefs that Aborigines were a childlike people who regarded Dunk simply as a larder for food (McCalman 2013: 173). But gradually Tom and Mickie, in particular, began to erode these prejudices by introducing Ted to the island's rich Indigenous cultural heritage. Tom led him, for example, to a series of exquisite hidden nature sites (Banfield [1908] 2006: 260–75). One was a cavern near Brammo Bay that Tom called *Coobee cotanyou*, or Falling Star Hole, because it had been created by a meteor fall. An impressed later visitor, the Australian writer-naturalist Charles Barrett, described it as "a cave whose mouth is overhung by ferns and jungle vines, and the lintel green with moss, a filter for water that falls upon rocks tufted with orchids the colour of dull gold" (Barrett 1939: 172).

Barrett was still more impressed by another of Tom's revelations on adjacent Bedarra Island, another cave hidden ten yards above the watermark that Ted named the "Cave of Swiftlets," after more than fifty nests of gray-rumped swiftlets that were glued to its rock faces with bird saliva, each containing a "pearly white egg." These rare little birds, had been found in the 1840s by the naturalist Jock MacGillivray, but thenceforth lost to Europeans until Tom brought the cavern to light sixty-one years later (173; Banfield 1912: 200–4).

Furthermore, Tom alone knew the whereabouts of Dunk's two major Aboriginal rock art galleries, which had been overgrown by the island's rainforest, and are now lost once again. Ted had not known of their existence and was moved to write: "Here is the sheer beginning, the spontaneous germ of art" (Banfield [1908] 2006: 233).

Ted also grew to venerate his guides' astounding natural knowledge and marine skills. Here were Indigenous men who could swim huge distances unfazed by a fear of sharks; who could sail the crankiest of sailboats in any sea; who could spear fish and turtle with preternatural speed and accuracy. In an instant they could also improvise traps and nets to snare fish of all sizes and speeds. They could spot tiny objects in the water at a distance and with a clarity that exceeded the range of Ted's binoculars. They could catch a ninety-kilogram bull turtle using a roped remora suckerfish, which clamped onto the creature's shell (McCalman 2013: 174). They knew the art of stunning fish by crushing an array of "wild dynamite" plants, in a process so recondite that Ted declared: "the Australian aboriginal has to his credit as a chemist, the results of successful original research and [...] is also a herbalist from whom it is not condescension to learn." Indeed, Ted's condescension had now turned to awe (Banfield [1917] 2010: 107–20):

> Mickie's bush craft, his knowledge of the habits of birds and insects and the ways of fish is enviable. Signs and sounds quite indeterminate to "white fellas" are full of meaning to him [...] The scratching of a scrub fowl among decayed leaves is heard in the jungle at an extraordinary distance, and a splash or ripple far out on the edge of the reef tells him that a shark or kingfish is driving the mullet into the lagoon, where he may easily spear them. He can tell to a quarter of an hour when the fish will leave off biting [...] and knows when the giant crabs will be "walking about" in the mangroves. He is trustworthy and obliging, and ready to impart all the lore he possesses, an expert boomerang thrower, a dead shot with a nulla-nulla, and an eater of everything that comes in his way except "pigee-pigee" [nutmeg pigeon].
>
> (Banfield [1908] 2006: 260)

When Tom was killed suddenly by spearing in a mainland melee of 1911, Ted allowed his admiration to spill over into genuine grief. This broad-chested, big-limbed, coarse-handed warrior had been as gentle and funny as he was brave, as tender as he was tough, as learned as he was skilled. "Among his mental accomplishments was a specific title for each plant and tree," Ted wrote. "His almanac was floral. By the flowering of trees and shrubs so he noted the time of year, and he knew many stars by name and could tell when such and such a one would be visible." Penning an impromptu epitaph for Tom, Ted summoned his highest words of praise: "he [was] an Australian by the purest lineage and birth—one whose physique was example of the class that tropical Queensland is capable of producing, a man of brains, a student of Nature who had stored his mind with first-hand knowledge unprinted and now unprintable" (Banfield 1912: 281).

Above all, it was these Aboriginal mentors who led Ted to a foundational belief of his beachcomber philosophy: that humans needed to develop "a sense of fellowship with animated and inanimate things" within their country. Such knowledge must draw on the complete spiritual, material, emotional, sensual, and intellectual composition of one's being (McCalman 2013: 175). Dunk Island, Ted proclaimed, was more than just a habitat or environment: it was a fusion of nature and culture, a heartland, a Dreaming. When Ted wrote of his desire "to exhaustively comprehend" the island, he was referring to an Aboriginal rather than a European way of comprehending country:

> If you would read the months off-hand by the flowering of trees and shrubs and the coming and going of birds; if the inhalation of scents is to convey photographic details of the scenes whence they originate; if you would explore miles of sunless jungle by ways unstable as water; if you would have the sites of camps of past generations of blacks reveal the arts and occupations of the race, its dietary scale and the pastimes of its children; if you desire to have exact first-hand knowledge, to revel in the rich delights of new experiences.
>
> (Banfield 1912: 28–9)

If you really wanted to learn all these things, then you must put yourself under the tutelage of an Aboriginal sage such as Tom or Mickie.

In the end, however, it proved to be an intervention from across the oceans that enabled Ted to take this philosophy out to the Western world. On October 10, 1904, the weekly steamer disgorged a scruffy red-faced Englishman of fifty-two, who'd invited himself to Dunk by letter for a two-week visit. Notwithstanding his eccentric appearance, Walter Strickland was the son of a wealthy Yorkshire landed baronet and had been educated at Trinity College, Cambridge. He was fluent in several languages, had a string of publications to his name, and was well versed in natural history. Impervious to hardship, he spent his time scrabbling over reefs, peering into rock pools, and quizzing Ted on his Aboriginal-acquired knowledge of island nesting and migration patterns.

Strickland pressed Ted to make a systematic census of all the bird species on Dunk Island, an undertaking that eventually produced a tally of 128 species (Banfield 1907–8: 60–1), and he urged Ted to lobby the Queensland government to take action against the slaughter by hunters of Torres Strait pigeons and to have Dunk and other islands in the Family Group officially designated as bird sanctuaries. Ted was thus granted official recognition as ranger of the Dunk and Family islands sanctuaries in June 1905 (Noonan 1986: 148–50).

Moreover, Strickland not only admired Ted's nature journalism but he also had the resources and connections in England to propel the beachcomber to national and international fame. After urging Ted to gather his occasional nature pieces together for possible publication, he suggested a perfect title, *The Confessions of a Beachcomber*, and then in 1907 recommended the manuscript to the London publishing firm that specialized in naturalist and travel works, T. Fisher Unwin. Even so, the publisher's demand for a 150 pound subsidy would have been prohibitive had Strickland not loaned Ted the money.

After months of frenetic writing and revision, *Confessions* appeared in London bookstores on September 17, 1908, and in New York the following year, to a stream of heady reviews that compared him to legendary figures such as Robert Louis Stevenson and Thoreau. Down-to-earth Bertha felt, though, that he needed to prune his prose style; and Ted's modern readers would probably agree. Even so, there were times his disparate influences of Romanticism, science, and Indigenous naturalism came together in a harmonious whole (see McCalman 2013: 177). As a literary romantic, for example, he described the multicolored parrot fish on Dunk's fringing coral reef as the "jewel of the sea" with iridescent scales of "blue outlined with pink, sometimes golden-yellow combined with green; […] [in] colours that flash and change with indescribable radiance." As a scientist, he described the fish as a member of the scaroid family, with a beaklike mouth, a row of pharyngeal interior teeth for grinding hard shell, and a gizzard "composed of an intensely tough material, lined with membrane resembling shark's skin." Further, as a professed disciple of the "natives of the island," he recorded that the parrot fish was known by the euphonious name of "Oo-ril-ee" and that its flesh made good eating (Banfield [1908] 2006: 146).

Ted lived on Dunk Island as an internationally celebrated Great Barrier Reef writer until he suddenly succumbed to peritonitis on the night of June 2, 1923, at the age of seventy-one. Bertha, isolated by storms, had to stay with his body for three nights before she managed to attract the notice of a passing steamer. The captain and sailors came ashore, built a rough coffin of ship's timber, and laid the beachcomber to rest on the island he so loved. Later, Bertha built a stone cairn over his grave and eventually joined her "dear laddie" there in August 1933. His greatest legacy was both to have inspired a specific movement of "escape artists" to live similar beachcomber lives on the Family Island group from the 1930s to the 1980s, and more widely to have been the father of the Great Barrier Reef's modern mass tourism industry. Sadly, though he left no memorials to Tom, Mickie, Willie, Nellie, Jinny, and Jenny, the Indigenous descendants of Coonanglebah who had made his Dunk Island Paradise possible.

* * *

These four stories of castaway experiences living with Indigenous maritime societies of the Great Barrier Reef during the period 1770 to 1923 span a dramatic shift in European perceptions of this vast constellations of coral reefs, sand beaches, lagoons, and islands.

The view of Captain Cook and his crew that its seas were threaded by a lurking labyrinth of terror, its beaches barren of freshwater and food, and its coasts inhabited by hostile Indians prevailed for much of the century and were only partially dented by little-read accounts of the rescue and succor by friendly maritime clans such as the Guugu Yimithirr, Kaurareg, and the Wanthaala of European castaways like Cook and his crew, Barbara Thompson, and Narcisse Pelletier.

By the time that Ted Banfield published his "Beachcomber" books recounting an idyllic life as a voluntary castaway on Dunk Island, it had become possible for literate Westerners and Australian colonials to imagine that living on a Reef island in easy proximity to small coastal towns could offer a safe, healthy, relaxed, and sensually rich experience of coral, lagoon, forest, and sun. By this time, however, the independent Indigenous maritime communities who had succored Giom and Anco were disappearing, their lands stolen, their seas and resources commercialized by Europeans, and their clans moved into missions or fragmented by ill-paid wage labor like that of Tom, Mickey, and Jinny. The ancient traditions and practices entailed in their spiritual and ecological care of reef and sea country would never disappear but would have to fight to survive under extreme duress.

For a few sympathetic nineteenth-century European seafarers and Australian colonials—as well as for today's readers—the castaway experiences of Cook, Thompson, Pelletier, and Banfield can perhaps help to throw some light on the lost stories of how Australia's Indigenous peoples managed the seas, islands, corals, and coasts of the Great Barrier Reef as places of sustainable ecological and spiritual nurture for thousands of years. At a time when the supposedly indestructible Great Barrier Reef has become both fragile and endangered, we need somehow to recover the nurturing ethos of its traditional maritime peoples before it is too late.

CHAPTER SIX

Travelers

On the Diverse Voyagers of the Northern Waters

ADRIANA CRACIUN

Who traveled the world's oceans in the nineteenth century? Oceanic travelers included naval crew, merchants, tourists, naturalists, explorers, whalers, and the seamen whose labor made all this maritime travel possible. The Atlantic and Pacific Oceans are the most studied among the world's seas, but I want to shift our attention northwards: to the Arctic Ocean that connects the Atlantic and Pacific via the Northwest Passage through the Arctic archipelago, and the Northern Sea Route over the top of Asia. By looking to this less familiar, sometimes frozen, watery world we can free our expectations of oceanic travelers and travel. Alongside the familiar European travelers mentioned above, Indigenous Arctic voyagers traveled on the sea and sea ice of Arctic archipelagos for a range of reasons, from curiosity to necessity, and generated new artforms and new transoceanic relations in the process. Furthermore, considering not only who but what traveled these seas—from molecules to animalcules, to icebergs, whales, crates, flotsam, and seeds—shifts our visions of maritime mobilities far from terrestrial paradigms and human agents, and toward a richer cultural history of seas.

One of the age's great travelers by any measure was Alexander von Humboldt, the Prussian naturalist whose epic five-year voyage across the Americas began in 1805 and produced thirty volumes of words and images revolutionizing the scientific and humanistic understandings of an entire hemisphere. Driven by an intense curiosity, a vast personal fortune, and a commitment to illuminating the cosmopolitan and indeed cosmic connections of all earthly living and nonliving things, Humboldt began his *Personal Narrative of a Voyage to the Equinoctial Regions* with a comparison of terrestrial and maritime travelers. The latter dominated late Enlightenment scientific expeditions such as the circumnavigations led by Cook and La Pérouse: "Maritime expeditions, voyages round the world, have conferred just celebrity on the names of those naturalists and astronomers," wrote Humboldt, but oceanic exploration favors the sciences of "geography and nautical astronomy," to the detriment of other inquiries (Humboldt 1814: vi):

> During a navigation of several years, the land but seldom presents itself to the observation of the mariner; and when, after lengthened expectation, it is descried, he often finds it stripped of its most beautiful productions. Sometimes beyond a barren coast he perceives a ridge of mountains covered with verdure, but its distance forbids his examination, and the view serves only to increase his regrets.
>
> (vii)

Humboldt's epic terrestrial and riverine expedition, by contrast, would replace oceanic distance with an intense intimacy between the natural and the human.

Setting out across the Atlantic Ocean to reach this new world, Humboldt began his *Personal Narrative* with a characteristically multidimensional analysis of the dynamic forces at work in the ocean, focusing first on the Gulf Stream, a current studied for centuries but still little understood. For Humboldt, the ocean is not an empty space or surface to traverse, but rather a dynamic agent of global movements. The Gulf Stream current

> deposits every year on the western coasts of Ireland and Norway the fruit of trees, which belong to the torrid zone of America. On the shores of the Hebrides, we collect seeds of mimosa scandens, of dolichos urens, of guilandina bonduc, and several other plants of Jamaica, the Isle of Cuba, and of the neighbouring continent. The current carries thither also barrels of French wine, well preserved, the remains of the cargoes of vessels wrecked in the West Indian Seas. To these examples of the distant migration of the vegetable world, others no less striking may be added. The wreck of an English vessel, the Tilbury, burnt near Jamaica, was found on the coasts of Scotland. On these same coasts various kinds of tortoises are sometimes found, that inhabit the waters of the Antilles. When the western winds are of long duration, a current is formed in the high latitudes, which runs directly towards the east-south-east, from the coasts of Greenland and Labrador, as far as the North of Scotland. Wallace relates, that twice, in 1682 and 1684, American savages of the race of the Esquimaux, driven out to sea in their leathern canoes, during a storm, and left to the guidance of the

currents, reached the Orcades [Orkney]. This last example is so much the more worthy of attention, as it proves at the same time how, at a period when the art of navigation was yet in its infancy, the motion of the waters of the ocean would contribute to disseminate the different races of men over the face of the globe.

(59–60)

The long-distance travelers alongside Humboldt on the ocean include plants (he names legumes, beans, and liana vines), barrels of wine, wrecked ships of war (the *Tilbury*), giant tortoises, and Inuit in kayaks.[1] The seventeenth-century Inuit were the most remarkable oceanic travelers to Humboldt because they attested to the ability of humans to migrate globally long before the age of sail and of modern navigation.

Humboldt sailed to South America in the aptly named *Pizarro* and represented himself as rediscovering the New World in the name of science, a myth of "anti-conquest" that situated the forces of nature as the central agents of both human and natural history.[2] Humboldt was a wealthy European elite traveling during a war fought across the globe's oceans, but, unusually, he envisioned himself as one traveler among others—beans, flotsam, tortoises, ships of war, Indigenous craft, and sailors.

This diversity of travelers riding the world ocean included the tiniest known to science, individual water molecules:

> We have just seen that between the parallels of 11 and 43 degrees, the waters of the Atlantic are drawn on by the currents in a continual whirlpool. Supposing that a molecule of water returns to the same place from which it departed, we can estimate, from our present knowledge of the swiftness of currents, that this circuit of 3800 leagues is not terminated in less than two years and ten months.
>
> (Humboldt 1814: 56)

Humboldt's zeal for quantification was only matched by his zeal for sublime aesthetics, and here perhaps he approaches the infinitesimal sublime, by calculating the length of time it would take for a water molecule to circumnavigate the Atlantic basin.

On land and at sea, Humboldt illuminated the vertiginous depths of natural processes—at sea, he wanted metropolitan readers to understand that the ocean's depths are variegated and alive not only with creatures but with energy:

> In the conflict of currents, as in the oscillation of the waves, our imagination is struck by those movements which seem to penetrate each other, and by which the ocean is continually agitated.
>
> (69)

The nature and origin of currents were widely debated in the early nineteenth century, and the Gulf Stream in particular would be the subject of new analyses by Sabine in 1825, James Rennell in 1832, and numerous others, arguing cases for competing models of how different kinds of currents were generated (by wind? temperature variations? the sun? salinity? water density at the poles?; see Peterson, Stramma, and Kortum 1996).

While Humboldt conjured for our imaginations the smallest travelers on these currents using the language of mathematics, it was the largest travelers circulating the world oceans that had captured the European imagination for many years—icebergs. Experienced Arctic voyagers knew that icebergs often moved against prevailing winds, sailing on the invisible currents deep below. Their accounts of iceberg mobility often highlighted this remarkable feature that challenged assumptions of the ocean as a surface to be traversed by human ingenuity and imperial intentions. The Danish missionary to Greenland Otto Fabricius wrote in his extensive "On the Floating Ice in the Northern Waters":

> It is really surprising to see the rapidity with which such mountains sometimes move even against the wind, of which the reason is that, the base running deep in the water, the current operates on it with greater force than the wind on the smaller part above the surface, and [...] it may happen that the current which runs deep under the surface may be quite opposite to the current which is caused on the surface by the wind. Thus from the base being of different depth, one may conceive how one mountain may move with greater velocity than another, or even in an opposite direction.
>
> (Fabricius n.d.)

For travelers willing to spend time among Arctic coastal people, the Arctic seas offered unique glimpses of the ocean as a varied, three-dimensional space. Fabricius was a naturalist and missionary who gained his extensive knowledge of Greenlandic fauna and sea ice by living in a Greenlandic sod house among Inuit, wearing Greenlandic clothing, and hunting seal in a kayak, for which he became known as *Erisaalik* ("the man in the [...] kayak-dress") (Adolf Jensen, quoted in Kapel 2005: 13). Fabricius readily credited Greenlanders with superior natural knowledge about these seas: "I never asked a free Greenlander in vain about any work of nature; he was not only able to immediately give it a name, but was also [able] to tell a story about it which was usually found reliable" (Fabricius n.d.).

Such observations of icebergs moving at varying speeds and directions through what Humboldt had described as "the conflict of currents" provided valuable knowledge to nineteenth-century scientists and navigators refining complex theories of how water and wind circulated globally. They could even help voyagers in danger of being trapped by ice by suggesting an ingenious method of propulsion. While searching for the lost John Franklin expedition in the 1850s, American explorer Elisha Kane described narrowly escaping being crushed by ice floes in Melville Bay, Greenland, by harnessing their ship to an iceberg (a common whaling practice) and hitching a ride: "Fearing a besetment, I determined to fasten to an iceberg; and after eight hours of very heavy labour, warping, planting ice-anchors succeeded in effecting it" (1856: 33). The excruciating labor of accessing this "ice road" paid off with rapid sailing and an aesthetic epiphany:

> On our road we were favoured with a gorgeous spectacle, which hardly any excitement of peril could have made us overlook. The midnight sun came out over the northern crest of the great berg, our late "fast friend," kindling variously-coloured fires on every part of its surface, and making the ice around us one great resplendency of gem work, blazing carbuncles, and rubies and molten gold [...]. Our brig went crunching through all this jewellery; and, after a tortuous progress of five miles, arrested here and there by tongues which required the saw and ice-chisels, fitted herself neatly between two floes.
>
> (37–8)

Kane's accounts of his Arctic voyages were beautifully illustrated by high-quality engravings based on his own sketches, and he included one of *Advance* "Fastened to an Iceberg" (Figure 6.1).

Whalers remained Europe's experts on sea ice and icebergs, their northern exploits regularly and quietly exceeding the furthest north celebrated by voyages of exploration such as Kane's, which often employed whalers as ice masters on their ships. One well-known example was William Scoresby, whose maritime expertise helped inspire the British naval Arctic voyages of 1818, while he himself was patronizingly dismissed from any visible role in the project. Scoresby's influential *Account of the Arctic Regions* (1820) and *Journal of a Voyage to the Northern Whale-Fishery* (1823) offered an encyclopedic vision of the northern seas' biodiversity, hydrography, meteorology, geography, commercial wealth, technological innovations, and the spectacular properties of its cryosphere—ice in all its forms and properties. As with his admirer Humboldt, Scoresby's scale of attention was expansive—he lavished visual attention on the astonishing variety of the smallest ice crystals and microorganisms visible under his microscope, and on the largest movements of ice that could be mapped on innovative ice maps covering thousands of kilometers. From the "extreme beauty and endless variety of the microscopic objects procured in the animal and vegetable kingdoms," to the "particulars of beauty and variety" (Scoresby 1820: 426) of snow crystals, icebergs, and atmospheric phenomena, the devout Scoresby saw everywhere the sublime workings of his god, "even [in] the most minute and evanescent, and in regions the most remote from human observation" (477).

FIGURE 6.1 "Fastened to an Iceberg," engraving in Elisha Kent Kane, *Arctic Explorations in the Years 1854, '54, '55* (Philadelphia: Childs and Peterson, 1856), vol. 1, p. 34. © Biodiversity Heritage Library (public domain).

Scoresby's unique range of scientific, commercial, and religious approaches moved readily "from industrial whaling in pursuit of profit to disinterested whaling in pursuit of science and exploration"; as Michael Bravo has shown, Scoresby pursued both in the interest of seeing "the northern ocean as a national space over which control was increased by a range of military, commercial, regulatory, and rhetorical means" (2006: 522). A deeply religious and sensitive writer, Scoresby approached Arctic maritime science and commerce with a consistent sense of wonder, one that famously inspired *Moby-Dick*'s effusions on the whiteness of the whale and cetology. Melville was deeply read in Scoresby, but scholars and readers well versed in the former and not in the latter over-rely on Ishmael's patronizing account of Scoresby's "mechanical outlines of things":

After giving us a stiff full length of the Greenland whale, and three or four delicate miniatures of narwhales and porpoises, [Scoresby] treats us to a series of classical engravings of boat hooks, chopping knives, and grapnels; and with the microscopic diligence of a Leuwenhoeck submits to the inspection of a shivering world ninety-six fac-similes [sic] of magnified Arctic snow crystals.

([1851] 2001: 292)[3]

The objects of Scoresby's keen observation are in fact alive in the precise outlines of their form and function, illuminating a range of maritime practices. For example, plate II in *Account of the Arctic Regions*, titled modestly "Instruments," assembles the multifaceted approach to the northern ocean that Melville learned from but derided in his "veteran" precursor (Figure 6.2). The "Marine Diver" was Scoresby's own invention, an improvement upon an instrument given to him by Sir Joseph Banks, and used in a series of shipboard experiments on water pressure, specific gravity, and temperature at great depths; the "Improved Magnetic Needle" was likewise Scoresby's attempt to solve the oldest problem in northern navigation, namely coping with magnetic variation and how it is exacerbated by local attraction (to shipboard iron); the "Lines of Temperature"

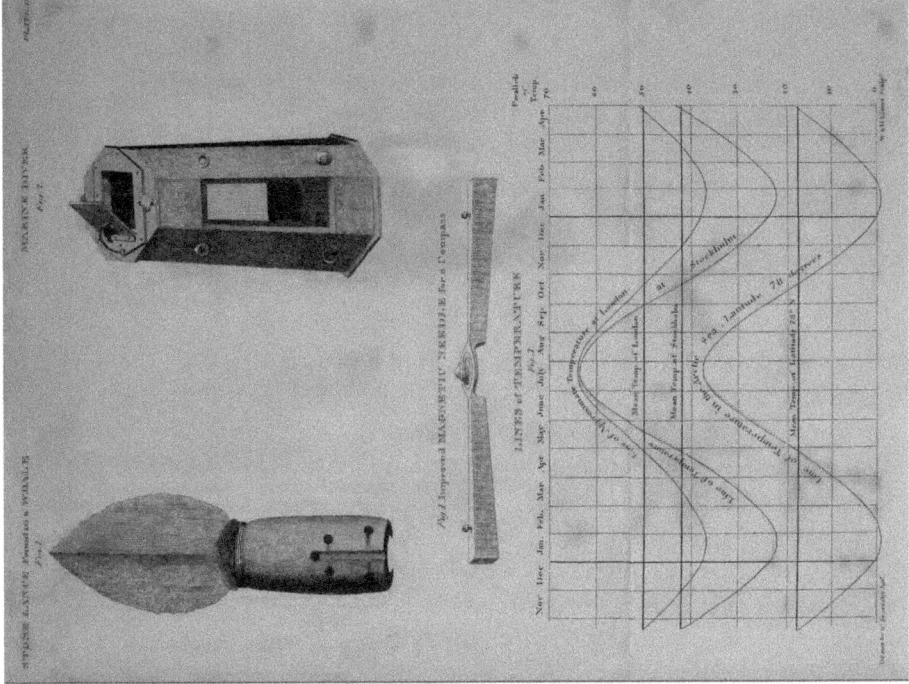

FIGURE 6.2 "Instruments," from William Scoresby, *An Account of the Arctic Regions* (Edinburgh, 1820), vol. 1, plate II. © Internet Archive (public domain).

visualized the temperature shifts Scoresby charted using his Marine Diver, and confirmed the dramatic convergence of southern and northern currents in the Greenland seas, and for the first time the temperature variability of Arctic currents; the "Stone Lance found in a Whale" in Spitsbergen was an Inuit instrument embedded in the body of a whale whose death drew together two radically different and distant cultures of Arctic technological mastery. Scoresby situates these instruments in the heterogeneous matrix of northern maritime life, incorporating imperial science, artisan craft, Indigenous traditional knowledge, and the bodies of leviathans.

The text, charts, tables, and maps accompanying these instruments compose a vision of northern seas rich with spiritual wonder, the terrors of life at sea, the confidence of national projects, the profusion of biodiversity, the meticulous care required to produce pages of invaluable climatological data, and yes, of "magnified Arctic snow crystals" visualized in their shivering world for the first time. The so-called "boring parts" of *Moby-Dick*, for which literary scholars and modern readers seek credit for enduring, are only boring in a novel where the richness of Scoresby's predisciplinary exploration culture has been erased by an author seeking, paradoxically, credit for inventing a hybrid form he is in fact helping to obscure.[4]

In observing and illustrating for the first time microscopic organisms in the northern seas and then identifying them as the food of the ocean's largest travelers, the baleen whales, Scoresby discovered a divinely inspired "dependent chain of existence, one of the smaller links of which being destroyed, the whole must necessarily perish" (1820: 546). These microscopic animalcules (medusae and other jellies), "beautifully transparent" with "quite a crystalline appearance," (546) were brought up in the Marine Diver, illustrated by Scoresby for the first time, and calculated by him to the same exponential degrees that Humboldt used for his intrepid water molecule. The numbers of these iridescent creatures "exceed all the powers of the mind to conceive," admitted the modest Scoresby (547), but he nevertheless attempted the mathematical sublime anyway: "In this proportion, a cubic inch of water must contain 64 [medusae]; a cubic foot 110,592; a cubic fathom 23,887,872; and a cubical mile about 23,888,000,000,000,000!" (179).

The scales of life in the northern seas reached their grandest scope in the accounts of this early marine ecologist who wrote for a large audience, reaching novelists like Melville and men of science such as Darwin. It would be the encyclopedic accounts of ice itself that Scoresby's work remains known for, and here again Scoresby approached the question of the life of icebergs by contemplating their potentially immense age: "what might be the effect of fifty or sixty centuries, affording an annual increase" in the size of bergs (1820: 261)? Scoresby imagined that icebergs may be as old as the earth itself (roughly six thousand years, as he, like many contemporaries believed), and thus that he was sharing the seas with not only the smallest and largest travelers, but also the most ancient.

The vast temporal scale of iceberg voyages in northern seas is important to recognize when relying on seemingly self-evident periods such as "the nineteenth century." Like the iceberg that gave Kane's *Advance* a lift, "the iceberg that sank the *Titanic* began its journey as a rough contemporary of King Tutankhamun, entire civilizations rising and falling while it made its slow march to infamy" (Wilkins 2012). Not only are the life cycles of icebergs conducted on scales of millennia, but their voyages shape their environment in ways perceptible across thousands and even millions of years. Submarine geologists have located and imaged thousands of iceberg drift marks tracing these eccentric travelers back in time (Dowdeswell et al. 2016). Drift marks inscribed into the Arctic seabed reveal the movements of ice and currents at the end of the last Ice Age, when the first Arctic travelers, the Paleo-Eskimo people that preceded the Inuit by thousands of years, began to arrive along the northern shores of the High Arctic archipelago and northern Greenland. Inuit travelers on sea ice continue to use icebergs as navigational markers, sources of fresh water, and shelter (Gearheard et al. 2013: 298). Today, scientists name and track individual bergs across oceans, and like the Inuit (and Kane and Scoresby) understand that "the iceberg can be regarded as an enormous scientific instrument" (Jacobs 1992: 32). We have come to think of nineteenth-century long-distance exploration vessels such as the *Beagle*, the *Advance*, and the *Investigator* as floating laboratories, and more specifically as the largest instruments on earth. Icebergs, in contrast, have been arrested as the nineteenth century's iconic objects of the so-called Arctic sublime, blank surfaces upon which to project our varied Arctic dreams (see Loomis 1977; Lopez 1986). But the mobility of icebergs, their roles in shaping the sea ice–land boundary crucial to Arctic peoples' occupancy and the voyages of explorers, and the wealth of differentiated knowledge about their structures and life cycles from Inuit and European sources, reveal their voyages in time and space to be far richer than the symbolic value the Arctic sublime imagined.

While European travelers in northern seas considered ice as a bitter foe, to be overcome with the "tortuous" labor Kane described using ice chisels and saws, Inuit travelers used sea ice as a highway connecting communities across great distances. One of the greatest nineteenth-century northern voyages of any kind was that of Qillaq or Qitdlarssuaq. Qitdlarssuaq's extraordinary voyage from southern Baffin Island in the Canadian Arctic to the northwest of Greenland in the 1850s reverses not only the direction of Eurocentric models of Arctic voyages (from European centers to Arctic peripheries) but also unsettles southern conceptions equating oceanic space with liquidity, and liquidity with mobility (see Craciun 2010). Qitdlarssuaq's voyage across frozen oceanic space reestablished centuries-old links between circumpolar Inuit communities, at precisely the same moment when European searchers for the John Franklin expedition struggled to move their cumbersome ships through ice as hard as granite.

As Shelley Wright notes, "like many European explorers, from Eric the Red and Martin Frobisher to Franklin himself, Qitdlarssuaq headed out on his travels for less than noble reasons" (2014: 87). A powerful but unscrupulous shaman, Qitdlarssuaq murdered a rival in the 1830s and fled community retribution with a number of families, a testament to the esteem he enjoyed as shaman. After further violent episodes and flights across the Arctic archipelago, Qitdlarssuaq encountered a British searcher for the Franklin expedition in 1853 (Ingleford) and again in 1859 (McClintock), and learned of a distant Inuit community in the far north of Greenland. Merqusaq, Qitdlarssuaq's companion, later told Knud Rasmussen of Qitdlarssuaq's intense curiosity:

> After Qitdlarssuaq had once heard that there were Inuit over on the other side of the sea, he could never settle down to anything again. He held great conjurations of spirits in the presence of all the people of the village. He made his soul take long journeys through the air, with his helping spirits, to look for the country of the strange Inuit. At last one day he informed his fellow-villagers that he had found the new country! And he told them, that he was going to journey to the strange people, and he exhorted them all to follow him.
>
> "Do you know the desire for new countries? Do you know the desire to see new people?" he said to them.
>
> (Merqusaq, quoted in Rasmussen [1905] 1908: 27)

Qitdlarssuaq put his desire for the unknown into action and persuaded his wife Agpaq and thirty-seven men, women, and children to accompany him across one thousand kilometers on six-meter-long whalebone sledges and kayaks. Guided by powerful helping spirits (*tuurngait*), Qitdlarssuaq led his expedition through two winters, hunting and camping along the way until dissent within the group led twenty-four of the Inuit to turn back, never to be heard from again. The remaining group successfully crossed the sea ice from Ellesmere Island to northern Greenland in 1862 and located the Inughuit community in the Avanersuaq (Thule) area (famously dubbed "Arctic Highlanders" in 1818 by the John Ross expedition). There they stayed for six years, revitalizing the travel and hunting skills and technologies of the more isolated Inughuit (who had forgotten how to build and use kayaks), and intermarrying with them, so that to this day, most of the population is descended from this inter-Inuit encounter.

Anthropologists like Rasmussen have tended to characterize Qitdlarssuaq's voyage as one of "tribal migration," but we can also think of it as a voyage of discovery with far-reaching effects. One result of this high-risk "journey of exploration," writes Robert McGhee, was that travelers' descendants in northern Greenland became "prominent members of most of the polar expeditions that set out from northern Greenland from 1860 to 1910," that is, the so-called heroic age of the race to the North Pole (2007: 232). While this heroic model of Arctic voyaging is typically presented as a completely masculine affair, the centrality of Inuit women to all these Arctic travel efforts expands the ranks of oceanic travelers significantly. Without the technological expertise of Inuit women in constructing weatherproof sealskin clothing and preparing the animal food provided by hunters, none of these voyages would have been possible.

The mobilities that Qitdlarssuaq and his family reestablished between these northern communities, made possible by this unique oceanic space, also have a heightened international significance in the twenty-first century, beyond the dangerous legacy of the race to the North Pole. The sea between Ellesmere and Thule is known as the North Water Polynya (Pikialasorsuaq in Greenlandic, the North Water to nineteenth-century whalers) and is one of the largest marine oases on the planet. Today the ice bridge bordering the polynya that Qitdlarssuaq's expedition crossed is severed by an international boundary impeding Inuit travel, and its biosphere is increasingly destabilized by global warming and intensifying marine shipping and extraction efforts. Air travel, with its expense and international bureaucracy, has in some respects made travel more difficult, paradoxically, than in the nineteenth century for the Inuit who followed Qitdlarssuaq and strengthened the transoceanic connections he established (Report of the Pikialasorsuaq Commission 2017: A6). This is an important corrective to the popular notion (derived in part from Marx's famous proposition that train travel initiated a speed-up of time that would annihilate space) that modern globalization will inevitably draw closer together traditional communities and erase their differences, for better or worse (an "aspatial globalization," according to Doreen Massey, because it fails "to recognise the multiplicities of the spatial" [2005: 83]). In 2017 the Inuit Circumpolar Council began to push for an Inuit-led international management of this unique oceanic space, arguing for differentiated kinds of mobilities. Critical to this unique international proposal is the right to free travel: "Inuit on both sides are expressing a strong desire for free movement, once again, across the Pikialasorsuaq" (Report of the Pikialasorsuaq Commission 2017: x). Indigenous travelers such as Qitdlarssuaq and his group transformed the neat boundaries between exploration and migration that inform both colonialist and postcolonial conceptions of travel and mobility, and the repercussions of their travels can shape in unpredictable ways those spaces, their legal regimes, and thus the cryosphere as a whole across centuries.

"Indigenous agency in long-distance travel is prone to being overlooked," writes Michael Bravo in a fascinating study of Inuit-missionary maritime "co-travel" (2019). In 1810 Moravian missionaries enlisted converted Christian Inuit families and an Inuit shaman to lead them on a voyage for spiritual, commercial, and geographical ends, from the Labrador peninsula to the Ungava region of the Canadian Arctic. The published narrative, *Journal of a Voyage from Okkak* (1814), reveals the complex entanglements of this diverse body of travelers, from global network building, to inter-Inuit regional networks of trade and power, to spiritual journeys both Christian and shamanic. Like Qitdlarssuaq and his knowledge exchanges with European voyagers, the Inuit men and women in the voyage from Okkak enjoyed both overlapping and competing interests with these European newcomers, and traveled together for mutual advantage. Our taxonomies of travelers and voyages need significant revising if we are to understand the richness of these entanglements, beyond colonial vs. Indigenous, or exploration vs. migration.

Oceania has received much greater attention that the Arctic in this regard, especially regarding the numerous Polynesian voyagers who joined European ships following the famous examples of Ahutoru aboard Bougainville's 1768 voyage, and Mai and Tupaia aboard the Cook voyages a few years later. "By the end of the eighteenth century," writes Nicholas Thomas, "dozens and certainly maybe hundreds of Islanders had joined whalers, traders and other ships":

> most worked as crew, but some were what the navy called supernumeries [*sic*], the guests of explorers or missionaries. In many cases they visited British outposts like Sydney, and Asian ports such as Canton, Macau and Manila. Some returned to their ships' home bases in New England or Europe [...]. It is striking that many also became temporary or permanent residents of Pacific Islands other than their own.
>
> (2010: 4)

Curiosity about distant Polynesian communities was a great driving factor in Islanders joining such long-distance European ships. As with Qitdlarssuaq and the Okkak voyagers, these diverse Polynesian travelers "were excited by the political practices that were akin but distinct, by new rites that might be imported, by unfamiliar and prestigious objects, by the scope of new sorts of trade," and by the prospect of renewing distant kin relations (Thomas 2010: 4). The convergence of Indigenous and European travelers on the seas sometimes produced aesthetic innovations as well, a feature of their shared roles in fashioning modernities. The best-known example is Tupaia, the Raiatean priest and navigator aboard Cook's first circumnavigation, wherein Tupaia produced a series of drawings and a map of Oceania by merging European and Oceanic technologies and techniques (see Smith 2005). The shipboard work of Indigenous voyagers has in the past been read in the limited sense of the production and donation of Indigenous knowledge, "itself a trope of imperial encounter" (Bravo 2019). This reduction of Indigenous cultural production like Tupaia's to a gift of knowledge obscures a host of possibilities for rethinking nineteenth-century maritime travel and its representations, as the work of Thomas, Bravo, and other scholars show.

Qitdlarssuaq was not the first Inuk to seek out the Inughuit (Polar Inuit) of Qaanaaq in northern Greenland. The voyages and artwork of an extraordinary Greenlander known as John Sacheuse in the early nineteenth century illustrates the richness of underexamined materials in our transoceanic archives. The Inughuit "exist in a corner of the world by far the most secluded which has yet to be discovered," wrote naval captain John Ross, the first European to make contact with them aboard his Northwest Passage expedition in 1818; "until the moment of our arrival," Ross asserted, the Inughuit "believed themselves to be the only inhabitants of the universe" (1819: 123).[5] The encounter between Ross's men and the Inughuit had been orchestrated by Sacheuse, Ross's official interpreter who had been converted by missionaries in Ilulissat ("Icebergs" in the West Greenland language) and voluntarily came to Edinburgh aboard a whaler in 1816. In Edinburgh, Sacheuse had met two prestigious figures in the arts and sciences: Alexander Nasmyth, the leading landscape painter of the age, and Sir Basil Hall, a naval captain and brother to the president of the Royal Society of Edinburgh. He studied painting in Nasmyth's renowned school, and accompanied Ross as a paid interpreter onboard the *Isabella*. We know that the *Isabella* was searching for the Northwest Passage, but what was Sacheuse searching for?

Sacheuse returned to Edinburgh with Ross and immediately began preparing for another expedition, aboard Parry's 1819 search for the Northwest Passage: "he looked forward with the utmost keenness and anxiety to the sailing of the expedition, [...] being perfectly aware, at the same time, of his own value upon the occasion" (Anonymous 1818: 4). Before the ship sailed, Sacheuse died of an illness in February 1819, aged twenty-two. Sacheuse made several paintings while onboard the *Isabella* and one of them survives in the form of a colored lithograph, offering us a glimpse of his perspective: "First Communication with the Natives of Prince Regent's Bay, Drawn by John Sackheouse [*sic*]" (Figure 6.3).[6] This image enjoyed pride of place in the official voyage publication at a time when visual knowledge was one of the most highly valued artifacts collected. Whereas Ross stressed priority, discovery, and the otherness of the Inughuit in his narrative, Sacheuse focused on encounter and exchange on the sea ice. "Everything in the picture tells of a meeting," writes one of the few art historical accounts of Sacheuse's work (Kaalund 1983: 158). Working as one of the earliest known Inuit artists trained in European practices, Sacheuse combined "Inuit traditions for visual storytelling with European representational techniques to arrive at a synthesis that testifies to the ways in which [he] himself lived and moved in both cultures" (Høvik 2013: 237).

FIGURE 6.3 "First Communication with the Natives of Prince Regent's Bay, Drawn by John Sackheouse [sic]," lithograph after a drawing by John Sacheuse, from John Ross, *A Voyage of Discovery* (London: John Murray, 1819). © The John Carter Brown Library at Brown University (public domain).

Sacheuse had devised a novel, hybrid technique suited for a singular "first communication" and, even more significantly, he placed himself in the center of the encounter in what appears to be the first extant Inuit self-portrait. Having given the Inughuit mirrors, Sacheuse then pictured them in the act of self-reflection, a carefully drawn Inuk's face smiling in the mirror. These fleeting glimpses of Inuit self-reflection and storytelling appear in an image otherwise devoted to ceremonies of possession—Ross's title, the associated map, and the narrative all rename Qaanaaq as Prince Regent's Bay, and the people as Arctic Highlanders.

Sacheuse then led Ross and Parry, captains of the *Isabella* and *Alexander*, to meet the Inughuit on the sea ice of Pikialasorsuaq, and pictures them exchanging narwhal tusks for knives. But Sacheuse actually included three distinct encounters in "First Communication": an initial meeting between himself and the Inughuit in the distance, the meeting of Sacheuse again wearing a naval uniform (holding the shirt) with the Inughuit who see themselves in the mirror he has given them, and in the foreground Parry and Ross exchanging gifts with two Greenlanders. The series of three meetings is unusual in Western encounter pictures and suggests a temporal progression, with "the figures positioned closer to the foreground not only growing in size but representing events that occurred closer to the present" (Høvik 2013: 238). Sacheuse's lively vision of plural encounters reflects one of this volume's central tenets, that "conquest, exploration, voyages of discovery are about the meeting up of histories, not merely a pushing-out 'across space'" (Massey 2005: 120).

As lead intermediary, Sacheuse had devised an innovative composition for imagining their encounters and pictured himself as a central figure wearing naval clothing. He included the expected elements of this genre of history painting—the ships at anchor with their prominent ensigns, the submissive posture and astonished faces of the Native people. But he also shows us two sources of European astonishment in the Arctic: the sublime icescape surrounding the bay, and the Inuk on the sledge commanding his dogs without hands or reins, using only his voice and whip, as Ross had marveled in his account (1819: 102). European wonder at the technical skill and arts of Indigenous people was a common feature of Pacific and Arctic exploration accounts, and "First Communication" highlights this, creating a subtle symmetry of wonder.

Sacheuse produced other ship-board drawings, now lost: a self-portrait with a broken arm, a drawing of Inughuit aboard the *Isabella* interacting with the crew and instruments, another encounter picture featuring himself planting a flag on the ice in an effort to attract the attention of the Inughuit.[7] We do not know how much freedom Sacheuse enjoyed over the formal composition of "First Communication," over the depiction of the Inughuit, or how representative this brief catalog of images was in its repeated motif of self-representation. But what had initially appeared as a stolidly imperial vision of the discovery of an exotic and "unknown" people in Ross's *Voyage of Discovery*, has revealed a rich archive of encounters and travelers. Naval voyagers such as Ross and Parry saw themselves as pushing out into empty oceanic spaces, driven by scientific curiosity and sometimes a desire for conquest. But their partial visions should not frame our inquiries, lest we repeat the imperial histories that cast Europeans as history's mobile agents of global change and Indigenous peoples as "firmly situated in place and culturally coherent" (Thomas 2010: 3). Sacheuse was converted by missionaries, had family in Denmark, traveled aboard a British whaling ship and joined a naval expedition of geographical discovery bound for North America and, beyond that, the Pacific. He probably spoke two European and two Greenlandic languages, was highly skilled with a kayak and harpoon, and had started to study with artists and men of science in the Scottish Enlightenment. The interesting possibility is not how his perspective helps us see "both sides" of maritime exploration but how voyagers such as Sacheuse shared a cosmopolitanism and curiosity that too often we consider exclusively European (see Thomas 2010: 3–6).

Sacheuse's maritime art had innovated a series of perspectives on encounter on the Greenland sea ice. The most remarkable example of aesthetic and technological innovations as a result of such encounters happened also in Greenland, a few decades later. At nearly the same time as Qitdlarssuaq led his followers across a frozen Northwest Passage toward Greenland, a Danish colonial administrator at Nuuk (Godthab) introduced a printing press into the Greenlandic community and set up a Greenlander-run press in Kalaallisut (the West Greenlandic Inuit language). In 1861 they began to publish a monthly newspaper illustrated with colored engravings, *Atuagagdliutit*—the first color-illustrated periodical in the world. The first editor, Rasmus Berthelsen, was a Greenlander catechist, and the lead artist was the legendary Aron of Kangeq. The subject matter of *Atuagagdliutit* ranged from traditional Greenlandic tales gathered from across Inuit communities, to accounts of violent clashes with the ancient Norse, contemporary European cities and events, notices and illustrations of explorers passing through en route to their searches for Franklin and later to the North Pole, and retellings of classic European fictional and nonfictional travel accounts. While other colonial Indigenous presses predated *Atuagagdliutit,* this was also the first secular, Native-run press in the world.

Aron's dynamic illustrations of Inuit oral tales brought to life for a Pan-Greenlandic audience an emerging sense of cultural unity: *Atuagagdliutit* "played an important role as a means of binding Greenland together and gave the scattered population the impression of being one people and distinct from the other nations of the world" (Thisted 2001: 255). One of the ways *Atuagagdliutit* did this was by also retelling and picturing exotic materials from a global archive of travels. Beginning in 1862, they began retelling *Robinson Crusoe* with a long series of illustrations. Episodes highlighted included the most highly charged and violent ones, as well as iconic scenes popular in European illustrations of Defoe's novel, such as Crusoe with his umbrella and goatskin, Crusoe and Friday, Crusoe's sighting of the cannibal feast, and Crusoe shipwrecked (Figure 6.4).[8] *Atuagagdliutit* also featured images of European and Eastern cities, customs, pastimes, and even European travels. Aron's watercolor illustrations and their color engravings are prized as artifacts of Greenlandic identity and art, innovations in global print culture, and instruments for generating an Indigenous global perspective in the age of high empire. Like Sacheuses's visual art and the long-lived oral tales of Qitdlarssuaq's exploits that continue to circulate today, the innovations of *Atuagagdliutit* reposition Greenland as a fruitful site of Indigenous modernity and unpredictable cultural encounter, far from the remote and timeless periphery imagined by Europeans.

The question of who could travel on the Arctic seas was for centuries limited to the Indigenous coastal people, whalers, commercial traders, and naval crews we have considered thus far. In the nineteenth century they began to include civilian naturalists and occasionally trained artists. Arctic maritime voyagers aboard state-funded expeditions included professionally trained artists such as the Briton George Back in the 1820s to 1830s in the North American Arctic,

FIGURE 6.4 Aron of Kangeq, illustration from serialized *Robinson Crusoe*, in *Atuagagdliutit* 2.8 (1862). The caption in Kalaallisut (Greenlandic) reads "Robinson from his ship by the waves carried/run (to shore)" (thanks to Nelson Graburn for this translation). © Nunatta Atuagaateqarfia, Central Library of Greenland (public domain); Landsobasafn Islands, National Library of Iceland (public domain).

the Frenchman François-Auguste Biard in the 1830s in Spitsbergen, and the Bohemian Julius von Payer in the Austro-Hungarian expedition that discovered the Frantz Joseph Land archipelago in 1872. Like the engravings for Kane's illustrations, the paintings of these skilled artists amplified a distinctive Arctic sublime by emphasizing the dreamlike and hallucinatory aspects of icebergs, sea ice, and aurora borealis. Displayed in academies and salons, but also in more diverse public interiors such as popular panoramas, science museum interiors, and other popular science spectacles, Arctic travelers' sublime visions helped fuel the emergence of Arctic tourism.

The 1838 French state scientific expedition to the Spitsbergen archipelago and northern Scandivania that included three artists also included the writer Léonie d'Aunet, the eighteen-year-old lover of the painter Biard who would become Victor Hugo's long-term mistress. D'Aunet later published a narrative of her voyage, *Voyage d'une femme au Spitzberg*, in which her xenophobic descriptions of Sami people coexist with sublime effusions about a romanticized, unpeopled Arctic archipelago, the kind of increasingly conventional vision that drew more private travelers, artists, and adventurers north. Biard meanwhile painted an extraordinary seascape as a result of this voyage, *Vue de l'Océan Glacial, pêche aux morses par des Groënlandais* (1841) (Figure 6.5), which is unusual in featuring Greenlanders, not Europeans, heroically struggling in an animated icescape, hunting walrus. Biard's icescapes have been described accurately as

FIGURE 6.5 François-Auguste Biard, *Vue de l'Océan Glacial: pêche aux morses par des Groënlandais*, 1841. Oil on canvas. Chateau de Dieppe. © Wikimedia Commons (public domain).

protosurrealistic and hallucinatory, but in the case of *Vue de l'Océan Glacial* the most extraordinary feature is the presence of Indigenous Greenlanders as the central actors at home in this imagined struggle (Matilsky 1985: 82). Better-known mid-nineteenth-century visions of northern seas such as Church's *The Icebergs* or George Back's *The Perilous Position of H.M.S. Terror* (1837) featured either massive ships in epic struggles against the frozen ocean, or the wreckage left behind, in visions dominated by a rhetoric of northern seas as empty wastelands testing the imperial, scientific, or spiritual resolve of European men. But as Sacheuse and d'Aunet's presence aboard state scientific voyages indicate, public interest in these remote seas continued to create opportunities for more diverse kinds of travelers.

Tourism was slower to arrive in the northern seas than elsewhere because of the extreme difficulties and expense of travel, but wealthy tourists, sport hunters, artists, and journalists began to arrive in the mid-nineteenth century, chasing the visions that these earlier travelers had popularized in illustrated periodicals, published narratives, novels, paintings, panoramas, and museum exhibitions. Lord Dufferin was a pioneer of Arctic tourism, sailing in his yacht *Foam* in 1856 and producing a crowd-pleasing, often humorous account in *Letters from High Latitudes*. Dufferin amplified the aesthetic commodities available to gentlemen

FIGURE 6.6 "Et Ego in Arctis," from Lord Dufferin, *Letters from High Latitudes: Being Some Account of a Voyage, in 1856, in the Schooner Yacht "Foam" to Iceland, Jan Mayen, and Spitzbergen* [sic], 6th edn. (London: John Murray, 1873). © Biodiversity Heritage Library (public domain).

travelers in such illustrations as "Et Ego in Arctis" (Figure 6.6). This example of Arctic picturesque at English Bay, Spitsbergen, evokes both a classical trope and reinscribes the Arctic as a site of disaster and now disaster tourism. English Bay and Magdalena Bay were sites of seventeenth- and eighteenth-century whaling stations and graveyards, that had drawn both naval travelers passing through (such as John Franklin in 1818, who removed grave goods as souvenirs) and tourists like Dufferin, chasing aesthetic opportunities in ever more dramatic settings.

Far from the more muted and collectively oriented rhetoric of naval voyagers, Dufferin's overwrought prose suited audiences such as Kane's who enjoyed more literary allusion and subjective effusion by charismatic career explorers. "It was no brother mortal that lay at our feet, softly folded in the embraces of 'Mother Earth,'" reflected Dufferin on the whaler's beachside grave, "but a poor scarecrow, gibbeted for ages on this bare rock, like a dead Prometheus" ([1856] 1873: 193).[9] The Dutch whaler had traveled with hundreds of other men for grueling labor in the world's first global oil rush. Thousands of exposed remains of these earlier maritime laborers, their elaborate infrastructure and environmental footprints, and the whales they hunted, littered the shores of the archipelago and became in the nineteenth century a major draw for adventurers such as Dufferin, who may not have been able to access the more remote fields of disaster souvenirs left behind by the John Franklin expedition along the Northwest Passage but were content to transform the remains of "brother mortals" into broken Titans.

By the late nineteenth century, the shores and seas of the Spitsbergen archipelago had been actively transformed into the newest playground of the rich, complete with a luxury hotel, yachts, hunting guides, and probably the world's northernmost illustrated periodical, the *Spitsbergen Gazette* (Figure 6.7). "Our pleasures these days seem to lead us northwards," wrote Miss H.E. Hearn in the *Spitsbergen Gazette* of July 1897, "and Spitzbergen [sic] is the one accessible place where one may make acquaintance with really arctic scenery and arctic life at comparatively little trouble and expense" (1897: 1).[10] Luckily now one could choose from several different steamers leaving Europe weekly during the summer season, and the *Gazette* was full of advertising featuring furs, fine wines, hunting equipment, cigars, photographic supplies, and prepared game—all the comforts of home for its discerning readership.

Most travelers sailing to Spitsbergen were not seeking the sporting life but rather naked profits, as the archipelago remained *terra nullius* until 1925, meaning that any nation, individual, or company could prospect for resources unhindered by laws save that of first come first served. By the late nineteenth century, it was mining (chiefly coal, but also asbestos, marble, gold, and other minerals) that generated a new resource scramble, meaning that most of the occupants that the yacht and steamer set would have seen on the land

FIGURE 6.7 *Spitsbergen Gazette* (July 1897). © Photograph by Adriana Craciun, copy from Scott Polar Research Institute, University of Cambridge.

were speculators, hunters, and miners living and traveling in vastly different conditions than those advertised in the *Spitsbergen Gazette*. Spitsbergen (today Svalbard) has retained this hybrid, uneasy identity as a site of luxury tourism and harsh resource extraction, a shared modernity that continues to attract innovators of all kinds.

One thing the yachting set and the hunters and miners shared in traveling to Spitsbergen was their dependence on bringing most supplies and building materials aboard their ships, as no edible vegetation grew on the islands and the only trees were dwarf willows, which reach only 2.5 centimeters high. From the mass of accumulated shipping crates was born another innovation, the first modular do-it-yourself furniture. Bostonian designer Louise Brigham was one of few women to spend two summers in Spitsbergen at the turn of the twentieth century. All were servants or wives, but the well-to-do Brigham came to the fledgling mining colony of Bostonian coal magnate John Munro Longyear out of curiosity. Finding herself among a glut of empty wooden shipping crates in 1906, Brigham was inspired to create a new kind of Arts and Crafts furniture made from recycled materials:

> Cut off from other materials, the possibilities of the box seemed greater than ever [...]. As I worked in that far-off marvelous land of continuous day, surrounded by mountains and glaciers, I felt anew the truth, so familiar to all, that work to be of real value must be honest, useful, and beautiful, and Ruskin and Morris spoke as clearly in the arctic regions as in the settlements or studio in New York.
>
> (1909: Preface)

All Arctic travelers found this furniture beautiful, from the American aeronaut Walter Wellman to "The Prince of Monaco, who visited our arctic home, [and] seemed as much pleased as the Danish peasant who watched by the workbench" (Brigham 1909: Preface). Brigham dedicated her resulting book *Box Furniture* to Joseph Riis, the pioneering photographer and urban reformer, and herself became a leading philanthropist and reformer among urban, immigrant populations. Her designs that grew from her Spitsbergen travels went on to influence Rudolf Schindler and other leading modernists (Banham 1997:1137).

Thanks to the accumulated voyages of these diverse travelers across the century, the islands of Spitsbergen and Manhattan were much closer at the end of the nineteenth century than at the beginning. The Arctic seas, their inanimate and animate travelers, and the unfamiliar and extraordinary scales of their journeys, made possible this dynamic understanding of space and time, which in familiar seas is harder to appreciate. Heterochronic and heterotopic, Arctic seas transformed nineteenth-century southern travelers, their arts and imaginations, their sciences, and their distant cities.

CHAPTER SEVEN

Representations

Lascars, Drifters, Aquanauts

CHARNE LAVERY

INTRODUCTION

We begin with a moment in Joseph Conrad's *Lord Jim*, a novel of the sea published in 1900. At the end of the novel the narrator Marlow is talking in the murky dusk to Jim's widow, the woman he calls Jewel. Marlow is discomfited by her emotion, forced to face, in her face, the not-us of the novel. Jewel is "half-caste," not "one of us" in imperial, racial or gendered terms, yet her visible grief speaks too closely to a shared humanity. Suddenly, Marlow is overwhelmed—and describes that psychological moment in oceanic terms:

> An inconceivable calmness seemed to have risen from the ground around us, imperceptibly, like the still rise of a flood in the night, obliterating the familiar landmarks of emotions. There came upon me, as though I had felt myself losing my footing in the midst of waters, a sudden dread, the dread of unknown depths.
>
> ([1900] 2008: 227)

The passage relies both on familiar tropes of the ocean as disconcerting fluidity and also on specific oceanic phenomena: the flood in the second line refers to the tide, rising by imperceptible degrees during the dark of the night, so that, with dawn, the landscape appears fundamentally changed; the landmarks have been submerged, so that the navigating observer cannot take his bearings, is lost and uncertain. This image of rising waters is paired in the next sentence with an image of falling into the sea, losing contact with the bottom and a clear sense of how far the ocean extends below. The landmarks and the swimmer are both literally overwhelmed by the sea. The passage describes forms of deep uncertainty using metaphors of oceanic verticality, in a racialized moment of encounter that is a result of the lateral networks of maritime empire.

Marlow's invocation of slipping beneath the surface of the sea as a metaphor for existential uncertainty also, less metaphorically, recalls the dramatic maritime events of the novel—the plot of *Lord Jim* in fact turns on encounters with the submarine. Jim's life-defining crisis precipitates from two points of contact with the deep: the submerged object—possibly "a waterlogged wreck" or "floating derelict"—that rears up randomly and strikes his ship, the *Patna*, in the night; and the submarine telegraph cable that carries the fateful telegraph bearing news of Jim and his fellow-officers' cowardly abandonment of their eight hundred passengers from Aden, along the floor of the Indian Ocean, to surface in an "Eastern port" before they arrive (Conrad [1900] 2008: 21). The telegraph signal travels along the same route, but in the opposite direction, to the *Patna*'s originally intended itinerary—from Singapore to Aden—tracing the route of the Indian Ocean transoceanic submarine telegraph that was laid in 1870, just four years after the successful completion of the pioneering transatlantic cable in 1866 (Huurdeman 2003: 137). Both the telegraph cable and submerged wreck point to incursions of the deep Indian Ocean into the surface world of the text.

The eastern direction and submarine encounters of Conrad's narrative, signaled by wreck and cable, point us toward a reading that centers the Indian Ocean as a literary space. The geopolitical significance of this oceanic region was largely overlooked until postcolonial writers looked back at empire, so that arguably the most robust historical sea fiction of the nineteenth-century Indian Ocean had to wait for the late twentieth century. Novels by Amitav Ghosh from India, such as the Ibis trilogy, *The Glass Palace*, and *The Circle of Reason*, and by Abdulrazak Gurnah from Zanzibar, such as *Paradise*, *Desertion*, and *By the Sea*, in particular but among others, have turned to the nineteenth-century Indian Ocean. Their writing produces alternative histories of maritime traffic that highlight African, Indian, and Arab participation, drawing attention to the oversights of their forbears and producing a more globally oriented view of nineteenth-century publics. However, while nineteenth-century sea writers had neither the agenda nor panoramic vision to write this neglected history into the canon in a fully imagined way, subjecting the earlier work to a different cultural geography of reading reveals more Indian Ocean material than is commonly conceived. Returning to the classical postcolonial method of contrapuntal reading theorized first by Edward W. Said, this chapter reads the most canonical of nineteenth-century writers of the sea in light of the "alternative modernities" represented by the Indian Ocean, those "formations of modernity that have taken shape in an archive of deep and layered existing social and intellectual traditions" (Hofmeyr 2007: 13).

The sea more widely forms a central focus of the nineteenth-century Anglophone literary imagination in a way that is distinct from both earlier and later centuries—the eighteenth century characterized by a paradoxical sublimation during the age of exploration, and the twentieth century marked by hydrophasia, or forgetting of the sea (Cohen 2010: 104, 14). The nineteenth century, in contrast, is a moment during which global trade and maritime empire are "dominant rather than emergent elements of world history" (Mentz and Rojas 2016: 2), and the century's cultural production is marked by an unparalleled interest in both the breadths and depths of the sea. Innovations in maritime technology work hand in hand with the virulent expansion of maritime empire, developments that are central to its most popular and widely read fictions. The depth of the seafloor, anybody's guess at the beginning of the century, is not only mapped but overlaid with telegraph cables by its end; sailing ships reach their technological peak only to give way by late century to the predictability of steam; maritime traffic enables the lucrative violence of empire while also facilitating transoceanic anti-colonial networks. Much of this is reflected in literary production from the period, sometimes in cursory but crucial detail (Dickens and Austen), sometimes as primary setting and subject (Melville, Conrad, Stevenson, Verne).

To give readers a good sense of the rich potential for decentering imperialist geographies of fiction-reading, this chapter focuses on just two masters of the craft of sea fiction from the nineteenth century—a narrative form dominated by Anglophone readers at the time. It shows how productive it is to read their work through a decentered decolonial-ecological lens, as a model for readings that could be done to countless other works of the era, from canonical novels by James Fenimore Cooper and Robert Louis Stevenson, to popular fiction by R.M. Ballantyne and the French Jules Verne—authors I mention in passing to give readers a sense of the possibilities opened by such an approach. The focus, though, is on Joseph Conrad and Herman Melville, known as the "two great English-language writers of sea stories," because the sea is consistently at the heart of their works and because they have been deemed "first-rate novelists" (Peck 2001: 107). Melville's *Moby-Dick* is paradigmatic of Western representations of the sea, published precisely in the middle of the nineteenth century and described by D.H. Lawrence as "the greatest book of the sea ever written" ([1923] 2003: 146). Conrad's experiences as a sailor feed into his writing, producing a body of work that offers a retrospective overview on nineteenth-century maritime culture, and that forms a hinge between the age of empire and postcolonial writing of the twentieth century in ways that are both fraught and far-reaching. His career ends at the end of British maritime domination and the beginning of the demise of its empire, and he is known, for much of this period and despite his protestations, as "our greatest sea-writer" (Simmons 2004: 5).

Conrad's work in particular continues to haunt postcolonial writers of the sea. Amitav Ghosh, as a writer of historical sea fiction of the nineteenth century, is often compared to Conrad, an association that, however well intended, he rejects. As he explains in an interview, pointing to key figures of Indian Ocean sailing, who will be discussed below, "what really vitiates Conrad's work for me is that in the background is always this lascar—but never does the lascar in Conrad have a voice except as some sort of maligned presence. To me, that's a failure of imagination" (Boehmer and Mondal 2012: 32).[1] Ghosh prefers both James Fenimore Cooper's writing and, most significantly, Melville's, for example referencing "that wonderful Melville piece [in *Redburn*] about the lascar that he meets" (32). Reading the canonical EuroAmerican writers contrapuntally in light of later authors such as Ghosh, reminds us that gaps in representation should not be considered inevitable.

The sections that follow examine canonical writing of the sea in light of these concerns, reading for overlooked oceans, underrepresented voices, and submerged worlds. What do we learn about this writing, first of all, if we turn our focus from the North Atlantic to the Indian Ocean? The North Atlantic has been the dominant focus of Anglophone critics as the region that sees the most well-known part of the slave trade, the location of the first telegraph cable, and, with American independence and ascendancy, the site of well-worn paths of circulation between the New World and the old.[2] However, Britain's maritime empire during this period is in fact centered on India after the loss of its American colony in the eighteenth century, and both the rounding of the Cape and the Suez Canal are key gateways to this Indian Ocean-centered imperial domain. After the experimental success of the first transatlantic telegraph cable, the second submarine cable to be laid was across the Indian Ocean linking Aden to Bombay (present-day Mumbai), as can be seen in Figure 7.1. Further, while the North Atlantic-based slave trade was dominant in previous centuries, the drawing in of Indian Ocean slave networks served a crucial role in prolonging the trade, while indentured labor from the East represented its change into a new form (Lavery 2020a; Tinker 1992).

Reading for the Indian Ocean is to look "underneath the as-it-were dome of empire," following figures that elude its borders, shadow its edges, and give the lie to its narratives of all-dominance (Amitav Ghosh, quoted in Boehmer and Mondal 2012: 34). This chapter also explores what lies otherwise underneath or at the margins, the deep-sea marine environment of the Indian Ocean in its three dimensions, in the spirit of the submarine cables betraying the betrayers in *Lord Jim*, granting significance to what lies beneath the surface of the sea. Figure 7.2 is suggestive of these modes of approaching the submarine, bringing

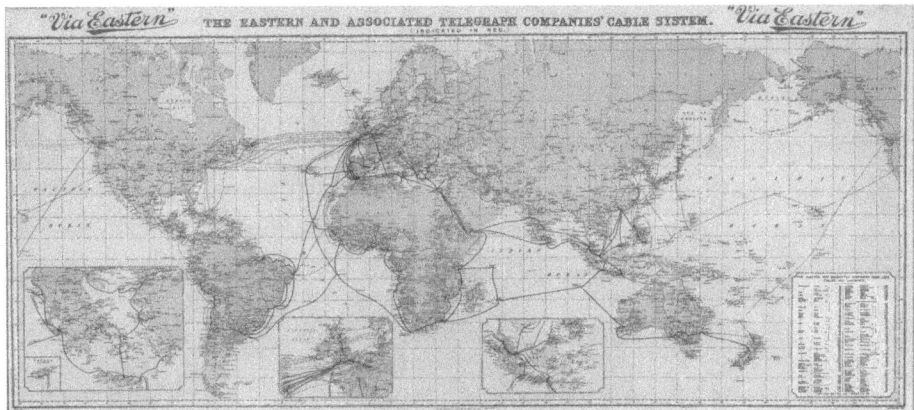

FIGURE 7.1 Eastern and Associated Telegraph Companies map depicting global coverage by 1914, including the submarine Indian Ocean telegraph cable that connected Europe to India in 1858 (London: Waterlow & Sons Limited, September). © David Rumsey Map Collection, David Rumsey Map Center, Stanford Libraries.

FIGURE 7.2 "A whale entangled in the submarine telegraph cable, Persian Gulf," illustration from *The Illustrated London News*, vol. 63, September 13, 1873. © DEA/Biblioteca Ambrosiana/Getty Images.

together a whale, a telegraph cable, and the Indian Ocean. As Hester Blum asks, "what would happen if we take the ocean's nonhuman scale and depth as a first critical position and principle?", even while contending with the limits imposed on perception and experience by the ocean's physical properties, like its opacity to light and inhospitability to human life (2014: 24, 30). One way is to follow representations of various forms of direct and indirect engagement with the seas—sailing, drifting, whaling, diving, telegraphing, sounding, wrecking—each of which is marked to varying degrees in the sections to follow.

Reading for the Indian Ocean is a lateral shift, while reading for the ocean's three-dimensional volumes is a shift vertically. Shifts in perspective reflect, in fact, what the sea allows writers of this period to do—to explore the edge of human experience in both geographic and psychic terms, to introduce strangeness and improbability into the bounds of realism, and to roam widely across vast scales of breadth and depth, with often destabilizing results. The sea's representation is as manifold as the sea itself, with many moods and countercurrents. I've selected from this vast manifold of instances those that occur in works at once well known and overlooked, to encourage similar readings against the critical grain. The first section addresses underrepresented voices, particularly the lascar sailors who formed a large percentage of the maritime workforce but are rarely depicted; the second section looks beyond the ideal imperialists, travelers and sailors, to the underworld of failures, drifters, and beachcombers; and the third section dives beneath the opaque surface of the sea to the largely invisible submarine depths—following the imaginative dive of the aquanauts aboard the *Nautilus* to the pearl divers of Ceylon.

LASCARS

Conrad's writing of the sea is diagnostic of what Jameson describes as the fundamentally dyadic nature of the ocean in literature, between a romanticized abstraction and a material place of work. His fiction deploys the more stereotypical oceanic tropes of "light literature," but also clearly represents the sea as "the very element by which an imperial capitalism draws its scattered beachheads and outposts together, through which it slowly realizes its sometimes violent, sometimes silent and corrosive, penetration of the outlying precapitalist zones of the globe" (Jameson [1981] 2002: 201). The Indian Ocean, as such a place of both romance and work in Conrad's fiction, is here read through depictions of its particular workforce, the lascar sailors who made up often the majority of sailing crews in this period. In nineteenth-century English the word "lascar" referred to "all indigenous sailors of the Indian Ocean region," whether Arabs, South Asians, Malays, East Africans, Filipinos, or Chinese (as opposed to "kanaka," a term that pointed to the Indigenous sailors of the Pacific Ocean) (Ghosh 2008: 4) (Figure 7.3). While Indigeneity is a tricky concept in an Indian Ocean context of ancient and extensive travel and trade,

FIGURE 7.3 Photograph of the crew of *Cawdor* including four African Lascar crew members, 1884. © National Maritime Museum, Greenwich, London.

it is useful in describing the pre- and coexisting oceanic worlds that subtend European maritime networks.

Conrad's maritime oeuvre provides an imaginative map of the ocean in Anglophone culture—while also a map of a specific oceanic terrain. For instance, in the first portion of *The Nigger of the "Narcissus,"* both the abstract ocean and a particular, material ocean are in evidence:

> The passage had begun, and the ship, a fragment detached from the earth, went on lonely and swift like a small planet. Round her the abysses of sky and sea met in an unattainable frontier. A great circular solitude moved with her, ever changing and ever the same, always monotonous and always imposing. Now and then another wandering white speck, burdened with life, appeared far off—disappeared; intent on its own destiny.
>
> (Conrad [1897] 1974: 29–30)

Here the sea is vast, abyssal, infinite; it represents violent flux but also stasis and boredom; the horizon recedes in every direction creating a sense of a "borderless immensity" that is nevertheless circular, shaped to the horizon from a sea-level perspective. The sea is atmospheric and immaterial, a blank context for the human drama yet to unfold on the microcosmic ship. All this is entirely in keeping with the oceanic Romanticism invented in the first part of the century, which Conrad happily exploits—but also undermines. Alongside these familiar evocations of a romanticized oceanic sublime, the passage also suggests a particular ocean with its peculiar geographic, social, and historical characteristics. The *Narcissus* is leaving Bombay to sail across the Indian Ocean and back to England. Later on, the particulars of this first part of the voyage are overshadowed by a storm-ridden rounding of southern Africa such that coming out on the other side was like "dying and being resuscitated," so that "all the first part of the voyage, the Indian Ocean on the other side of the Cape, all that was lost in a haze, like an ineradicable suspicion of some previous existence" (Conrad [1897] 1974: 100). The dematerialized language partially ironizes the earlier description, in which the vastness of the ocean is measured by the apparently total solitude of the British ship. In fact, however, one of the "wandering white specks" in the distance, the narrator explains a little later, is "the pointed sail of an Arab dhow [that,] running for Bombay rose triangular and upright above the sharp edge of the horizon, lingered and vanished like an illusion" (30). Rather than a generic ocean, the dhow represents a long history of Indian Ocean trade between Africa, India, and the Arab world, as well as resilient contemporary competition with European capital (Pearson 2003: 114, 319; Hofmeyr 2012) (Figure 7.4).

FIGURE 7.4 "Giving chase to a dhow in the distance," from *The Illustrated London New,* December 17, 1881. © Wikimedia Commons (public domain).

Like the dhows in *Narcissus*, figures from the Indian Ocean world shadow the edges of *Lord Jim*. Jim's transoceanic routes are overlaid upon Indigenous maritime networks, like the Muslim pilgrims from the Malay world, who follow ancient routes of pilgrimage to Mecca in the Middle East, traveling on a steamship under Chinese ownership. The pilgrims are the moral problem at the heart of the novel, revealing, when they are abandoned to their deaths by the European officers, a brutal imperial hypocrisy. Their abandonment is a move consistent with imperial practice based on hierarchized racial value but horrifyingly inconsistent with its rhetoric of paternalistic care. As Captain Brierly, nautical assessor at the inquiry into the case, explains: "Frankly, I don't care a snap for all the pilgrims that ever came out of Asia, but a decent man would not have behaved like this to a full cargo of old rags in bales" (Conrad [1900] 2008: 49). Notably, Jim's action is not only a private shame but also a public disgrace, compounded by the fact of witness. It is the "publicity" that distresses Brierly, the fact that, in his words, "all these confounded natives, serangs, lascars, quartermasters, are giving evidence that's enough to burn a man to ashes with shame" (48). Something about the nature of this audience drives Brierly to suicide less than a week after the inquiry, jumping overboard "as though on that exact spot in the midst of waters he had suddenly perceived the gates of the other world flung open wide for his reception" (43). It is the second disastrous submersion in the novel, linking the "Asian" pilgrims abandoned by Jim's leap to wider Indian Ocean publics of "natives, serangs, lascars."

The Muslim pilgrims in *Lord Jim* can be seen as what Conrad, in the "Author's Note" to *Typhoon* calls "the human element below her decks" (Conrad [1919] 2008: 218).³ In *Typhoon*, it is not the weather—the storm that is a feature of the material ocean's most extreme capacity—that constitutes the challenge in the story, as it would certainly have been in much of sea adventure fiction. The challenge rather is the way in which the "remarkable occurrence" of the storm is complicated by the human element of maritime empire (Cohen 2010: 23). In *Typhoon* the human element is a cargo of "two hundred Chinese coolies, returning to their village homes in the province of Fo-kien, after a few years of work in various tropical colonies" (Conrad [1902] 2008: 5). Indentured labor, largely from the Indian Ocean region, is the solution to which Britain turned to make up for the shortfall in free or cheap labor after outlawing slavery in the Atlantic (Tinker 1992). During the storm, the indentured laborers are thrown about violently as the ship tosses, their chests coming loose so that their hard-won earnings become hopelessly confused (Conrad [1902] 2008: 52). In *Lord Jim*, the remarkable occurrence of striking a submerged object in a clear sea is complicated by the shortage of life boats on which to offload the eight hundred pilgrims, just as the matter of determining the nautical facts of the case in the inquiry is secondary to the fact of native witness, which extends far beyond the crowded courtroom full of lascars. As Marlow recounts, invoking an expanded imperial public, "you heard of it in the harbour office, at every ship-broker's, at your agent's, from whites, from natives, from half-castes, from the very boatmen squatting half naked on the stone steps as you went up" (Conrad [1900] 2008: 27).

However, while Conrad writes the lascars, coolies, and pilgrims, figures of the Indian Ocean world, as the moral center of the story, they are by no means its narrative focus. Ghosh argues for contemporary interest in and attempts to imagine the lives of lascars, as "possibly the first Asians and Africans to participate freely, and in substantial numbers, in a globalized workspace" (2008: 1). He cites—as one of a myriad of examples—the ship's manifest of the *William Stewart*, a vessel that sailed from England to Australia in 1854, and that lists the majority of the crew as lascars (only seven or eight were white sailors, out of a crew of forty-four) (6). They hail from all over what is now South Asia, Arab Africa, Malaysia, and the Philippines—a diversity of origin that, Ghosh suggests, is only surprising when viewed from a land-centric and contemporary perspective. As a postcolonial writer of the sea, Ghosh writes lascar experience—and even lascar language, *laskari*—into his groundbreaking Ibis trilogy, a project in which he cites Melville, rather than Conrad, as a more useful model.

At the start of Melville's *Moby-Dick*, New Bedford is described as populated with "the queerest nondescripts from foreign parts. Regent Street is not unknown to Lascars and Malays; and at Bombay, at the Apollo Green, live Yankees have often scared the natives" (Melville [1851] 2002: 28).[4] There is later in the novel the rarity of these "foreign" sailors being given voice. Along with the French, Icelandic, Maltese, Tahitian, Sicilian and Danish sailors, in "Chapter 40: Harpooners and Sailors," the "China Sailor" and the "Lascar Sailor" each have their lines, in an equivalence of cultural stereotyping (144–5).[5] However, the more substantial engagement with lascar life appears in Melville's novel *Redburn*—a minor moment in a relatively minor work, but significant as a corrective to the dominant representation of the world's sailors. The narrator, a novice sailor from New York who has undertaken his first transatlantic voyage and arrived in the bustling port of Liverpool, finds that his interest is most engaged by encountering sailors from the next ocean on, the Indian Ocean.

> Among the various ships lying in Prince's Dock, none interested me more than the Irrawaddy, of Bombay, a *"country ship,"* which is the name bestowed by Europeans upon the large native vessels of India. Forty years ago, these merchantmen were nearly the largest in the world; and they still exceed the generality.
>
> ([1849] 1969: 170)

The ship from Bombay begins the opening sentence as a curiosity and ends as a symbol of an alternative maritime world, which, even if dominated at this time by British sea power, points to a pre- or coexisting Indian maritime culture.

The ship is manned by "native seamen," some forty or fifty lascars, and built by native shipwrights of India (170).

While the narrator is not immune from racist discourse, describing how the lascars, "hopped about aloft, chattering like so many monkeys" (172), he shifts quickly to an emphasis on a shared seamanship, what Margaret Cohen calls, following Conrad, "craft" (2010: 4, 58). The passage comments with revealing irony on more insidious forms of racist thought, by noting that a young English cabin boy speaks of the death of seven lascars as a "farmer would about the loss of so many sheep from a murrain," and how "old women with umbrellas" come to the quay to stare at the lascars, "even when they desired

FIGURE 7.5 William Lionel Wyllie (1851–1931), *Lascars Manning the Sails*. Watercolour. © The National Maritime Museum, Greenwich, London.

to be private" (Melville [1849] 1969: 171). But the spectators—who "regard the strange sailors as a species of wild animal, whom they might gaze at with as much impunity, as at leopards in the Zoological Gardens" (171)—are watched in turn by the narrator, presented to the reader as the stranger of the two and most in error. The narrator himself responds to strangeness with curiosity; for him, the lascar he encounters is primarily a fellow smoker. They sit to smoke and talk, a conversation so lengthy that he complains of there being no room in the narrative to describe all the topics they covered. Rather than a horror, it is a "Godsend to fall in with a fellow like this," who could add considerably to a sailor's stock of knowledge (172). Their shared humanity is highlighted by their shared craft: the lascar, when above in the rigging, demonstrates the kind of embodied skill known as "sea legs"; he reveals his "compleat" knowledge by detailing precisely the method for making the rigging; and so on (Cohen 2010: 20, 37).

Craft in this sense, however, is a characteristic of the age of sail. The fact that Jim's dereliction is so inexplicable to Marlow stems not only from its exposure of increasingly untenable imperial hypocrisies but also a fundamental historical shift in the technologies of seafaring:

> There is a historical explanation for Marlow's inability to make sense of Jim's obscurity. Jim is the bearer of a message Marlow does not want to hear, but Jim is its symptom rather than its cause. There is no spark of glamour illuminating Jim because craft has disappeared. It has, however, disappeared at the level of a historical conjuncture, rather than as a circumstance specific to Jim's personality.
>
> (Cohen 2010: 207)

The large teams of men needed to man sailing ships produced both the communities of a global maritime labor market, including diverse lascar crews, and their shared knowledge and skill in arts of seamanship and navigation. By mid-century, however, the age of sail was giving over to the age of steam, and its eventual dominance might explain the fading of the ocean from cultural production in the twentieth century. Conrad's elegiac description of sailing ships in *The Mirror of the Sea*—the successor to *Lord Jim* (Cohen 2010: 208)—points to a technology engaged with its medium, and therefore both an art and a science. Steamship travel is divorced from the winds and currents, no longer subject to the vicissitudes of the sea, and therefore no longer requiring language-assisted teamwork—even across racial divides.

However, while coal makes steamships largely independent of the sea's power, they also are unable to make use of that power in moments of breakdown. The power and vulnerability of the sea remain in fact very much in play, as do the "human elements" that it draws together. The next section begins with another story of a steamship, in Conrad's "Falk," which introduces maritime images of breakdown and drifting, of both ships and men.

DRIFTERS

Lascars and other characters from diverse communities across the Indian Ocean world are brought together onboard ship as minor characters in these Eurocentered narratives—despite being often numerically in the majority and representative of a coexisting world of South–South maritime trade and travel. But this decentered mode of reading also highlights alternative aspects of the main characters themselves, who—largely white, male, of European origin—reveal a shadowy underside to glorified imperial itineraries. The sea, as the theater not only of empire but its various underworlds, also provides the images of drifting and beaching that represent these listless lives. For while the sea is the key means and metaphor for imperial expansion in the nineteenth century, it is also, in its literary representation, the imaginative site for counternarratives to progress. Imperialism demanded a set of bold voyages out from the metropole and the return of vessels loaded with wealth. This is reflected in the structure of sea adventure fiction, in which a hero ventures out and is tested in a maritime context, eventually returning home with newfound wisdom or wealth—for instance, Jack London's *Sea Wolf* (1904), Henry Dana's *Two Years Before the Mast* (1840), or even Rudyard Kipling's *Captains Courageous* (1897). But significant late nineteenth-century and early modernist tales are rather of aimless wandering, lostness, failure, and death (Peck 2001: 166). In *Moby-Dick* the clear financial motive for a whaling voyage is superseded by the vengeful whim of the Captain, following a single whale's path in a largely pointless and ultimately fatal mission.[6] Similarly, in Conrad's writing and the late work of Robert Louis Stevenson, as discussed below, sea adventure fiction is invoked but undermined: challenges invariably defeat the hero, puzzles remain unexplained, and there is no triumphant return. Rather, characters drift onwards from place to place, sometimes washing up on far-flung beaches like so much imperial flotsam, as wanderers, drifters, or beachcombers.

In Conrad's short story "Falk," a steamship breaks down and, with no capacity to harness the power of the wind, drifts aimlessly on the currents further and further south. The story up until that point has been a slightly labored romance, a domestic tale set in a nominally maritime context. Falk is a pilot employed to guide ships up to the river harbor in which the narrator and several other captains are at anchor. He falls in love with the niece of a Dutch captain in port, but puts off asking for her hand until he has confessed a mysterious past crime. After all the procrastinations and delays—the bulk of the story—Falk's admission of cannibalism, "in his ordinary voice," is a shock (Conrad [1903] 2008: 129). The narrative opens suddenly out onto the high seas, sweeping the tale into the Southern Ocean (Lavery 2020b: 312). Importantly, the cause of the crime "'was no shipwreck,'" as Falk forcefully asserts (134). The narrator is initially confused, having assumed that Falk and his crewmates would have been starving in boats or a raft, as would have been familiar from so many tales of shipwreck. Instead, Falk asserts, it was a "break down" (134). A shipwreck is the kind of disaster likely to befall a sailing ship, while only steam powered vessels are subject to break down.[7] With the ship's only internal means of powering itself incapacitated, there is nothing at all to be done, no artful harnessing of the elements to effect a rescue and just as importantly no communal task around which to rally the crew. As the formerly purposeful, predictable steamship is left to drift with the currents, the crew drifts into lethargy, starvation, and finally over the border of civilization into cannibalism.

In *The Mirror of the Sea*, Conrad describes the track of a similarly disabled and drifting ship. A steamer, likewise on her way to New Zealand, loses her propeller in the southern Indian Ocean, so that "from her stubborn, arrogant existence she passed all at once into the passive state of a drifting log" ([1906] 1924: 78). The steamer is disabled all on its own rather than through a battle with the elements, revealing a tragicomic disconnection with the medium through which it travels. This is, for Conrad, a comeuppance for having gone on "in disregard of wind and wave," emitting black smoke; now, the ocean in turn disregards the steamer, as it drifts into the wildest ocean. Later on, Conrad is treated to a birds-eye, synchronic image of that journey:

> The track she had made when drifting while her heart stood still within her iron ribs looked like a tangled thread on the white paper of the chart. It was shown to me by a friend, her second officer. In that surprising tangle there were words in minute letters—"gales," "thick fog," "ice"—written by him here and there as memoranda of the weather. She had interminably turned upon her tracks, she had crossed and recrossed her haphazard path till it resembled nothing so much as a puzzling maze of pencilled lines without a meaning.
>
> ([1906] 1924: 78)

The laying out of a ship's track by using positions determined on successive days underlies the spatiotemporal technology of the chart, and corresponds to the link between space and time established by the narrative structure of the novel (Foulke 2002: 74). But in this track of a drifting ship, the inscriptions of weather are the only reminders of the usual orderliness of a ship's chart. Instead, this is a "puzzling maze" and "tangled thread," its nonlinear form reflecting a subjection to wind and current and otherwise "without a meaning."

In that tangled track there can be no reflected history of linear imperial progress or, in a parallel between the lives of characters and fictional direction, no teleological *Bildung* of character maturation. Drifting ships are matched by drifter lives in this sea fiction. The maritime characters who form the bulk of Conrad's interest are described most explicitly in "Travel," the preface to Richard Curle's *Into the East*:

What about mere wanderers?—those individuals that one meets in various fairly well known localities, but who come upon one round unexpected corners, often shabby and depressed, sometimes haggard and jaunty, with tales in their mouths of the flattest description or of a comic quality bordering on tears; with, now and then, a story that would frighten you to death if you were one of those men who don't know how to smile in time. I would class them as an outcast tribe if it did not sound so rude.

(Conrad 1926: 66)

These "mere wanderers" are the shadow side of the ideal imperialist, a contrastingly competent and authoritative figure. They are outcast from the purposive community of imperial sailors; theirs is a kind of *flanerie*, but played out on an oceanic rather than an urban scale, and leading to cannibalism rather than discovery (Hayes 2007: 34). Their itineraries are not vectors imagined as straight lines, but, like broken-down ships, they travel in curves, zigzags, and circles, like Nielsen of "Freya of the Seven Isles" who is described as "trading and sailing in all directions through the Eastern Archipelago, across and around, transversely, diagonally, perpendicularly, in semi-circles, and zigzags, and figures of eights, for years and years" (Conrad 1912: 57). The haphazard itineraries of wanderers create the effect of a complicated and congested cobweb—a lateral maritime network that entraps as much as it connects.

The beach is where all drifting flotsam from circulating currents eventually washes up. The word "beachcomber" is first used by Dana and then Melville when he tells his readers that *Omoo*, the unusual-sounding word he chose for the title of his second novel, comes from the dialect of the Marquesas Islands and means "a rover, or rather, a person wandering from one island to another" (Hayes 2007: 34).[8] Drifters, wanderers, beachcombers: all are represented either as those who have given up even the minimum of imperial morality to become the worst of criminals—one thinks of Kurtz and Gentleman Brown— or, as those who have refused its exclusionary categorizations in favor of a more egalitarian set of relations, however relative; perhaps Jim at the end, Stein in moments, and even in some ways Falk, who is shunned by his white fellows for having a lascar crew and a vegetarian cook from Madras (Conrad [1903] 2008: 97).

Robert Louis Stevenson, himself a wanderer across the Pacific due to his health but also perhaps temperament, became at the end of these travels and toward the end of his life a narrator of sea tales highlighting imperial drifters whose passivity shades into cruelty. Thus, among other stories in *South Sea Tales* (1894), "The Ebb-Tide" evokes both the viciousness as well as the haplessness of empire, in which "scattered men of many European races and from almost every grade of society carry activity and disseminate disease" (Stevenson [1870] 2008: 123). The story centers on three men who are "on the beach," a "telling

South Sea phrase" that designates both their location and their state (123). All three have changed their names, deserted their families at home, and live by charity or crime. Their plot to steal a smallpox-ridden ship is foiled by a prior fraud committed by its former officers—the stolen cases of champagne are discovered to have been deceitfully filled with water—portraying imperial trade as a tissue of layers of criminality (178). The beachcombers, in addition to being inept in their attempted crime, are ignorant and negligent mariners, and find themselves forced by a shortage of food upon an island where a strange missionary, Attwater, gives them a reluctant welcome. The motley crew discovers that the mysterious island has been kept hidden, its details imprecise on the charts, because it is a valuable pearl fishery. Attwater came upon it by chance, and has managed it for ten years by forcing Polynesian divers to work as slaves (216). Like Jim, Attwater is white, authoritative, clear-eyed, described as a perfect specimen of an imperial subject; but soon this veneer too is stripped away, revealing only a maniacal slaver.

Stevenson's writing has produced a powerful association between the figure of the beachcomber and the Pacific, as though the quality of this particular figure was a product of geography rather than empire. But the beachcomber qualities of maritime mixing and aimless criminality can be applied to a critique of empire more widely, across comparative oceanic geographies. This view of Stevenson is shaped by the gaze thrown back on the age of empire by Zanzibari author Abdulrazak Gurnah, whose historical fiction connects the Pacific with the Indian Ocean, gathering together drifter-figures into an under-acknowledged imperial underworld. His novel *Desertion*, set in east Africa in the nineteenth century, centers on a series of characters whose lives are given shape by maritime travel, although this fluidity leads less to adventure and discovery than to loss, violence, and abandonment. In *Desertion*, a British officer on the Kenyan coast, Frederick Turner, invokes beachcombers when he describes the bedraggled appearance of a white stranger who has been rescued by locals: he had the "look of a beachcomber, an educated idler, one of those R.L. Stevenson South Sea ruins, especially with the bare feet and the straggly beard on him" (2005: 48). Gurnah highlights the dominance of a Pacific genealogy of beachcombing and drifting that he draws into this Indian Ocean literary world: "Those chaps in R.L. Stevenson who abandon ship for a bit of a fling with the native girls. Or am I thinking of Melville again? But R.L.S. has plenty of beachcombers as well" (2005: 93; see Lavery 2017).

For Gurnah, however, recentering the drifter or beachcomber figure in an Indian Ocean context allows for subtle shifts in characterization. One is a decoupling of the relationship between beachcombing and whiteness, a deracialization that troubles the imperial divide represented by the beach. In *Desertion*, the character of Hassanali is a Muslim sailor from India who settles in Kenya. From the point of view of his homeland, he is merely an unreturned wander, known in India as "the young man who went away to the black coast and never returned" (Gurnah 2005: 60). However, his is a positive choice to marry and settle, and he explains his cross-cultural migration by invoking the capaciousness of *dar-al-Islam* (the house of Islam). On the morally darker side too are characters such as Azad, who abandons his wife in an act of cruel desertion that reverberates through several generations (60). Another shift in emphasis is the linking of the imperial beachcomber figure with environmental destruction. The white stranger whose bedraggled appearance earns him a beachcomber reference at the start, had been part of a hunting expedition that began by sailing from Aden to Brava and ended in four weeks of "slaughtering our way across Southern Somalia," killing "as many as four or five lions in a day, and leopards and rhino and antelope," an imperial act of "unbearable destruction" (52). Here the desertion of the title is linked also to desertification, the wasting of multispecies life.

Rereading Stevenson's novella in the light of *Desertion* draws out the violence perpetrated on the silent pearl-fishing slaves and "kanaka" crew, while the pearl fishery itself points to a wider ocean-ecological violence. At the start of part 2, Herrick, the Oxford-educated wastrel, looks down from the boat into the lagoon, where "below, in the transparent chamber of waters, a myriad of many-coloured fishes were sporting, a myriad pale flowers of coral diversified the floor" (Stevenson [1870] 2008: 188). The seafloor view foreshadows his later attempt to commit suicide by intentional drowning, a task that, unlike Brierly, he fails to complete. Later, Attwater takes him to see the diving-shed, which contains a "large display of apparatus, neatly ordered: pumps and pipes, and the leaded boots, and the huge snouted helmets shining in rows along the wall; ten complete outfits" (202). Attwater describes the suited divers as "marine monsters" who "kept appearing and reappearing in the midst of the lagoon," their diving suits a metaphor for either self-conceit (Herrick's guess) or God's grace (Attwater's) (202) (Figure 7.6). Attwater has become immensely wealthy because "I have had as many as ten divers going all day long; and I went further than people usually do in these waters, for I rotted a lot of shell" (202).[9] The sentence draws together the human oppression of forced labor with the ecological destruction of rotting oysters, thereby connecting the lateral contact zone of the beach and the vertical contact zone of the sea surface. The rotted oysters on Stevenson's slave-run, ecologically demolished island are the doubly silenced backdrop to the surface story of cruelty and greed. They remind us that drifting ships and drifter characters are overwhelmed in number by the real drifters of the sea, the plankton which are famously addressed in Melville's chapter "Brit." Pearls and plankton, diving and drowning—these point to an ecological submarine kingdom that is the last of the underworlds to be explored here.

FIGURE 7.6 "Divers Preparing for Work," from *The Illustrated London News*, 1873—becoming the "marine monsters" of Stevenson's story. © Wikimedia Commons (public domain).

AQUANAUTS

The transition from sail to steam is marked not only by a paradoxical interest in the less predictable journeys of sailing ships but also by an incipient awareness of the environmental costs of such overweening speed and certainty. Conrad evokes the relative cleanliness and sustainability of sailing ships in *The Mirror of the Sea*, while *Moby-Dick* is at least partly an account of unchecked plunder of a scarce resource (a kind of peak whale oil) and the danger of extinction (Rozwadowski 2005: 31). What emerges from these anxieties is a glimpse of the sea itself, as a thing not only of vastness and power, but also of finitude and vulnerability. This is for the most part a haunting presence, as the deep sea is so little understood and out of sight as to be largely ignored. Until, for instance, that object strikes the *Patna* on an otherwise calm sea in the dead of night, figuring the incursion of the deep sea into the surface maritime world of the narrative. We return to this moment here in the final section.

The narrator of *Lord Jim* sets up the incursion of the marine depths early in the novel. In a dreamy but foreboding passage, the Indian Ocean is described, typically, as calm, warm and easy. Jim looks to the pencil line drawn on the ship's chart that is used to log its progress.

> From time to time he glanced idly at a chart pegged out with four drawing-pins on a low three-legged table abaft the steering-gear case. The sheet of paper portraying *the depths of the sea presented a shiny surface* under the light of a bulls-eye lamp lashed to a stanchion, a surface as level and smooth as the glimmering surface of the waters.
>
> (Conrad [1900] 2008: 76, my emphasis)

The chart both suggests the opaque surface of the sea, with its level smoothness, and also belies it by portraying the three-dimensional ocean below. The presence of the bathymetrical chart, portraying the depths of the sea, is a grim reminder of the volumes of underlying water into which the rickety steamship is nearly to sink.

Interest in the deep sea grew rapidly during the nineteenth century until by 1900 the sea was no longer a "blank space," like the central Africa of the maps of Conrad's boyhood, but a basin with knowable characteristics (Rozwadowski 2005: 4, 73). Primary among these was its depth. Before the mid-nineteenth century the ocean's depth was unknown, with soundings used only to rule out shallowness for navigational purposes (33). Melville calls it the "bottomless deep" (Melville [1851] 2002: 57)—and for much of this era he is not wrong. For some time the most extreme estimates were made by whalers, which also turned out to be the most accurate (Rozwadowski 2005: 4). Answers about the depth of the ocean were finally motivated by the profitable potential of transoceanic telegraphs, along with their military and political possibilities. Matthew Fontaine Maury published the first contour map of the North Atlantic as part of *The Physical Geography of the Sea* in 1855. The imaginative possibilities of the deep ocean were explored in fiction, too. R.M. Ballantyne, adventure fiction writer, wrote *The Battery and the Boiler*, subtitled *Adventures in Laying of Submarine Electric Cables* (1883), based on W.H. Russell's 1865 *The Atlantic Telegraph* as well as J.C. Parkinson's 1870 *The Ocean Telegraph to India* (see Shelangoskie 2017: 92). Hans Christian Andersen's last fairy tale is called "The Great Sea Serpent" (1872), and describes the laying of a telegraph cable from the perspective of fish and whales. Jules Verne's *Twenty Thousand Leagues Under the Sea* ([1870] 2017) was inspired by a voyage on the *Great Eastern*, which laid both the transatlantic and the Indian Ocean cables (Rozwadowski 2005: 27). Telegraph cables and whaling both also provided the first hints that life could be found in the darker and deeper parts of the sea, beyond the reach of sunlight and at the immense pressures that had made it seem impossible. Whalers consistently reported whales diving to great depths as measured by harpoon lines, and telegraph cables brought up for repair were found to be encrusted with marine life (Rozwadowski 2005: 44–5) (Figure 7.7). Telegraphy is interlinked with literary soundings of the depth of the ocean, whether through extrapolation beyond the limits of science, as in Verne, or as an exploration of the edges of ignorance, as in Conrad.

The first submarine cable was the transatlantic laid by John Pender on the *Great Eastern* in 1866. Hardly less experimental, the second submarine telegraph cable ever to be laid was the Indian Ocean cable, when the British Indian Submarine Telegraph Company connected Suez via Aden to Bombay, a line completed only four years later in 1870 (Huurdeman 2003: 136). An Extension

FIGURE 7.7 A piece of the 1873 submarine telegraph cable, encrusted with marine life. © Science & Society Picture Library/Getty Images.

Company continued the link overland to Madras (present-day Chennai) and then again as a submarine cable to the Malaysian peninsula, with landing points at Penang, Malacca, and Singapore, where the cable arrived in 1871 (136).[10] Jim's initial journeys in the novel follow this route very closely, as noted earlier. The telegraph arrived ahead of the deserting officers, bringing the news of the abandoned but still-floating *Patna* to the notice of the maritime community, who traveled more slowly on their rescuing ship. The telegraph cable as a plot point functions by this asynchronicity, the difference in time it takes for information to travel from one end of the Indian Ocean to the other, via ship and telegraph, respectively. The various landing points of the extension cable mirror Jim's harbors on his eastward flight, as he tries to stay ahead of gossip about his *Patna* shame, "known successively in Bombay, in Calcutta, in Rangoon, in Penang, in Batavia" (Conrad [1900] 2008: 4). Marlow's invocation of slipping beneath the surface of the sea as a metaphor for existential uncertainty, at the end of the novel, is therefore matched by these underwater material correlates, submarine telegraph cable and submerged wreck.

Moby-Dick is more conspicuously cognisant of the materiality of the deep sea, conveying, in a way that is unusual even in sea fiction, a rich sense of the sea itself (Peck 2001: 115). While the novel is from the first "launched upon the deep," at the start of the "Cetology" chapter it becomes "lost in its unshored harbourless immensities" (Melville [1851] 2002: 109). Blum suggests that this first line "inaugurates a shift in the novel's setting from the land or coastal shelf to the open sea," where it remains, remarkably, for the rest of the novel (2014: 10). *Redburn*, in contrast, is set on a merchant ship, and is more concerned with the ship as a microcosm of life on land than with the sea that flows beneath. Most types of ship—merchant, military, even pirate—are, as Conrad also shows, extensions of the land. This gives the whaling ship, and the whaling novel, a peculiarly oceanic character. As Melville himself asserts, out of all the many kinds of maritime vessels, "it is only whaling ships which seek to draw their living from the bottomless deep itself" ([1851] 2002: 55). Whalers live out on the ocean during much of the nineteenth century, whereas until the late eighteenth century whaling was conducted mostly from bases on shore (Rozwadowski 2005: 42).

In Melville just as in Conrad, there is no innocence to the depiction of dark, unknown, and dangerous depths, mirroring from below the colonial construction of terra nullius. The growth in interest in the deep sea in the nineteenth century is an expression of the extension of the imperial frontier in a new, vertical direction, along with other frontiers such as the polar regions (Cohen 2010: 49–51, Rozwadowski 2005: 29). In *Moby-Dick*, whaling is explicitly entangled with a representation of maritime empire. While the novel's lascar characters and cosmopolitan crews point to the lateral expansions of empire, its depiction of whaling is a prescient representation of vertical, environmental imperialism.[11]

Melville explicitly compares imperial political and military conquests on land to the ecological conquest of the oceans:

> Let America add Mexico to Texas, and pile Cuba upon Canada; let the English overswarm all India, and hang out their blazing banner from the sun; two thirds of this terraqueous globe are the Nantucketer's. For the sea is his; he owns it as the Emperors own empires; other seamen having but a right of way through it.
>
> (Melville [1851] 2002: 54)

The Nantucketers, those "sea-hermits," have colonized the "watery world" (54). But the comparison goes the other way too. The bloodiness and slaughter of whaling reflect the bloody military conquests of EuroAmerican empire, such that imperialism is represented as violent conquest and war rather than by the apologetics of paternalism. In gruesome interspecies metaphor, Ishmael comments on the hypocrisy of a peace-loving Quaker being able to justify a career in whaling: "Though refusing, from conscientious scruples, to bear arms against land invaders, yet himself had illimitably invaded the Atlantic and Pacific; and though a sworn foe to human bloodshed, yet had he in his straight-bodied coat, spilled tuns upon tuns of leviathan gore" (Melville [1851] 2002: 64).

New Bedford's status as an implausible city of wealth is premised on this bloody conquest of the deep. The wild and scraggy coast somehow hosts a town known for its opulent houses and gardens, its brilliant weddings. Unfit for agriculture with its scouring wind and poor soil, New Bedford is instead a "land of oil" (Melville [1851] 2002: 29). Melville makes the stark material point that "all the brave houses and flowery gardens came from the Atlantic, Pacific and Indian Oceans" (29). It is an oil-wealth that was "dragged up hither from the bottom of the sea" (29). Nevertheless, the bottom of the sea remains mostly a mystery, encountered only indirectly through the lengths of a harpoon line.

Jules Verne, finally, takes a perspective on the submarine world that is not indirect at all, but dives directly beneath the waves. The novel follows the aquanaut Captain Nemo and the trapped narrator Pierre Aronnax on a scientifically informed journey around the world's deep oceans. Their journey on a near-futuristic submarine, *The Nautilus*, follows many of the conventions of adventure fiction, although it turns these toward a new, submarine frontier. This is signaled at the start by the narrator's role as a marine scientist who is working on "a two-volume in-quarto work entitled *The Mysteries of the Great Ocean Depths*"—a mirror of the two-part, mystery-filled novel (Verne [1870] 2017: 3). The novel, while taking a more conservative approach to narrative structure by keeping close to the traditions of sea adventure fiction and avoiding the oceanic forms pioneered by Conrad and Melville, is experimental in other ways. Primarily, it is unusual for taking a fully submarine perspective, directly apprehending the three dimensions of the sea by deploying cutting-edge nineteenth-century marine science.

Still, Verne's emphasis on the material submarine does not preclude the political. In the sequel, *The Mysterious Island,* Verne reveals that Nemo is Prince Dakkar, driven from land by the British murder of his family and destruction of his society in the Rebellion of 1857. Like the lascars, coolies, pilgrims, and pearl divers, the most advanced and well-known aquanaut of nineteenth-century literature is also a non-European oceanic traveler, with Indian Ocean origins. Similarly, the main focus of the *Nautilus*'s Indian Ocean sojourn is an extended sequence about pearl diving. The fantastical dive of the *Nautilus* finds here its more humble precedents, in the practice of unaided human free-diving, as the submarine halts just off the coast of Ceylon (present-day Sri Lanka), "that pearl hanging from the earlobe of the Indian subcontinent" (Verne [1870] 2017: 3). Even though it is early in the season, the visiting party is able to watch the activities of a single diver, "a living man, an Indian, a Black—a poor devil of a diver no doubt" (3). The Captain exclaims, "That Indian, professor, is the inhabitant of an oppressed country. I am his compatriot, and shall remain so to my very last breath!" (3). Aronnax describes the scene in terms of visibility and imaginability: "The diver did not see us. We were hidden by the shadow of a rock. And besides, how could this poor Indian imagine that beings like himself were underwater watching his every movement, not losing a single detail of his fishing?" (3). "Beings like himself" suggests the ambiguous "one of us" from Conrad—here all divers, all human, all men. But unequal visibility is reflected in unequal imaginability, as the "poor devil" cannot imagine the technological advances of the diving-suited observers.

If Conrad and Melville accurately depict ignorance about the submarine world, Verne proceeds by filling in the gaps in scientific knowledge by extrapolating from existing facts in vivid visualizations. The underwater forest of Crespo, for instance, is a preternatural realm of bright colors and strange shapes (Figure 7.8). It also exemplifies the strange verticality of a submarine perspective:

> None of the grasses carpeting the ground, none of the branches multiplying on the shrubs crept or drooped, and none stretch out horizontally. All rose towards the surface. There was not a single filament, not a single blade, however thin, which did not stand up as straight as iron stalks. The wracks and creepers grew in rigid perpendicular lines determined by the density of the element that had given them birth. The plants were motionless, but when I shifted them with my hand, they immediately moved back to their original positions. It was the realm of the vertical.
>
> (Verne [1870] 2017: 3)

The verticality of this biological regime is reflected by similarly vertical layers of submarine history. For the observers aboard the *Nautilus* the ocean is littered with the remains of maritime histories, shipwrecks that float and settle at various depths: "we often sighted sunken hulls, completely rotten and hanging in the water, or, deeper, cannons, cannonballs, anchors, chains, and a thousand other

FIGURE 7.8 The vertical structure of the submarine world, as in this illustration of "Hunting in underwater forests of Crespo," engraving after a drawing by Alphonse de Neuville and Edouard Riou, from Jules Verne, *Twenty Thousand Leagues Under the Sea* (1870). © De Agostini Picture Library/Getty Images.

iron objects being devoured by rust" (3). Part 2 of the novel begins with "Chapter 1: The Indian Ocean," as the *Nautilus* crosses "a vast liquid plain covering 550 million hectares, with waters so transparent that anyone looking down from the surface feels dizzy" (3). The ocean introduces a sense of enormous scale, in both directions, producing a kind of oceanic vertigo.

The vertiginous effects of oceanic apprehension might be summed up in Aronnax's observation that "on the surface of the sea, your chief sensation is the constant feeling of an underlying chasm." The effect is relatively abstract for Aronnax and fleeting for Marlow, but for the young Black boy of Melville's *Moby-Dick*, Pip, it is annihilating. Pip, left behind after jumping in terror from the harpooner Stubb's boat, becomes "another lonely castaway" on the "shoreless ocean" (Melville [1849] 1969: 390). The sea is calm enough that he is able to stay afloat until his rescue, but although the "sea had kept his finite body up" it had "drowned the infinite of his soul":

> Not drowned entirely, though. Rather carried down alive to wondrous depths, where strange shapes of the unwarped primal world glided to and fro before his passive eyes; and the miser-merman, Wisdom, revealed his hoarded heaps; and the multitudinous, God-omnipresent, coral insects, that out of the firmament of waters heaved the colossal orbs. He saw God's foot upon the treadle of the loom, and spoke it; and therefore his shipmates called him mad.
>
> (390)

The passage merges Verne's material with Conrad's metaphoric sense of the sea, linked by Pip's sea-level perspective also to a racialized maritime imperialism.

CONCLUSION

We return at the end to the moment of encounter between Marlow and Jewel with which we started, a moment of disturbing cross-racial encounter that is imagined in terms of sinking into the unknown depths of the sea. While Marlow recovers quite quickly from this momentary existential panic—unlike Brierly whose mysterious existential malady ends in a gesture of fatal immersion, or Pip whose experience of submersion results in madness—the immanent metaphorics of that passage echo back through the novel as a whole, and outward, as has been shown, to the wider representations of the sea in nineteenth-century fiction. The superficiality of Jim's racially perfect looks and the insidious cowardice of his deeper character are described by Marlow in another well-known phrase: "I would have trusted the deck to that youngster on the strength of a single glance, and gone to sleep with both eyes—and, by Jove! It wouldn't have been safe. There are depths of horror in that thought" (Conrad [1900] 2008: 34). The depths of the waters, a persistent metaphor for disorienting fluidity, is connected sonically to the depths of horror that arise from Jim's failure to protect the pilgrims—inhabitants of an underlying Indian Ocean maritime world, along with lascars and indentured laborers. Furthermore, if *Lord Jim* can be read, as V.S. Naipaul suggests, as a novel about the theme of a "racial straggler" (1974), then the sea is not only the medium for a callous maritime imperialism but also the metaphor for those figures that give the lie to its racist hierarchies, its stragglers, failures, and drifters. Finally, the sea, with its submarine inhabitants, its pearl oysters, and whales, is represented as the victim of ecological imperialism.

The sea's representation in this oceanic century is, like the sea itself, shaped by eddies, countercurrents, submerged and invisible seamounts. Reading Conrad and Melville, as well as Stevenson, Verne, and others, in light of the Indian Ocean interests of later, postcolonial writers, we see hints of underlying worlds that complicate and color the oceanic picture. The ocean's well-established, unparalleled cosmopolitanism in the nineteenth century can be widened to include a greater number of non-European characters whose lives are at the center of these oceanic stories. Narratives of imperial control and paternalistic care—persistent even today—should be continually troubled by highlighting the ineptitude, greed, and criminality that make up the greater part of the story. Further, the ocean itself, in its three-dimensional depths and multispecies life, can shed luminescent and variegated light on all of this.

CHAPTER EIGHT

Imaginary Worlds

Sea of Ink

CANNON SCHMITT

The sea has long served as the locus of imaginary worlds—as something to speculate on, meditate over, fantasize about, lose oneself in. The truth of that claim may be so obvious as to require no evidence. If one were looking, however, a good place to start would be the final paragraph of a 1967 lecture by Michel Foucault titled "Of Other Spaces." "Heterotopias," Foucault calls those spaces, sites set apart from the rest of a society that mirror that society's principles of order, simultaneously reflecting and inverting them. Touching briefly on prisons, cemeteries, gardens, and colonies, the lecture builds to a concluding discussion of "the heterotopia par excellence," the ship (Foucault 1986: 27). Since the Renaissance, Foucault declares, the ship has been "the great instrument of economic development" as well as "the greatest reserve of the imagination": "In civilizations without boats, dreams dry up, espionage takes the place of adventure, and the police take the place of pirates" (27). But of course it isn't really the ship that merits that grand title, "the greatest reserve of the imagination." Although boats may crowd the daydreams of sailors, for them as well as for swimmers, oceanographers, skin divers, surfers, utopianists, explorers, wave scientists, maritime painters, marine biologists, and beachcombers the not at all obscure object of desire is the sea itself.

Add continental philosophers to the list, for Foucault's own lyricism suggests that, even as he awards the distinction to the ship, for him too the paramount imaginary world was and remains salt water. Witness not only his association of boats with dreams and adventure but also his description of the ship as a special kind of place because "closed in on itself and at the same time [...] given over to the infinity of the sea" (27). The infinity of the sea! The phrase echoes across centuries, millennia of human history in which "oceanic" and "limitless" could be used as synonyms. Contemplating that aqueous infinity, Foucault joins innumerable others in adopting what Christopher Connery identifies as a "recurring figure" for the search for knowledge: "the gaze to the ocean from shore: the westerner's confrontation with limits and limitlessness, and with what is fundamentally other than itself" (2006: 506). The sea has been the greatest reserve of the imagination due in large part to this fancied infinitude and otherness. But if we study how the sea was imagined in the nineteenth century, we find something remarkable: it often wasn't conceived of as limitless or other at all. Instead, it was an increasingly finite and known place—accommodating, yes, both economic development and imagination, but somehow also espionage as well as adventure, police as well as pirates. One could go still further: the sea in the nineteenth century was a place of dreams and adventure exactly to the extent that it was also a place of finitude; of practice; of concrete, hard-won knowledge; of operable details.

Consider, as an initial example, a book the existence of which somewhat confounds Foucault's resonant dictum about civilizations without boats: a spy novel in which the main characters spend the bulk of their time at sea. Erskine Childers's *The Riddle of the Sands* (1903) takes place mostly onboard the *Dulcibella*, a nine-meter yawl whose fictional voyages in the Baltic and the North Sea retrace the author's travels in a converted lifeboat named *Vixen*. Novel and life align so closely that sections of *Riddle* reproduce entries in *Vixen*'s log nearly verbatim (Schmitt 2014: 79n57) (Figure 8.1). But Childers, extraordinary as he was (about which more below), did not discover a secret German plan to invade England, as do *Riddle*'s narrator, Carruthers, and his friend, Davies. The centrality of that discovery to its plot makes the novel an early instance of espionage fiction as well as an example of a lesser-known subgenre, invasion fiction, in which Britain is attacked or threatened—often by Germans, as in *Riddle* and George Tomkyns Chesney's *Battle of Dorking* (1871), generally considered the first invasion novel, but sometimes by undead Eastern European nobility, as in Bram Stoker's *Dracula* (1897), or Martians, as in H.G. Wells's *The War of the Worlds* (1898). Compared to other works in both subgenres, *Riddle* stands apart for the pride of place it gives to the ocean: the key site for both espionage and warfare in the novel, its waves, winds, and tides are rendered with an exactitude as loving as it is lavish.

Drawing deeply on a sailor's knowledge and experience, *The Riddle of the Sands* deserves inclusion in any cultural history of the sea. More than simply belonging to such a history, however, Childers's novel contains one in its own pages: the *Dulcibella* has a library, and every item in that library concerns the

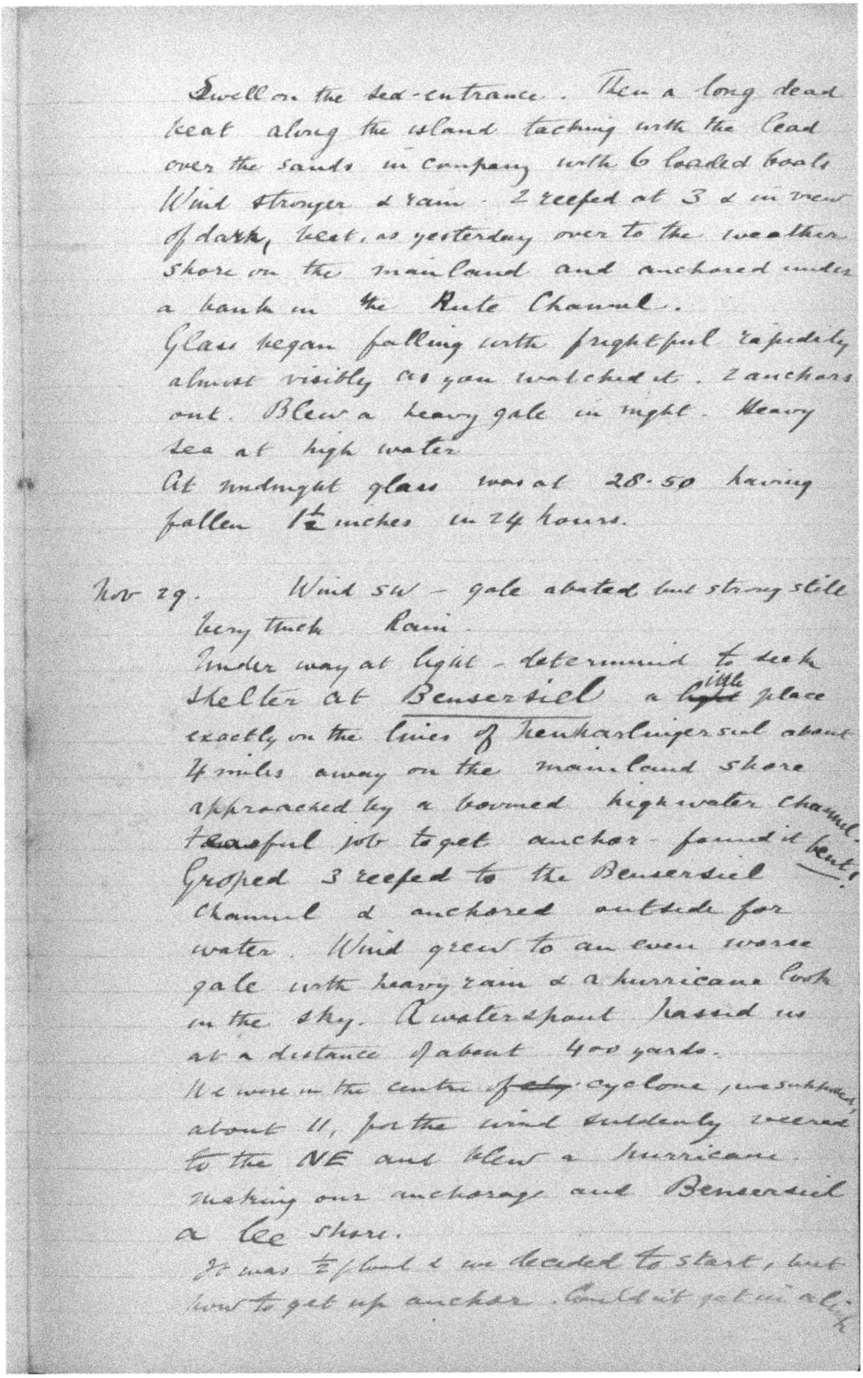

IMAGINARY WORLDS

> Swell on the sea-entrance. Then a long dead beat along the island tacking with the lead over the sands in company with 6 loaded boats. Wind stronger & rain. 2 reefed at 3 & in view of dark, beat, as yesterday over to the weather shore on the mainland and anchored under a bank in the Rute Channel.
>
> Glass began falling with frightful rapidity almost visibly as you watched it. 2 anchors out. Blew a heavy gale in night. Heavy sea at high water.
>
> At midnight glass was at 28.50 having fallen 1½ inches in 24 hours.
>
> Nov 29. Wind SW – gale abated, but strong still. Very thick rain.
>
> Under way at light – determined to seek shelter at Benzersiel a little place exactly on the lines of Neuharlingersiel about 4 miles away on the mainland shore approached by a boomed high-water channel. Fearful job to get anchor – found it bent. Groped 3 reefed to the Benzersiel channel & anchored outside for water. Wind grew to an even worse gale with heavy rain & a hurricane look in the sky. A waterspout passed us at a distance of about 400 yards.
>
> We were in the centre of the cyclone, we supposed, about 11, for the wind suddenly veered to the NE and blew a hurricane making our anchorage and Benzersiel a lee shore.
>
> It was tj hard & we decided to start, but how to get up anchor. Could it get in at

FIGURE 8.1 Extract from Erskine Childers's *Vixen* log, November 29, 1897. © National Maritime Museum, Greenwich, London and the Royal Cruising Club.

sea. Readers first learn about the books onboard when Carruthers narrates a scene in which Davies "pull[s] down (in two pieces) a volume of Mahan's *Influence of Sea Power*" from a shelf attached to the forward bulkhead:

> I had not hitherto paid attention to the medley on our bookshelf, but I now saw that, besides a Nautical Almanack and some dilapidated *Sailing Directions*, there were several books on the cruises of small yachts, and also some big volumes crushed in anyhow or lying on the top. Squinting painfully at them I saw Mahan's *Life of Nelson*, Brassey's *Naval Annual*, and others.
> (Childers [1903] 2011: 42–3)

We are not told which almanac or sailing directions, and Carruthers waits until a later chapter to itemize some of those "books on the cruises of small yachts." That leaves three titles: Alfred Thayer Mahan's *The Influence of Sea Power Upon History* (1890), which, as its preface states, "is an examination of the general history of Europe and America with particular reference to the effect of sea power upon the course of that history" (iii); Mahan's *Life of Nelson* (1897), a biography of the preeminent English naval hero of the Napoleonic Wars, Vice Admiral Horatio Nelson; and a volume of Brassey's *Naval Annual*, a yearly omnibus of facts and figures pertaining to British naval vessels, personnel, and preparedness initially edited by Thomas Brassey and first appearing in 1886. There is much to be said about each, but for the moment the key point is that on this fictional bookshelf in a fictional yawl sailed by fictional characters sit actual books—or at least books with titles that encourage readers to take them as representative of actual books. A photograph of the log of *Vixen* illustrates this section of the chapter because no photograph of the log of the *Dulcibella* exists or could exist. Dublin's Glasnevin Cemetery holds Childers's remains, but the graves of Carruthers and Davies are to be found nowhere on earth. Brassey's annuals and Mahan's books of naval history and biography, however, can readily be located, read, and quoted from—as I've quoted from *The Influence of Sea Power Upon History* just above. Like the North Sea through which the *Dulcibella* sails, these books belong to two worlds at once, fictional and factual.

Riddle is far from unusual in this regard: the invented and actually existing commonly coexist in the pages of fiction. The tribulations of Ralph Rover and his friends, the purely imaginary protagonists of R.M. Ballantyne's children's adventure novel *The Coral Island* (1858), take place in a Polynesia visible on any chart of the Pacific. Disko Troop and his schooner, the *We're Here*, belong solely to Rudyard Kipling's *Captains Courageous* (1897), but the Grand Banks off the coast of Newfoundland where they fish for cod are a permanent feature of the North Atlantic Ocean. And so on: the "mixing of fictional and factual elements" in novels, Elaine Freedgood has pointed out, is so familiar, and so "naturalized," that it seems not to need scrutiny (2010: 408). But such mixing can pose thorny problems of reference. For instance, although it would be absurd to draw conclusions about the historical Kaiser Wilhelm II, the ruler of Germany and Prussia during the time the book is set, from the cameo appearance in Childers's novel of a character evidently based on him, *Riddle* almost ceases to be readable if its "Germany" does not in some way correspond to the European nation that bears the same name. As for the books in the library of the *Dulcibella*: because we are given only titles, and for many of them not even that, there would be a certain rigor in limiting discussion to titles alone. But the gambit of this chapter will be to assume that Carruthers's mention of a title brings with it the entirety of the book in question as it exists outside the novel. We *can* locate and read these books—and so I have. Inverting the usual procedure whereby historical context is invoked to interpret fiction, I take the fictional ship's library in *The Riddle of the Sands* as material for a cultural history of the sea in the age of empire.

If that history were comprised of only three books it would be an anemic one. But there are more. Returning to the shelf later in the novel, Carruthers repeats his initial account with a different emphasis and additional specifics: "Davies's library, excluding tide-tables, 'pilots,' etc., was limited to two classes of books, those on naval warfare, and those on his own hobby, cruising in small yachts. He had six or seven of the latter, including Knight's *Falcon in the Baltic* [sic], Cowper's *Sailing Tours,* Macmullen's [sic] *Down Channel*, and other less-known stories of adventurous travel" ([1903] 2011: 179). Like Mahan's biography of Nelson and Brassey's *Naval Annual*, Knight's, Cowper's, and McMullen's books exist both inside and outside the pages of *Riddle*. Moreover, they belong to one category, books about "cruising in small yachts," in a tripartite taxonomy into which everything in the library of the *Dulcibella* may be sorted. Brassey's and Mahan's volumes fit into a second category, books on war at sea. The tide tables and pilots constitute a third, unlabeled by Carruthers but that might be called technical sailing aids. Taken together, these categories and the texts that exemplify them provide a rich, evocative record of the sea in the nineteenth-century imagination.

A record: one of many possible, and far from complete. Even if we consider only what might be found in books and not, say, music, visual arts, ship design, and so on, omissions are immediately evident. Where are the volumes on empire, emigration, trade, fishing, deep-sea exploration? Of course, their absence itself tells us something: the association between the sea and empire, or the sea and any other topic on my list of what has been left out, may have been so commonsensical, so woven into the fabric of existence, that it need not be explicitly invoked. Still, any aspiration to provide something like encyclopedic coverage of the nineteenth-century sea would require supplementing the handful of volumes Carruthers mentions with more titles from additional categories; and not just categories: languages. Apart from a set of German charts, all the printed matter onboard the *Dulcibella* is in English. Further, with the exception of Mahan, an American, all the authors and editors are British. The sea in other tongues, the sea according to other national traditions, goes missing. From the outset, then, it must be acknowledged that any cultural history of the sea derived from the library of the *Dulcibella* will be a partial one.

Encyclopedism, however, has its own shortcomings. The impossibility of total coverage, although among them, is not the most damaging. The more grievous problem has to do with the difficulty of discerning, amongst the welter of details in a would-be complete and even-handed survey, patterns of significance, knots or nodes of denser meaning or greater emphasis. Furthermore, should such knots or nodes even appear, they might well be anachronistic: a testament to what visitors from the future (by which I mean: to what we) find compelling, not what those living at the time obsessed over or were moved by. Carruthers's threefold taxonomy may not provide an exhaustive picture of the sea in the age of empire; it does, however, offer something arguably more needful: evidence of some of the main lines along which the nineteenth-century sea was imagined by contemporaries. The technical sailing aids testify to a sea increasingly known by science: its depths sounded, its hazards charted, its tides predictable. The books on naval warfare indicate a sea that continued to be, as historically, the scene of military conflict, particularly among nation-states vying for regional dominance. Finally, and perhaps most strikingly, the books in the library of the *Dulcibella* on the cruises of small yachts show a sea newly open to individuals: democratized (at least to a certain extent), available as never before as a place to travel for pleasure—and, consequently, as a subject to write about. In what follows I'll take each category in turn, exploring them in themselves and demonstrating the extent to which they implicate one another. To grasp how the library of the *Dulcibella* so eloquently conveys these different facets of a distinctive nineteenth-century imagination of the sea, however, we must first understand the existence and characteristics of onboard libraries as such.

OF SHIPS' LIBRARIES

An ocean-going vessel with a library is a metaphor waiting to happen. But which metaphor? We might say it is a toolbox filled with useful items, like the one Robinson Crusoe rescues from his wrecked ship: "And it was after long searching that I found out the Carpenter's Chest, which was indeed a very useful Prize to me, and much more valuable than a Ship Loading of Gold would have been at that time" (Defoe [1719] 1998: 50). But that requires conceiving of onboard books as tools—which might be accurate for some of them but is certainly not the case for all. In a different register, we could say a ship with a library is a kind of Noah's Ark with books instead of animals saved from the Flood. Unlike on the Ark, however, there is no possibility of carrying two of everything, or even one. No matter how large the vessel, room for books, or tools, or anything at all, is in short supply. As Samuel Johnson famously quipped, "being in a ship is being in a jail, with the chance of being drowned": going to sea means not only danger but also loss of space, privacy, and possessions (Boswell [1791] 1998: 247). Johnson recoiled from such a paring down, but Roland Barthes saw it as the chief pleasure boats have to offer—with the proviso that, to be fully relished, limited shipboard space must be thronging with things: "An inclination for ships always means the joy of perfectly enclosing oneself, of having at hand the greatest possible number of objects, and having at one's disposal an absolutely finite space" ([1957] 1993: 66). The *Nautilus*, Captain Nemo's submarine in Jules Verne's *Twenty Thousand Leagues Under the Sea* (1870), perfectly incarnates the paradox: "the most desirable of all caves," Barthes calls it, but a cave that somehow finds shelf space for twelve thousand volumes of "science, moral philosophy and literature, in many languages," including the scientist-narrator Professor Arronax's own "monograph on the great ocean depths" (Barthes [1957] 1993: 66; Verne [1870] 2017: 81, 89, 87). Powered by electricity, capable of reaching speeds of fifty knots, feeding and clothing its crew only from what may be found in the sea: the *Nautilus* stretches credulity in many of its particulars but perhaps none more so than in boasting an onboard library with so many books.

Outside of the pages of speculative fiction, to stock a library at sea is a matter of extreme parsimony, an earnest variant on that breezy cocktail-party question, "What book would you take with you if you were going to be cast away on a desert island?" The shift from one book (on the island) to several (on a boat) does not much dissipate the intensity of the selective pressure. Nor does it rid the question of its essential point, which is to reveal what the selector most values. Every ship's library is symptomatic: its volumes, a handful selected from myriads, are the distillation of the meaningful and the treasured. Or just the practical, to go back to tools: for if the desert-island question seems intended to elicit answers along the lines of George Eliot's *Middlemarch* (1872) or Marcel Proust's *Du côté de chez Swann* (1913), there is always that contrarian who, deliberately missing the point, replies: the *Boy Scout Handbook*.

Historically, many ships' libraries seem to have been assembled by those of similar mind. Take HMS *Beagle*, aboard which Charles Darwin circumnavigated the globe between 1831 and 1836. John van Wyhe, the editor of Darwin Online, estimates that the *Beagle* library contained 180 works, totaling just over 400 separate volumes, of which 36 percent were travels; 33 percent natural history; 15 percent geology; 7 percent atlases and charts; 3 percent reference; and 2 percent history (Van Wyhe 2002–). Only the remaining 4 percent, categorized as "literature" and including Milton's *Paradise Lost* (1667) and Samuel Richardson's *The History of Charles Grandison* (1781), would seem to allow for George Eliot or Proust (if George Eliot had written anything yet, or Proust been born). But the conclusion to be arrived at may not be that the *Beagle* library made room for the practical at the expense of the treasured. For Darwin as well as for Robert FitzRoy, the *Beagle*'s captain during the voyage, the two were often identical. The question that must be asked becomes: treasured in what way? To put a different interpretation on the choice of the *Boy Scout Handbook*, it may not result from deliberate misconstrual but simply be the answer of a person who values the practical above all else.

It might seem as though all sailors would be such people when choosing the few books scant space on ship allows. As it turns out, however, the *Beagle*'s collection represents one end of a broad spectrum. Other ships' libraries held volumes ranging well beyond sheer practicality, as Harry Skallerup documents in *Books Afloat and Ashore* (1974). Naval vessels such as the *Beagle* were particularly likely to stock titles with immediate pertinence for life at sea, but even they included exceptions. A book list from the US Navy dated 1839, for instance, predictably includes Euclid's *Elements of Geometry* and Nathaniel Bowditch's *Practical Navigator* but also finds room for James Feninore Cooper's *Naval History of the US* (1839) along with four of his maritime novels (Skallerup 1974: 143). In the nineteenth century, both naval and merchant vessels also commonly stocked religious materials, largely due to the efforts of the British and Foreign Sailors' Society and the American Seaman's Friend Society (ASFS). By mid-century the ASFS began assembling and loaning out entire small collections "packed in strong cases with locks and hinges made of brass (so the hardware would not rust)" (Skallerup 1974: 102). The first of these, from 1843, contained fifty books, many with an explicitly Christianizing aim: John Bunyan's *Pilgrim's Progress* (1678), William Paley's *Natural Theology* (1802), and Hannah More's *The Shepherd of Salisbury Plain* (1795), among others (Skallerup 1974: 99).[1] But even those titles that appear to promise entirely secular content often promoted religious views. Edward Hitchcock's *Elementary Geology* (1841), for example, included in the 1843 library, makes the Paleyan argument that from geological facts "we infer the absolute perfection, and especially the immutable wisdom of the Divine character" (1841: 276). Given that sailors did not possess an especially high reputation for piety, if these books were read at all they may have fit into a category not yet anticipated in my treatment of the desert-island question: neither the treasured nor the practical but simply the available.

Ships' libraries, however, provide only a partial glimpse of what titles went to sea. There were also the books seamen themselves brought. "Much of the cheap and popular literature of the day," writes Skallerup, "found its way aboard ships in the sea chests of sailors" (1974: 208). In *The View From the Masthead* (2008), Hester Blum makes precise what some of that literature was: "the novels of Cooper, [Walter] Scott, [Edward] Bulwer-Lytton, Marryat, and [William] Godwin as well as travel narratives, conduct manuals, reform tracts, 'flash' papers, pamphlet novels, and other ephemeral works" (20; see also Blum 2015: 129).² Regardless of how cheap or costly, practical or pious, all printed matter was precious at sea. In *Two Years Before the Mast* (1840), famous for the light it shed on mistreatment of sailors, Richard Henry Dana, Jr. repeatedly demonstrates how much so—compelling readers to add scenes of reading to their imagination of life afloat and to conceive of sailors as possessed of imaginations that, like their own, gravitated to what print has to offer. In one episode the crew of the *Alert*, separated from their chests, can find only a single book among them: Scott's novel *Woodstock* (1826) (Figure 8.2). "As all could not read it at once," writes Dana, "I, being the scholar of the company, was appointed reader. I got a knot of six or eight about me, and no one could have had a more attentive audience" ([1840] 1986: 338).³ In another, when a whaling ship out of New Bedford anchors near the *Alert*, Dana and the rest of the crew obtain leave to visit it as soon as they have finished their duties: "we exchanged books with them,—a practice very common among ships in foreign ports, by which you get rid of the books you have read and re-read, and a supply of new ones in their stead" (282). Read and reread: due to the scarcity of reading material, many books on ship must have suffered the fate of Davies's copy of *The Influence of Sea Power*, returned to again and again until they broke "in two pieces."

Naval libraries, merchant vessel libraries, the miscellany possessed by individual sailors and avidly traded: each set of texts tells a different story

FIGURE 8.2 E. Boyd Smith, "Reading *Woodstock* aloud," illustration from Richard Henry Dana, Jr., *Two Years Before the Mast: A Personal Narrative* (Boston: Houghton Mifflin Co., 1911). © Thomas Fisher Rare Book Library, University of Toronto (public domain).

about the sea in the nineteenth century. But not only the sea. That Bunyan and Paley were to be found onboard so many ships cannot be understood apart from the resurgence of Protestant Christianity that took the shape of the Great Awakening in the United States and the Evangelical Revival in Britain. Similarly, that the names Scott and Cooper on Blum's list remain familiar but Bulwer-Lytton and Godwin less so testifies to a change in canonical novelists between the nineteenth and twenty-first centuries. And so on: "The history of books among seamen in the days of sail," Skallerup observes with careful understatement, "is not unrelated to the cultural history of the world" (1974: x).

To turn from the sea of ink conjured up by the phrase "books among seaman in the days of sail" to the contents of a single ship's library in a novel published at the beginning of the twentieth century entails a profound loss of scope, and not merely because of the (much!) smaller number of texts. As I've already mentioned, there's also something peculiar about the library of the *Dulcibella* in that every volume it contains has to do with the sea. This sets it apart from most ships' libraries. Captain Nemo declares of his books: "They are the only links I still have with the land" (Verne [1870] 2017: 87–9). Despite its fantastic immensity, the library of the *Nautilus* has in common with libraries on actual ocean-going vessels a more or less promiscuous mix of volumes pertaining to terra firma as much as or more than to life afloat: "masterpieces of the great writers of Antiquity and the Modern world," from Homer to George Sand, as well as "books about mechanics, ballistics, hydrography, meteorology, geography, geology" (89). Other fictional libraries from the period range as widely. In Jack London's *The Sea-Wolf* (1904), the narrator Humphrey Van Weyden reports that Wolf Larsen's contained "such names as Shakespeare, Tennyson, Poe, and De Quincey [...]. Tyndall, Proctor, and Darwin. Astronomy and physics were represented, and I remarked Bulfinch's *Age of Fable*, Shaw's *History of English and American Literature*, and Johnson's *Natural History*" (London [1904] 2000: 43). In *The Riddle of the Sands*, however, despite Carruthers's use of the word "medley" in connection with the items on the bookshelf, the singular focus of every bit of printed matter gives testament to monomania: obsessed with all things nautical, Davies carries books about the sea over the sea; water within, water without. To focus on those books means a loss of scope, to be certain, but a concomitant gain in intensity. *Whatever else one might say about the library of the* Dulcibella, *this much is clear: it imagines the sea as the only world worth reading about—almost as the only world there is.*

TIDE-TABLES, PILOTS, ETC.

Amongst the variability in the content of ships' libraries and sailors' chests, one constant: no vessel puts to sea without technical sailing aids. The least particularized of Carruthers's categories, it is nonetheless the most indispensable. One could go so far as to say that the offhand way he refers to those aids while setting them aside confirms that indispensability, the sheer unthinkability of their not being onboard. Consider again the first account of the bookshelf, which begins: "besides a Nautical Almanack and some dilapidated *Sailing Directions.*" And the second, which sets out similarly: "excluding tide-tables, 'pilots,' etc." (Childers [1903] 2011: 42, 179). The rhetorical figure here, used twice to identical effect, is paralepsis: mentioning something by stating that you won't be mentioning it. Like the connection between the sea and empire, the presence of sailing aids onboard the *Dulcibella* goes without saying—not because those aids are unimportant but, on the contrary, because they are the most frequently consulted printed matter to be found on any sea-going vessel.

Take charts, not even named by Carruthers but, in a kind of second-order paralepsis, implied by that capacious "etc." tacked onto the end of the list of what is to be excluded from his inventory. The nautical chart is a technology with a long and storied history. Originating in but distinct from the ancient Greek *periplus,* a list of ports with distances between them for use while at sea, the chart as such makes its initial appearance in late medieval Europe in the form of the portolan chart, a dramatic innovation in that it provided details of the coast and featured compass lines that could be used to set course headings (Whitfield 1996: 7, 19). The chart of the nineteenth century, a direct descendant of the portolan chart, contained still more technical information—so much that, in the words of Edwin Hutchins, such a chart amounts to "an analogue computer." A chart's function exceeds representationality: "All maps are spatial analogies in the sense that they preserve some of the spatial relationships of the world they depict, but navigation charts depict spatial relationships in special ways that support certain specialized computations" (Hutchins 1995: 61). Ships carry charts not simply because they are portable models of the water to be traveled over and the land to be avoided or made for but because they allow courses to be plotted, positions to be fixed, magnetic compass readings to be converted to true, and so on. They allow sailing to be done.

Which is to say: although many use "chart" and "map" as interchangeable terms (no doubt the same people who fail to distinguish between paddles and oars), the two differ in significant ways. Some of those differences are on view in the pages of *The Riddle of the Sands* itself: Carruthers may not bother to name charts in his itemization of the contents of the library, but his creator Childers took the unusual step of inserting two of them in the novel (and two maps as well). According to a note in the first edition, they are "reproductions, on a slightly reduced scale, and omitting some confusing and irrelevant details, of British and German Admiralty Charts" (Childers 1903: ix). Even thus simplified, they contain an enormous amount of information, evident at a glance in the "Chart of Juist, Memmert, and part of Norderney"

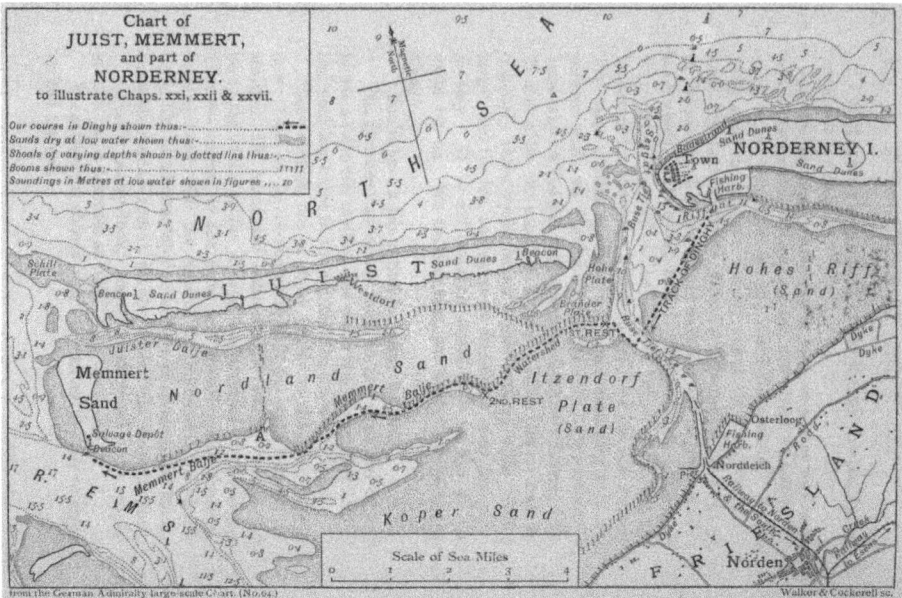

FIGURE 8.3 "Chart of Juist, Memmert, and part of Norderney," from Erskine Childers, *The Riddle of the Sands: A Record of Secret Service Recently Achieved* (London: Smith, Elder, & Co., 1903). © Thomas Fisher Rare Book Library, University of Toronto (public domain).

(Figure 8.3): water depths (at mean low tide probably, although this is nowhere spelled out), the direction of magnetic (as distinct from true) north, the location of beacons and lights, distances in nautical miles. In addition, comparing this to the map of "East Friesland, and the German or East Frisian Is[lands]" (Figure 8.4), which covers some of the same area and is also included in the novel, reveals the fundamental difference of focus between all maps and charts: whereas the sea on the map is blank space, on the chart it bristles with detail while the land is relatively featureless. Both the charts and the maps add verisimilitude to the novel; both are also integral to the plot. But the charts alone communicate to readers what a complex, difficult place the sea is—as well as the degree to which its complexities have been accounted for, its difficulties defanged.

The same may be said about the pilots, guides to navigation in crowded waters such as harbors or particularly dangerous waters such as river mouths. No specific pilot is named by Carruthers, but texts along the lines of what the *Dulcibella* would have carried were ubiquitous in the nineteenth century, and not only for the coasts of Britain, Europe, and the United States. Robert Louis Stevenson, himself the creator of a famous fictional map, the one in *Treasure Island* (1883), left San Francisco for the South Pacific in 1888 carrying the fifth

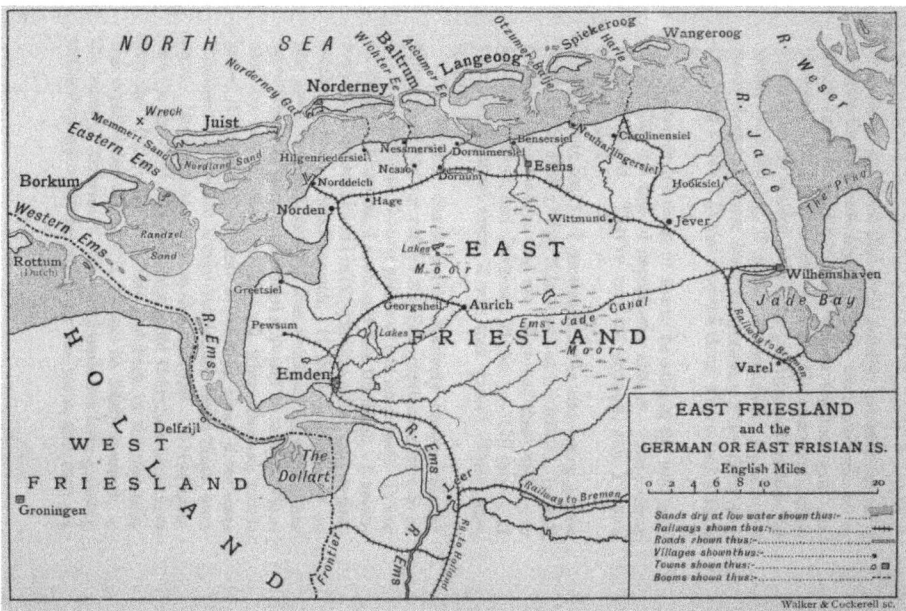

FIGURE 8.4 "East Friesland and the German or East Frisian Is.," from Erskine Childers, *The Riddle of the Sands: A Record of Secret Service Recently Achieved* (London: Smith, Elder, & Co., 1903). © Thomas Fisher Rare Book Library, University of Toronto (public domain).

edition of Alexander George Findlay's *A Directory for the Navigation of the South Pacific Ocean* (1884) in his ship, *Casco* (F. Stevenson 2004: 199–200; R. Stevenson [1870] 2008: 284n184). Running to more than twelve hundred pages, the *Directory* provides pilotage information for scores of islands as well as charts of the South Pacific marked with magnetic variation, prevailing winds subdivided by season and region, prevailing currents, and the location of known icebergs. Somewhat ironically, the book concludes with a warning about the increasing propensity to take the representation of the ocean for the ocean itself:

> There is one misfortune attendant on the advancement of science, that by following out to minute particulars each special branch of it, the mind is more or less diverted from the simple first principles [...]. [For instance,] the great principles of the sphere were then [in former times] better considered than now, when the universality of charts causes the surface of the earth to be rather viewed as a plane in hydrographical problems.
>
> (Findlay 1884: 1157)

Like charts, and like other pilots, Findlay's *A Directory for the Navigation of the South Pacific Ocean*, an immense, comprehensive, and authoritative compendium of maritime expertise, threatens to overwrite sea with text.

To turn to tide tables is to witness the command evidenced by charts and pilots over the ocean in the present extended into futurity. The ability accurately to predict tides is essential to the action of *Riddle*, much of which chronicles strandings or close calls with stranding. As the "Chart of Juist" shows, the waters around the Frisian Islands abound with hidden shallows potentially catastrophic even for vessels with as little draft as the *Dulcibella*. Carruthers's and Davies's lives often depend on tide tables, which they consult incessantly and with confidence. We can begin to grasp how remarkable this is by noting that one hundred years earlier it would have been impossible even to conceive of a novel such as *The Riddle of the Sands*—because it would have been impossible to imagine that tides could be so accurately predicted or that tidal information could be so widely disseminated.

Isaac Newton formulated an essentially correct theory of tides at the end of the seventeenth century, but another two hundred years of work was required to enable reliable predictions for any given spot along the littoral or out in blue water. The problem occupied some of the greatest scientific minds of the nineteenth century, including the polymath historian and philosopher of science William Whewell and the physicist Lord Kelvin. As the culmination of his tidal researches for the British Admiralty, in the 1830s Whewell produced maps of the North Sea showing cotidal lines, lines connecting points that experience high tide simultaneously. In *Tides of History* (2008), Michael Reidy writes of those maps that their "efficient and rational ordering of the ocean fit perfectly with the Admiralty's own designs. The ocean and coastlines now looked regimented and ordered, reduced to a single visual that could be printed, reproduced, and dispersed throughout the sea-lanes of the world. Science was helping to control the ocean" (2008: 191). In *Tides: A Scientific History* (1999), David Edgar Cartwright reveals the orderly, completed aspect of these tidal maps to be partly illusory insofar as they were contested by contemporaries, including the Astronomer Royal, G.B. Airy, and Robert FitzRoy (the same who captained the *Beagle* while Darwin was aboard) (110–18). Nonetheless, it was clear that a definitive solution to the problem of tidal prediction was not only possible but close to being worked out. If the ocean was not yet as regimented as it appeared in Whewell's maps, it was well on its way to being so.

Charts, pilots, tide tables: taken together, the technical sailing aids in the library of the *Dulcibella* convey an ocean imagined as fully known. The sense of completed or nearly completed knowledge, that there would soon be nothing more to be discovered, was ubiquitous in the second half of the nineteenth century. As early as 1854, Darwin's champion and the great popularizer of science T.H. Huxley declared of his own 1846 to 1850 voyage in HMS *Rattlesnake* that it was the last in the "great series of ocean explorations for the discovery of new and untrodden lands, within the habitable globe" (1854: 115). Joseph Conrad, writing about arctic journeys that took place at nearly the same time as the *Rattlesnake*'s visit to the Torres Strait and Papua New Guinea, identifies them as belonging to a period of geographical exploration "already conscious of its approaching end" (1926: 18). Marlow, in Conrad's *Heart of Darkness* (1899), echoes this sentiment: as a boy, he tells us, he longed to visit the interior of Africa, "the biggest, the most blank" part of the map of the world; by the time he reached adulthood, however, "it had got filled [...] with rivers and lakes and names. It had ceased to be a blank space of delightful mystery" ([1899] 2002: 108). Huxley, Conrad, and Conrad's creation Marlow all bear witness to the coming to pass of that phenomenon Rosalind Williams refers to as "the triumph of human empire": the advent, clearly in prospect at the end of the nineteenth century, of a fully mapped, rationalized, humanized globe, "a planet dominated by the human presence, so that we are constantly encountering ourselves" (2013: 33). Williams documents not the completion of that dominance but the realization that it was occurring—an "event of consciousness," as she calls it, for which she finds evidence in the work of Verne, Stevenson, and William Morris (x). Childers, born in 1870 and thus a generation younger than Stevenson and two younger than Verne and Morris, must have perceived this equivocal triumph still more sharply than his illustrious predecessors. Without it, *The Riddle of the Sands* could not have been written.

At the same time, the novel insists that in the interstices of apparently complete knowledge the unknown persists: regardless of charts, pilots, and tide tables, in any given situation the actual sea may escape understanding or defy prediction. Quoting bits and pieces of *Riddle* to illustrate the point would give the inaccurate impression that the novel is only occasionally concerned with the sea's resistance to being brought to book. In fact, that resistance undergirds *Riddle* as fully as do predictable tides. Here is Davies explaining to Carruthers the difference between a chart and that which is charted, as though continuing Findlay's line of thought: "'That chart may look simple to you'—('simple!' I thought)—'but at half flood all those banks are covered; the islands and coasts are scarcely visible, they are so low, and everything looks the same'" (Childers [1903] 2011: 35). Carruthers finds ample confirmation of these claims in a book in the library of the *Dulcibella* different from all the rest because handwritten on-board each day: Davies's log. "The bulk," he relates, "dealt with channels and shoals with weird and depressing names, with the centre-plate, the sails, and the wind, buoys and 'booms,' tides and 'berths' for the night. 'Kedging off' appeared to be a frequent diversion; 'running aground' was of almost daily occurrence" (43–4). In the first place the passage functions as a form of characterization: placing quotation marks around words like "booms" (poles inserted into the sand to indicate safe passage through a shallow area) and "kedging off" (using a kedge anchor to provide leverage for pulling a vessel that has run aground back into water deep enough to float in), Carruthers calls attention to his former ignorance. But it also functions as a testament to how frequently the *Dulcibella* gets into trouble in spite of all the sailing aids it carries: running aground, a sailor's nightmare, "was of almost daily occurrence."

The *Riddle of the Sands*, then, shows both the triumph and the limits of human empire. Given those limits, it also shows the continued need for "craft," Conrad's term, adopted and developed by Margaret Cohen to mean "the power of embodied reason, creative improvisation, and the honor of labor" (2010: 58). Craft relies on an array of tools and instruments: compass, chronograph, barometer, sounding lead. It also relies on the texts in ships' libraries. But it is more than those texts. Drawing on human experience and intelligence, it fills the gap between what charts, pilots, and tide tables tell about the sea and the sea itself. At once a paean to and a dense illustration of craft, *Riddle* gives us a sea that continues to elude attempts to know and control it. This is not an addlepated maritime romanticism. It is, instead, an insistence on the sea as always and everywhere a place of particularity and contingency—as well as on the virtues of imagining it as such a place.

BOOKS ON NAVAL WARFARE

Books on naval warfare similarly body forth the sea as above all the locus of contingency. Weather may influence a battle on land, but naval contests can be entirely decided by wind and waves—as most famously in the role played by storms in the English defeat of the Spanish Armada in 1588. To reduce such contingency, war at sea puts a premium on sailing aids: using them, of course, but also making them. We may remember the 1831 to 1836 voyage of the *Beagle* in connection with natural history and evolutionary theory, but its principal aim was to create accurate charts of the waters around the southern cone of South America. In her biography of Darwin, Janet Browne writes that the Admiralty charged the *Beagle* with this task "to enable informed decisions to be made on naval, military, and commercial operations along the unexplored coastline south of Buenos Aires and to enable Britain to establish strong footholds in these areas, so recently released from their commitment to trade only with Spain and Portugal" (1995: 181). It was also the Admiralty that commissioned Whewell's tidal maps, and ocean science continued to be the handmaiden of war up through the twentieth century and beyond. During the Second World War, to give one instance among many, the US military enlisted oceanographers in wave forecasting to prepare for landings in Normandy and elsewhere (Helmreich 2015a: 79; Schlee 1973: 206). In short, Carruthers's first and second categories are intimately intertwined.

The books on naval warfare in the library of the *Dulcibella* also bear a close connection to Erskine Childers himself. *Riddle*, autobiographical in a number of ways, may be most so in its thoroughgoing militarism. Up to and including his execution by firing squad during the Irish Civil War, Childers lived the life of a soldier. In 1899 to 1900 he volunteered in an artillery company in the Boer War, an experience recounted in his first book, *In the Ranks of the C.I.V.* (1900). He went on to write two short books arguing for the modernization of cavalry warfare, *War and the Arme Blanche* (1910) and *German Influence of British Cavalry* (1911). A volunteer in the Royal Navy Reserve during the First World War, among other things he helped to plan the Cuxhaven Raid, the bombing of a German North Sea port. Furthermore, in a celebrated episode that combined soldiering with his gift for and love of sailing, in 1914 he smuggled rifles from Germany to nationalist Irish Volunteers in his sixteen-meter gaff-rigged yacht *Asgard*.[4] (The weapons were used in the 1916 Easter Rising, and the *Asgard* now rests on the hard in a permanent display in Collins Barracks, Dublin.) In Davies, the sailor obsessed with war at sea, Childers put much of himself. But Childers's life and works, as well as the existence of the books on naval warfare that Davies reads until they break in two, attest to a wider context: that of a militarized ocean.

As an invasion novel, *The Riddle of the Sands* assumes such militarization. Its essential claim, however, is that many do not, and specifically that Britons possess an insufficiently keen sense of how susceptible they might be to attack from across the North Sea. *Riddle*'s subgenre-founding predecessor, *The Battle of Dorking*, had also made the British lack of military preparedness its keynote: looking back half a century to the defeat of Britain by Germany, the narrator laments that "the bitterest part of our reflection is that all this misery and decay might have been so easily prevented [...]. There, across the narrow Straits, was the writing on the wall; but we would not choose to read it" (Chesney ([1871] 1977: 47). *Riddle* seeks to magnify that writing, although the novel's specific concern, naval preparedness, was largely ignored by Chesney. Posing as editor of a manuscript brought to him by an anonymous author who writes under the pen name "Carruthers," Childers condenses his argument into the final sentence of a postscript, a rhetorical question delivered *in propria persona*: "Is it not becoming patent that the time has come for training all Englishmen systematically either for the sea or for the rifle?" (Childers [1903] 2011: 301). The body of *Riddle* as well as the rest of its several paratextual elements—preface, epilogue, maps, charts—underscore the extra-fictional purpose of sounding the alarm about Britain's maritime vulnerability, and there is some evidence that the Admiralty took notice (Boyle 1977; Piper 2003: 139; Ring 1996: 15).

Despite Childers's anxieties, however, belief in the possibility of an imminent attack on Britain was in fact widespread. The library of the *Dulcibella* itself may contain a book with a warning similar to *Riddle*'s. Carruthers does not say which volume of Brassey's *Naval Annual* Davies owns, but there is a certain satisfaction in imagining it to be the one for 1902, the year during which the action of the novel is set. The eighth chapter of that volume, "The Invasion of England," begins: "It is impossible to follow the discussion of many international questions debated on the Continent without realising that there exists, in the military mind of Europe, a conviction that the invasion of England is an operation within the bounds of reasonable possibility. The belief is especially prevalent in France and Germany" (1902: 130). Canvassing the evidence for such a conviction, the chapter reaches the conclusion that it is correct, and as a consequence that "a sufficient and efficient Navy is the essential factor in national as in Imperial defence" (143). Like *Riddle* itself, the *Naval Annual* for 1902 contends that the sea is more militarized, and more dangerous as a potential avenue of invasion, than most Britons realize.

The sea as a scene of conflict in *Riddle* and the *Naval Annual* is that of the present and the immediate future. Two of Davies's books on naval warfare, however, focus on the past: Alfred Thayer Mahan's *Influence of Sea Power* and his *Life of Nelson*. Mahan, who combined the roles of historian and strategist, remains an inevitable point of reference when considering war at sea, so much so that in 1993 a collection was published with the title *Mahan Is Not Enough* and the remit of expanding the study of naval strategy and tactics beyond this single towering figure (see Goldrick and Hattendorf 1993). In an earlier collection, *The Influence of History on Mahan*, US Navy Rear Admiral Ronald J. Kurth refers to *The Influence of Sea Power* as "one of the most influential American books of the 19th century" and Mahan as "a man whose name everybody in the Navy has heard" (Hattendorf 1991: 3). Still more indicative of Mahan's status is the quotation Kurth gives from Henry L. Stinson, US Secretary of War under Presidents Taft, Franklin D. Roosevelt, and Truman: "the peculiar psychology of the Navy Department [...] frequently seemed to retire from the realm of logic into a dim religious world in which Neptune was God, Mahan his prophet, and the United States Navy the only true church" (Stinson quoted in Hattendorf 1991: 3). In his devotion to Mahan, Davies presciently seizes upon a writer who was to be the most significant theorist of war at sea for a century or more.

One reason for that significance is to be found in Mahan's insistence, early in *The Influence of Sea Power*, on the ability to derive principles from precedent, and on the aim of naval history as precisely such a derivation: "a precedent is different from and less valuable than a principle. The former may be originally faulty, or may cease to apply through the change of circumstances; the latter has its root in the essential causes of things, and [...] remains a standard to which action must conform to attain success" (1890: 7). After an initial chapter laying out the basic principles of sea power and the factors influencing its operation in Europe and the United States, there follow nearly five hundred pages explicating one by one the key European and American naval engagements between 1660 and 1783, frequently accompanied by maps and battle plans. A

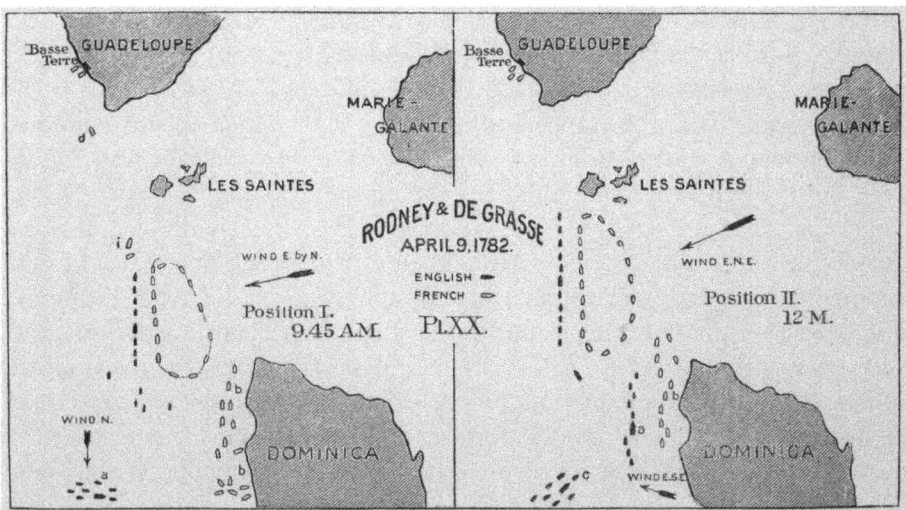

FIGURE 8.5 "Diagrams illustrating the Battle of the Saintes," from Captain A.T. Mahan, *The Influence of Sea Power Upon History, 1660–1783* (London: S. Low, Marston, Searle & Rivington, 1890). © Thomas Fisher Rare Book Library, University of Toronto (public domain).

sense of the stance the book takes to all of these engagements may be gleaned from Mahan's comments on the moment when French commander Comte de Grasse, in an April 1782 encounter with the British fleet known as the Battle of the Saintes (Figure 8.5), fails to attack nine British ships despite having a numerical advantage: "Had those nine been thoroughly beaten, [British commander Admiral George] Rodney's further movements must have been hopelessly crippled" (483). Note the conditional mood ("Had ... must have been"): here and throughout, Mahan concerns himself not only with the way historical naval engagements actually transpired but also with how they might have gone differently. Although he does not cite Carl von Clausewitz, he shares what Catherine Gallagher has shown to be the Prussian military theorist's conviction that "perfecting the art of warfare entailed knowing not only what had occurred in previous wars but also everything that *could have* occurred"; such "counterfactual speculation" promised "the ability to gain knowledge from the past for the sake of future planning" (2018: 5, emphasis in original). Mahan's counterfactuals undo the apparent fixity of the past; conversely, in doing so they lend solidity both to the principles of war at sea and to the sea on which that war takes place.

The counterfactuals in *The Influence of Sea Power* also emphasize the decisive role played by individual naval commanders. This is the entire burden of the other title by Mahan in the library of the *Dulcibella*, *The Life of Nelson*. Addressing the question of why he undertook to write yet another biography of Nelson, Mahan explains the relation between his two books: "it is essential to the author's discussion of the Influence of Sea Power, that he present a study [...] of the one man who in himself summed up and embodied the greatness of the possibilities which Sea Power comprehends" (1897: 1:v). But it often seems as though Sea Power sums up and embodies Nelson rather than the reverse: *The Life of Nelson*, nearly as thick with diagrams and densely technical discussions of strategy and tactics as *Influence*, elides the distinction between naval history and biography. Recreating not only past sea states but also the motivations and calculations of a historical personage as he seeks to use those states to advantage, the book instantiates the complex role imagination plays in oceanic practice. The whole builds to a concluding discussion of the October 21, 1805, Battle of Trafalgar, during which Nelson dies—but not before assuring British victory over a combined French and Spanish fleet. In the course of his lengthy treatment of the battle, Mahan provides two plans of attack and quotes extensively from a letter by Nelson explaining his assumptions and concomitant actions: "I will only suppose that the Enemy's Fleet being to leeward, standing close upon a wind on the starboard tack, and that I am nearly ahead of them, standing on the larboard [i.e., port] tack, of course I should weather them"—and so on (2:342). The plans, the letter, and Mahan's discussion of them, like *The Life of Nelson* as a whole, imagine a sea of principles as well as contingency, a sea at once known and unknown.

They also give us something like craft, in so doing making space for the outsize influence of a single individual. Mahan embarks on this biography with the intent of "showing clearly not only what he [Nelson] did, but the principles which dominated his military thought, and guided his military actions" (1:vii). But if the appeal to principles makes it seem as though anyone who took the trouble could discern them, the rest of the book insists on Nelson's singularity. "Beyond all question or competition," ensuring Britain's dominance at sea "was Nelson's great achievement"—and Nelson's alone (2:398). For Mahan, although naval warfare necessarily involves institutions such as the Admiralty as well as the sailors who fought in each of the battles chronicled in *The Influence of Sea Power* and *The Life of Nelson*, the definitive factor is a single man. That emphasis on the discernment and effectiveness of the individual is repeated on a much smaller scale in the plot of *Riddle*, in which Davies and Carruthers, amateurs in a small boat, find evidence of a planned invasion of which neither the Admiralty nor the Foreign Office, with all the resources at their command, has any idea. Transpose the figure of the singular heroic naval commander still further, this time into the minor key of the middle-class sailor on a holiday at sea, and we arrive at the last set of books onboard the *Dulcibella*.

BOOKS ON CRUISING IN SMALL YACHTS

To move from navies at war deciding the fate of nations to Davies's "hobby, cruising in small yachts" may seem a stark shift. But many of those who first took up such cruising had ties to the navy. The first circumnavigation of the globe in a private yacht, for example, was accomplished in 1876 to 1877 by none other than the founding editor of the *Naval Annual*, Thomas Brassey (Bender 2017: 85, 148–9, 190n58; Phillips-Birt 1974: 146–7). Naval officers swelled the ranks of the amateur yachtsmen who began to make increasingly frequent journeys around the coasts of Britain and beyond. *Riddle* itself acknowledges as much via the presence of the one bit of *fictional* print in the library of the *Dulcibella*, the work of a character named Dollman, an Englishman in the pay of the German Empire. Although Carruthers provides no title, he does briefly describe the book's contents: "A preface explained that it had been written during a spell of two months' leave from naval duty, and expressed a hope that it might be of service to Corinthian sailors. The style was unadorned, but scholarly and pithy. There was a certain subdued relish in describing banks and shoals, which reminded me of Davies himself" (Childers [1903] 2011: 189). Marking the overlap between naval officer and amateur yachtsman, this fictional text also contains two details that go far to illuminate the actual ones with which it shares shelf space—as well as the momentous shift they signal in imagining the sea: the word "Corinthian" and the tone of "subdued relish in describing banks and shoals."

To begin with the former: "A Corinthian yachtsman," writes Tyrell Biddle in explanation of his 1886 book of that title, "is one who has never been engaged in any professional capacity for pecuniary emolument on board a yacht. It means the same as amateur" (Biddle 1886: v). Actually, however, it means (or meant) much more. Deriving from the Greek Isthmian Games, close cousin to the Olympic Games and so called because held on the isthmus of Corinth, the term "Corinthian" could be used in the nineteenth century simply to denote amateur rather than professional (Kemp 1878: 522; Mayne 2000: 75). But in its nautical application it referred more specifically to a "new way of sailing [that] had a strong moral and emotional undertone," according to Mike Bender in his *New History of Yachting*: "it gained much of its attractiveness from its incorporation of key Victorian work-related values" such as "frugality, hard work, self-help, and 'pluck'" (2017: 154).⁵ Dollman's book, addressed to Corinthian sailors, finds its ideal reader in Davies, who exemplifies the type in everything he does and says. Newly arrived onboard, Carruthers admits he knows nothing about how to sail because he has always been on boats worked by a crew. Davies gives the requisite Corinthian reply: "'Crew!'—with sovereign contempt—'why, the whole fun of the thing is to do everything oneself'" (Childers [1903] 2011: 27). Later, as Davies describes the complexities of navigating among the Frisian

Islands, Carruthers interrupts: "Didn't you ever take a pilot?" (a person with local expertise brought onboard to guide vessels through dangerous waters). "Pilot?" asks Davies; "Why, the whole point of the thing … " (35). The whole point of the thing, per the dictates of Corinthian sailing, is to rely entirely on oneself.

And, if at all possible, to enjoy doing so. Variants on Dollman's tone of "subdued relish" in describing dangers at sea are to be found in each of the books on cruising in small yachts in the library of the *Dulcibella*. The Corinthian attitude in literary form, such a tone makes light of or even takes pleasure in difficulty and discomfort. No better example exists than the moment in *The Falcon on the Baltic* (1888), another of Davies's books on cruises in small boats, when E.F. Knight observes of the tiny, low cabin on his nine-meter ketch: "If one wishes to assume an erect position one can always go on deck" ([1888] 1951: 27). The same wry self-deprecation is on view in Knight's comment about the leak that plagued him for much of the voyage: "it was the great feature of the cruise" (41). More than simply playing down suffering, however, the ideal of Corinthian sailing embraces, even requires it. Knight raises this theme explicitly during a particularly trying stretch aboard *Falcon*: "As I kept my watch in dripping oilies, pumping hard with one hand, holding on with the other, and peering through the obscurity on the look-out for those murderous nuisances the screw steamers, I became meditative […]. I asked myself, 'Is this pleasure?'" (60–1). The answer is clearly yes, this *is* pleasure, at least of a kind—that kind akin to what goes by the name "Type 2 Fun" in a popular twenty-first-century taxonomy of outdoor adventure: enjoyable in retrospect even if more or less miserable while happening.

But to read Knight is to understand the insufficiency of the common definition of Type 2 Fun, or at least to glimpse an explanation for why a certain amount of discomfort can not only be relished but necessary. Knight's pleasure, the pleasure of Corinthian sailing as such, is that attendant on momentarily finding oneself outside an entirely managed, humanized, charted world. The cruise of the *Falcon*, book and voyage, lives in the shadow of that world, the triumph of human empire in its quotidian aspect. Knight undertakes a journey in which nothing is discovered, in the course of which nothing even unfamiliar is encountered. His constant refrain is that he will not bother to give a full account of what he sees because everything has already been "written up in the books of Murray, Baedeker, and the rest" (Knight [1888] 1951: 74). Widely consulted travel guides in the nineteenth century, Murrays and Baedekers serve as shorthand for the very beaten track—beaten to death, as it were. "But there was nothing very new in all this, and it has been described over and over again": Knight's remark after a short description of Hellevoetsluis, Holland, could have served as his book's epigraph (68). In a world thoroughly explored and repeatedly written about, a world in which travel has been made comfortable and quick (at least for those who can afford it), pleasure inheres in moments of uncertainty and discomfort because such moments are all that remain of adventure.[6]

Finding adventure in the familiar: an apt characterization of the accomplishments of one of Knight's key predecessors, R.T. McMullen, who, from 1850 to his death at sea in 1891, sailed small boats around Britain and across to France, at first with crew but later single-handed. *Down Channel*, the book of McMullen's in the library of the *Dulcibella*, documents these voyages, although with a tone quite different from Knight's gentle self-mockery. That difference may begin to be conveyed via McMullen's comments on his own ship's library, or that part of it he actually made use of: "What time was found for reading was generally devoted to the study of charts, books of sailing directions, and an occasional newspaper" ([1893] 1986: 27). Knight, despite his frequent caustic remarks about Baedekers, evidently spent a lot of time reading them. McMullen, altogether more Davies-like in his total devotion to the sea, pores over his charts and sailing directions.

McMullen's enjoyment, although akin to Knight's, is of a somewhat different sort as well: altogether more bound up in the technical. But the two men share the sense of the desirability of difficulty. Evident on nearly every page of *Down Channel*, that sense is clearest in McMullen's repeated use of the word "problem" as something to be hoped for and cherished. He writes of the "insatiable pleasure in the art of sailing, which, especially in strong weather, offers such an endless variety of problems for solution that there is always something fresh to engage the attention" (McMullen [1893] 1986: 235). Or again: "manoeuvres strictly belonging to the 'marine department' (getting under way on a tideless lee shore without sternway, for instance), carried out with precision, are among the most interesting problems of sea-sailing" (252). Accordingly, and in this like large swaths of *The Riddle of the Sands*, *Down Channel* concerns itself almost entirely with the minutiae of weather conditions and boat-handling: the book is, McMullen writes in a preface, "little more than a bare record of sailing"—a prose incarnation of the Corinthian ideal (25).[7]

Down Channel documents the early days of Corinthian sailing; *The Falcon on the Baltic*, a moment from its second generation. After McMullen and Knight (and, to be fair, a handful of others), the deluge—as indicated by the presence onboard the *Dulcibella* of Frank Cowper's five-volume set, *Sailing Tours: The Yachtsman's Guide to the Cruising Waters of the English Coast* (1892–6). Knight, who constantly refers his readers to Baedekers and Murrays, insists he has not written that sort of book. McMullen likewise declares that *Down Channel* "is not intended to trespass on the ground occupied by Murray's handbooks" ([1893] 1986: 25). But Cowper, matter-of-factly acknowledging "the trammels of that monotonous humdrum which civilisation imposes upon our existence," offers as a means of escape his "guide" to "the grand possibilities, from a sailing point of view, of the smaller harbours and creeks which crowd along our coasts" (1892–6: 1:v). Addressing the "large and ever-increasing brotherhood of 'corinthian sailors,'" he aspires to provide that oxymoronical thing, a guidebook to adventure (1:2).[8]

If he achieves this aim it is largely because he writes his guidebooks as though they were travel narratives intended to be read by rank amateurs. After a night spent in the Suffolk Hamlet Pin Mill, for instance, Cowper begins the first volume's fourteenth chapter, "The Stour," as follows: "With much regret we shortened in our chain and got up the mainsail the next morning. Pinmill is such a delightful little nook that we could spend a week here with much profit. But the charms of beauty must be disregarded, however peaceful and alluring they may seem. So break out the anchor and set the jib" (1892–6: 1:114). That the whole is cast in the first-person plural brings readers along, including them as though they, too, were on the voyage. The impression is made stronger by the appearance of a kind of faux imperative that instructs readers to up anchor and set sail as a means of reporting that Cowper did so himself. Both strategies steer well clear of wooden guidebook prose. So does the mention of hazards. The opening of the chapter on the Stour continues with this warning about the east side of the River Orwell below Pin Mill: "The tide is now full, and as the wind heads us a bit we have to be very careful not to reach over too far on either side, but especially on the eastern shore, where the mud lies out a long way and is very flat" (1:114). That the chart accompanying this section of the book, "Approaches to Harwich, Hanford Water, the Stour, Orwell, and Deben Rivers" (Figure 8.6), is too small-scale to show those mud flats clearly suggests the degree to which Cowper has attempted to strip out precisely those technical aspects of cruising that McMullen coveted (1:facing page 98). And how much more so the following recommendation: "There are plenty of craft about, and one has only to follow a vessel, drawing a little more water than we do, and we are sure to be all right" (1:115). No bothersome chart reading or casting of the lead required! If Cowper is to be believed, anyone and everyone can sail.

The explosive growth in recreational sailing in the twentieth century: this is what not *Sailing Tours* alone but all the books in the library of the *Dulcibella* on cruising in small yachts presage. We might say that, along with such innovations as fiberglass hulls, mass-produced boats, and GPS, they made such growth possible. They also made possible the efflorescence of twentieth- and twenty-first-century writing about sailing. The sea as imagined by McMullen, Knight, and Cowper is the sea of countless later books of maritime travel, from—to instance a very few highlights—Hilaire Beloc's *The Cruise of the Nona* (1925) and the sailing-mountaineering books of H.W. Tilman (1898–1977) up through Jonathan Raban's *Coasting* (1987) and beyond. And not only travel narratives: this sea is also the sea of fiction, including especially Arthur Ransome's Swallows and Amazons series. Following the camping and

IMAGINARY WORLDS 227

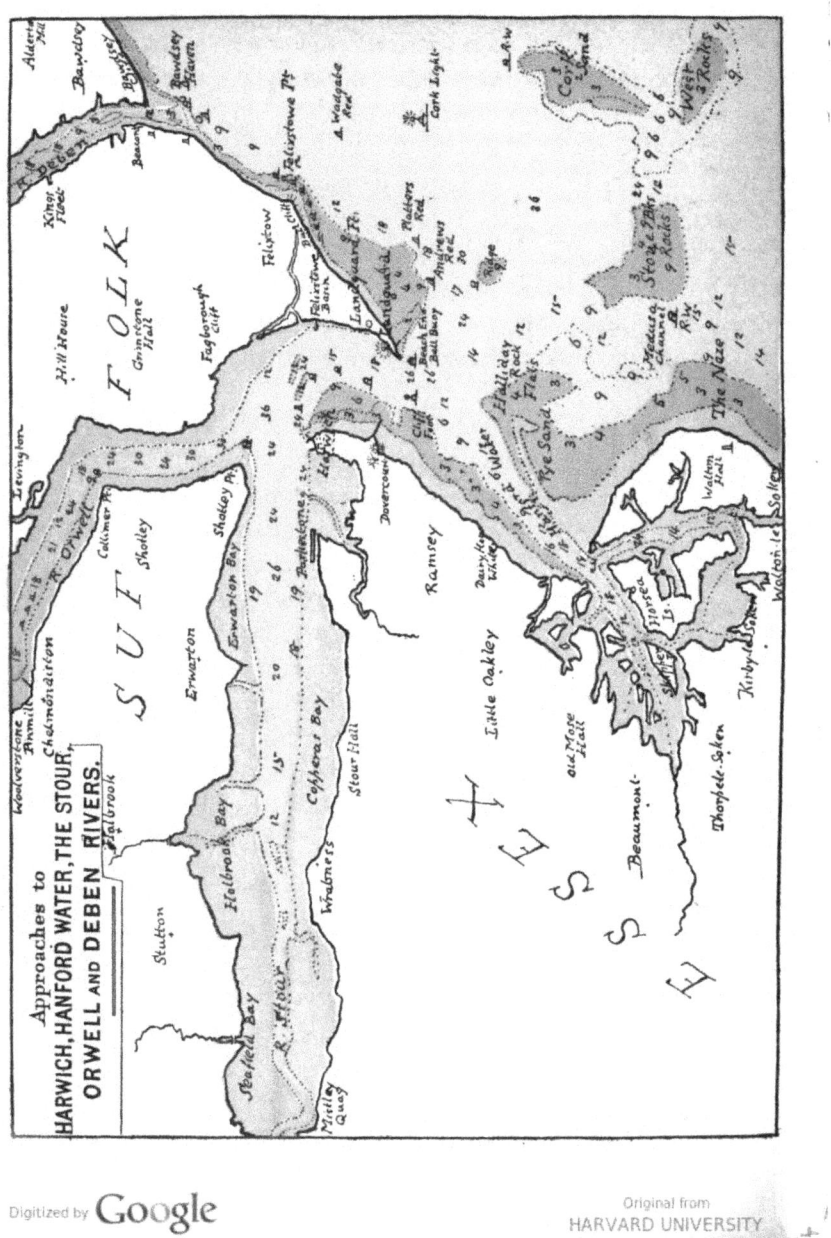

FIGURE 8.6 "Approaches to Harwich, Hanford Water, the Stour, Orwell, and Deben Rivers," from Frank Cowper, *Sailing Tours: The Yachtsman's Guide to the Cruising Waters of the English Coast*, 5 vols (London: L. Upcott Gill, 1892–6) (public domain).

sailing exploits of four children, at first close to home but increasingly further afield, these novels push the democratization of cruising still further (at least for age; class is another matter). Moreover, they demonstrate the continued, even intensified attraction of the cultivation of difficulty and discomfort. The tie to the library of the *Dulcibella* is direct: Ransome wrote the biographical note to a twentieth-century reprint of *Down Channel* and the preface to a reprint of *The Falcon on the Baltic*.[9] In the latter, he mentions Knight's other books but declares that *Falcon on the Baltic* is to be preferred because it provides readers with "stories that tell of adventures that might happen, with luck, to themselves" (Ransome 1951: 5). The sea in Davies's books on cruises in small yachts is a sea at once welcoming and dangerous, welcoming because potentially dangerous; a sea that many might, with luck, set out on, but that anyone and everyone can read about.

With the publication of *The Riddle of the Sands*, writes Douglas Philips-Birt in *The History of Yachting*, "the young art of yacht cruising was given literary expression." "The hero of the book," he goes on, is neither Carruthers nor Davies but "*Dulcibella*, the tiny centreboard cruiser converted from a ship's lifeboat" (1974: 137). But by 1903 that young art had already been given ample literary expression, not least in the books on cruising in Davies's library. Moreover, and in this like Foucault, Philips-Birt awards a boat the title that ought by rights to go to the sea itself. Hero, heroine, antagonist, foil, setting, love interest: the sea in *Riddle* is all in all. It can be so not because it is infinite or other but because—as given to us by charts and tide tables, by Brassey and Mahan, by McMullen and Knight and Cowper and Childers—it is known but not fully; predictable but capable of surprises; thankfully uncomfortable and trying; above all a place of contingent practice, where dreams are realized in and through timely action and mastery of technical details. The imaginary world of the sea in the age of empire: even if, only if for these counterintuitive reasons, still the greatest reserve of the imagination.

NOTES

Preface

1 This phrase is the title of a Walcott poem "The Sea Is History" (Walcott 2007).

Chapter 1

1 *Translator's note:* my translation of Schleiden.
2 *Translator's note:* my translation.
3 For the discovery of deep time and the beginnings of geology, cf. Albritton (1980); Ariew (1991); Geikie (1897); Gould (1987); Rossi (1984); Rudwick (2005: ch. 5); Schneer (1967); Toulmin and Goodfield (1982).
4 The flying reptile described is the *Pterodactyl*, or "Wing Finger."
5 Epistemic things are uncertain, provisional things, "to which the effort of knowledge applies. [...] these things present themselves as epistemic in the irreducible haziness and vagueness characteristic to them" (Rheinberger [2001] 2006: 27) *Translator's note*: my translation of Rheinberger.
6 In addition to Gosse's famous works were, for example, "The Aquarium Simplified" (1856); Bateman (1870); Butler (1858); Damon (1879); Furneaux (1896); Harper (1856, 1858); Humphreys (1857); Materlinck (1889); Ortleb and Ortleb (1885); Simmons (1874); Sowerby (1865); Wood (1868).
7 *Translator's note*: my translation of Simon.
8 A selection of classical texts: Campbell (1988); Friedman (1981); Gerald of Wales (*c*. 1188); Gervaise of Tilbury ([*c*. 1211] 2002); Mandeville ([1480] 1983); Polo ([1298/9] 2016); Romm (1992).
9 *Comptes rendus hebdomadaires des séances de l'Academie des Sciences*, 53 (July–December 1861): 1265–7, 1265f.
10 Indeed, there are three illustrations in which a kraken is clearly depicted: the title page of *Vingt Mille Lieues sous les mers*, an illustration in the fourth chapter of volume 2, which shows a sponge diver, and an illustration in the ninth chapter of the same volume, which shows Captain Nemo and Monsieur Aronnax on the way to Atlantis.

11 For this reason, the Giant Squid is often conflated with a kraken, because it first appeared in literature under the Norwegian designation *kraken*.
12 Larger still than *Architeuthis* is the Colossal Squid (*Mesonychoteuthis hamiltoni*). It belongs to the family *Cranchiidae* and lives in the waters of the Antarctic, which is why European stories of Giant Squids do not refer to it, but rather to Architeuthis.
13 The longest measured squid to date was 17.4 meters long. It was beached in 1887 on the coast of New Zealand (see Ellis 2002: 13).
14 *Translator's note*: my translation of Müller.
15 *Comptes rendus hebdomadaires des séances de l'Academie des Sciences*, 117 (1–17) (July–December 1893): 286–9.

Chapter 2

1 Melville's narrator in *White-Jacket* got several historical details about the early history of navigating Cape Horn incorrect. For example, Schouten and Le Maire had earlier lost their ship *Hoorn* to accidental fire while careening the ship a few months earlier. They went around aboard their second and larger vessel, the *Eendracht*.
2 Melville oddly substituted the *Sultan* for the *Natchez*, another merchant ship that was out at sea at the time, but over two thousand nautical miles away (Anderson 1966: 138).
3 Having just turned forty-one years old only days earlier, his sailing days long over, Melville saw the Cape Horn region as the sailor's underworld in part because in the months before and after he was in his cabin aboard the *Meteor* reading his copies of Dante and Spenser. Melville inscribed "C. Horn 1860" in the front of the first volume of Milton that he'd brought along on the voyage (Parker 2002: 434).
4 For a summary of all Melville's voyages, see Madison (2016: 263–7).
5 For example, see a discussion of the hazards of steam travel through the Straits of Magellan and a proposal of a line tug-steamers to help vessels through in "Interesting from Chile ... " (1858: 1).
6 Sailing ships may also gybe, or "wear ship," which is to turn their ship by moving their stern through the wind rather than the bow as with a tack. This maneuver can be safer for the crew and the rig of the ship, but it requires more sea room and often loses a bit of the windward progress.
7 In Irving Johnson's famous 1980 narration of his 1929 film of his voyage around *Cape Horn,* he mentions Captain Jürgen Jürs of the *Peking*, who doubled Cape Horn fifty-six times, which is the most Johnson had ever heard of.
8 This is perhaps where Melville derived his "fleet of icebergs" for *White-Jacket*, if he never experienced this for himself.

Chapter 3

1 For the bottle's initial discovery by a Black man, see Halliday (1837: 26–7).
2 For more on the *kalapani* taboo, see Claveyrolas (2018: 27–8).
3 Unless otherwise indicated, all information reflecting Duncan MacGregor's perspective is taken from the copy of his March 7, 1825 letter to his father, John MacGregor, in the John MacGregor Papers, National Maritime Museum, Greenwich, 1–19.
4 Information reflecting Joanna Agnes Dick's perspective is taken from a copy of her 1825 letter to her aunt, Mary Dick, in the John MacGregor Papers, National Maritime Museum, Greenwich, 25–85.

5 All information from David Pringle's perspective is taken from a copy of his April 1825 letter to Mary A. Pringle in the John MacGregor Papers, National Maritime Museum, Greenwich, 25–85.
6 See Tracy (2014: 180–81) for the narrative's international afterlife.

Chapter 5

1 The suggestion of a turtle prohibition was made to me by the late Eric Deeral, MP, Guugu Yimithirr elder and clan custodian, when I visited Cooktown with the *Endeavour* replica in 2001, but I have been unable to verify it one way or another.
2 This was also explained to me by Eric Deeral. It was later confirmed and elaborated on by another Guugu Yimithirr scholar, Alberta Hornsby, when we were making a documentary film version of Cook's environmental crisis at Endeavour River. See video interview with Alberta Hornsby at the Reef (2014).
3 Banfield's correspondents included F. Manson Bailey, author of *The Queensland Flora*, and the zoologist C.W. de Viss of the Queensland Museum.

Chapter 6

1 The *Tilbury* was a ship of the line that actually wrecked in Cape Breton (1757) with four hundred men aboard. But she was popularly imagined to have been burnt in Jamaica, as Humboldt relates, because of Thomas Pennant's well-known *A Tour in Scotland and Voyage to the Hebrides* (1772), from which Humboldt gleans these details of transoceanic plant migration to the Hebrides.
2 On scientific anti-conquest, see Pratt (2008).
3 Melville's chapter 56 is titled "Less Erroneous Pictures of Whales, and the True Pictures of Whaling Scenes." Leeuwenhoek was a self-taught seventeenth-century savant who pioneered the use of the microscope in biology.
4 On the shift in material and disciplinary forms in exploration accounts from the eighteenth through the nineteenth centuries, see Craciun (2013).
5 In fact the Inughuit had a longer history of Inuit contact, see Vaughan (1987).
6 Ross discusses Sacheuse's picture in detail and insists that the lithograph is "without the slightest variation from the original, the scale only being reduced to accommodate the size of the work" (1819: 87). The original paintings have not been found but are described in Anonymous (1818).
7 An anonymous newspaper account of the Inughuit encounters drawn from shipboard witnesses was published before Ross's *Voyage of Discovery* and provided details of these images, now lost (Anonymous 1818: 4). See Craciun and Terrall (2019) for more details.
8 The caption for Aron's illustration reads "Robinson from his ship by the waves carried/run (to shore)" (my thanks to Nelson Graburn for this translation).
9 On Dufferin's transformation of Arctic travel into a leisure pursuit, see Hansson (2009).
10 Hearn's story was dated 1896, as the *Gazette*, which was actually printed in Tromsø, often featured writing produced by travelers in the previous summer.

Chapter 7

1 This is similar to the most damning, and brilliant, critique of Conrad and by implication EuroAmerican writing more generally, in that it is deeply racist in its portrayal of Indigenous characters as setting rather than subjects (Achebe 1977).

2 The recent collection by Steve Mentz and Martha Elena Rojas, *The Sea in Nineteenth-Century Literature and Culture,* takes "transatlantic Anglophone literary culture" as its "relatively constrained geographic, linguistic, and cultural borders" (2016); Paul Gilroy situates the Atlantic as the center of an incipient modernity born of the middle passage (1993); and John Peck's *Maritime Fiction* takes British and American novels as the basis for an argument about the ability for maritime material to frame a debate about the identity of the nation, based largely on the maritime dominance of these two nations during the nineteenth century (2001: 4).

3 The "below decks" suggests a vertical arrangement that symbolizes hierarchical organizations of racial value, and also points further down to the wreckage of slave bodies and shipwrecks below the surface of the sea, as will be discussed in the final section.

4 The startling cosmopolitanism of the novel is reflected not only in ethnicity and origin, but spatially in the names of pubs, such as "Bombay." It is also cosmopolitan, in an ethical sense, in its sometimes critical attitude to racist prejudice. As Ishmael notes, while musing on having to share his room at the whaler's Spouter Inn with the Polynesian Queequeg, "Better to sleep with a sober cannibal than a drunken Christian" (see Peck 2001: 112).

5 The Pacific is at first the most prominent ocean to appear in the novel, a Queequeg is its irresistible representative for the first half of the novel, and the ultimate goal of the voyage is to find Moby Dick in the Pacific. However, much of the action of the novel is set during the rounding of the Cape and in the Indian Ocean. Feddallah could be considered its representative character, in turn (see Birns 2012).

6 This is true of all Melville's various sea fictions, as it is of twentieth-century works such as Virginia Woolf's *The Voyage Out.*

7 A mechanical breakdown does not entirely disallow the possibility of "jury-rigging," a term for the creative improvisations of survival at sea derived from the term for fashioning of a temporary mast after dismasting,—and "survival cannibalism" could be considered a form of jury-rigging in some cases, which is in essence Falk's argument in the story (Cohen 2010: 30, 32).

8 Also see Pratt (2007).

9 The rotting of oysters to get at the pearls is vividly described by Leonard Woolf in a short story, "Pearls and Swine," as a noxious process symbolizing imperial waste (1921).

10 Ten years later, Pender founded the Eastern and South African Telegraph Company, which linked to the British Indian line at Aden, extended south through Zanzibar, Mozambique, and the Cape of Good Hope, connecting across then the full extent of the Indian Ocean (Huurdeman 2003: 137).

11 Melville is far from alone in making this connection. Between 1840 and 1880, the ocean's meaning shifted to become perceived as an arena for "national accomplishment and imperialist influence" (see Rozwadowski 2005: 62 onwards).

Chapter 8

1 David H. Stam describes the bibliographic mission of the American Seaman's Friend Society as "the provision of Bibles and uplifting literature for the salvation of the sinful sailor and the conversion of the heathen" and estimates that "about 1,150,000 volumes [were] sent to sea by the [...] Society from 1859 to 1967" (2012: 45, 52). On the books available on Richard Evelyn Byrd's several twentieth-century Antarctic expeditions, see Stam (2016).

2   In *The View from the Masthead*, Blum stresses the literariness of being at sea in her effort "to reimagine the maritime world as a sphere of both manual and intellectual labor" (2008: 2). In "Floating Worlds: Poetry and the Voyage Out," the first chapter of *Imagined Homelands* (2017), Jason Rudy similarly stresses the sea voyage as a place of literary production, although in this case by passengers rather than sailors (19–42). In "First-Person Nautical," Blum and Rudy together argue that "Poetical communities at sea occupied a place of paradox between the exceptional intimacy of production and circulation, and the limitlessness of the surrounding ocean" (2013: 193).

3   The literary nature of being at sea as well as the responsibility maritime fiction bore for sending people to sea in the first place is frequently represented in novels of the period. Joseph Conrad's novels and short stories, for instance, make frequent reference to the love of reading by sailors before the mast. In *Lord Jim* (1900), a desire to go to sea is itself a product of such novels: "when after a course of light holiday literature his vocation for the sea had declared itself, he was sent at once to a 'training-ship for officers of the merchant marine'" (Conrad [1900] 2002: 4–5). In this Jim resembles his creator. About the sea fiction of Marryat and Cooper, Conrad wrote: "Perhaps no two authors of fiction influenced so many lives and gave to so many the initial impulse towards a glorious or useful career. Through the distances of space and time those two men of another race have shaped also the life of the writer of this appreciation" (1925: 56).

4   For Childers's various military engagements, see several extant biographies: Boyle (1977); Drummond (2016); McInerney (1971); Piper (2003); Ring (1996).

5   Drummond, in *The Riddle*, characterizes Childers as a Corinthian sailor and writes of the term: "The description 'Corinthian' was an American import that had become part of the language in the United States in the second half of the nineteenth century, where it was used to describe the ways of well-to-do amateur sportsmen. These men relied on their own expertise and prowess rather than enjoying the sport second-hand by watching a hired champion perform" (2016: 97). Corinthian disdain for second-hand pleasures as well as pomp often took the form of cutting remarks on yacht racing, particularly as exemplified by the Royal Yacht Club at Cowes, Isle of Wight. Knight, writing of a man he hired as crew, is typical: "John Wright has luckily had nothing to do with Cowes and yachts" ([1888] 1951: 30).

6   Knight's book was a key source for *The Riddle of the Sands*: Knight covered much the same ground as Carruthers and Davies. Moreover, the way he wrote of the Frisian Islands anticipates Childers's title and plot: "the sands on this coast are constantly shifting, so that a stranger can place no reliance on the recorded bearings and soundings" ([1888] 1951: 155).

7   McMullen on *Down Channel* as "a bare record of sailing" and Carruthers on the style of Dollman's book as "unadorned" both recall the plain style that had characterized mariners' narratives for centuries, a style Cohen calls "the language of work at sea" in which "efficiency and economy were paramount" (Childers [1903] 2011: 189; Cohen 2010: 42; McMullen [1893] 1986: 25).

8   Bender writes of *Sailing Tours*: "Pioneering yachting authors, such as McMullen, [John] MacGregor, [E.E.] Middleton, and E.F. Knight expanded yachtsmen's imaginations and horizons, but it was Cowper's endeavours that allowed the Corinthian philosophy to be put into practice around the British, Irish, and North Brittany coast" (2017: 158).

9   Bender goes further, arguing that Ransome, "very much a Corinthian," constructed the canon of cruising books in his own image when he chose the forty-seven volumes that were to be included in Rupert Hart-Davis's *Mariner's Library* (2017: 159).

BIBLIOGRAPHY

Achebe, Chinua (1977), "An Image of Africa: Racism in Conrad's Heart of Darkness," *Massachusetts Review*, 57 (1): 14–27.
Albion, Robert Greenhalgh (1939), *The Rise of New York Port (1815–1860)*, New York: Charles Scribner's Sons.
Albritton, Claude C. (1980), *The Abyss of Time: Changing Conceptions of the Earth's Antiquity after the Sixteenth Century*, San Francisco: Freeman, Cooper & Co.
Aldrich, Frederick A. (1992), "Some Aspects of the Systematics and Biology of Squid of the Genus *Architeuthis* Based on a Study of Specimens from Newfoundland Waters," *Bulletin of Marine Science*, 49 (1–2): 457–81.
Allen, David Elliston (1969), *The Victorian Fern Craze*, London: Hutchinson & Co.
Allingham, William (1904), "Neptune's Ocean Mail," *Gentleman's Magazine*, 296 (2078): 168–77.
Andersen, Hans Christian (1872), "The Great Sea Serpent: A New Wonder," *Scribner's Monthly*, 3 (3) (January): 325–9.
Anderson, Charles Robert, ed. (1966), *Journal of a Cruise to the Pacific Ocean, 1842–1844, in the Frigate United States, with notes on Herman Melville*, New York: AMS Press, Inc.
Anderson, Stephanie (2008), "'Three Living Australians' and the Société d'Anthropologie de Paris, 1885,'" in Bronwen Douglas and Chris Ballard (eds.), *Foreign Bodies: Oceania and the Science of Race, 1750–1940*, 229–55, Canberra: ANU Press.
Anderson, Stephanie (2009), *Pelletier: The Forgotten Castaway of Cape York*, Melbourne: Melbourne Books.
Anonymous (1818), "The Newly Discovered Nation," *Hereford Journal*, December 23: 4.
Anonymous (1855), "Wie er- und behält man den Ocean auf dem Tische, oder das Marine-Aquarium," *Die Gartenlaube*, 38: 503–5.
Anonymous (1856), "The Aquarium Simplified," *Home Friend*, 1: 130–2.
Ariew, Roger (1991), "A New Science of Geology in the Seventeenth Century?," in Peter Barker and Roger Ariew (eds.), *Revolution and Continuity: Essays in the*

History and Philosophy of Early Modern Science, 81–94, Washington, DC: Catholic University of America Press.
Armitage, David (2007), *The Declaration of Independence: A Global History*, Cambridge, MA: Harvard University Press.
Armitage, David, Alison Bashford, and Sujit Sivasundaram (2017), *Oceanic Histories*, New York: Cambridge University Press.
Armstrong, Carol (2004), *Ocean Flowers: Impressions from Nature*, Princeton, NJ: Princeton University Press.
Arnold, David (2006), *The Tropics and the Traveling Gaze: India, Landscape, and Science, 1800–1856*, Seattle: University of Washington Press.
Atholl, Katharine Marjory Stewart-Murray Duchess of (1908), *Military History of Perthshire*, Perth: R. A. & J. Hay.
Auden, W.H. (1951), *The Enchafèd Flood or the Romantic Iconography of the Sea*, London: Faber and Faber.
Bakhtin, Mikhail (1995), *Rabelais und seine Welt: Volkskultur als Gegenkultur*, Frankfurt: Suhrkamp.
Ballantyne, R.M. (1883), *The Battery and the Boiler*, London: James Nisbet & Co.
Banfield, Edmund J. (1898–1901), *Diary*, Edmund Banfield Collection, John Oxley Library, State Library of Queensland, Brisbane, Box 16031.
Banfield, Edmund J. (1907–8), "Dunk Island—Its General Characteristics," *Proceedings of the Geographical Society of Queensland*, 23: 51–64.
Banfield, Edmund J. ([1908] 2006), *The Confessions of a Beachcomber*, Rowville: Five Mile Press.
Banfield, Edmund J. (1912), *My Tropic Isle*, London: T. Fisher Unwin.
Banfield, Edmund J. ([1917] 2010), *Tropic Days* [e-book], Adelaide: University of Adelaide.
Banham, Joanna, ed. (1997), *Encyclopedia of Interior Design*, New York: Routledge.
Banks, Joseph (1963), *The Endeavour Journal of Joseph Banks*, 2 vols, ed. J.C. Beaglehole, Sydney: Trustees of Public Library of NSW in Association with Angus and Robertson.
Barrett, Charles (1939), *Koonwarra: A Naturalist's Adventures in Australia*, London: Oxford University Press, H. Milford.
Barthes, Roland ([1957] 1993), *Mythologies*, trans. Annette Lavers, London: Vintage.
Bateman, Gregory C. (1870), *Fresh-Water Aquaria: Their Construction, Arrangement, and Management*, London.
Bates, Claire and Robert Spencer (2016), "Who, What, Why: How Dangerous for Ships Is the Bay of Biscay?," *BBC News*, February 1. Available online: https://www.bbc.com/news/magazine-35461135 (accessed October 12, 2020).
Bayly, C.A. (2004), *The Birth of the Modern World: 1780–1914*, Oxford: Blackwell.
Beale, Howard K. (1967), *Theodore Roosevelt and the Rise of America to World Power*, New York: Collier Books.
Belon, Pierre (1555), *La Nature et Diversité des Poissons*, Paris.
Bender, Mike (2017), *A New History of Yachting*, Woodbridge: Boydell Press.
Benson, Keith, Helen Rozwadowski, and David van Keuren, eds. (2004), *The Machine in Neptune's Garden: Historical Perspectives on Technology and the Marine Environment*, Sagamore Beach, MA: Watson Publishing International LLC.
Betts, Jonathan (2017), *Marine Chronometers at Greenwich: A Catalogue of Marine Chronometers at the National Maritime Museum, Greenwich*, Oxford: Oxford Scholarship online.

Biddle, Tyrrel (1886), *The Corinthian Yachtsman, or Hints on Yachting*, London: Norie & Wilson.
Birns, Nicholas (2012), "'Thickly Studded Oriental Archipelagoes': *Figuring the Indian and Pacific Oceans in Moby-Dick*," *Leviathan: A Journal of Melville Studies*, 14 (2): 4–24.
Blum, Hester (2008), *The View from the Masthead: Maritime Imagination and Antebellum American Sea Narratives*, Chapel Hill: University of North Carolina Press.
Blum, Hester (2014), "Melville and Oceanic Studies," in Robert S. Levine (ed.), *The New Cambridge Companion to Herman Melville*, 22–36, Cambridge: Cambridge University Press.
Blum, Hester (2015), "A List of Books That I Did Not Read on the Voyage," *Leviathan: A Journal of Melville Studies*, 17 (1): 129–32.
Blum, Hester and Jason R. Rudy (2013), "First-Person Nautical: Poetry and Play at Sea," *J19: The Journal of Nineteenth-Century Americanists*, 1 (1): 189–94.
Boehmer, Elleke and Anshuman Mondal (2012), "Networks and Traces: An Interview with Amitav Ghosh," *Wasafiri*, 27 (2): 30–5.
Bolster, W. Jeffrey (2012), *The Mortal Sea*, Cambridge, MA: Harvard University Press.
Boswell, James ([1791] 1998), *Life of Johnson*, Oxford: Oxford University Press.
Bouquillard, Jocelyn (2007), *Hokusai's Mount Fuji: The Complete Views in Color*, New York: Harry N. Abrams.
Boutan, Louis (1898), "Submarine Photography," *Century Magazine*, 34: 42–9.
Boutan, Louis (1900), *La Photographie sous-marine et les progrès de la photographie*, Paris, Schleicher Frères.
Bowen, James and Margarita Bowen (2002), *The Great Barrier Reef: History, Science, Heritage*, New York: Cambridge University Press.
Boyle, Andrew (1977), *The Riddle of Erskine Childers*, London: Hutchinson.
Brassey, T.A., ed. (1902), *The Naval Annual*, Portsmouth: J. Griffin and Co.
Braswell, William (1937), "Melville as a Critic of Emerson," *American Literature*, 9 (3): 317–34.
Braudel, Fernand ([1969] 1980), "History and the Social Sciences, The *Long Durée*," in *On History*, 25–55, trans. Sarah Matthews, Chicago: University of Chicago Press.
Bravo, Michael (2006), "Geographies of Exploration and Improvement: William Scoresby and Arctic Whaling, 1782–1822," *Journal of Historical Geography*, 32: 512–38.
Bravo, Michael (2019), "Indigenous Voyaging, Authorship, and Discovery," in Adriana Craciun and Mary Terrall (eds.), *Curious Encounters: Voyaging, Collecting, and Making Knowledge in the Long Eighteenth Century*, 71–112, Toronto: Toronto University Press.
Brigham, Louise (1909), *Box Furniture*, New York: Century Co.
Brontë, Charlotte ([1853] 2001), *Villette*, New York: Modern Library.
Browne, Janet (1995), *Charles Darwin: Voyaging*, New York: Knopf.
Brunsman, Denver (2013), *The Evil Necessity: British Naval Impressment in the Eighteenth-Century Atlantic World*, Charlottesville: University of Virginia Press.
Burg, B.R. (1997), "'Women and Children First': Popular Mythology and Disaster at Sea, 1840–1860," *Journal of American Culture*, 20 (4): 1–9.
Burnet, Thomas (1864), *The Theory of the Earth*, London.
Burton, James, ed. (2018), *The State of the Polar Oceans 2018: Making Sense of Our Changing World*, British Antarctic Survey, July 17. Available online: https://www.bas.ac.uk/wp-content/uploads/2018/07/State-of-the-Polar-Oceans-2018_final.pdf (accessed October 12, 2020).

Butler, Henry D. (1858), *The Family Aquarium; or, Aqua Vivarium. A New Pleasure for the Domestic Circle*, New York: Dick & Fitzgerald.
Byron, George Gordon, Lord (1819), *The Complete Works of Lord Byron*, vol. 1, London: John Murray.
Cadbury, Deborah (2001), *Dinosaur Hunters: A True Story of Scientific Rivalry and the Discovery of the Prehistoric World*, New York: Harper Collins.
Campbell, Mary (1988), *The Witness and the Other World: Exotic European Travel Writing 400–1600*, Ithaca, NY: Cornell University Press.
Cappon, Lester J., ed. ([1959] 1987), *The Adams – Jefferson Letters: The Complete Correspondence between Thomas Jefferson & Abigail & John Adams*, Chapel Hill: University of North Carolina Press.
Carson, Rachel ([1951] 2003), *The Sea Around Us*, New York: Oxford University Press.
Cartwright, David Edgar (1999), *Tides: A Scientific History*, Cambridge: Cambridge University Press.
"Charles W. Morgan" (n.d.), Mystic Seaport Museum. Available online: https://www.mysticseaport.org/explore/morgan/ (accessed September 19, 2019).
Chesney, George Tomkyns ([1871] 1977), *The Battle of Dorking: Reminiscences of a Volunteer*, in I.F. Clarke (ed.), *The Battle of Dorking and When William Came*, Oxford: Oxford University Press.
Childers, Erskine (1897–9), Cruising Log of the Yacht *Vixen*, RCC/2, Royal Cruising Club Collection, National Maritime Museum, Greenwich, UK.
Childers, Erskine (1900), *In the Ranks of the C.I.V.: A Narrative and Diary of Personal Experiences with the C.I.V. Battery (Honourable Artillery Company) in South Africa*, London: Smith, Elder, & Co.
Childers, Erskine (1903), *The Riddle of the Sands: A Record of Secret Service Recently Achieved*, London: Smith, Elder, & Co.
Childers, Erskine ([1903] 2011), *The Riddle of the Sands: A Record of Secret Service*, London: Penguin.
Childers, Erskine (1910), *War and the Arme Blanche*, London: Edward Arnold.
Childers, Erskine (1911), *German Influence on British Cavalry*, London: Edward Arnold.
Christopher, Emma (2006), *Slave Ship Sailors and Their Captive Cargoes, 1730–1807*, New York: Cambridge University Press.
Christopher, Emma, Cassandra Pybus, and Marcus Rediker, eds. (2007), *Many Middle Passages: Forced Migration and the Making of the Modern World*, Berkeley: University of California Press.
Christopher, Emma (2007), "'The Slave Trade Is Merciful Compared to [This]': Slave Traders, Convict Transportation, and the Abolitionists," in Emma Christopher, Cassandra Pybus, and Marcus Rediker (eds.), *Many Middle Passages: Forced Migration and the Making of the Modern World*, 109–28, Berkeley: University of California.
Clark, A. Howard (1887), "History and Present Conditions of the [Whale] Fishery," in George Brown Goode (ed.), *The Fisheries and Fishery Industries of the United States*, vol. 2, pt. 15, 2–218, Washington, DC: Government Printing Office.
Clark, Arthur H. (1912), *The Clipper Ship Era*, New York: G. P. Putnam's Sons.
Claveyrolas, Mathieu (2018), "From the Indian Ganges to a Mauritian Lake: Hindu Pilgrimage in a 'Diasporic' Context," in Simon Coleman and John Eade (eds.), *Pilgrimage and Political Economy: Translating the Sacred*, 21–39, New York: Berghahn Books.

Cleveland, Richard J. (1842), *A Narrative of Voyages and Commercial Enterprises*, 2 vols, Cambridge, MA: Published by John Owen.
Cohen, Margaret (2010), *The Novel and the Sea*, Princeton, NJ: Princeton University Press.
Cohen, Margaret (2014), "Underwater Optics as Symbolic Form," *French Politics, Culture & Society*, 32 (3): 1–23.
Cohn, Raymond (2005), "The Transition from Sail to Steam in Immigration to the United States," *Journal of Economic History*, 65 (2): 469–95.
Connery, Christopher (2006), "*There Was No More Sea*: The Supersession of the Ocean, from the Bible to Cyberspace," *Journal of Historical Geography*, 32: 494–511.
Conrad, Joseph ([1897] 1974), *The Nigger of the "Narcissus,"* London: Dent.
Conrad, Joseph ([1899] 2002), *Heart of Darkness*, in *Heart of Darkness and Other Tales*, ed. Cedric Watts, 103–87, Oxford: Oxford University Press.
Conrad, Joseph ([1899] 2006), *Heart of Darkness*, ed. Paul Armstrong, New York: W. W. Norton.
Conrad, Joseph ([1899] 2016), *Heart of Darkness*, New York: W.W. Norton.
Conrad, Joseph ([1900] 2002), *Lord Jim: A Tale*, New York: Oxford University Press.
Conrad, Joseph ([1900] 2008), *Lord Jim: A Tale*, Oxford: Oxford University Press.
Conrad, Joseph ([1902] 1953), *Typhoon*, in *Tales of Land and Sea*, with an introduction by William McFee 287–347, Garden City, NY: Hanover House.
Conrad, Joseph ([1902] 2008), *Typhoon*, in *Typhoon and Other Tales*, ed. Cedric Watts, 3–74, Oxford: Oxford University Press.
Conrad, Joseph ([1903] 2008), "Falk: A Reminiscence," in *Typhoon and Other Tales*, ed. Cedric Watts, 75–145, Oxford: Oxford University Press.
Conrad, Joseph ([1906] 1924), *The Mirror of the Sea*, New York: Doubleday.
Conrad, Joseph (1912), *A Personal Record*, New York: Harper & Brothers.
Conrad, Joseph ([1912] 1921), *'Twixt Land and Sea*, London: Heinemann.
Conrad, Joseph ([1919] 2008), "Author's Note," in *Typhoon and Other Tales*, ed. Cedric Watts, 218–20, Oxford: Oxford University Press.
Conrad, Joseph (1921), "Tales of the Sea," in *Notes on Life and Letters*, 73–8, London: William Heinemann.
Conrad, Joseph (1925), *Notes on Life and Letters*, Edinburgh: John Grant.
Conrad, Joseph (1926), *Last Essays*, London: J. M. Dent and Sons.
Conybeare, William (1824),"On the Discovery of an Almost Perfect Skeleton of the Plesiosaurus," *Transactions of the Geological Society of London*, 1: 412–21.
Cook, James (1955), *The Journals of Captain James Cook on His Voyages of Discovery*, vol. 1, ed. J.C. Beaglehole, Cambridge: Published for the Hakluyt Society at the University Press.
Cooper, James Fenimore ([1824] 1986), *The Pilot*, in *Sea Tales*, 1–422, New York: The Library of America.
Corbin, Alain (1994), *The Lure of the Sea: The Discovery of the Seaside in the Western World*, trans. Jocelyn Phelps, Berkeley: University of California Press.
Cowper, Frank (1892–6), *Sailing Tours: The Yachtsman's Guide to the Cruising Waters of the English Coast*, 5 vols, London: L. Upcott Gill.
Craciun, Adriana (2010), "The Frozen Ocean," *PMLA*, 125 (3): 693–702.
Craciun, Adriana (2013), "Oceanic Voyages, Maritime Books, and Eccentric Inscriptions," *Atlantic Studies*, 10 (2): 170–96.

Craciun, Adriana and Mary Terrall (2019), "Introduction," in Adriana Craciun and Mary Terrall (eds.), *Curious Encounters: Voyaging, Collecting, and Making Knowledge in the Long Eighteenth Century*, 3–18, Toronto: Toronto University Press.
Cushman, Gregory T. (2013), *Guano and the Opening of the Pacific World*, New York: Cambridge University Press.
Cutler, Carl C. (1930), *Greyhounds of the Sea: The Story of the American Clipper Ship*, Annapolis, MD: United States Naval Institute.
Damon, William E. (1879), *Ocean Wonders: A Companion for the Sea Side; Aquaria*, New York: D. Appleton and Company.
Dana, Richard Henry, Jr. (1840), *Two Years Before the Mast: A Personal Narrative of Life at Sea*, New York: Harper and Bros.
Dana, Richard Henry, Jr. ([1840] 1911), *Two Years Before the Mast: A Personal Narrative*, Boston: Houghton Mifflin Co.
Dana, Richard Henry, Jr. ([1840] 1986), *Two Years Before the Mast: A Personal Narrative of Life at Sea*, Harmondsworth: Penguin.
Dana, Richard Henry, Jr. (1936), *Two Years Before the Mast*, New York: Modern Library.
Darwin, Charles (1851), *A Monograph of the Sub-class Cirripedia, with Figures of All the Species*, London: Ray Society.
Davie, John (1804), *Observations and Instructions for the Use of the Commissioned, the Junior, and Other Officers of the Royal Navy*, London: P. Steel at the Navigation Warehouse.
Davis, Lance E., Robert E. Gallman, and Karin Gleiter (1997), *In Pursuit of Leviathan: Technology, Institutions, Productivity, and Profits in American Whaling, 1816–1906*, Chicago: University of Chicago Press.
Deacon, Margaret (1997), *Scientists and the Sea: 1650–1900; A Study of Marine Science*, Aldershot: Routledge.
Defoe, Daniel ([1719] 1998), *Robinson Crusoe*, Oxford: Oxford University Press.
Delumeau, Jean ([1978] 1989), *Angst im Abendland: Die Geschichte kollektiver Ängste im Europa des 14. bis 18. Jahrhunderts*, Hamburg: Rowohlt.
Derham, William (1726), *The Philosophical Experiments and Observations of the Late Eminent Dr. Robert Hooke*, London: W. and J. Innys.
Dias, João Ferreira and Patrice Guillotreau (2004), "Nearly Two Centuries of Fish Canning: An Historical Look at European Exports of Fish," in *Proceedings of IIFET 2004*. Available online: https://www.researchgate.net/publication/280945477_Nearly_two_centuries_of_fish_canning_an_historical_look_at_european_exports_of_canned_fish (accessed September 26, 2019).
Dick, Joanna Agnes (1825), "Letter to Mary Dick," John MacGregor Papers, National Maritime Museum, Greenwich, 25–85.
Douglass, Frederick (1845), *Narrative of the Life of Frederick Douglass, An American Slave, Written by Himself*, Boston: Published at the Anti-Slavery Office. Available online: http://utc.iath.virginia.edu/abolitn/dougnarrhp.html (accessed September 26, 2019).
Douglass, Frederick (2015), *The Heroic Slave*, eds. Robert S. Levine, John Stauffer, and John R. McKivigan, New Haven, CT: Yale University Press.
Dow, George Francis (1927), *Slave Ships and Slaving*, Cambridge, MD: Cornell Maritime Press.

Dowdeswell, J.A., M. Canals, M. Jakobsson, B.J. Todd, E.K. Dowdeswell, and K.A. Hogan, eds. (2016), *Atlas of Submarine Glacial Landforms: Modern, Quaternary and Ancient*, Memoirs 46, London: Geological Society of London.

Druett, Joan, ed. (1992), *"She Was a Sister Sailor": Mary Brewster's Whaling Journals, 1845–1851,* Mystic, CT: Mystic Seaport Museum.

Drummond, Maldwin (2016), *The Riddle: Illuminating the Story Behind* The Riddle of the Sands, 2nd edn., London: Uniform.

Ducruet, C. (2013), "Mapping Global Urban Interactions: Maritime Flows and Port Hierarchies since the Late Nineteenth Century," *GaWC Research Bulletin*, 429, September 18. Available online: https://www.lboro.ac.uk/gawc/rb/rb429.html (accessed September 26, 2019).

Dufferin, Lord ([1856] 1873), *Letters from High Latitudes*, 6th edn., London: John Murray.

Ellis, Joseph J. (1998), *American Sphinx: The Character of Thomas Jefferson*, New York: Vintage Books.

Ellis, Joseph J. (2002), *Founding Brothers: The Revolutionary Generation*, New York: Vintage Books.

Ellis, Richard (1994), *Monsters of the Sea*, New York: Knopf.

Emerson, Ralph Waldo (1847), *Essays: First Series*, new edn., Boston: James Munroe and Co.

"Exhibition of the Royal Academy" (1840), *The Times*, May 6.

Fabricius, Otto (n.d.), "On the Floating Ice in the Northern Waters," Joseph Banks Manuscript Collection, Sutro Library, San Francisco.

Falconer, William (1762), *The Shipwreck: A Poem; In Three Cantos; By a Sailor*, London: Printed for the Author; and sold by A. Millar.

Findlay, Alexander George (1884), *A Directory for the Navigation of the South Pacific Ocean*, 5th edn., London: Richard Holmes Laurie.

Flexner, James Thomas (1962), *That Wilder Image*, Boston: Little, Brown and Co.

Forest, J. (1996), "Henri Milne Edwards," *Journal of Crustacean Biology*, 16 (1): 207–13.

Foucault, Michel (1986), "Of Other Spaces," trans. Jay Miskowiec, *Diacritics*, 16 (1): 22–7.

Foulke, Robert (2002), *The Sea Voyage Narrative*, New York: Routledge.

Franklin, Wayne (2007), *James Fenimore Cooper: The Early Years*, New Haven, CT: Yale University Press.

Freedgood, Elaine (2010), "Fictional Settlements: Footnotes, Metalepsis, and the Colonial Effect," *New Literary History*, 41 (2): 393–411.

Friedman, John Block (1981), *The Monstrous Races in Medieval Art and Thought*, Cambridge, MA: Harvard University Press.

Frumer, Yulia (2018), *Making Time: Astronomical Measurement in Tokugawa Japan*, Chicago: University of Chicago Press.

Furneaux, William (1896), *Life in Ponds and Streams*, London: Longmans & Green.

Gallagher, Catherine (2018), *Telling It Like It Wasn't: The Counterfactual Imagination in History and Fiction*, Chicago: University of Chicago Press.

Gearheard, Shari Fox, Lene Kielsen Holm, Henry Huntington, Joe Mello Leavitt, Andrew Mahoney, Margaret Opie, Toku Oshima, and Joelie Sanguya, eds. (2013), *The Meaning of Ice: People and Sea Ice in Three Arctic Communities*, Hanover, NH: International Polar Institute Press.

Geikie, Archibald (1897), *The Founders of Geology*, London: Macmillan.

Gerald of Wales (c. 1188), *Topographia Hiberniae, sive de mirabilibus Hiberniae*, British Library (BL), Royal MS 13 B VIII.

Gervaise of Tilbury ([c. 1211] 2002), *Otia Imperialia*, eds. S.E. Banks and J.W. Binns, Oxford: Oxford University Press.

Gesner, Conrad (1558), *Historiae Animalium: Liber 4 qui est de Piscium & Aquatilium Animantium natura*, Tiguri.

Ghosh, Amitav (2008), "Of Fanás and Forecastles: The Indian Ocean and Some Lost Languages of the Age of Sail," *Economic and Political Weekly*, 43 (25): 56–62.

Gibson, Gregory (2002), *Demon of the Waters*, Boston: Little, Brown and Co.

Gillis, John (2004), *Islands of the Mind: How the Human Imagination Created the Atlantic World*, New York: Palgrave Macmillan.

Gilroy, Paul (1993), *The Black Atlantic: Modernity and Double Consciousness*, Cambridge, MA: Harvard University Press.

Goldrick, James and John. B. Hattendorf, eds. (1993), *Mahan Is Not Enough: The Proceedings of a Conference on the Works of Sir Julian Corbett and Admiral Sir Herbert Richmond*, Newport, RI: Naval War College Press.

Golinski, Jay (2007), *British Weather and the Climate of Enlightenment*, Chicago: University of Chicago Press.

Gosse, Philip Henry (1853), *A Naturalist's Rambles on the Devonshire Coast*, London, John Van Voorst.

Gosse, Philip Henry (1854), *The Aquarium: An Unveiling of the Wonders of the Deep Sea*, London, John Van Voorst.

Gould, Stephen Jay (1987), *Time's Arrow, Time's Cycle: Myth and Metaphor in the Discovery of Geological Time*, Cambridge, MA: Harvard University Press.

Graham, Gerald S. (1956), "The Ascendancy of the Sailing Ship 1850–85," *The Economic History Review*, n.s., 9 (1): 74–88.

Grocott, Terence (2002), *Shipwrecks of the Revolutionary & Napoleonic Eras*, London: Caxton Editions.

Gurnah, Abdulrazak (2005), *Desertion*, London: Bloomsbury.

Halley, Edmond (1715), "A Short Account of the Cause of the Saltiness of the Ocean," *Philosophical Transactions of the Royal Society*, 29: 296–300.

Halley, Edmond (1716), "The Art of Living Under Water: Or, a Discourse Concerning the Means of Furnishing Air at the Bottom of the Sea, in Any Ordinary Depths," *Philosophical Transactions of the Royal Society*, 349: 492–9.

Halliday, Andrew (1837), *The West Indies: The Natural and Physical History of the Windward and Leeward Colonies*, London: J. W. Parker.

Hansson, Heidi (2009), "The Gentleman's North: Lord Dufferin and the Beginnings of Arctic Tourism," *Studies in Travel Writing*, 13 (1): 61–73.

Hantschk, Andreas and Stephanie Kruspel (2001), "With Sketchbook and Diving Bell: A Viennese Painter Underwater," *Historical Diver*, 9 (3): 40–3.

Harley, C. Knick (1988), "Ocean Freight Rates and Productivity, 1740–1913: The Primacy of Mechanical Invention Reaffirmed," *Journal of Economic History*, 48 (4): 851–76.

Harper, John (1856), "Parlour Aquaria," *Family Friend*, 2: 192–7.

Harper, John (1858), *The Sea-Side and Aquarium; or; Anecdote and Gossip on Marine Zoology*, Edinburgh: William P. Nimmo.

Hattendorf, John (1970), "Westward 'Round Cape Horn: A Study of Americans in the Navigation of Cape Horn En Route to the Pacific," Mystic Seaport, unpublished, MS RF122.

Hattendorf, John. B., ed. (1991), *The Influence of History on Mahan: The Proceedings of a Conference Marking the Centenary of Alfred Thayer Mahan's* The Influence of Sea Power upon History, 1660–1783, Newport, RI: Naval War College Press.

Hawkesworth, John, D., Warrington Evans, and James Cook (1969), *An Account of a Voyage Round the World with a Full Account of the Voyage of the Endeavour in the Year MDCCLXX along the East Coast of Australia*, Brisbane: Smith & Paterson.

Hayes, K.J. (2007), *The Cambridge Introduction to Herman Melville*, Cambridge: Cambridge University Press.

Hearn, H.E. (1897), "Letters from Spitsbergen," *Spitsbergen Gazette* 4 (July 20): 1.

Heflin, Wilson (2004), *Herman Melville's Whaling Years*, eds. Mary K. Bercaw Edwards and Thomas Farel Heffernan, Nashville, TN: Vanderbilt University Press.

Helmreich, Stefan (2015a), "Old Waves, New Waves: Changing Objects in Physical Oceanography," in John Gillis and Franziska Torma (eds.), *Fluid Frontiers: New Currents in Marine and Maritime Environmental History*, 76–88, Cambridge: White Horse Press.

Helmreich, Stefan (2015b), *Sounding the Limits of Life: Essays in the Anthropology of Biology and Beyond*, Princeton, NJ: Princeton University Press.

Hibberd, Shirley (1869), *The Fern Garden*, London: Cambridge University Press.

Hitchcock, Edward (1841), *Elementary Geology*, 2nd edn., New York: Dayton and Saxton.

Hobsbawm, Eric (1977), *The Age of Revolution: 1789–1848*, London: Abacus.

Hofmeyr, Isabel (2007), "The Black Atlantic meets the Indian Ocean: Forging New Paradigms of Transnationalism for the Global South—Literary and Cultural Perspectives," *Social Dynamics*, 33 (2): 3–32.

Hofmeyr, Isabel (2012), "The Complicating Sea: The Indian Ocean as Method," *Comparative Studies of South Asia, Africa and the Middle East*, 32 (3): 584–90.

Hohman, Elmo Paul (1928), *The American Whaleman*, New York: Longmans, Green and Co.

Howard, Warren S. (1963), *American Slavers and the Federal Law, 1837–1862*, Berkeley: University of California Press.

Hough-Snee, Dexter Zavalza and Alexander Sotelo Eastman (2017), *The Critical Surf Studies Reader*, Durham, NC: Duke University Press.

Høvik, Ingeborg (2013), "Arctic Images 1818–1859," PhD diss., University of Edinburgh.

Hu-DeHart, Evelyn (2007),"La Trata Amarilla: The 'Yellow Trade' and the Middle Passage, 1847–1884," in Emma Christopher, Cassandra Pybus, and Marcus Rediker (eds.), *Many Middle Passages: Forced Migration and the Making of the Modern World*, 166–83, Berkeley: University of California Press.

Hugo, Victor ([1866] 2002), *The Toilers of the Sea*, trans. James Hogarth, New York: Modern Library.

Humboldt, Alexander von (1814), *Personal Narrative of Travels to the Equinoctial Regions of the New Continent During the Years 1799–1804*, trans. Helen Maria Williams, London: Longman, Hurst, Rees, Orme, and Brown.

Humphreys, H. Noel (1857), *River Gardens; Being an Account of the Best Methods of Cultivating Fresh-Water Plants in Aquaria*, London: Sampson Low, Son, and Co.

Hutchins, Edwin (1995), *Cognition in the Wild*, Cambridge, MA: MIT Press.

Huurdeman, Anton A. (2003), *The Worldwide History of Telecommunications*, Hoboken, NJ: John Wiley and Sons.

Huxley, Thomas H. (1854), "Science at Sea," *Westminster Review*, 61: 98–119.
Huxley, Thomas H. (1883), *Inaugural Meeting of the Fishery Congress: Address by Professor Huxley*, London: W. Clowes and Son.
"Interesting from Chile ... " (1858), *The New York Times*, March 2: 1.
Israel, Jonathan (2017), *The Expanding Blaze: How the American Revolution Ignited the World, 1775–1848*, Princeton, NJ: Princeton University Press.
Jacobs, Stan (1992), "The Voyage of Iceberg B-9," *American Scientist*, 80 (1): 32–42.
Jäger, Gustav (1908), *Das Leben im Wasser und das Aquarium*, Stuttgart: Gesellschaft der Naturefreunde.
Jameson, Fredric ([1981] 2002), *The Political Unconscious: Narrative as a Socially Symbolic Act*, London: Routledge.
Jasanoff, Maya (2017), *The Dawn Watch: Joseph Conrad in a Global World*, London: William Collins.
"John MacGregor ('Rob Roy')" (1895), *The Leisure Hour*, 44: 43–7.
Jung, Michael (1999), *Das Handbuch zur Tauchgeschichte: Techniken, Geräte, Berufe, Erfindungen*, Stuttgart: Delius Klasing.
Kaalund, Bodil (1983), *The Art of Greenland*, Berkeley: University of California Press.
Kane, Elisha Kent (1856), *Arctic Explorations in the Years 1854, '54, '55*, vol. 1, Philadelphia: Childs and Peterson.
Kapel, Finn (2005), *Otto Fabricius and the Seals of Greenland*, Copenhagen: Danish Polar Center.
Kelly, John (2012), *The Graves Are Walking: The History of the Great Irish Famine*, London: Faber and Faber.
Kemp, Dixon (1878), *A Manual of Yacht and Boat Sailing*, London: "The Field" Office.
Kemp, Peter (1988), *The Oxford Companion to Ships and the Sea*, New York: Oxford University Press.
Kingsley, Charles (1859), *Glaucus; or, the Wonders of the Shore*, Cambridge, MacMillan and Co.
Kipling, Rudyard ([1897] 1995), *Captains Courageous*, New York: Oxford University Press.
Kirker, James (1970), *Adventures to China, Americans in the Southern Oceans 1792–1812*, New York: Oxford University Press.
Knight, E.F. [Edward Frederick] ([1888] 1951), *The Falcon on the Baltic: A Coasting Voyage from Hammersmith to Copenhagen in a Three-Ton Yacht*, London: Rupert Hart-Davis.
Korhs, Donald G. (2015), *Chautauqua: The Nature Study Movement in Pacific Grove, California*, [Pacific Grove, CA]: Donald G. Kohrs.
Kubodera, Tsunemi and Kyoichi Mori (2005), "First-Ever Observations of a Live Giant Squid in the Wild," *Proceedings of the Royal Society: Biological Sciences*, 272: 2583–6.
Kubodera, Tsunemi and Kyoichi Mori (2007), "Observations of Wild Hunting Behaviour and Bioluminescence of a Large Deep-Sea, Eight-Armed Squid, *Taningia danae*," *Proceedings of the Royal Society: Biological Sciences*, 274: 1029–34.
Landes, David (1988), *The Unbound Prometheus: Technological Change and Industrial Development in Western Europe from 1750 to the Present*, New York: Cambridge University Press.
Larabee, Mark (2018), *The Historian's Heart of Darkness; Reading Conrad's Masterpiece as Social and Cultural History*, Santa Barbara, CA: Praeger.
Lavery, Brian (2015), *Empire of the Seas*, London: Bloomsbury.

Lavery, Charne (2017), "The Indian Ocean Meets the South Seas: Abdulrazak Gurnah's *Desertion* and Robert Louis Stevenson's Beachcombers," *Wasafiri: A Journal of Postcolonial Studies*, 32 (1): 33–9.

Lavery, Charne (2020), "Diving into the Slave Wreck: The *São José Paquete d'Africa* and Yvette Christiansë's *Imprendehora*," *Eastern African Literary and Cultural Studies*, published online ahead of print September 10, 2020: 1–15.

Lawrence, D.H. ([1923] 2003), *Studies in Classic American Literature*, Cambridge: Cambridge University Press.

Laxton, Edward (1997), *The Famine Ships: The Irish Exodus to America 1846–51*, London: Bloomsbury.

Lewis, David (1994), *We, the Navigators: The Ancient Art of Landfinding in the Pacific*, Honolulu: University of Hawaii Press.

Linebaugh, Peter and Marcus Rediker (2000), *The Many-Headed Hydra: The Hidden History of the Revolutionary Atlantic*, London: Verso.

Logkeeper (1845–9), Logbook of the *Commodore Morris* (capt. Silas Jones), Falmouth Historical Society, 2013.076.09.

London, Jack ([1904] 2000), *The Sea-Wolf*, Oxford: Oxford University Press.

Lonicer, Adam (1551–5), *Historiae Naturalis opus novum*, 2 vols., Frankfurt.

Loomis, Chauncey (1977), "The Arctic Sublime," in U.C. Knoepflmacher and G.B. Tennyson (eds.), *Nature and the Victorian Imagination*, 95–112, Berkeley: University of California Press.

Lopez, Barry (1986), *Arctic Dreams: Imagination and Desire in a Northern Landscape*, New York: Charles Scribner's Sons.

Lowes, John Livingston (1927), *The Road to Xanadu: A Study in the Ways of the Imagination*, Boston: Houghton Mifflin.

MacGregor, Duncan (1825a), "*Kent* Letter," John MacGregor Papers, National Maritime Museum, Greenwich.

MacGregor, Duncan (1825b), "Letter to John MacGregor (Copy)," John MacGregor Papers, National Maritime Museum, Greenwich, 1–19.

MacGregor, Duncan (1825c), *A Narrative of the Loss of the Kent East-Indiaman, in the Bay of Biscay, by Fire, March 1, 1825: In a Letter to a Friend by a Passenger*, Edinburgh: Waugh and Innes.

MacGregor, Duncan (1826), "Letter to Miss Joanna Dick (Copy)," John MacGregor Papers, National Maritime Museum, Greenwich, 110–16.

Mack, John (2011), *The Sea, A Cultural History*, London: Reaktion Books.

Madison, James (1999), "War Message to Congress," in Jack N. Rakove (ed.), *Writings*, 685–92, New York: Library of America.

Madison, R.D., ed. (2016), *The Essex and the Whale: Melville's Leviathan Library and the Birth of Moby-Dick*, Santa Barbara, CA: Praeger.

Mahan, A.T. ([1889] 2016), *The Influence of Sea Power upon History 1660–1783*, New York: Dover.

Mahan, Captain A.T. [Alfred Thayer] (1890), *The Influence of Sea Power Upon History, 1660–1783*, London: S. Low, Marston, Searle & Rivington.

Mahan, Captain A.T. [Alfred Thayer] (1897), *The Life of Nelson: The Embodiment of the Sea Power of Great Britain*, 2 vols, Boston: Little, Brown and Co.

Mangin, Arthur (1868), *The Mysteries of the Ocean*, trans. W.H. Davenport Adams, London: T. Nelson and Sons.

Mandeville, John ([1480] 1983), *The Travels of Sir John Mandeville*, trans. C.W.R. D. Mosley, Harmondsworth: Penguin.

Marsilli, Luigi Ferdinando (1725), *Histoire physique de la Mer*, Amsterdam: aux dépens de la Compagnie.
Marx, Robert (1990), *A History of Underwater Exploration*, New York: Dover.
Massey, Doreen (2005), *For Space*, London: Sage.
Materlinck, Maurice (1889), "Aquarium," in *Serres chaudes*, Belgium.
Matilsky, Barbara (1985), "François-Auguste Biard: Artist-Naturalist-Explorer," *Gazette des Beaux-Arts*, 105: 75–88.
Maury, M.F. (1834), "On the Navigation of Cape Horn," *American Journal of Science and Arts (Silliman's Journal)*, 26 (1): 54–63.
Maury, M.F. (1855), *The Physical Geography of the Sea*, London: Sampson Low, Son & Co.
Mayne, Richard (2000), *The Language of Sailing*, Manchester: Carcanet Press.
McCalman, Iain (2013), *The Reef: A Passionate History—From Captain Cook to Climate Change*, New York: Scientific American/ Farrar, Straus and Giroux.
McGhee, Robert (2007), *The Last Imaginary Place: A Human History of the Arctic*, Chicago: University of Chicago Press.
McInerney, Michael (1971), *The Riddle of Erskine Childers*, Dublin: E. & T. O'Brien.
McMullen, R.T. [Richard Turrell] ([1893] 1986), *Down Channel*, London: Grafton.
Melville, Herman ([1845] 1968), *Typee: A Peep at Polynesian Life*, eds. Harrison Hayford, Hershel Parker, and G. Thomas Tanselle, Evanston and Chicago, IL: Northwestern University Press and The Newberry Library.
Melville, Herman ([1847] 1968), *Omoo: A Narrative of Adventures in the South Seas*, ed. Harrison Hayford, Hershel Parker, and G. Thomas Tanselle, Evanston and Chicago, IL: Northwestern University Press and The Newberry Library.
Melville, Herman ([1849] 1969), *Redburn: His First Voyage*, Evanston and Chicago: Northwestern University Press.
Melville, Herman ([1850] 1979), *White-Jacket, Or the World in a Man-of-War*, New York: Signet Classic.
Melville, Herman ([1850] 1988), *White-Jacket, or The World in a Man-of-War*, eds. Harrison Hayford, Hershel Parker, and G. Thomas Tanselle, Evanston and Chicago, IL: Northwestern University Press and The Newberry Library.
Melville, Herman ([1851] 1981), *Moby-Dick*, Berkeley: University of California Press.
Melville, Herman ([1851] 1988), *Moby-Dick or The Whale*, eds. Harrison Hayford, Hershel Parker, and G. Thomas Tanselle, Evanston and Chicago, IL: Northwestern University Press and The Newberry Library.
Melville, Herman ([1851] 2001), *Moby-Dick, or The Whale*, New York: Penguin.
Melville, Herman ([1851] 2002), *Moby Dick; or, The Whale*, Ware: Wordsworth.
Melville, Herman (1989), *Journals*, eds. Howard C. Horsford and Lynn Horth, Evanston and Chicago, IL: Northwestern University Press and The Newberry Library.
Melville, Herman (1993), *Correspondence*, ed. Lynn Horth, Evanston and Chicago, IL: Northwestern University Press and The Newberry Library.
Mencken, H. L. ([1917] 1930), "Joseph Conrad," in *A Book of Prefaces*, 11–66, New York: Knopf.
Mentz, Steve and Martha Elena Rojas (2016), *The Sea and Nineteenth-Century Anglophone Literary Culture*, London: Taylor & Francis
Merland, Constant ([1876] 2009), "Dix-sept Ans chez les sauvages. Les Aventures de Narcisse Pelletier," trans. Stephanie Anderson, in *Pelletier: The Forgotten Castaway of Cape York*, 132–281, Melbourne: Melbourne Books.

"Messages from the Sea" (1890), *Chambers's Journal of Popular Literature, Science and Arts*, 7 (363): 795–8.

Michelet, Jules (2012), *The Sea*, trans. Katia Sainson, Los Angeles: Green Integer.

Mollard, Claude and Gilles Gauthier (2018), *The Epic of the Suez Canal, from the Pharoahs to the 21st Century* (press kit), Paris: Institut du Monde Arabe.

Moore, David R. (1979), *Islanders and Aborigines at Cape York: An Ethnographic Reconstruction Based on the 1848–50 "Rattlesnake" Journals of O. W. Brierly and Information Obtained from Barbara Thompson*, Canberra: Australian Institute of Aboriginal Studies.

Müller, Irmgard (1976), *Die Geschichte der Zoologischen Station in Neapel von der Gründung durch Anton Dohrn (1872) bis zum Ersten Weltkrieg und ihre Bedeutung für die Entwicklung der modernen Biologischen Wissenschaften*, Düsseldorf: Universität Düsseldorf.

Murphy, Dallas (2004), *Rounding the Horn*, New York: Basic Books.

Mustakeem, Sowande' M. (2016), *Slavery at Sea: Terror, Sex, and Sickness in the Middle Passage*, Urbana: University of Illinois Press.

Naipaul, V.S. (1974), "Conrad's Darkness and Mine," *New York Review of Books*, October 17.

Neill, Peter, ed. (2000), *American Sea Writing*, New York: Library of America.

Nesbitt, Nick (2008), *Universal Emancipation: The Haitian Revolution and the Radical Enlightenment*, Charlottesville: University of Virginia Press.

Noonan, Michael (1986), *A Different Drummer: The Story of E. J. Banfield, Beachcomber of Dunk Island*, St. Lucia: University of Queensland Press.

Norton, Trevor (1999), *Stars Beneath the Sea: The Extraordinary Lives of the Pioneers of Diving*, London: Century.

Novak, Barbara (1969), *American Painting of the Nineteenth Century*, London: Pall Mall Press.

Ortleb, Alexander and Gustav Ortleb (1885), *Das Süßwasseraquarium und Terrarium: Anleitung zur Herstellung von Aquarien und Terrarien, Springbrunnen, Laubfrosch- und Goldfischgläsern nebst Beschreibung der dazu gehörigen Tiere und Pflanzen*, Berlin: Mode.

Osterhammel, Jürgen (2014), *The Transformation of the World. A Global History of the Nineteenth Century*, trans. Patrick Camiller, Princeton, NJ: Princeton University Press.

Oxford English Dictionary (OED) Online (2008), s.v. "network, n. and adj.," July 2018, Oxford: Oxford University Press. Available online: https://www.oed.com/ (accessed October 12, 2020).

Parker, Hershel (2002), *Herman Melville: A Biography*, vol. 2, *1851–1891*, Baltimore: Johns Hopkins University Press.

Pearson, Michael (2003), *The Indian Ocean*, London: Routledge.

Peck, John (2001), *Maritime Fiction: Sailors and the Sea in British and American Novels, 1719–1917*, New York: Palgrave.

The Penny Cyclopædia of The Society for the Diffusion of Useful Knowledge (1836), vol. 6, London: Charles Knight and Co.

Peterson, R.G., L. Stramma, and G. Kortum (1996), "Early Concepts and Charts of Ocean Circulation," *Progress in Oceanography*, 37: 1–115.

Peterson, William N. (1989), *"Mystic Built": Ships and Shipyards of the Mystic River, Connecticut, 1784–1919*, Mystic, CT: Mystic Seaport Museum.

Philbrick, Thomas (1961), *James Fenimore Cooper and the Development of American Sea Fiction*, Cambridge, MA: Harvard University Press.
Phillips-Birt, Douglas (1974), *The History of Yachting*, London: Elm Tree Books.
Piddington, Henry ([1846] 1864), *The Sailor's Horn-Book for the Law of Storms ...*, London: Williams and Norgate.
Piper, Leonard (2003), *Dangerous Waters: The Life and Death of Erskine Childers*, London: Hambledon and London.
Polo, Marco ([1298/9] 2016), *Il Milione: Book of the Marvels of the World*, trans. Nigel Cliffe, London: Penguin.
Pratt, Mary Louise (2007), *Imperial Eyes: Travel Writing and Transculturation*, London: Routledge.
Pratt, Mary Louise (2008), *Imperial Eyes: Travel Writing and Transculturation*, 2nd edn., London: Routledge.
Pringle, David (1825), "Letter To M. A. P. (Copy)," John MacGregor Papers, National Maritime Museum, Greenwich, 25–85.
Purdy, John and Alexander George Findlay (1861), *Memoir, Descriptive and Explanatory, of the Northern Atlantic Ocean*, 11th edn., London: Richard Holmes Laurie.
Pybus, Cassandra (2007), "Bound for Botany Bay: John Martin's Voyage to Australia," in Emma Christopher, Cassandra Pybus, and Marcus Rediker (eds.), *Many Middle Passages: Forced Migration and the Making of the Modern World*, 97–104, Berkeley: University of California.
Quatrefages, Armand de (1857), *The Rambles of a Naturalist on the Coasts of France, Spain, and Sicily*, London: Longman, Brown, Green, Longmans and Roberts.
Quinton, René. *L'eau de mer milieu organique: constance du milieu marin originel, comme milieu vital des cellules, à travers la série animale*, Paris: Encre, 1904.
Raban, Jonathan, ed. (1993), *The Oxford Book of the Sea*, Oxford: Oxford University Press.
Randier, Jean (1969), *Men and Ships Around Cape Horn 1616–1939*, New York: David McKay Co.
Ransome, Arthur (1951), "Introduction," in E.F. [Edward Frederick] Knight (ed.), *The Falcon on the Baltic: A Coasting Voyage from Hammersmith to Copenhagen in a Three-Ton Yacht*, 5–18, London: Rupert Hart-Davis.
Ransonnet-Villez, Baron Eugen von (1868), *Ceylon: Skizzen seiner Bewohner, seines Thier- und Pflanzenlebens und Untersuchungen des Meeresgrundes nahe der Küste*, Braunschweig, Westermann.
Rasmussen, Knud ([1905] 1908), *People of the Polar North*, comp. and ed. G. Herrig, Philadelphia: J. P. Lippincott Co.
The Reef, Encounters with the Great Barrier Reef and Its People: From Cook to Climate Change (2014). Available online: http://thereef.iainmccalman.com.au (accessed October 14, 2020).
Rees, Siân (2011), *Sweet Water and Bitter Water: The Ships that Stopped the Slave Trade*, Durham: University of New Hampshire Press.
Rehbock, Philip F. (1979), "The Early Dredgers: 'Naturalizing' in British Seas, 1830–1850," *Journal for the History of Biology*, 12 (2): 293–368.
Rediker, Marcus (2013), *The Amistad Rebellion: An Atlantic Odyssey of Slavery and Freedom*, New York: Penguin.
Reidy, Michael S. (2008), *Tides of History: Ocean Science and Her Majesty's Navy*, Chicago: University of Chicago Press.

Reiß, Christian (2012), "Gateway, Instrument, Environment. The Aquarium as a Hybrid Space between Animal Fancying and Experimental Zoology," *NTM Zeitschrift für Geschichte der Wissenschaften, Technik und Medizin*, 20 (4): 309–36.
Report of the Pikialasorsuaq Commission (2017), *People of the Ice Bridge*. Available online: http://www.pikialasorsuaq.org/en/Resources/Reports (accessed October 12, 2020).
Rheinberger, Hans-Jörg (1992), *Experiment, Differenz, Schrift: Zur Geschichte epistemischer Dinge*, Marburg: Basilisken-Presse.
Rheinberger, Hans-Jörg (2001), "Objekt und Repräsentation," in Bettina Heintz and Jörg Huber (eds.), *Mit dem Auge denken. Strategien der Sichtbarmachung in wissenschaftlichen und virtuellen Welten*, 55–61, Zurich: Springer.
Rheinberger, Hans-Jörg ([2001] 2006), *Experimentalsysteme und epistemische Dinge: Eine Geschichte der Proteinsynthese im Reagenzglas*, Frankfurt: Suhrkamp.
Rigby, Nigel, Pieter van der Merwe, and Glyn Williams (2005), *Pioneers of the Pacific: Voyages of Exploration, 1787–1810*, Fairbanks: University of Alaska Press.
Ring, Jim (1996), *Erskine Childers*, London: John Murray.
Robertson, Roland (1992), *Globalization*, New York: Sage.
Rodger, N.A.M. (1988), *The Wooden World: An Anatomy of the Georgian Navy*, Hammersmith: Fontana Press.
Romm, James S. (1992), *The Edges of the Earth in Ancient Thought: Geography, Exploration, and Fiction*, Princeton, NJ: Princeton University Press.
Rondelet, Guillaume (1554), *Libri de Piscibus marinis, in quibus verae piscium effegies expressae sunt*, Lugduni.
Roper, Clyde F.E. (1998), *Architeuthidae*, Tree of Life Web-Project. Available online: http://tolweb.org/Architeuthis (accessed October 2, 2018).
Ross, John (1819), *A Voyage of Discovery, Made Under the Orders of the Admiralty, in his Majesty's Ships Isabella and Alexander for the Purpose of Exploring Baffin's Bay, and Enquiring into the Possibility of a North-West Passage*, London: John Murray.
Rossi, Paolo (1984), *The Dark Abyss of Time: The History of the Earth and the History of Nation from Hooke to Vico*, Chicago: University of Chicago Press.
Rozwadowski, Helen (2005), *Fathoming the Ocean: The Discovery and Exploration of the Deep Sea*, Cambridge, MA: Belknap Press, Harvard University.
Rozwadowski, Helen (2008), *Fathoming the Ocean: The Discovery and Exploration of the Deep Sea*, Cambridge, MA: Belknap Press, Harvard University.
Rudwick, Martin (2005), *Bursting the Limits of Time: The Reconstruction of Geohistory in the Age of Revolution*, Chicago: University of Chicago Press.
Rudwick, Martin (2008), *Worlds Before Adam: The Reconstruction of Geohistory in the Age of Reform*, Chicago: University of Chicago Press.
Rudy, Jason (2017), *Imagined Homelands: British Poetry in the Colonies*, Baltimore: Johns Hopkins University Press.
Rupke, Nicolaas A. (1983), *The Great Chain of History*, Oxford: Oxford University Press.
Russell, Lynette (2012), *Roving Mariners: Australian Aboriginal Whalers and Sealers in the Southern Oceans, 1790–1870*, Albany: State University of New York Press.
Saint-Pierre, Bernardin de (1788), *Paul and Virginie*, London.
Schleiden, Matthias Jakob (1858), *Die Pflanze und ihr Leben*, Leipzig: Engelmann.
Schlee, Susan (1973), *The Edge of an Unfamiliar World: A History of Oceanography*, New York: Dutton.
Schmitt, Cannon (2014), "Technical Maturity in Robert Louis Stevenson," *Representations*, 125: 54–79.

Schmitt, Carl (2015), *Land and Sea: A World-Historical Meditation*, trans. Samuel Garrett Zeitlin, Candor, NY: Telos Press.

Schneer, Cecil J., ed. (1967), *Towards a History of Geology*, Boston: MIT Press.

Schneider, David. P., Eric J. Steig, Tas D. van Ommen, Daniel A. Dixon, Paul A. Mayewski, Julie M. Jones, and Cecilia M. Bitz (2006), "Antarctic Temperatures Over the Past Two Centuries from Ice Cores," *Geophysical Research Letters*, 33 (L16707): 1–5.

Scoresby, William (1820), *An Account of the Arctic Regions*, vol. 1 of 2, Edinburgh: Archibald Constable & Co.

"A Scotch Heroine"(1878), *Wheeling Register*, May 23. Nineteenth Century U.S. Newspapers.

Shelangoskie, Susan (2017), "'Nerves of the Empire': Submarine Telegraph Technological Travel Narratives as Imperial Adventure," in Kate Hill (ed.), *Britain and the Narration of Travel in the Nineteenth Century: Texts, Images, Objects*, 91–108, Abingdon: Routledge.

Shelvocke, George (1726), *A Voyage Round the World by the Way of the Great South Sea*, London: J. Senex.

Sherburne, John Henry (1851), *The Life and Character of John Paul Jones, A Captain in the United States Navy during the Revolutionary War*, New York: Adriance, Sherman & Co.

Simmons, A.H. (2004), "The Art of Englishness: Identity and Representation in Conrad's Early Career," *The Conradian*, 29 (1): 1–26.

Simmons, William E. (1874), "The Aquarium," *Popular Science Monthly*: 687–95.

Simon, Hans-Reiner (1980), *Anton Dohrn und die Zoologische Station Neapel*, Frankfurt: Edition Erbrich.

Skallerup, Harry R. (1974), *Books Afloat and Ashore: A History of Books, Libraries, and Reading among Seamen during the Age of Sail*, Hamden, CT: Archon Books.

"The Slave Ship" (2020), Wikipedia, July 1. Available online: https://en.wikipedia.org/wiki/The_Slave_Ship (accessed October 12, 2020).

Smith, Jason (2018), *To Master the Boundless Sea: The U.S. Navy, the Marine Environment, and the Cartography of Empire*, Chapel Hill: University of North Carolina Press.

Smith, Keith Vincent (2005), "Tupaia's Sketchbook," *Electronic British Library Journal*. Available online: http://www.bl.uk/eblj/2005articles/article10.html (accessed September 26, 2019).

Sobel, Dava and William J. H. Andrewes (1998), *The Illustrated Longitude*, New York: Walker and Co.

Sowerby, George B. (1865), *The Aquarium: A Popular Account of Marine and Fresh-Water Animals and Plants*, London: Routledge, Warne and Routledge.

Stam, David H. (2012), "The Lord's Librarians: The American Seamen's Friend Society and Their Loan Libraries, 1837–1967: An Historical Excursion with Some Unanswered Questions," *Coriolis: An International Journal of Maritime History*, 3 (1): 45–59.

Stam, David H. (2016), "Byrd's Books: The Antarctic Libraries of Little America, 1928–1941," *Coriolis: An International Journal of Maritime History*, 6 (1): 26–44.

Starbuck, Alexander (1878), *History of the American Whale Fishery*, Waltham, MA: Published by Author.

Starr, Cindy (2016), "Annual Arctic Sea Ice Minimum 1979–2015, with graph," NASA Scientific Visualization Studio, March 10. Available online: https://svs.gsfc.nasa.gov/4435 (accessed October 9, 2020).

Stavridis, Admiral James (2017), *Sea Power: The History and Geopolitics of the World's Oceans*, New York: Penguin Press.
Sterling, Christopher H. (2007), *Military Communications from Ancient Times to the 21st Century*, Santa Barbara, CA: ABC-CLIO.
Stevenson, Fanny Van de Grift (2004), *The Cruise of the Janet Nichol among the South Sea Islands: A Diary by Mrs. Robert Louis Stevenson*, ed. Roslyn Jolly, Sydney: University of New South Wales Press.
Stevenson, Robert Louis ([1870] 2008), *South Sea Tales*, Oxford: Oxford University Press.
Stopford, Martin (2009), *Maritime Economics*, 3rd edn., New York: Routledge.
Stott, Rebecca (2000), "Through a Glass Darkly: Aquarium Colonies and Nineteenth-Century Narratives of Marine Monstrosity," *Gothic Studies*, 2 (3): 305–27.
Stott, Rebecca (2003), *Theatres of Glass: The Woman Who Brought the Sea to the City*, London: Short Books.
Sutton, Jean (1981), *Lords of the East: The East India Company and Its Ships*, London: Conway Maritime Press.
Tancred, George (1899), *The Annals of a Border Club*, Jedburgh: T. S. Smail.
Taylor, Eric Robert (2016), *If We Must Die. Shipboard Insurrections in the Era of the Atlantic Slave Trade*, Baton Rouge: Louisiana State University Press.
Thisted, Kirsten (2001), "On Narrative Expectations: Greenlandic Oral Traditions about the Cultural Encounter between Inuit and Norsemen," *Scandinavian Studies*, 73 (3): 253–96.
Thomas, Keith (1983), *Man and the Natural World: Changing Attitudes in England 1500–1800*, New York: Pantheon.
Thomas, Nicholas (2003), *Cook: The Extraordinary Voyages of Captain James Cook*, New York: Walker and Co.
Thomas, Nicholas (2010), *Islanders: The Pacific in the Age of Empire*, New Haven, CT: Yale University Press.
Thompson, Carl (2007), *Romantic-Era Shipwreck Narratives: An Anthology*, Nottingham: Trent Editions.
Thoreau, Henry David ([1854] 1995), *Walden, or Life in the Woods*, New York: Dover.
Thwaite, Ann (2002), *Glimpses of the Wonderful: The Life of Philip Henry Gosse 1810–1888*, London: Faber & Faber.
Thynne, Anna (1859), "On the Increase of Madrepores," *Annals and Magazine of Natural History*, 18: 449–61.
Tinker, Hugh (1992), *A New System of Slavery*, Oxford: Oxford University Press.
Toll, Ian W. (2006), *Six Frigates. The Epic History of the Founding of The U.S. Navy*, New York: Norton.
Torrens, Hugh (1995), "Mary Anning of Lyme; the Greatest Fossilist the World Ever Knew," *British Journal of the History of Science*, 28: 257–84.
Toulmin, Stephen and June Goodfield (1982), *The Discovery of Time*, Chicago: University of Chicago Press.
Tracy, Nicholas (2014), *The Miracle of the Kent: A Tale of Courage, Faith, and Fire*, Yardley: Westholme.
Tullibardine, Katharine Marjory Murray, Mise de. and Gustave De Ridder (1905), *A Military History of Perthshire, 1660–1902*, Perth: R. and J. Hay.
UN General Assembly (2015), *Oceans and the Law of the Sea: Report of the Secretary-General*, A/70/74. Available online: http://www.refworld.org/docid/558929624.html/ (accessed October 12, 2020).

United States Naval Meteorology and Oceanography Command (1995), *U.S. Navy Marine Climatic Atlas of the World*, ver. 1.1, Ashville, NC: Fleet Numerical Meteorology and Oceanography Detachment.

Van Wyhe, John (2002–), "Charles Darwin's *Beagle* Library," in Van Wyhe (ed.), *The Complete Work of Charles Darwin Online*. Available online: http://darwin-online.org.uk/BeagleLibrary/Beagle_Library_Introduction.htm (accessed May 22, 2018).

Vaughan, Richard (1987), "How isolated Were the Polar Eskimos in the Nineteenth Century?," in Louwrens Hacquebord and Richard Vaughan (eds.), *Between Greenland and America: Cross-Cultural Contacts and the Environment in the Baffin Bay Area*, 95–107, Groningen: University of Groningen, Arctic Centre.

Verne, Jules ([1870] 1998), *Twenty Thousand Leagues Under the Sea*, ed. and trans. William Butcher, Oxford: Oxford University Press.

Verne, Jules ([1870] 2017), *Twenty Thousand Leagues Under the Sea*, trans. David Coward, London: Penguin.

Villiers, J. A. J., de, ed. and trans. (1906), *The East and West Indian Mirror, Being an Account of Joris van Speilbergen's Voyage Round the World (1614–1617), and The Australian Navigations of Jacob Le Maire*, Series 2: No. 18, London: The Hakluyt Society.

Walcott, Derek (2007), "The Sea is History," in *Selcted Poems*, New York: Farrar, Straus and Giroux. Available online: https://poets.org/poem/sea-history (accessed October 9, 2020).

Wallis, John (1665), "An Essay of Dr. John Wallis, Exhibiting His Hypothesis about the Flux and Reflux of the Sea, Taken from the Consideration of the Common Center of Gravity of the Earth and Moon; Together with an Appendix of the Same, Containing an Answer to Some Objections, Made by Severall Persons against That Hypothesis," *Philosophical Transactions*, 1 (1–22): S. 263–81.

Walvin, James (2011), *The Zong: A Massacre, The Law & the End of Slavery*, New Haven, CT: Yale University Press.

Ward, Nathaniel Bagshaw (1837), "Reports on the Subject of the Growth of Plants in Closed Glass Vessels," *Report of the British Association for the Advancement of Science*, 1: 501–505.

Ward, Nathaniel Bagshaw (1842): *On the Growth of Plants in Closely Glazed Cases*, London: John Van Voorst.

Warington, Robert (1853), "On Preserving the Balance between the Animal and Vegetable Organisms in Sea-Water," *Annals of Natural History*, 12 (2): 319–24.

Warington, Robert (1854), "Memoranda of Observations Made in Small Aquaria, in which the Balance between the Animal and Vegetable Organisms Was Permanently Maintained," *Annals of Natural History*, 14 (2): 366–73.

Warington, Robert (1855), "On the Injurious Effects of an Excess or Want of Heat and Light on the Aquarium," *Annals of Natural History*, 16 (2): 313–15.

Warington, Robert (1857), "On the Aquarium," *Proceedings of the Royal Institution of Great Britain*, 2: 403–8.

"We Have Copied the Following from the Barbados Globe: 'The Currents of the Ocean'" (1827), *Louisiana Advertiser*, January 30. Nineteenth Century U.S. Newspapers.

Whitfield, Peter (1996), *The Charting of the Oceans: Ten Centuries of Maritime Maps*, London: British Library.

Whyte, Robert (1994), *Robert Whyte's 1847 Famine Ship Diary: The Journey of an Irish Coffin Ship*, ed. James J. Mangan, Cork: Mercier Press.

Wilkins, Alasdair (2012), "What Happened to the Iceberg that Sank the *Titanic*?," *Wired*, April 16. Available online: https://www.wired.com/2012/04/titanic-iceberg-history/ (accessed August 22, 2018).

Williams, Rosalind (2013), *The Triumph of Human Empire: Verne, Morris, and Stevenson at the Ends of the World*, Chicago: University of Chicago Press.

Williams, Thomas (1852), *Report on the British Annelida*, Report of the British Association for the Advancement of Science, 1851: 159–272.

Willis, Sam (2012), *The Fighting Temeraire: The Battle of Trafalgar and the Ship that Inspired J.M.W. Turner's Most Beloved Painting*, New York: Pegasus Books.

Wood, Gordon S. (2009), *Empire of Liberty: A History of the Early Republic, 1789–1815*, New York: Oxford University Press.

Wood, J.G. (1868), *The Fresh and Salt Water Aquarium*, London: Routledge.

Woolf, Leonard (1921), "Pearls and Swine," *Stories of the East*, 21–44, London: Hogarth Press.

Worrall, Simon (2018), "Clipper Ship Owners Made Millions: Others Paid the Price," *National Geographic*, August 31. Available online: https://www.nationalgeographic.com/science/2018/08/news-clipper-ship-opium-trade-gold-rush/ (accessed September 27, 2019).

Wright, Shelley (2014), *Our Ice is Vanishing/Sikuvut Nunguliqtuq: A History of Inuit, Newcomers, and Climate Change*, Montreal: McGill-Queen's University Press.

Zeuske, Michael (2015), *Amistad: A Hidden Network of Slavers and Merchants*, Princeton, NJ: Markus Wiener Publishers.

Zeuske, Michael (2018), "Out of the Americas: Slave traders and the *Hidden Atlantic* in the nineteenth century," *Atlantic Studies*, 15 (1) (March): 103–35.

Zottoli, Steven J. and Ernst-August Seyfarth (2015), "The Marine Biological Laboratory (Woods Hole) and the Scientific Advancement of Women in the Early 20th Century: The Example of Mary Jane Hogue (1883–1962)," *Journal of the History of Biology*, 48: 137–67.

Editor's Note: The blue humanities has only recently started to incorporate sound studies. Here are a few chapters and articles that suggest future directions for the field.

Carr, James Revell (2014), "A Wild Sort of Note," in *Hawaiian Music in Motion: Mariners, Missionaries and Minstrels*, Urbana: University of Illinois Press.

Cowgill, Rachel and Julian Rushton, eds. (2006), *Europe, Empire and Spectacle in Nineteenth-Century British Music*, London: Routledge.

Floyd, Samuel A. with Melanie L. Zeck and Guthrie P. Ramsey Jr. (2017), *The Transformation of Black Music: The Rhythms, the Songs, and the Ships of the African Diaspora*, New York: Oxford University Press.

Frey, Angelica (2015), "Eleven Beautiful Pieces of Classical Music Inspired by Water," *CMUSE*, September 4. Available online: https://www.cmuse.org/classical-music-inspired-by-water/ (accessed October 12, 2020).

Kelby, Rose (2012), "Nostalgia and Imagination in Nineteenth-Century Sea Shanties," *The Mariner's Mirror*, 98 (2): 147–60.

Milne, Graeme J. (2017), "Collecting the Sea Shanty: British Maritime Identity and Atlantic Musical Cultures in the Early Twentieth Century," *International Journal of Maritime History*, 29 (2): 370–86.

Schmidt, Arnold (2019), *British Nautical Melodramas 1820–1850*, London: Routledge.

CONTRIBUTORS

Natascha Adamowsky is Professor for Media and Culture, University of Passau, Germany. She previously held the positions of Professor for Media Culture at the Albert-Ludwigs-University, Freiburg, Germany, and Professor for Cultural History and Aesthetics at the Humboldt University, Berlin, Germany. Her primary research interests include media history, media aesthetics, intellectual culture, digital media, and game culture. Her most recent books include *The Mysterious Science of the Sea 1775–1943* (2016) and *Ozeanische Wunder: Entdeckung und Eroberung des Meeres in der Moderne* (2017).

William Boelhower is Visiting Professor in the Department of Linguistics and Comparative Culture Studies at the University of Ca' Foscari, Italy. He has recently published *Atlantic Studies, Prospects and Challenges* (2019), as editor, *New Orleans in the Atlantic World, Between Land and Sea* (2010), and the essays "Framing a New Ocean Genealogy: The Case of Venetian Cartography in the Early Modern Period" (*Atlantic Studies*, 2018) and "Three Early Modern Genres: A Microhistorical Approach to 'World Literature'" (*Atlantic Studies*, 2019). His book *Immigrant Autobiography* will be published in a revised and enlarged edition in 2021. He has translated the work of Lucien Goldmann and Antonio Gramsci.

Siobhan Carroll is Associate Professor of English at the University of Delaware, United States, where she teaches courses on nineteenth-century literature and science fiction. Her first book, *An Empire of Air and Water: Uncolonizable Space in the British Imagination, 1750–1850* (2015), describes the relevance of "uncolonizable" geographies such as the North Pole and the atmosphere to British imperialism. Her current book project examines the relationship between human agency and the natural world in the long nineteenth century.

Margaret Cohen holds the Andrew B. Hammond Chair of French Language, Literature, and Civilization at Stanford University, United States, where she teaches in the Departments of Comparative Literature and English. Her books include the award-winning *The Novel and the Sea* (2010) and *The Sentimental Education of the Novel* (1999) as well as *Profane Illumination: Walter Benjamin and the Paris of Surrealist Revolution* (1993). Her *The Underwater Eye*, a book on the poetics of underwater film, is forthcoming. Throughout her research and teaching, she emphasizes the enriching role of active engagement with the reality and specificity of marine environments.

Adriana Craciun is Emma MacLachlan Metcalf Chair of Humanities and Professor of English at Boston University, United States. Her most recent book, *Writing Arctic Disaster: Authorship and Exploration* (2016), was shortlisted for the 2016 Kendrick Book Prize by the Society for Literature, Science & the Arts. With Simon Schaffer she edited *The Material Cultures of Enlightenment Arts and Sciences* (2016), and with Mary Terrall, *Curious Encounters: Voyaging, Collecting and Making Knowledge in the Long 18th Century* (2019). She is writing a new book, *Arctic Enlightenments*, on deep time flora, seed vitality, and botanical collecting from the Enlightenment to the Svalbard Global Seed Vault.

Richard King is Visiting Associate Professor at the Sea Education Association in Woods Hole, United States. He is the author of *Lobster* (2011), *The Devil's Cormorant: A Natural History* (2013), and *Ahab's Rolling Sea: A Natural History of Moby-Dick* (2019).

Charne Lavery is a lecturer in the Department of English at the University of Pretoria, South Africa, and researcher on the Oceanic Humanities for the Global South project based at the Wits Institute for Social and Economic Research (WISER), University of the Witwatersrand, South Africa. She explores literary and cultural representations of the deep ocean, the Indian Ocean, and the Southern Ocean and Antarctic seas, researching oceanic underworlds of the Global South from a postcolonial-ecological perspective. She is the South African Humanities and Social Sciences delegate to the international Scientific Committee on Antarctic Research (SCAR), and coeditor of the series *Maritime Literature and Culture*.

Iain McCalman is Emeritus Professor at the University of Sydney and the Australian National University, and is currently working as a Research Professor at the Australian Catholic University. He is Fellow of four Learned Academies and is a former President of the Australian Academy of the Humanities. His award-winning book *Darwin's Armada* (2009) was the basis for the ABC–CBC

TV series, *Darwin's Brave New World*. He is the author of *The Reef: A Passionate History, from Captain Cook to Climate Change* (2013). His current book-in-progress is *The Grass Ceiling: A Human-Animal Saga. How two American women and a monkey challenged the male worlds of African exploration and science fiction.*

Cannon Schmitt is Professor of English and Director of Graduate Studies in English at the University of Toronto, Canada. He has published two books, *Darwin and the Memory of the Human: Evolution, Savages, and South America* (2009) and *Alien Nation: Nineteenth-Century Gothic Fictions and English Nationality* (1997), as well as essays in *Representations, ELH, Genre, Victorian Studies, Victorian Literature and Culture,* and elsewhere. At present he is completing a book on the sea in Victorian fiction and the possibilities of literal (and technical) reading.

INDEX

Note: Page locators in *italic* refer to figures.

Aboriginal and Torres Strait maritime societies 131–2, 152
  employment on Dunk Island 148–51
  Guugu Yimitthirr 135–8
  Kaurareg Islanders 139, 140, 141–2
  Wanthaala Aborigines 139–40, 141, 142–4
Acushnet 64
  abstract of log 60, *61*
  passage around Cape Horn 56, 57–62
Adams, John, correspondence with Jefferson 109–111
adventure
  amateur yachting and 225–226
  imagining ocean as space of 85, 111, 192, 203–204
  Type 2 fun and 224
albatrosses 62–3
amateur
  marine naturalism 20–1, 24, 25, 35–37
  yachting 23, 173, 176, 223–6
  (see also tourism)
American Seaman's Friend Society (ASFS) 210
Amistad rebellion 15, 115, *116*
Anco (*see* Pelletier, Narcisse (Anco))
Andersen, Hans Christian 196
Anning, Joseph and Mary 32, 33
Antarctic Convergence Zone 62
"aquarium mania" 39
aquariums 8–9, 35–9, 40, 51

Arctic exploration 126, 155, 158–76, 216–17
Atkins, Anna 24
Atuagagdliutit 170, *171*
Australia
  Botany Bay penal colony 117
  British colony 107
  surfing in 24
  (*see also* Aboriginal and Torres Strait maritime societies)
  Sydney as leading hub of maritime transport 2

Banfield, Ted
  Confessions of a Beachcomber 152
  dependence on Aboriginal workers 148–9, *148*
  as voluntary castaway 144–53, *147*
Banks, Joseph 134, 135, 136, 138, 161
Barbados Globe 83, 103
barnacles 41–3, *42*
Barthes, Roland 209
Battle of the Saintes 221, *221*
Battle of Trafalgar 10, 107, 222
Battle of Tushima 7–8
battleships 3, 7–8
Bay of Biscay 88–9
  currents 82, 103
  fire aboard *Kent* 91–4, 97
  storm 89–91

beachcombing
    on Dunk Island 146–7, 151, 152
    early marine science and leisure pursuit of 30–9
    of "mere wanderers" in Indian Ocean 191, 192–3
Beagle, HMS 4, 13, 57, 163, 209–210, 218
Biard, François-Auguste 172–3, *172*
Birkenhead, HMS 95
black seamen 15
    mutiny by 113
Bligh, Captain William 113
botanical study
    Aboriginal 151
    influence on aquariums 38
Botany Bay 117
Boutan, Louis Marie Auguste 52, 53–4
Brassey, Thomas 21, 206, 207, 219–20, 223
Bravo, Michael 160, 166, 167
Brierly, O.W. 141, *141*, 142
Brigham, Louise 176
British Empire
    abolition of slavery 3, 82, 115
    expansion 107–108
    importance of water networks 81
    in India 83–4, 85, 180
    interest in better understanding of oceans 82
    map *108*
    Pax Britannica 3, 20, 107–117
    policing the seas 108
    troubled relations with America 108–111
Brontë, Charlotte 78
Bruguière, Jean-Guillaume 35
Burnett, Thomas 29
Byron, Lord 21, 25, 111

cables, undersea 1, 7, 19, 180, *181*, 195, 196–7, *196*
Caisson's disease 6
Cambria 95, 96–7, 98, 100, 101
cannibalism 189, 191
canning 9
Cape Horn, voyaging around 18, 55–80
    charts *58*, *74*
    Dana's voyages 77–8, 123
    ecology 62–3
    extreme weather 62

Maury's scientific paper on 73
Melville's first passage 57–62
Melville's second passage 64–8, 70, 72
Melville's third passage 68–9
Melville's understanding of 78, 79
navigation in nineteenth century 74–6
nineteenth-century seamanship 65, 66, 69–74
a synonym for natural extremes at sea 79
Carson, Rachel 25
castaways, shipwreck
    Barbara Thompson 139, 140, 141–2, 144
    Narcisse Pelletier 139–40, *140*, 141, 142–3, 144
castaways, shipwreck of HMS *Endeavour* 132–9, 153
    Cook's admiration for skills of Guugu Timithirr 136–8
    dispute over turtles 135–6
    navigating out of coral reef 138–9
    search for fresh food 133–5
    stricken ship in Endeavour River 133, *133*
castaways, voluntary (*see* Banfield, Ted)
celestial navigation 75
Centurion, HMS 60
Challenger, HMS 18, 45
Charles W. Morgan 17
charts 14, 58, 74, 213
    The Riddle of the Sands 213–14, *214*, 217–18
Childe Harold's Pilgrimage 25, 111
Childers, Erskine
    biography 218–19
    The Riddle of the Sands. see The Riddle of the Sands
    Vixen log 204, *205*
China 3, 67, 107, 108, 116, 124
Cleveland, Richard J. 114
clipper ships 14, 15
    Meteor 18, 56, *56*, 68–9, 70, 72
    sailing around Cape Horn 68–9, 70, 72, 73, 74, *74*
coastal visits 9, 29–30
    beachcombing 30–9
Cobb, Captain Henry 85, 87, 88, 92, 94, 96, 99, 100–101
coffin ships 13, 117

Coleridge, Samuel Taylor 63, *64*
collecting 30, 35, 36, 38, 40
Commodore Morris, navigation of 72
communications technology 1, 7, 8, 19, 180, *181*, 195, 196–7, *196*
Confessions of a Beachcomber 152
Conrad, Joseph 79, 111, 119, 179–80, 216–17
   "Falk" 189
   Heart of Darkness 2, 19–20, 217
   Lord Jim 19, 111, 178–9, 185–6, 195, 197, 201–202
   The Mirror of the Sea 17, 188, 190, 194–5
   The Nigger of the "Narcissus" 79, 183–4
   A Personal Record 80
   "Travel" 190–1
   Typhoon 18, 79, 125, 129, 185
contrapuntal reading 221–222
contract laborers 116–17
convict ships 116, 117
Conybeare, William 33
Cook, Captain James
   on the Great Barrier Reef 132–9
   encounters of expedition with Guugu Yimitthirr 136–8
Cooper, James Fenimore 15, 119, 210
copper sheathing 17
Corbin, Alain 9, 28, 29
Corinthian yachtsmen 223–6, 233n5
Cowper, Frank 123, 207, 225–6, 227
Cruikshank, George *86*, 87
currents, study of ocean 82, 83, 103
   Gulf Stream 156–8

Dana, Richard Henry 77–8, 112, 118, 123, 211, *211*
Darwin, Charles 4, 41, 43
d'Aunet, Léonie 172
dead reckoning 75
declination 75
deep sea 4, 18, 44–54, 195, 195–7
   diving 50–4, *52*
   in literature 45–50, 197–201
   locating "depths of time" in 32
Defoe, Daniel 170, *171*, 208
Desertion 192–3
desertions 112–13
dhows 184, *184*

Dick, Agnes Joanna 84–5, 85–8, 89–91, 92–3, 93–4, 96, 101
Dickens, Charles 78
disaster tourism 174
discipline on board ships 112
diving
   chambers 6, 29
   early scientific 50–4, *52*
   helmet 6, 10, *194*
   pearl 193
   scuba 10
Dohrn, Anton 41, 50
Douglass, Frederick 15, 114–15
Down Channel 225, 228
Drake Passage 58, 59, 62, 63, 70, 72, 76
dredging, steam-powered 6
drifters 189–94
Dufferin, Lord 173, *173*, 174
Dulcibella library (*see* ship's library, *Dulcibella* fictitious)
Dunk Island 144–53

East India Company 85, 86
"East Indiaman" ships 85, 86, *86*
   (*see also* Kent)
"The Ebb-Tide" 191–2
ecology 50, 62–4, 153, 162, 193
Emerson, Ralph Waldo 78
emigrant ships 13–14, 117
Endeavour, HMS (*see* castaways, shipwreck of HMS *Endeavour*)
environmental issues 4, 9, 25, 194–5
extinct species 34–5, 36

Fabricius, Otto 158
Falcon on the Baltic 224, 228
Falconer, William 90
"Falk" 189
"Fallacies of Hope" 127
fiction, sea (*see* sea fiction)
The Fighting Temeraire tugged to her last berth to be broken up 10–11, *11*, 12
Findlay, Alexander George 215
"First Communication" (by Sacheuse) 167–9, *168*
fishing techniques 9, 150
Fitzroy, Robert 57, 216
floggings 112, 113
the Flood 29, 36

INDEX 259

fossils 32–5, 36
Foucault, Michel 87, 203–204
Franklin expedition 16, 158, 164, 170, 174
Fraser, Eliza 132
freight rates, lowering of 5
Friedrich, Casper David 126
furniture from ship containers 176

geological timescales 32, 34, 36
Géricault, Théodore 127
Germany 3, 207, 219
Gessner, Conrad 34
Ghosh, Amitav 178, 180, 182, 186
giant squid 47–9, *48*
Giom (*see* Thompson, Barbara (Giom))
Gosse, Philip Henry 37–8, 39, 43
Great Barrier Reef 16, 131–2, 146, 152–3
    Dunk Island 144–53
    (*see also* Aboriginal and Torres Strait maritime societies; castaways, shipwreck; castaways, shipwreck of HMS *Endeavour*)
Greenland 4, 158, 163
    Atuagagdliutit 170, *171*
    printing press 170
    Qitdlarssuaq's voyage to 163–5
    seeking out Inughuit in northern 164, 167–9, *168*
Greenwich prime meridian 14
Gulf Stream 156–8
Gurnah, Abdulrazak 178, 192–3
Guugu Yimitthirr 135–8

Halley, Edmond 29
Hawkesworth, John 132, 133, 134, 135, 136, 137, 138, 139
Heart of Darkness 2, 19–20, 217
heterotopias 87–8, 203
H.L. Hunley 8
Hokusai 123–4, *124*
Holmes, Joseph Warren 74, *74*
Homer, Winslow 127
Hugo, Victor 122
Humbolt, Alexander von 155–7
Huxley, Thomas 9, 216

icebergs 158–9, 162–3
    fastening ships to 159, *160*
Ichthyosaur 33

immigration 13–14, 117
impressment 108–109
indentured labor 116, 180, 185
India 84, 85
    British Empire in 83–4, 85, 180
    cable connections 19, 180, *181*, 196–7
Indian Ocean
    drifters 189–94
    lascars 182–8
    literary space of 178–9, 180–2
    monsoons and navigation 2, 88
    overlooked geopolitical significance of 178–179
    recovering history of 22, 178
    relevance for cultural and social history 180–182
    slave networks 180
    undersea cable networks 19, 180, *181*, 196–7
The Influence of Sea Power Upon History 206, 220–1
instruments 161–2, *161*
International Fisheries Exhibition 1883 9
Inughuit (Polar Inuit) 164, 167–9, *168*
Inuit 157, 158, 162
    kayaks 16, 158, 164, 169
    as members of polar expeditions 165
    -missionary maritime "co-travel" 166
    Qitdlarssuaq 16, 163–5
    Sacheuse 167–9, *168*
    travelers 163, 165
    women 165
invasion fiction 204, 219
Irish migrants 117
iron ships 5, 17, 76
ironclads 7
Isabella 167, 168, 169

Japan 3, 7–8, 14, 124
Jay's Treaty 110
Jefferson, Thomas, correspondence with Adams 109–111
Johnson, Samuel 209

Kane, Elisha 159, *160*
Kaurareg Islanders
    Brierly's interview with Thompson regarding 141–2
    rescue of Thompson 139, 140

kayaks 16, 158, 164, 169
Kent 82–103
    an "East Indiaman" 85, 86
    evacuation 95–9
    fire on board 91–4, *97*, 100
    global connections 89
    infants' funerals 89–90
    loss of life 100
    message in a bottle 82–3, *89*, 94, *102*, 103
    news story 100–101, 103
    oil lamps 90–1
    rescue by *Cambria* 95, 96–7, 98, 100
    storm in Bay of Biscay 89–91
    stowaways 88
Kingsley, Charles 35, 44
Knight, E.F. 224, 225, 228
kraken 47

lascars 21–2, 180, 182–8, *183*, 187
Le Gray, Gustave 11–12
libraries, ships' (*see* ships' libraries)
The Life of Nelson 206, 221–2
lifeboats
    evacuation of *Kent* 95–9
    "women and children first" rule 95–6
logbooks 60, *61*, 65, 71–2
    abstract logs 122
London, Jack 189, 212
Longitude, calculating 14, 75–6
Lord Jim 19, 111, 178–9, 185–6, 195, 197, 201–202
Lyme Regis 32, 33

MacGregor, Duncan
    Kent disaster and rescue 91–2, 93–4, 95, 96, 98, 99, 100, 101
    message in a bottle 82–3, *89*, 94, *102*, 103
    relationship with British Empire 83–4
Mahan, Alfred Thayer 3, 124–5, 206, 220–2
Mangin, Arthur 49
maps as distinct from charts 213–14
marine biology 38
    amateurs making advances in 20–1, 24, 35
    aquaria 35–9
    women's contributions to 20–1, 24–5

Marine Biology Laboratory (MBL) 25
    tide pools and 36, 43
marine chronometers 12–13, 75
marine fossils 32–5, 36
marine science
    of depths 4, 18, 195
    early scientific diving 50–4
    eighteenth century 29–30
    meteorology 118–21, 122
    seventeenth century 29
    sixteenth century 28–9
    voyaging around Cape Horn 62–4, 72–3
    wonderful facts 39–44
    (*see also* marine biology)
maritime art 125–7, 170–3, *172*
    Hokusai 124
    Homer 127
    Le Gray 11
    Sacheuse 167–9, *168*
    Turner 10–11, *11*, 125–7, *126*
    Wyllie 187
Marryat, Captain Frederick 87
Marsilli, Louis Ferdinand 29, *30*
Maury, Matthew Fontaine 73, 120, 121, 122, 128, *129*, 195
McMullen, R.T. 225
Melville, Herman 18, 56, 78, 79–80, 180, 193
    on *Acushnet* around Cape Horn 57–62
    on *Meteor* around Cape Horn 68–9, 70, 73
    Moby-Dick 70, 75, 79, 111–12, 128, 160, 162, 179, 186, 189, 195, 197–8, 201
    Omoo 78, 191
    Redburn 180, 186–8, 197
    Typee 63, 78
    on *USS United States* around Cape Horn 64–8
    White-Jacket 59, 67–8, 69, 70, 72, 73, 77, 79, 111, 112, 123
Merland, Constant 141, 142, 143, 144
Merrimack 7
message in a bottle 82–3, *89*, 94, *102*, 103
Meteor 18, 56, *56*
    accident aboard 70
    passage around Cape Horn 68–9, 70, 72, 73

meteorology 118–21, 122
Mexico 94–5
Michelet, Jules 121–2, 122–3
microscopes 41
microscopic organisms 162
Milne-Edwards, Henri 50
mining 95, 174, 176
The Mirror of the Sea 17, 188, 190, 194–5
Moby-Dick 70, 75, 79, 111–12, 128, 160, 162, 179, 186, 189, 195, 197–8, 201
modernization, technological 1–26
   complexity 5–10
   eccentricity 5, 21–6
   unevenness 5, 10–21
Monitor, USS 7
monstrosities 41–3, *42*
   of the deep 45–50, *48*
Moore, David R. 140, 141, 142
Muslim pilgrims 185
Mustakeem, Sowande' M. 115
mutinies 113

Natchez 65
Naval Annual 206, 219–20
naval warfare 3, 7–8
   books 207, 208, 218–22
navigation
   Cape Horn and nineteenth century 75–6
   combat of 122
   of HMS *Endeavour* off coral reef 138–9
   Marshall Island stick charts 118
   merging European and Indigenous technologies and techniques of 166–7
Nelson, Sir Horatio 107, 206, 221–2
networks
   Britain and water 81
   Kent and intersection of 82–103
   of print 103
   social 83, 84, 87, 97–8
   of trade and shipping 91, 94–5, 100
   of winds and currents 82, 83, 88, 103
Newton, Isaac 216
The Nigger of the "Narcissus" 79, 183–4
North Atlantic crossing times 1
North Water Polynya 165
North West Passage 16, 126, 155, 167, 170, 174

Omoo 78, 191
opium trade 15
Osterhammel, Jürgen 107, 108, 125
Ottley, Lieutenant 143
overfishing 9

Panama Canal 12, 20, 56
Parry, Sir William Edward 126, 168, 169
passenger transport 5–6, 13–14
Pax Britannica 3, 20, 107–117
pearl diving 193, *194*
Pearson, Michael 2, 184
Pelletier, Narcisse (Anco) 139–40, *140*, 141, 142–3, 144
penal colony 117
Philips-Birt, Douglas 228
photography 11, 24, 53
   underwater 10, *52*, 53
physical anthropology 143–4
Piddington, Henry 119
Pilgrim 77, 112
pilgrims 185
"pilots" (guides to navigation in coastal waters) 214–15
piracy 107
Plesiosaur 33
Polynesian voyagers 166
ports, expansion of 6
"primitives" 44
Pringle, David 87, 92, 96, 98–9, 100

Qitdlarssuaq 16, 163–5
Quinton, René 28

racial science of physical anthropology 143–4
racist discourse 44, 149, 187–8
Ransome, Arthur 226–8
Ransonnet-Villez, Eugen Freiherr von *51*, 53
Rasmussen, Knud 164
Rattlesnake, HMS 23, 139, 141, *141*, 216
recreational sailing, growth in 226–8
Red Rover 15
Redburn 180, 186–8, 197
reform movements 115
religious books 210
revolutionary ideas 114–15
The Riddle of the Sands

books on cruising in small yachts 207, 223–8
Dulcibella library 204–207, 212
an incomplete library of books 207–208
invasion fiction 204, 219
naval warfare books 207, 218, 219–22
spy fiction 204
technical sailing aids 207, 208, 212–14, *214*, *215*, 216, 217–18
"The Rime of the Ancient Mariner" 63, *64*
Robinson Crusoe 9, 170, *171*, 208
Romanticism 21, 119
Banfield's beachcomber lifestyle as 146, 149, 152
Cape Horn and 59, 79
Cook's view of noble savage as 136
sea imagery in 125–127
Ross, John 164, 167, 168, *168*, 169
Royal Navy 107, 108–109, 113
Rozwadowski, Helen 4, 40, 195, 196, 197
Russo-Japanese war (1904–5) 3, 7–8

Sacheuse, John 167–9, *168*
sailing, growth in recreational 226–8
sailing ships
immigrant transportation by 13–14, 117
interracial teams sharing skills and knowledge 188
persistence of 12, 13–14, 14–15, 17–18, 72
reading the weather 119–21
seamanship in nineteenth-century 69–74
transition to steam 10–12, *11*, 13–14, 188
watches 120–1
Sailing Tours 225–6, *227*
Saint-Domingue 114
Sandbeach people (Wanthaala Aborigines)
Merland's interview with Pelletier regarding 141, 142–4
rescue of Pelletier 139–40
Schleiden, Matthias Jakob 27
Schmitt, Carl 107
schooners 14, 15, 72
scientific voyages 13, 17–18, 57, *58*, 172, *173*
Scoresby, William 159–60
instruments 161–2, *161*

scurvy 133
sea fiction 119
aquanauts 194–201
drifters 189–94
imperialism reflected in structure of 189
lascars 182–8
literary space of Indian Ocean 178–9, 180–2
metaphors 178, 189, 197, 201–202
The Sea-Wolf 189, 212
sealers 63
seamanship, nineteenth-century 65, 66, 69–74
sexual aberration 41–3, *42*
Shelvocke, George 63
ship-of-state 107, 110–11
ships' libraries 208–212
ship's library, *Dulcibella* fictitious 18–19, 204–207, 212
cruising in small yachts 207, 223–8
incomplete 207–208
naval warfare 207, 218, 219–22
technical sailing aids 207, 208, 212–14, *214*, *215*, 216, 217–18
The Shipwreck 90
shipwrecks 13, 74, 81–2
(*see also* castaways, shipwreck; castaways, shipwreck of HMS *Endeavour*; Kent)
Skyfall 12
The Slave Ship 126–7, *126*
slave ships 15
deaths aboard 113–14, 116
duties of sailors on 113–14
insurrections on 116, *116*
Zong 126–7
slavery 115–16
abolition 3, 82, 115
Indian Ocean networks 180
second 15, 115
Slocum, Joshua 21
South Pacific Ocean Directory 215
Spitsbergen archipelago 172–6, *173*
Spitsbergen Gazette 174, *175*
spy fiction 204
steamships 2, 5, 7, 71–2, 125
break down of 188, 190
transition from sail to 10–12, *11*, 13–14, 188

Stevenson, Robert Louis 191–2, 193, 214–15
stone coral 36–7, 38
storms 88–9, 121–3
    Piddington's law of 119
Stott, Rebecca 36, 37, 39, 41, 43, 44
Straits of Magellan 57, 71, 77
Strickland, Walter 151–2
sublime 59, 85–86, 97, 159, 184
    Arctic as 163, 169, 172
    Humboldt and 157
    Maury and ocean as spectacle 120
    (*see also* Arctic, adventure, Romanticism)
submarines 8
    Verne's depiction of 8, 47, 198–199, 209
Suez Canal 6–7
surfing 24

technical sailing aids 207, 208, 212–18
telegrams 7
terminology, nautical 217–18
Thomas, Nicholas 166
Thompson, Barbara (Giom) 139, 140, 141–2, 144
Thynne, Anna 20, 24, 35–7, 38
tides 146, 177
    collecting specimens and 36, 43
    predicting 216
    tide tables 216
The Times 117, 127
timescales, geological 32, 34, 36
Torres Strait (*see* Aboriginal and Torres Strait maritime societies)
tourism, Arctic 172, 173–6
tramp steamers 7
"Travel" 190–1
Treaty of Ghent 109
Treaty of Kanagawa 124
The Tugboat 11–12
Tupaia 133, 134, 166, 167
Turner, J.M.W. 10–11, *11*, 125–7, *126*
turtles 135–6
Twenty Thousand Leagues Under the Sea 8, 10, 45–9, *48*, 198–201, *200*, 209, 212
Two Years Before the Mast 77, 118, 211, *211*

Typee 63, 78
Typhoon 18, 79, 125, 129, 185

undersea cable networks 1, 7, 19, 180, *181*, 195, 196–7, *196*
underwater photography 10, *52*, 53
United States
    Declaration of Independence 109, 114
    emigrant voyages to 117
    Revolution 114
    trade with China and Japan 124
    troubled relations with Britain 108–111
    US Navy victories 109
    War of 1812 109
United States, USS 56, *56*
    passage around Cape Horn 64–8
The United States v. the Schooner Amistad 15

Verne, Jules 21
    Twenty Thousand Leagues Under the Sea 8, 10, 45–9, *48*, 198–201, *200*, 209, 212
Villepreux-Power, Jeanette 20–1
Violence 105, 106, 114, 121–2, 192–3
Vue de l'Océan Glacial, pêche aux morses Groënlandais 172–3, *172*

Wanthaala Aborigines (Sandbeach people)
    Merland's interview with Pelletier regarding 141, 142–4
    rescue of Pelletier 139–40
War of 1812 109
Ward, Nathaniel Bagshaw 38
Warington, Robert 37, 38–9
water molecules 157
Waterman, Robert 67
The Wave 123–4, *124*
waves
    in Bay of Biscay 88
    compared to rabble 123
    representations of 122–3
    and swells in navigation 42
    swell forecasting of 218
    and wreck of the *Kent* 99
weather at sea
    Abstract Logs to chart 122
    around Cape Horn 62–3
    reports 89

scientific accounts 118–21, 122
storms 88–9, 119, 121–3
wild 106, 110, 118–30
Whale Chart 128, *129*
whaleships 17, 196, 197, 198
American 124
Arctic 159
Commodore Morris 72
Melville's passage on *Acushnet* 57–62
in Pacific Ocean 60
seamanship 71, 72–3
whaling stations 174
Whewell, William 216
White-Jacket 59, 67–8, 69, 70, 72, 73, 77, 78–9, 111, 112, 123
Williams, Rosalind 3, 19, 217
Williams, Thomas 41
Williamson, J,.E. 10
Wind 59, 62, 65, 66, 67, 70, 72, 73, 88–9, 118, 138, 158, 190

wind power as sustainable 17
women
on board ships 85, *86*, 87–8
contributions to marine biology 20–1, 24–5
Inuit 165
rescue of children and 94, 95–7, 98, 101
in Spitsbergen 176
treatment on convict ships 117
wives of officers 84
wonder 27, 35, 43
Arctic as source of 160, 162
European at Indigenous arts 169
science and 25
wonder-creatures 43
"wonders of the shore"` 35

Zong 126–7
Zoological Research Station, Naples 50–1